THE THRONE CARRIER OF GOD

THE THRONE CARRIER OF GOD

THE LIFE AND THOUGHT OF 'ALĀ' AD-DAWLA AS-SIMNĀNĪ

JAMAL J. ELIAS

STATE UNIVERSITY OF NEW YORK PRESS

Published by
State University of New York Press, Albany

Printed in the United States of America

For information, address State University of New York Press,
State University Plaza, Albany, N.Y. 12246

Production by M.R. Mulholland
Marketing by Bernadette LaManna

Library of Congress Cataloging-in-Publication Data

Elias, Jamal J.
    The throne carrier of God : the life and thought of 'Alā' ad
-dawlah as-Simnānī / Jamal J. Elias.
        p.   cm.
    Includes bibliographical references (p.   ) and index.
    ISBN 0-7914-2611-4 (acid free). -- ISBN 0-7914-2612-2 (pbk. :   acid
free)
    1. Simnānī, Aḥmad ibn Muḥammad, 1261–1336.   2. Sufism--Biography.
I. Title.
BP80.S58E55   1995
297'.4'092--dc20
    [B]   94-37174
                                                           CIP

10 9 8 7 6 5 4 3 2 1

من ندانم تا چه ام یا خود که ام یا بر چه ام
این قدر دانم که عرش شرع حق را حاملم

I do not know why I am, or who I am, or how I am;
All I know is I am carrying the throne of God's law.

—Dīwān-i ʿAlāʾ ad-dawla

CONTENTS

Illustrations   ix

Tables   xi

Preface   xiii

Notes on Transliteration   xv

1. Introduction   1
    Primary Sources of the Simnānī Tradition   4
    The Simnānī Tradition in Modern Scholarship   11

Part I

2. The Life and Times of 'Alā' ad-dawla as-Simnānī   15
    Early Life and Conversion to Sufism   17
    Conversion Experience   18
    Contact with Nūr ad-dīn al-Isfarā'inī   22
    Life in Simnān   28

3. Simnānī's Masters and Disciples   33
    Investiture with Sufi Robes (*Khirqas*)   39
    Associates and Disciples   44
    Conclusion   53

Part II

4. The Divine and Its Manifestation   61
    The Structure of God and the World   62
    Divine Manifestation   65
    The Spiritual and Physical Realms   68
    Emanation and the Compound Human Being   72

5. The Spiritual Body and the Mirror of God   79
    Composition of the Spiritual Body   81
    The Seven Climes of the Spiritual Realm   85
    Interior Ascent of the Subtle Substances   88
    Preeminence of the Subtle Substance of the "Real"   91

The Subtle Substance of I-ness 94
Conclusion 97

6. Traveling the Sufi Path 101
Islamic Foundations of the Path 105
Simnānī's Understanding of the Qur'ān 107
Simnānī's Understanding of Prophecy 110
Rules for the Novice 113
Rules for Sufi Practice 114

7. Seclusion and Recollection 119
The Rules of Recollection 124
The Hierarchy of Visions and Colors 135
Annihilation and Resurrection 141
Conclusion 144

8. Conclusion 147
Divine Emanation and the Islamic Philosophical Tradition 150
The Four Realms 154
The Concept of *Laṭā'if* 157
Simnānī's Legacy 160

Appendix A. The Written Works of Simnānī 165
Major Works 166
Minor Works 178
Correspondence 198
Works Attributed to Simnānī Not Known to be Extant 200
Simnānī's Titles Mentioned Only in *Maṭāf al-ashrāf* 201
Simnānī's Commentary on the Qur'ān 203

Appendix B. Chronology of Events 213

Glossary of Technical Terms 217

Bibliography 227

Index 243

ILLUSTRATIONS

Figure 1. *Silsila* of ʿAlāʾ ad-dawla as-Simnānī   40

Figure 2. Divine Manifestation   67

Figure 3. The Fourfold Scheme of Emanation   73

Figure 4. Emanation of the Celestial and Sublunar Realms   75

Figure 5. Emanation of the Compound Human Being   82

Figure 6. Simnānī's *Dhikr*   128

Figure 7. Levels of Death and Resurrection   143

TABLES

Table 1. The Four Dimensions of the Qur'ān   109

Table 2. Mystical Advancement and Divine Manifestation   151

PREFACE

This book would never have come to be had it not been for the support of a large number of individuals and institutions. Foremost among them is my teacher and friend, Professor Gerhard Böwering. His support and advice at all stages of this endeavor have proved invaluable. I would also like to thank Professors Ahmet Karamustafa, Carl Ernst, Wadad Kadi and Abbas Amanat for reading earlier versions of this work and commenting upon them. I am indebted to Professors Hamid Algar, Hermann Landolt and Adel Allouche for their advice and information during the research phase of this project.

Among the many others to whom I owe a debt of gratitude are Professors Alan Godlas and William Chittick, Doctors Hasan Javadi and Anthony Greenwood, Mr. Gerald Elmore, Mr. Arif Naushahi and Ms. Leyla Nişli; the reference librarians at Amherst College: Mr. Michael Casper, Ms. Margaret Groesbeck, Mr. Floyd Merritt, Mrs. Leeta Bailey and Ms. Susan Edelberg; Doctors Sha'bani, Tasbihi and Tamimdari of the Iran-Pakistan Institute for Persian Studies, Islamabad; the library staff of Kitābkhāna-yi Ganjbakhsh, Islamabad, and the Süleymaniye, Topkapı Sarayı Müzesi, İstanbul Üniversitesi and Beyazit libraries in Istanbul, with special thanks to the director and assistant director of the Süleymaniye Library, Mr. Müammer Ülker and Dr. Nevzat Kaya, for their friendship and gracious hospitality.

My research was greatly facilitated by grants from Amherst College, the American Research Institute in Turkey, the Yale Center for International and Area Studies, the National Endowment for the Humanities, and two research permits from the Turkish Ministry of Culture and Tourism.

Finally, I would like to thank Danielle for her patience, humor and encouragement, and Kamal and Kari for their material and moral support while this work was in its dissertation incarnation. To my parents, whom I owe a debt which can never be repaid, I wish to dedicate this work.

Amherst, Massachusetts

NOTES ON TRANSLITERATION

I have attempted to present transliterated terms in a form consistent with their pronounciation. Thus the Persian *wa* is written as *-u* where appropriate. Persian *iḍāfat* is always indicated, and in the Arabic *iḍāfa*, the final ة is shown when it is followed by a vowel. Similarly, Arabic terminal vowels are shown in instances when such vowels would commonly be pronounced. I show the assimilation of the *lām* of the definite article by the Sun letters, as in *as-Simnānī*. I also indicate elision of the definite article with a preceding vowel, as in *dhu'l-jalāl* (note that the long *ū* becomes short in such a construction). Transliterated terms contained in quotations from secondary sources are not brought into conformity with my system but are reproduced in their original form. The above-mentioned exceptions notwithstanding, the transliteration of Arabic letters closely follows the scheme used by the Library of Congress and the *International Journal of Middle East Studies*:

ا	a, ā	ط	ṭ
ب	b	ظ	ẓ
ت	t	ع	ʿ
ث	th	غ	gh
ج	j	ف	f
ح	ḥ	ق	q
خ	kh	ك	k
د	d	ل	l
ذ	dh	م	m
ر	r	ن	n
ز	z	ه	h
س	s	و	w, ū
ش	sh	ي	y, ī
ص	ṣ	ى	ā
ض	ḍ	ء	ʾ

For the sake of consistency, Persian, Turkish and Urdu letters have been transliterated using the same scheme, except that the Urdu 'big' *yā* is transliterated as *ē*, the undotted *nūn* as *ñ*, and aspirated consonants are underlined. Additional Persian characters are as follows:

Turkish proper names and terms have been transliterated using modern Turkish orthography.

1

Introduction

'Alā' ad-dawla as-Simnānī (Dhu'l-Ḥijja 659/November 1261 to 22 Rajab 736/6 March 1336) lived at a time when the Mongol dynasty of the Ilkhanids ruled over Iran and Iraq from the middle of the thirteenth to the middle of the fourteenth century. This period of history represents the only occasion until the advent of colonial empires in the eighteenth century when the central Islamic lands fell under non-Muslim rule. In the process of overrunning Iran and Iraq, the Mongols had not only destroyed the religious and governmental infrastructure of the region, but also Baghdad, the seat of the Caliphate and the most important Islamic city of its day. Having dispatched the Caliph and his immediate retinue, the Mongols then placed a few aristocratic and decidedly secular Persian families in administrative positions, the most famous of these being the Juwaynīs. But the name of another Khurāsānī family frequently appears along with that of the Juwaynīs, this one being from the town of Simnān. It was into this powerful clan of bureaucrats that 'Alā' ad-dawla as-Simnānī was born.

Raised in luxury and trained as a courtier, Simnānī's eventual abandonment of courtly life for one of piety, asceticism and mysticism constitutes a notable story in the annals of Islamic history. Although unusual, this Buddha-like transformation is by no means unique, since it bears many parallels to the biography of the legendary Ibrāhīm b. Adham. However, unlike this earlier prince-turned-ascetic, Simnānī's life exists within the parameters of recorded history, and his substantial corpus of teachings survives to this day.

A respected theologian, jurist and poet, Simnānī is best remembered for his contributions to Islamic mystical thought. He was deeply influenced by the visionary experiences and meditational practices (*dhikr*) of Najm ad-dīn al-Kubrā (d. 618/1221) and other visionary mystics associated with the latter, in particular Majd ad-dīn al-Baghdādī (d. 616/1219) and Nūr ad-dīn al-Isfarā'inī (d. 717/1317). Simnānī systematized their ideas and his own in a complex color symbolism of subtle substances (*laṭā'if*). His methodology is characterized by the construction of hierarchies and correspondences in the physical and spiritual realms, and by emphasis upon the polarity and complementarity between these two realms.

In an effort to balance the ideas of divine emanation and creation of the world, he developed the existing notion of *tajallī* (theophany) in terms of varying degrees of divine self-manifestation occurring through intermediaries, as opposed to the concept that all of creation shares in divinity. This facet of his thought placed him in opposition to the school of Ibn al-'Arabī (d. 638/1240) and its influential doctrine of the oneness of being (*waḥdat al-wujūd*), as is demonstrated by his correspondence with 'Abd ar-Razzāq al-Kāshānī (d. 736/1335), a disciple of Ibn al-'Arabī. Three centuries later, Aḥmad-i Sirhindī (d. 1033/1624) developed the doctrine of the oneness of witnessing (*waḥdat ash-shuhūd*) within the Naqshbandī Sufi order to check Ibn al-'Arabī's influence in India. Spreading from Sirhindī throughout the Mujaddidī phase of the Naqshbandiyya and beyond, this doctrine, derived from Simnānī's ontological theories, has become the major Sufi alternative to the concept of *waḥdat al-wujūd* for comprehending the relationship of God and the world.

'Alā' ad-dawla as-Simnānī was a prolific writer in both Arabic and Persian. One hundred and fifty-four titles are ascribed to him which refer to a total of one hundred and four works. Seventy-nine of these are known to be extant today (not counting his correspondence). These texts vary in length from substantial monographs to one or two-page treatises constituting works of spiritual counsel or brief explanations of particular terms and concepts, and include a highly crafted and frequently revised encyclopedic work on his mystical ideas, a commentary on the Qur'ān, a collection of poetry, a variety of short mystical treatises, and letters on controversial points of Sufism. Simnānī began his writing career well after meeting with Nūr ad-dīn al-Isfarā'inī, who formally introduced him to Kubrawī mysticism, and after having been authorized by Isfarā'inī to start instructing disciples of his own.

His writings cover a wide array of topics, although the emphasis is clearly upon the instruction of his disciples and of future generations of mystics. This instruction is both spiritual and practical in nature, covering theoretical aspects of mystical, theological, philosophical and legal thought as well as the finer points of everyday religious practice and social conduct. With this bipartite level of instruction in mind, Simnānī deals with mystical theories of the relationship of God to the universe, the form and function of the spiritual human body, the hierarchy of leadership in the mystical realm, and the nature and

manner of attainment of mystical states. In the course of his explanations of such points, he also discusses earlier Sufi, philosophical and
theological views, illustrating the reasons for his agreement with or
opposition to specific positions. Along with this spiritual instruction,
Simnānī provides practical direction on the appropriate forms of *dhikr*
performance, attitudes towards one's family and property, attitudes
towards the state, the correct manner of religious ritual, and such
apparent trivialities as the etiquette of eating and performing other
bodily functions. By his own admission, Simnānī's autobiographical
writings are intended to serve the didactic function of illustrating
these points through his personal experience.

Of all the existing works written by Simnānī, his commentary
on the Qur'ān entitled *Tafsīr najm al-qur'ān* provides the most perfect
summary presentation of his thought. Within the space of a lengthy
introduction, and commentary on the *Fātiḥa* and *sūras* 52–114 (roughly
one-sixth of the Qur'ān in terms of length), he addresses virtually all
the salient features of his thought. For this reason, Simnānī's *Najm
al-qur'ān* (supported by references to his other works) is a text worthy
of functioning as the primary representative of his teachings and
intellectual positions.

Despite his importance to the Kubrawiyya and Islamic mystical
thought in general, Simnānī has received scant attention in the works
of traditional Islamic biography and the critical studies of modern
scholars. The major reason for his relative obscurity may be that he
lived between the Mongol invasion and the reign of Tīmūr, which is
one of the most poorly understood periods of Islamic history. The
disregard of traditional Islamic scholars may also be explained in part
by his association with the Mongol court. There are some notable
exceptions to the lack of modern critical writings on Simnānī, in the
form of valuable studies on various aspects of Simnānī's thought by
H. Corbin, H. Cordt, N.M. Hirawī, H. Landolt, M. Molé, ʿAbd ar-Rafīʿ
Ḥaqīqat and S.M. Sadr. In addition, critical editions of a number of
his works have appeared in the last decade. A comprehensive monograph on Simnānī is still lacking, however, and it is the purpose of
this book to fill that gap. My principal goal has been to provide a
systematic presentation of a seminal Islamic figure. In my desire to
establish an accurate biography of Simnānī and to render his often
opaque and fragmented ideas as lucidly and coherently as possible,
I have minimized discussions assessing his life and teachings within
their historical or social context. The major exception to this is the
meaning of some concepts and terms which are central to his thought,

which have been discussed in the context of Islamic mystical and philosophical thought in the final chapter.

The eight chapters of this book naturally fall into two sections. The first consists of a study of Simnānī's life, while the second examines his ideas regarding Sufi thought and practice.

In the second and third chapters I have examined the accessible sources for information on his biography and teaching. Through a study of the works of Islamic historiography, biography and hagiography, as well as Simnānī's own writings and other miscellaneous religious texts, I have attempted to construct as accurate and critical a biography as is possible from the available sources.

The next four chapters deal with the content of Simnānī's works. Chapter 4 constitutes an analysis of his Sufi thought, emphasis being given to a coherent and ordered presentation of his key ideas, such as his teachings on God, creation, the human soul, while chapter 5 deals with the constitution of the mystical human body and the nature and importance of its highest state, referred to as the "subtle substance of I-ness" (*al-laṭīfa al-anā'iyya*). I have attempted to show how Simnānī organizes these ideas to provide a comprehensive theory justifying his belief that the highest human state is one of eternal servitude to God.

The next two chapters describe Simnānī's Sufi practice; in other words, the manner in which one attains the mystical knowledge described in chapters 4 and 5. After outlining the fundamental requirements of faith as understood by Simnānī in the sixth chapter, in the seventh I have examined his ways of meditation, retreat and prayer, as well as his methods of instruction and Sufi education.

In the absence of accurate critical editions of most of Simnānī's works, I have relied heavily upon sources in manuscript form. This is especially true in the case of the primary subject of this study, his *Tafsīr najm al-qur'ān*, for which I have referred to the most accurate (and relatively accessible) copy preserved in the Şehit Ali Paşa collection in the Süleymaniye Library, Istanbul. Appendix A lists Simnānī's writings and provides a brief critical description of each, inasmuch as is possible in chronological order. Emphasis has been given to a detailed external description of *Tafsīr najm al-qur'ān*, which has been discussed in terms of its manuscript tradition, its structure, and its place in the literature of Qur'ānic commentary.

Primary Sources of the Simnānī Tradition

Scholars interested in studying the life of 'Alā' ad-dawla as-Simnānī are fortunate in having a number of independent sources providing biographical details about him. This is due in the main to his status as a major religious figure and a member of a wealthy family which was involved in court politics in the Ilkhanid state. In addition, Simnānī wrote a large number of works, several of which provide autobiographical information.

Details on Simnānī's life are found in four distinct literary traditions: Arabic biographical works (*ṭabaqāt* literature), Persian political histories of the period, Sufi biographies and hagiographies, and Simnānī's autobiographical writings.

Simnānī was keenly aware of the narratibility of his own life, and provided information concerning himself in a number of his works, occasionally going into great detail concerning a specific topic. Most of Simnānī's treatises are written with the intention of guiding his disciples and future mystics. For this reason, the specific historical details of his autobiographical writings are unreliable since he clearly attempted to construct his biography not as an accurate chronology, but as an exemplary self-history providing a model of Sufi thought and practice for his disciples. Thus individual accounts are coherent within themselves, but inconsistent when compared to parallel ones written at other times. The conscious reorganization of his auto-biography as a didactic medium is most obvious in his *al-'Urwa li-ahl al-khalwa wa'l-jalwa*, a work which he revised at least twice, but also in other treatises in which he explains how he came to adopt his system of belief. Despite their shortcomings, these treatises never-theless provide a valuable picture of Simnānī's retrospective vision of his religious awakening, and of how he wished to present himself to posterity.

Some of the treatises written early in Simnānī's religious career cannot be precisely dated. Probably the earliest work to provide auto-biographical information is *al-Wārid ash-shārid*, which was completed in 699/1299–1300.[1] The stated purpose for providing this information is the "unveiling of the correct path from among the [varied] paths and the demonstration of the path of salvation from among the [various] sects."[2] This treatise provides a brief description of Simnānī's mystical conversion and some additional biographical details. The emphasis is not on the precise course of events in his life, but on how he came to become a disciple of Nūr ad-dīn al-Isfarā'inī (d. 717/1317) and a mystical teacher in his own right, and upon the chain of religious

---

1. Simnānī states that at the time he was writing this work, he was forty years old (*al-Wārid ash-shārid*, MS. A1588 (Catalog no. 5226), Topkapı Sarayı Müzesi Kütüphanesi, Istanbul, 27a).

2. Ibid., 26b.

authority which he derived from Isfarā'inī. Two other short works
written before 28 Ṣafar 714/13 June 1314 have a similar emphasis: an
undated treatise entitled *Hadiyyat al-muhtadī wa-hidāyat al-mubtadi'*,
and the *Risāla fatḥ al-mubīn*, written some time between Shawwāl
712/February 1313 and 19 Ramaḍān 713/7 January 1314.[3] Both treatises
mention his mystical conversion and emphasize the underlying importance of this experience in his decision to quit government service.
Additional information on the names of his teachers and associates
is found in an untitled treatise of three folios preserved in one of the
earliest collections of Simnānī's work.[4]

A work entitled *Risāla fī-dhikr asāmī mashāyikhī* and datable
to 712/1312–13 provides even more details on Simnānī's mystical
affiliation and gives valuable information on the chain of transmission
of various Sufi robes (*khirqa*) in the Kubrawī order.[5] Similar information is also found in a short published work entitled *Tadhkirat
al-mashāyikh*.[6]

Much of Simnānī's autobiographical information is repeated in
these treatises with slight variations. It is also recorded in the *'Urwa*,
Simnānī's major prose work, which he took pains to revise twice
during his life time. The final version of the text was completed late
in his life (probably in 728/1328) and is therefore removed in time from
the information it purportedly conveys. Given the temporal distance
between the events themselves and their description in the *'Urwa*,
and the author's obvious intention of leaving an exemplary and crafted
account of his life for later readers, it is not surprising that the autobiographical details found in this text seem the most artificial. Simnānī's
personal history is streamlined, and actions and liaisons of his youth
which were inconsistent with activities in his later life are omitted.

The *Chihil majlis* is even further removed in time and has the
added problem of being a collection of Simnānī's sayings and actions

<hr>

3. *Hadiyyat al-muhtadī*, MS. 353, Karaçelebizade, Süleymaniye
Kütüphanesi, Istanbul, 80b–86a; *Risāla fatḥ al-mubīn*, MS. 1, Fiqh ḥanafī fārsī,
Dār al-kutub, Cairo, 193b–211a.

4. MS. 11-mīm, Majāmi' fārsiyya, Dār al-kutub, Cairo, 145a–147a. The
majmū'a is dated 3 Rabī' I, 887/22 April, 1482 (hereafter referred to as Dār
al-kutub, untitled). See appendix A for details on this and other works by
Simnānī.

5. MS. 11-mīm, Majāmi' fārsiyya, Dār al-kutub, Cairo, 72a–76b.

6. M.T. Dānishpazhūh, "Khirqa-yi hazār mīkhī," *Collected Papers on
Islamic Philosophy and Mysticism*, ed. H. Landolt and M. Mohaghegh (Tehran:
La branche de Téhéran de l'institut des études islamiques de l'Université
McGill, 1971), 147–78.

compiled in "sessions" (*majālis*) by his student Iqbāl-i Sīstānī (Sijistānī) and authorized by Simnānī. The biographical information contained therein is anecdotal and somewhat hagiographical in nature as a result of Sīstānī's editorial judgement and feelings of extreme admiration and affection for Simnānī. Nevertheless, it is valuable as a record of Simnānī's interaction with his students and of his students' perception of his identity.

The earliest references to Simnānī's life in biographical works are found in the *Kitāb al-wāfī bi'l-wafayāt* and *A'yān al-'asr* of Salāh ad-dīn as-Safadī (d. 764/1362).[7] Safadī's information on Simnānī is both accurate and detailed, and is obtained in part from Safadī's teacher, Shams ad-dīn adh-Dhahabī (d. 748/1347).[8]

A second strand of biographical material on Simnānī is found in the *tabaqāt* works of the Shāfi'ī school. There is a brief entry in the *Tabaqāt ash-shāfi'iyya* of Asnawī (d. 772/1370–71) which does not draw any information from Safadī's works.[9] From Asnawī's short reference, Simnānī finds his way into other compilations of Shāfi'ī biographies, including that of Taqī ad-dīn Ibn Qādī Shuhba (d. 851/1447).[10]

A brief entry on Simnānī also exists in the *Tā'rīkh 'ulamā' Baghdād* by Ibn Rāfi' (d. 774/1372–73).[11] This is neither closely based upon the work of Safadī, nor on that of Asnawī. With Ibn Hajar al-'Asqalānī (d. 852/1448), the biography of Simnānī begins to take a formulaic shape. He provides more details about Simnānī than are found in the Shāfi'ī *tabaqāt*, but his information consists mainly of extracts culled from Safadī's work and presented in summary form, compounding the mistakes found in manuscripts of Safadī's work.[12] Biographical works after *ad-Durar al-kāmina* do not contribute any new material to the study of Simnānī, but simply repeat entries found

---

7. *Kitāb al-wāfī bi'l-wafayāt*, vol. 7, ed. Ihsān 'Abbās (Wiesbaden: Franz Steiner Verlag, 1969), 356; *A'yān al-'asr*, MS 1809, Atif Efendi, Süleymaniye Kütüphanesi, Istanbul, 48b–49a.

8. Simnānī does not appear in any of Dhahabī's major works. Nevertheless, Safadī mentions that he received some information on Simnānī from Dhahabī.

9. Jamāl ad-dīn al-Asnawī, *Tabaqāt ash-shāfi'iyya*, 2 vols., ed. K.Y. al-Hūt (Beirut: al-Maktaba al-'ilmiyya, 1987), 1:349, no. 664.

10. *Tabaqāt ash-shāfi'iyya*, 4 vols., ed. 'Abd al-'Alīm Khān (Beirut: 'Alam al-kutub, 1987), 2:248–49, no. 530.

11. Ed. 'Abbās al-'Azzāwī (Baghdad: Matba'at al-ahālī, 1938), 162, no. 136.

12. *ad-Durar al-kāmina*, 5 vols., ed. M. Sayyid Jādd al-Haqq (Cairo: Dār al-kutub al-hadītha, 1966), 1:266, no. 663.

in earlier texts, particularly in that of Asnawī. The references for Simnānī in both the *Ṭabaqāt al-mufassirīn* and the *Shadharāt adh-dhahab* are based upon this work.[13]

Political histories of the Ilkhanid and Timurid periods prove to be almost as rich a source for information regarding Simnānī's life as the biographical works described above. References to Simnānī's family are found in all historical works of the Ilkhanid era. Incidental references with some value for the study of ʿAlāʾ ad-dawla as-Simnānī are found in the *Taʾrīkh-i Uljāytū* (completed ca. 716/1316),[14] *Taʾrīkh-i Waṣṣāf* (ca. 728/1328),[15] and the *Taʾrīkh-i guzīda* (ca. 730/1329–30).[16] Similar anecdotal references are also found in the *Ẓafarnāma* of Yazdī (completed 828/1424–25).[17]

The *Mujmal-i faṣīḥī* of Faṣīḥ Aḥmad-i Khwāfī (d. 849/1445) is extremely valuable for establishing a chronology of the events in Simnānī's life.[18] The *Taʾrīkh-i ḥabīb as-siyar* (ca. 940/1533–34) of Khwānd Amīr is equally useful for its detailed treatment of Simnānī.[19] It is the most important and well-regarded work of Persian history to provide a substantial biography of Simnānī.

In addition to political histories, references to Simnānī are also found in works of historical geography. The most important of these are the *Haft iqlīm* (1002/1593–94) and the *Riyāḍ as-siyāḥa* (1237/1821–22).[20]

The above-mentioned historical and biographical works are crucial for establishing a critical biography of ʿAlāʾ ad-dawla as-Simnānī because they are independent sources: they are neither

13. Shams ad-dīn ad-Dāwūdī (d. 945/1538), *Ṭabaqāt al-mufassirīn*, 2 vols., ed. ʿAlī Muḥammad ʿUmar (ʾĀbidīn: Maktaba Wahba, 1972), 1:66, no. 61; ʿAbd al-Ḥayy Ibn al-ʿImād (d. 1089/1678), *Shadharāt adh-dhahab fī-akhbār man dhahab*, 8 vols. (Cairo: Maktabat al-Qudsī, 1932), 6:125.

14. Abuʾl-Qāsim ʿAbd Allāh b. Muḥammad al-Qāshānī, *Taʾrīkh-i Uljāytū*, ed. Mahin Hambly (Tehran: Bungāh-i tarjuma wa nashr-i kitāb, 1969).

15. Shihāb ad-dīn Shīrāzī Waṣṣāf, *Taʾrīkh-i Waṣṣāf* (Tehran: 1967).

16. Ḥamd Allāh Mustawfī al-Qazwīnī, *Taʾrīkh-i guzīda*, ed. ʿAbd al-Ḥusayn Nawāʾī (Tehran: Intishārāt-i Amīr-i Kabīr, 1983).

17. Sharaf ad-dīn ʿAlī Yazdī, *Ẓafarnāma*, 2 vols., ed. M. ʿAbbāsī (Tehran: Amīr-i Kabīr, 1957).

18. Ed. Maḥmūd Farrukh (Mashhad: Kitābfurūshī-yi bāstān, 1960).

19. Ghiyāth ad-dīn al-Ḥasanī (Khwānd Amīr), *Taʾrīkh-i ḥabīb as-siyar*, 4 vols. (Tehran: Kitābkhāna-yi Khayyām, 1964).

20. Amīn Aḥmad Rāzī, *Haft iqlīm*, 2 vols., ed. Jawwād Fāḍil (Tehran: Kitābfurūshī-yi ʿAlī Akbar ʿIlmī, n.d.); Zayn al-ʿābidin Shīrwānī, *Riyāḍ as-siyāḥa*, ed. Asghar Ḥamid Rabbānī (Tehran: Kitābfurūshī-yi Saʿdī, 1960).

dependent on information provided by Simnānī himself nor written within the Sufi tradition and thus potentially hagiographical in nature. The writings of Ṣafadī and the *ṭabaqāt* works of the Shāfiʿī school shed light on Simnānī's involvement in non-mystical endeavors, and reflect his contacts with individuals who are overlooked in the writings of the Sufi historical tradition. This tradition emphasizes Simnānī's religious career only within the context of Kubrawī mystical circles along with his well-known contacts with ʿAbd ar-Razzāq al-Kāshānī (d. 736/1335), the disciple of Muḥyī ad-dīn Ibn al-ʿArabī (d. 638/1240).[21]

The first major reference to Simnānī in Sufi biographical literature is in the *Nafaḥāt al-uns* of ʿAbd ar-Raḥmān-i Jāmī (d. 898/1492).[22] Jāmī bases most of his information on Simnānī's autobiographical writings and the works of his disciples, in particular the *Chihil majlis* of Iqbāl-i Sīstānī.[23] Several anecdotes concerning his life and thought are recorded, although Jāmī fails to show the critical judgement displayed by Ṣafadī.

The information about Simnānī's life and thought found in the *Rawḍat al-jinān* of Ibn al-Karbalāʾī (completed 975/1567) is also extremely important.[24] Although he relies on the *Nafaḥāt*, Ibn al-Karbalāʾī also consults Simnānī's own writings and is a better source than Jāmī for Simnānī's disciples as well as his thought and place in the Sufi tradition.

Later Sufi biographical works rely upon Jāmī and do not make any significant contribution to one's knowledge of Simnānī's life. Significant among them are the *Safīnat al-awliyāʾ* of Dārā Shikūh (d. 1069/1658–59), completed in 1049/1639, and the *Khazīnat al-aṣfiyāʾ* of Ghulām Sarwar Lāhūrī, dated 1281/1864–65.[25] Both these works

---

21. See below, p. 44–55, 199.

22. Ed. Mahdī Tawḥīdīpūr (Tehran: Kitāb furūshī-yi Saʿdī, 1958), 439–43. The *Nafaḥāt*, completed in 881/1476, is also a valuable source of information on several of Simnānī's most important teachers and disciples.

23. For further information see below, pp. 176–78. Cf. Ivanow, "More on the Sources of Jāmī's Nafahat," *Asiatic Society of Bengal*, new series, 19 (1923), 299–303. Very little is known about Sīstānī's life, and the dates of his birth and death are not recorded in any known work. For whatever information can be found on him, see H. Cordt, *Die Sitzungen des ʿAlāʾ ad-Dawla as-Simnānī*, (Zurich: Juris, 1977).

24. Ḥusayn Ibn al-Karbalāʾī-yi Tabrīzī, *Rawḍat al-jinān wa jannāt al-janān*, ed. Jaʿfar al-Qurrāʾī (Tehran: Bungāh-i tarjuma wa nashr-i kitāb, 1970).

25. *Safīnat al-awliyāʾ* (Cawnpore: 1906), 107; *Khazīnat al-aṣfiyāʾ*, tr. Iqbāl Aḥmad Fārūqī (Lahore: Maktaba-yi nabawiyya, 1983), 264–65.

provide summary extracts from the *Nafaḥāt* and are inaccurate in their details. As such, they constitute hagiographies rather than historical references.

A more recent Sufi biographical work containing valuable information is the *Ṭarā'iq al-ḥaqā'iq* (dated 1333/1915) of Ma'ṣūm 'Alī Shāh.[26] This source combines information found in earlier biographies like the *Nafaḥāt* with primary writings, particularly better known Simnānī texts such as *al-'Urwa li-ahl al-khalwa wa'l-jalwa* and the *Chihil majlis*.[27]

Simnānī's substantial poetical writings have caused him to be included in works devoted to the biographies of poets, in particular the *Tadhkirat ash-shu'arā* (892/1487) of Dawlatshāh Samarqandī and the *Riyāḍ al-'ārifīn* (1260/1844) and *Majma' al-fuṣaḥā'* (1288/1871), both by Riḍā Qūlī Khān (d. 1288/1871).[28] Dawlatshāh's work is based upon Simnānī's own writings and is of some value, while the latter two provide brief extracts from the *Nafaḥāt*.

As a result of Simnānī's possible connections with the Sarbadār movement[29] and his affiliation with the Kubrawī order (which had an ambiguous relationship with Shī'ism),[30] he has been included in Shī'ī biographical works as well. The substantial entry in the *Majālis al-mu'minīn* of Nūr Allāh Shushtarī (d. 1019/1610) is primarily based upon the *Nafaḥāt*. However, Shushtarī greatly exaggerates Simnānī's devotion to the *Imāms*.[31] Not only was his hatred for the Umayyads not as visceral as is described in the *Majālis al-mu'minīn*, but Simnānī also criticized the Shī'īs for their lack of respect for the first three caliphs and for 'Ā'isha, the wife of Muḥammad. From the *Majālis al-mu'minīn*, Simnānī enters larger Shī'ī biographical works, most significantly the *A'yān ash-shī'a* of Muḥsin al-Amīn.[32]

---

26. 3 vols., ed. M. Ja'far Maḥjūb (Tehran: Kitābkhāna-yi Bārānī, 1921).

27. See appendix A for a discussion of these and other works by Simnānī.

28. *Tadhkiratu'sh-Shu'arā*, ed. E.G. Browne, Persian Historical Texts, no. 1 (London: Luzac and Co., 1901), 250–52; *Tadhkira-yi riyāḍ al-'ārifīn*, ed. S. Ahmad-i Muhadhdhab (Tehran: Kitābkhāna-yi mahdiyya, 1937), 178; *Majma' al-fuṣaḥā'*, 6 vols., ed. Maẓāhir Muṣaffā (Tehran: Chāp-i Mūsawī, 1960), 2:869.

29. See below, p. 51.

30. For further information, see Marijan Molé, "Les Kubrawiya entre sunnisme et shiisme aux huitième et neuvième siècles de l'hégire," *Revue des études islamiques* 29 (1961), 61–142.

31. Shushtarī, *Majālis al-mu'minīn*, 2 vols. (Tehran: Kitābfurūshī-yi islāmiyya, 1956), 2:134.

32. 3rd ed. (Beirut: Maṭba'at al-inṣāf, 1961), 9:213–15, no. 1566.

The Simnānī Tradition in Modern Scholarship

Scant attention has been paid to the study of Simnānī throughout this century. This is surprising in light of his stature as one of the most important intellectual figures of Ilkhanid Iran, and the state's foremost religious authority during the reign of Abū Saʿīd. However, the last decade has witnessed an increase in the scholarly attention paid to Simnānī in the form of editions of his works and the compilation of preliminary biographies. A thorough analytical study of his life and thought is still lacking.

The first modern piece of scholarship is an article in Persian by Saʿīd Nafīsī.[33] This was followed by a brief but valuable monograph by Sayyed Mozaffer Sadr entitled *Sharḥ-i aḥwāl-u afkār-u āthār-i shaykh ʿAlāʾ ad-dawla as-Simnānī*.[34] Both these preliminary studies are valuable for their attempts to place Simnānī within the Kubrawī tradition, but an over-reliance on Sufi hagiographical literature detracts from their scholarly accuracy.

Simnānī's life was discussed by Molé in light of his relationship with Shīʿism,[35] and shortly after this Nazif Ṣahinoğlu attempted a study of his biography in his dissertation on Simnānī.[36] Further study of Simnānī's life in the context of his mystical thought has been conducted by Henry Corbin in his monumental work entitled *En Islam iranien*.[37] Important advances were also made by Hermann Landolt in the critical study of Simnānī and his relationship with his mystical guide, Nūr ad-dīn al-Isfarāʾinī.[38]

---

33. "ʿAlāʾ ad-dawla-yi Simnānī," *Yaghmā* 7 (1954), 358–62. Cf. the brief extracts from Simnānī's commentary on the Qurʾān and the *Chihil majlis* of Iqbāl-i Sīstānī found in L. Massignon, *Recueil de textes inédits concernant l'histoire de la mystique en pays d'Islam* (Paris: Librairie orientaliste Paul Geuthner, 1929), 143–45.

34. (A Study of the Life, Thought and Works of Shaykh ʿAlāʾ ad-dawla as-Simnānī), Tehran: Dānish, 1955.

35. Molé, "Les Kubrawiya."

36. "*Alâ al-Davla al-Simnânî: Hayatı, Eserleri, Kelâm Telâkkisi, Tasavvuf Alanındaki Görüşleri ile Beyân al-İhsân li ahl al-îkân*, (Istanbul: Şarkiyat Araştırma Merkezi Kitapları, no. 6, 1966). Cf. Şahinoğlu's article in the new *İslam Ansiklopedisi* which is extracted from this monograph ("Alâuddevle-i Simnânî." *Türkiye Diyanet Vakfı İslam Ansiklopedisi*, vol. 2, ed. Kemal Güren et al. (Istanbul: Türkiye Diyanet Vakfı, 1989), 345a–47b).

37. (Paris: Gallimard, 1972), 3:275ff.

38. *Correspondence spirituelle échangée entre Nuroddin Esfarayeni et son disciple ʿAlaoddawleh Semnani* (Tehran: L'institut franco-iranien de recherche, 1972). Cf. also Landolt's *Le révélateur des mystères* (Lagrasse: Verdier, 1986), which provides additional information.

More recently, Hartwig Cordt has included a brief biography of Simnānī in his analytical examination of the *Chihil majlis*. In addition, a renewed interest in the study of 'Alā' ad-dawla as-Simnānī in Iran has yielded one useful biographical essay by 'Abd ar-Rafī' Ḥaqīqat in his *Khumkhāna-yi waḥdat,* a work which supplants Sadr's book as the most comprehensive monographical essay on Simnānī.[39] Less valuable biographical essays have also been written by Najīb Māyil-i Hirawī, who has edited a number of Simnānī's works.

In addition to the biographical accounts mentioned above, preliminary studies on Simnānī are found in the accurate and informative encyclopedia articles by Fritz Meier and Josef Van Ess.[40]

---

39. *Khumkhāna-yi waḥdat* (Tehran: Shirkat-i mu'allifān-u mutarjimān-i Īrān, 1983).

40. F. Meier, "'Alā' al-Dawla al-Simnānī," *Encyclopaedia of Islam,* new edition, vol. 1 (Leiden: E.J. Brill, 1960), 346b–47b; J. Van Ess, "'Alā' al-dawla Semnānī," *Encyclopaedia Iranica,* vol. 1, ed. Ehsan Yarshater (London: Routledge and Kegan Paul, 1985), 774b–77a. Brief accounts of Simnānī's life are contained in a number of other works, most significantly: F. Meier, *Die Fawā'iḥ al-Ǧamāl wa Fawātiḥ al-Ǧalāl des Naǧm ad-Dīn al-Kubra* (Wiesbaden: Franz Steiner Verlag, 1957); *Abū Saʿīd-i Abū l-Ḥayr* (Leiden: E.J. Brill, 1976); 'Alī Akbar Dihkhudā, *Lughatnāma* (Tehran: Dānishkada-yi adabiyyāt wa 'ulūm-i insānī, 1958); M.H. adh-Dhahabī, *at-Tafsīr wa'l-mufassirūn,* 2 vols., 2nd ed. (Cairo: Dār al-kutub al-ḥadītha, 1976); J.S. Trimingham, *The Sufi Orders in Islam* (Oxford: Clarendon Press, 1971); S. Ateş, *İşârî Tefsîr Okulu* (Ankara: Ankara Üniversitesi Basımevi, 1974); 'Isā b. Junayd Shīrāzī, *Tadhkira-yi hazār mazār,* ed. Nūrānī Wiṣāl (Shiraz: Kitābkhāna-yi Aḥmadī, 1985).

PART I

2

THE LIFE AND TIMES OF
'ALĀ' AD-DAWLA AS-SIMNĀNĪ

Abu'l-Makārim Rukn ad-dīn 'Alā' ad-dawla Aḥmad b. Muḥammad b. Aḥmad al-Biyābānakī as-Simnānī was born in Dhu'l-Ḥijja 659/November 1261 into a Persian family of wealthy landlords from the village of Biyābānak, located approximately fifteen kilometers southwest of Simnān in the direction of Rayy (Tehran). Jāmī states that Simnānī's ancestry was from the feudal lords (*mulūk*) of Simnān.[1] The title *malik* was used by his father and uncles, and theirs appears to have been the family with the second largest land-holding in the Simnān area. The largest landowner during Simnānī's lifetime was Sayyid Ibrāhīm-i Simnānī, a minor Sufi figure in his own right who died at least ten years before Simnānī. He was succeeded by his son, Ashraf Jahāngīr-i Simnānī (d. ca. 808/1404–5), who left his property to his younger brother, Sayyid 'Imād ad-dīn, in order to become a disciple of 'Alā' ad-dawla, and later of 'Abd ar-Razzāq al-Kāshānī.[2]

Simnānī's family belonged to the Sunnī landed aristocracy of Khurāsān, which was characterized by political quietism and allegiance to any regime that came to power. He was apparently descended on his mother's side from Ḍiyā' al-mulk (also called Ḍiyā' ad-dīn) Muḥammad b. Mawdūd, a courtier of Muḥammad Khwārazmshāh, who was in the service of Jalāl ad-dīn Khwārazmshāh when he was defeated by the Mongols and fled across the Indus.[3] His maternal uncle,

---

1. Jāmī, 439. The statement is repeated by Shushtarī (2:134), Dārā Shikūh (107) and Ma'ṣūm 'Alī Shāh (2:653).

2. Waḥīd Ashraf Kachawchawī, *Ḥayāt-i Sayyid Ashraf Jahāngīr-i Simnānī* (Lucknow: Sarfarāz Qawmī Press, 1975), 12ff.

3. Khwānd Amīr, *Ḥabīb as-siyar*, 3:208; *Dastūr al-wuzarā'*, ed. Sa'īd Nafīsī (Tehran: Kitābfurūshī-yi Iqbāl, 1938), 323; Shihāb ad-dīn al-Khwāfī Ḥāfiẓ-i Abrū, *Dhayl jāmi' at-tawārīkh*, ed. Khānbābā Biyānī (Tehran: Shirkat-i taḍāmunī-yi 'ilmī, 1938), 116.

Khwāja Rukn ad-dīn-i Ṣā'in, held the office of *qāḍī-yi jumlat al-mamālik* (chief magistrate) until his execution by order of Ghāzān on 22 Dhu'l-Ḥijja 700/28 August 1301.[4] Simnānī's paternal great-grandfather, Ḍiyā' ad-dīn Biyābānakī-yi Simnānī, was also a member of the Khwārazmid court, having been appointed one of five *wazīrs* by 'Alā' ad-dīn Muḥammad in 596/1200.[5] Both Simnānī's father, Malik Sharaf ad-dīn, and paternal uncle, Jalāl ad-dīn-i Mukhliṣ, entered the service of Arghūn when he was ruling Khurāsān. Simnānī's father served intermittently as *ulugh tupakchī* (master of the guards), *ṣāhib-i dīwān* (master of the exchequer) of Iraq and *malik* of Baghdad under Ghāzān from 687/1288 until his execution in 695/1295–96. His paternal uncle became a *wazīr* in 683/1284, and was elevated to *wazīr* of Iran upon the death of Shams ad-dīn Muḥammad-i Būqā in 685/1286, but was removed from this post in 697/1297–98 and executed in the following year.[6]

Both sides of Simnānī's family were deeply involved in the court intrigues and political conspiracies of their day. Rukn ad-dīn-i Ṣā'in was an enemy of Sa'd ad-dīn Muḥammad-i Awajī, who had succeeded Jamāl ad-dīn-i Dastirjānī (or Dastgirdānī) as Ghāzān's *wazīr*, and probably met his end as a result of this conflict.[7] Sharaf ad-dīn and Jalāl ad-dīn-i Simnānī were closely associated with Arghūn loyalists such as Amīr Nawrūz who were accused (with very little substantiation) of conspiring with the Mamluks during Ghāzān's reign.[8] They also incurred the wrath of Sa'd ad-dawla (d. 690/1291), the most

---

4. Mustawfī, *Tā'rīkh-i guzīda*, 605; Khwāfī, 2:382. There is some confusion in the sources between Rukn ad-dīn Ṣā'in-i Simnānī, and Nuṣrat Allāh 'Ādil, also known as Rukn ad-dīn Ṣā'in. The latter was the deputy (*nā'ib*) of Amīr Chūbān and advanced in his service until he became a *wazīr* under Abū Sa'īd in 724/1324. He was later implicated in the execution of Chūbān's son, Dimashq Khwāja (Mustawfī, 624–6; Khwānd Amīr, *Ḥabīb as-siyar*, 3:208–9; *Dastūr al-wuzarā'*, 323).

5. The other four were Tāj ad-dīn-i Nīshāpūrī, Sharīf Muḥammad an-Nasawī, Najm ad-dīn-i Kalābādhī, and Majd ad-dīn-i Hishmī (Khwāfī, 2:277). Cf. Josef Van Ess, "'Alā' al-dawla Semnānī," *Encyclopaedia Iranica*, ed. Ehsan Yarshater (London: Routledge and Kegan Paul, 1985), 1:774b–77a, where the date is listed as 614/1218.

6. Khwāfī, 2:353, 359, 687, 362, 374; Rashīd ad-dīn, *Jāmi' at-tawārīkh*, ed. Bahman Karīmī (Tehran: Kitābfurūshī-yi Iqbāl, 1959; rpt. 1988), 2:819–20; Khwānd Amīr, *Ḥabīb as-siyar*, 3:125; *Dastūr al-wuzarā'*, 295; Mustawfī, 597; Sadr, 21.

7. Khwānd Amīr, *Dastūr al-wuzarā'*, 314.

8. Mustawfī, 603.

important administrator during Arghūn's reign, and fell prey to his machinations.

Arghūn maintained a policy of discrimination against Muslim—particularly Sunnī—courtiers, and appointed Jews and Christians whenever feasible. Among his closest advisors was Sa'd ad-dawla, the son of Ṣafī ad-dīn-i Abharī. Jalāl ad-dīn-i Simnānī was discredited and killed as a result of conspiracies involving Sa'd ad-dawla, who succeeded him as *wazīr*. Over time, Sa'd ad-dawla became the most powerful person after the Ilkhan himself and appointed his own relatives to important posts: his brother Fakhr ad-dawla became governor of Baghdad, other brothers the rulers of Diyārbakr, Rabī'a and Azarbāyjān, and a cousin that of Fārs.[9] By 688/1289 Sa'd ad-dawla had become open in his anti-Islamic rhetoric and temporarily convinced Arghūn not to appoint Muslims to positions at the court and to bar them from the royal camp.[10]

Early Life and Conversion to Sufism

Considering the nature of his family, it is not surprising that 'Alā' ad-dawla as-Simnānī was raised to occupy a position at the Ilkhanid court. When he was four years old his father sent him to a local teacher named Ṣadr ad-dīn-i Akhfāsh with whom he studied for almost eleven years.[11] This is probably the same individual as the teacher of grammar named Sayyid-i Akhfāsh mentioned in the *Chihil majlis*.[12] Simnānī emphasizes this man's vehement opposition to Sufism in order to stress his own ignorance of it in the years preceding his mystical conversion. Although he had not been formally educated in Sufism at an early age, Simnānī came in contact with a number of Sufis during his childhood. In addition to Sayyid Ibrāhīm-i Simnānī mentioned above, he also met a number of wandering mystics as they passed through Simnān. These wandering dervishes cannot be identified on account of the scarce biographical information that is available. The first was a certain Siyāwash ash-Shirwānī, who came from Turkestan

-----

9. Khwānd Amīr, *Dastūr al-wuzarā'*, 296ff.; *Ḥabīb as-siyar*, 3:125; Rashīd ad-dīn, 2:819–20.

10. Khwānd Amīr, *Dastūr al-wuzarā'*, 301. For more information on Sa'd ad-dawla and the religious situation under Arghūn, see Kamil M. Al-Shaibi, *Sufism and Shi'ism* (Surbiton: LAAM, 1991), 109ff.

11. *al-Wārid ash-shārid*, 27a.

12. Iqbāl-i Sīstānī (Sijistānī), *Chihil majlis*, ed. N. M. Hirawī (Tehran: Intishārāt-i adīb, 1987), 188.

when Simnānī was eleven, and stayed in Simnān for one year before
going to Iṣfahān and dying there four years later (675/1276–77).[13] He
also met a certain mystic named Mahdī-yi Ḥajjī when he was fourteen,
and visited Ḥajjī-yi Abharī at his mosque in Abhar.[14]

At the age of fifteen (674/1275–76) and with the encouragement
of his paternal uncle, Simnānī joined the court of Arghūn (reigned
683/1284 – 691/1292), a committed Buddhist known for his hostility
towards Islam.[15] Very little is known about his life at the court in
Tabriz, except that Buddhist monks (*bakhshīyān*) held a prominent
position and engaged in debates with Muslim scholars for the benefit
of Arghūn.[16]

Conversion Experience

On 16 Ṣafar 683/4 May 1284 Simnānī participated in a battle at
Aqkhwāja outside Qazwīn between Arghūn and 'Alīnāq, the general

---

13. Dār al-kutub, untitled, 145a; *Risāla fī-dhikr asāmī mashāyikhī*, MS.
11-mīm, Majāmī' fārsiyya, Dār al-kutub, Cairo, 75b.

14. *R. fī-dhikr asāmī mashāyikhī*, 75b.

15. Bertold Spuler, *Die Mongolen in Iran* (Berlin: Akademie Verlag, 1955),
184ff.; Manūchihr Murtaḍawī, *Masā'il-i 'aṣr-i Īlkhānān* (Tabriz: Intishārāt-i
mu'assasa-yi tā'rīkh wa farhang-i Īrān, 1979), 176.

16. Simnānī uses *bakhshī* (plural *bakhshīyān*) as a generic term for all non-
Muslim religious figures from Central and South Asia. From Simnānī's
references to their beliefs, one can gather that the most influential ones were
Buddhists, which is not surprising since Arghūn was himself a Buddhist and
the eastern front of the Ilkhanid empire probably still had a measurable
Buddhist population.

Simnānī's autobiographical writings display a degree of antipathy
towards Buddhists. A significant exception is the case of a certain Bakhshī
Parinda mentioned in the *Chihil majlis*. Simnānī allegedly knew him from
Arghūn's court and acknowledged that Bakhshī Parinda was spiritually very
advanced despite his non-Muslim status. Later on, when Bakhshī Parinda came
to Biyābānak, Simnānī concocted an excuse not to see him, but used a ruse
to enlist the monk's help in guiding one of Simnānī's own disciples. (*Chihil
majlis*, 81ff.; Molé, "Les Kubrawiya," 79ff.). The implications of this instance
of Buddhist-Muslim collaboration are interesting; however, the *Chihil majlis*
very consciously minimizes the extent of contact. Bakhshī Parinda relates
in his own words how other monks in Somnāth ostracized him and accused
him of being closer to Islam in his religious beliefs than he was to Buddhism.
He is also credited with turning Arghūn away from idol-worship towards a
quasi-Islamic belief in the oneness of God, judgement and an afterlife (*Chihil
majlis*, 84).

and son-in-law of Aḥmad Takūdar (reigned 681/1282 to 683/1284).[17] At this time Simnānī was twenty-four years old. When the battle lines were drawn, as soon as he said the battle-cry of *"Allāhu akbar!"* ("God is Great") Simnānī underwent a mystical experience.[18] "When I was busy saying the *takbīr*, God (may He be praised and exalted) removed the veil of this world from in front of these blind eyes and revealed the beauty of the world to come."[19] This mystical state (*ḥāl*) lasted through the battle and into the next day, after which Simnānī slowly returned to normalcy.

Simnānī's religious crisis on the battle field was one of the most momentous incidents in his life. It was the occasion of his first visionary experience, and the event to which he attributes his religious conversion. It is not surprising, therefore, that this occasion is alluded to in all major autobiographical accounts written by Simnānī although, perhaps out of embarrassment, he seldom refers directly to the battle. This incident is recognized as an important event in his life in Sufi biographical works as well. For Simnānī, the main feature of this experience was its noetic quality, enabling him to catch a fleeting glimpse of the world in its true nature. This feeling was so strong that he could not participate in the battle, feeling as if God had placed an obstacle in his way, preventing him from fighting.[20]

"When God cast into my heart the light of will (*nūr al-irāda*) and awakened me from the slumber of heedlessness, my soul turned away in disgust from the pleasures of this world and I became weary of the company of the Sultan."[21] This awareness of the "errors" of his

---

17. *Fatḥ al-mubīn*, 2b; 'Alī Īnāq according to Dawlatshāh Samarqandī (252); for details of the battle, see Khwāfī, 2:353; Spuler, 80–81; Khwand Amīr gives the date as 687/1288 (*Ḥabīb as-siyar*, 3:220; Nawā'ī, ed., *Rijāl-i kitāb-i ḥabīb as-siyar* [Tehran: Sahāmī, 1946], 30).

18. *Fatḥ al-mubīn*, 2b; *al-Wārid ash-shārid*, 27a; *R. fī-dhikr asāmī mashāyikhī*, 72; cf. *Hadiyyat al-muhtadī wa-hidāyat al-mubtadi'*, according to which he would have been nineteen at this time (81b).

19. *Fatḥ al-mubīn*, 2b ff.

20. *R. fī-dhikr asāmī mashāyikhī*, 72b. There is no mention of the battle in this account. On no occasion does Simnānī mention whether he left the battlefield at that moment or continued to command his troops. Historical references to the Battle of Aqkhwāja, which ended in an ambiguous defeat of the forces loyal to Takūdar, do not mention this incident in Simnānī's life. The fact that he continued to be a welcomed member of Arghūn's court suggests that Simnānī continued to command his troops despite his agitated spiritual state.

21. *Hadiyyat al-muhtadī*, 81a.

past life, including his employment at the court of Arghūn, seems to have been clearly articulated in his writings years after he actually underwent the experience. Shortly after this time, he suffered a second mystical experience in which he encountered the Prophet Muḥammad and Abū Yazīd al-Bisṭāmī (d. 261/875) in a dream. Simnānī then consciously began to compensate for neglected religious duties by adopting an ascetic life, saying ten days' worth of prayers each night to make up for the prayers forfeited in his youth, and memorizing five verses from the Qur'ān each day.[22] He journeyed to seek out mystical guides, two of whom were named Mahdī-yi Kiyā and Khwāja-yi Ḥājjī.[23] The former resided at Āmul and had renounced the world to live in seclusion, while the latter was an ascetic (*zāhid*) living in Abhar. They are almost certainly the same individuals as the wandering mystics named Mahdī-yi Ḥājjī and Ḥājjī-yi Abharī whom Simnānī encountered in his youth.[24] Simnānī confided in Khwāja-yi Ḥājjī about his wish to leave the service of Arghūn, but Khwāja-yi Ḥājjī told him to stay, because "we pray that God may increase the number of people like you among them, meaning among the Sultan and his courtiers."[25] Simnānī took his advice and continued his life of asceticism and renunciation in Tabriz for another year and a half. He repented, gave up alcohol, spending his nights in prayer and his days memorizing the Qur'ān, accompanied in worship by Sharaf ad-dīn Ḥasan b. 'Abd Allāh al-Qarwānī.[26]

His rigorous life of asceticism took its toll and he was struck by a prolonged illness which the Sultan's physicians found impossible to cure. He asked permission to return to Simnān, and was allowed to do so by Arghūn. Simnānī left the encampment (*urdū*) of Uljāytū Khudābanda on the sixteenth of Sha'bān 685/7 October 1286, reaching Simnān in Ramaḍān of the same year.[27] When he had traveled only

---

22. *al-'Urwa li-ahl al-khalwa wa'l-jalwa*, ed. N. Māyil-i Hirawī (Tehran: Intishārāt-i Mawlā, 1983), 298.

23. Dār al-kutub, untitled, 145b.

24. *R. fī-dhikr asāmī mashāyikhī*, 75b; see above, p. 18.

25. Dār al-kutub, untitled, 145b.

26. *al-Wārid ash-shārid*, 27a. Simnānī does not mention him at any other time and no further information about him is known. In his youth Isfarā'inī was a disciple of a certain Shaykh 'Abd Allāh, a student of Rashīd ad-dīn-i Ṭūsī, who in turn was a disciple of 'Alī-yi Lālā (Landolt, *Révélateur*, 25–26). Sharaf ad-dīn could conceivably be the son of this Shaykh 'Abd Allāh.

27. *Fatḥ al-mubīn*, 3a; *R. fī-dhikr asāmī mashāyikhī*, 72b; *'Urwa*, 299; Faṣīḥ Khwāfī, 2:358.

a short distance from Tabriz, his fever grew worse and he sat in freezing water at Ūjān for an hour. After leaving the water he began to pray and was completely cured.

> And I knew that God had cured me on the outside without the efforts of a physician, and that he was going to cure me on the inside of the sickness of love for this world and obedience to desires.[28]

This constituted Simnānī's third involuntary mystical experience, and clearly reinforced his belief that God had guided him away from an undesirable worldly life to that of a true believer. Upon reaching Simnān in the beginning of Ramaḍān, 'Alā' ad-dawla abandoned his courtly robe, hat and belt , symbolically turning away from his worldly past, and adopted Sufi dress at the tomb of Ḥasan-i Sakkāk.[29]

Simnānī claims that at the time he had entered the service of Arghūn, although he had been well-versed in the rational and traditional sciences ('ulūm-i 'aqlī wa naqlī), he was sadly lacking in a religious education, having only memorized six short chapters from the Qur'ān.[30] To make up for this deficiency he studied the legal sciences and familiarized himself with the principles of belief of the Indians, Greeks, Turks, Persians and Arabs, as well as the teachings of the Sunnī schools. He also studied a number of different sects (e.g., the Qalandariyya, Ibn al-I'rābiyya, and Nuṣayriyya), none of which pleased him.[31] Lacking a spiritual guide, Simnānī attempted to acquire mystical knowledge from books, in particular the Qūt al-qulūb of Abū Ṭālib al-Makkī (d. 383/993 or 386/996). He based his religious practice upon such works; however, he remained dissatisfied with them because the religious knowledge he acquired from books was rational, attained through scholarly learning and reason, rather than exper-

---

28. *Hadiyyat al-muhtadī*, 81b. Cf. Dār al-kutub, untitled, 146a, according to which he was cured upon reaching Simnān.

29. *Fatḥ al-mubīn*, 3a; *R. fī-asāmī mashāyikhī*, 72b. Ḥasan-i Sakkāk-i Simnānī was a student of Abu'l-Ḥasan al-Bustī, one of the disciples of Abū 'Alī al-Fārmadhī (d. 477/1084–85) (Jāmī, 413–14).

30. The *Fātiḥa*, *an-Naṣr* (110) and the four *Qalāqil* (109, 112–114) (*'Urwa*, 297).

31. *al-Wārid ash-shārid*, 27b–28a. Detailed descriptions are given of the shortcomings of these groups; cf. *Hadiyyat al-muhtadī*, 81ff., where Simnānī outlines his examination of a variety of religions and Islamic sects.

iential, acquired by way of witnessing (*mushāhada*) and inner discovery.[32] He grew increasingly discontented with his progress until
Muḥarram 686/February 1287 when he had a major mystical experience.[33]

Contact with Nūr ad-dīn al-Isfarā'inī

During this early period of Sufi education Simnānī engaged in
mystical exercises of his own design. He allegedly prayed three
hundred prayer cycles (*rak'āt*) each day and repeated *dhikr* formulae
twelve thousand times, consisting of *tasbīḥ, taḥmīd, tahlīl* and
takbīr.[34] This state of affairs continued until the arrival in Simnān
of a disciple of Nūr ad-dīn al-Isfarā'inī named Akhī Sharaf ad-dīn Sa'd
Allāh al-Ḥanawayh.[35] There is some confusion as to the exact time
of his arrival in Simnān on his way from Khurāsān to Baghdad. Three
separate dates are given for his arrival, of which one, Ramaḍān
685/October 1286,[36] is chronologically impossible as this is the time
of Simnānī's return from the court of Arghūn. The second date of
Dhu'l-Ḥijja 685/January 1287[37] is also highly unlikely since Simnānī

---

32. *al-Wārid ash-shārid*, 29a.

33. *Hadiyyat al-muhtadī*, 81b–82a. "God opened before me the doors of
discovery and witnessing, which the tongue cannot describe, and about which
the fingers are incapable of writing."

34. Dār al-kutub, untitled, 146a; saying "Glory be to God" (*subḥān Allāh*),
"Praise be to God" (*al-ḥamdu li'llāh*), "There is no God but Allāh" (*lā ilāha
illa'llāh*), and "God is Greatest" (*Allāhu akbar*). These are the same *dhikr*
formulae which Isfarā'inī's father taught him to say (Landolt, *Révélateur*, 20).
Cf. *'Urwa*, 313, according to which he prayed ten days' worth of ritual prayer
(*namāz*) each day plus one hundred supererogatory *rak'āt* (*nawāfil*).

35. No biographical information has been found on this man independent
of the writings of Simnānī and Isfarā'inī. The *nisba* Ḥanawayh most probably
derives from the town of Ḥanā near Diyārbakr (Abū Sa'd as-Sam'ānī, *Kitāb
al-ansāb*, ed. 'Abd ar-Raḥmān al-Yamānī (Hyderabad: Dā'irat al-ma'ārif, 1962),
4:290; Ibn al-Athīr al-Jazarī, *al-Lubāb fī-tahdhīb al-ansāb* (Beirut: Dār Ṣādir,
1972), 1:397–98; cf. Yāqūt ar-Rūmī, *Mu'jam al-buldān* (Beirut: Dār Ṣadir, 1979),
2:208, where the name of the town is listed as al-Ḥānī). The name could
possibly also derive from *ḥanwatun*, meaning "a stooping of the head, and
bowing of the back, in prayer" (Lane, *Arabic-English Lexicon*, 2:660), thus
implying someone characterized by constant prayer; cf. *al-Wārid ash-shārid*,
29b, where it is Ḥabawayh.

36. *R. fī-dhikr asāmī mashāyikhī*, 73a.

37. Dār al-kutub, untitled, 146a.

spent more than three months engaged in mystical exercises of his own design. Thus the probable date of Simnānī's initial contact with Sharaf ad-dīn al-Ḥanawayh is the beginning of Ramaḍān 686/October 1287.[38]

It is difficult to ascertain the exact identity of Sharaf ad-dīn al-Ḥanawayh. He was a wandering mystic who claimed to have performed the Ḥajj three times, had lived in Mecca for the purpose of being near the Ka'ba, and had served as an attendant to various Sufis.[39] At some point in Mecca he had become a disciple of Isfarā'inī who had instructed him in Jumādā II 685/August 1286 to go to Khurāsān, and told him that when he found a nobleman who had undergone a religious experience (*jadhba-yi makramat-yi ḥaqq*), Ḥanawayh was to become his companion and attendant.[40]

Ḥanawayh became Simnānī's prayer companion during this period in Simnān. It was Ḥanawayh who introduced Simnānī to the *dhikr* practice of Isfarā'inī, an event which Simnānī described in great detail.[41] One day the two of them were praying side by side when, after finishing his prayers, Simnānī noticed that his companion was engaged in an exercise which involved throwing his head from side to side. When Ḥanawayh was done, Simnānī asked him if he was doing this because his head hurt. He replied that he was engaged in *dhikr*, upon which Simnānī reprimanded him and told him that it was better to engage in the *dhikr* of the Caliph Abū Bakr aṣ-Ṣiddīq, which involved repeating the formula "There is no God but Allāh, the Master, the Real, the Apparent; Muḥammad is His messenger, true to what he

---

38. *Fatḥ al-mubīn*, 3a. The date does not appear in the MS. 11-mīm, Majāmī' fārsiyya copy of the treatise.

39. *'Urwa*, 314.

40. Ibid., 318–19. A person named Sharaf ad-dīn-i Badī' appears in the correspondence between Isfarā'inī and Simnānī (Landolt, *Correspondence*, 12, 76). This is most probably the same individual as Akhī Sharaf ad-dīn al-Ḥanawayh. The latter of the two letters in which he is mentioned, written in 693/1294, refers to him as deceased (Landolt, *Correspondence*, 37, note 34). It is unlikely that Akhī Sharaf ad-dīn is the same person as Sharaf ad-dīn Ḥasan b. 'Abd Allāh al-Qarwānī who had been Simnānī's prayer companion at the court (see above, p. 20). Simnānī states repeatedly and clearly that he had never met Akhī Sharaf ad-dīn before the latter's arrival in Simnān.

41. *Fatḥ al-mubīn*, 3a. Accounts, varying in detail, of Simnānī's introduction to the *dhikr* practice of Isfarā'inī are to be found in *Fatḥ al-mubīn*, 3a ff.; Untitled MS. 11-mīm, 146; *R. fī-dhikr asāmī mashāyikhī*, 73; *al-Wārid ash-shārid*, 29; *'Urwa*, 314ff.

promised, the trustworthy."[42] Ḥanawayh stated that his *shaykh* had taught him the practice and he did not dare alter it. Then he explained the significance of moving his head:

> With the *lā ilāha* (There is no god) I negate everything besides God, and with the *illa'llāh* (except Allāh) I affirm the love of God in the heart. I move so that the energy of the *dhikr* reaches the pineal [physical] heart which is located in the flank of the human body. As a result, the transparency (*shaffāfī*) which lies between this [physical] heart and the real [mystical] heart becomes actualized, and the light of faith casts a ray from the real heart upon the human body.[43]

Upon hearing this, Simnānī beseeched Ḥanawayh to teach him this *dhikr*. On his first night of practice, Simnānī underwent mystical experiences that made him doubt his own sanity. He described them to Ḥanawayh who informed Simnānī that these were states that normally could be attained only after a long period of labor.[44] Simnānī then asked Ḥanawayh the name of his *shaykh* and so became acquainted with the identity of Nūr ad-dīn al-Isfarā'inī for the very first time. Through Ḥanawayh he became a follower of Isfarā'inī, and continued his religious exercises according to the method of his new master as it was described to him by Ḥanawayh.[45]

As a result of his association with Sharaf ad-dīn and the mystical states he attained under this man's guidance, Simnānī came to the conclusion that in order to develop his spiritual side he had to rid himself of worldly concerns such as his land, property, and even his family.[46] Simnānī gives the distinct impression that he gave away all

---

42. *Fatḥ al-mubīn*, 3a. "True to what he promised" is missing in this manuscript, but is to be found in MS. 11-mīm, Majāmī' fārsiyya, Dār al-kutub, 195a. The attributes of God and Muḥammad appearing in this formula are extracted and combined from phrases appearing in a number of Qur'ānic verses (19:54, 20:114, 23:112, 24:25 and 27:79).

43. Ibid., 3b.

44. *Fatḥ al-mubīn*, 3b; *Tafsīr najm al-qur'ān*, MS. 165, Şehit Ali Paşa, Süleymaniye Kütüphanesi, Istanbul, 25b.

45. Isfarā'inī himself learnt the *dhikr* of his *shaykh*, Aḥmad-i Gūrpānī (or Jūrfānī, d. 669/1270), through an intermediary named Pūr-i Ḥasan (Landolt, *Révélateur*, 20).

46. *al-Wārid ash-shārid*, 29b.

his worldly possessions and adopted the life of a penniless ascetic. In the *'Urwa* he states that he had already done so in the winter following Ramaḍān 685/October 1286 (probably on the occasion of his mystical experience of Muḥarram 686/February 1287).

> I became eager to divest myself of all the money I possessed. I returned what was due to whomsoever I knew. That [money] about which I did not know, I gave all of it in religious endowments and charity. I freed all my bondsmen and women. I provided for my wife and for my son more than my father had provided for me. And I built the Khānaqāh-i Sakkākiyya which is named after Ḥasan-i Sakkākī.[47]

In actual fact, Simnānī appears to have retained control over the land endowments which were his major source of income. According to Ṣafadī, he used to derive 90,000 dirhams annually from his land which he spent in pious enterprises.[48] Ibn Ḥajar al-'Asqalānī corroborates the claim that Simnānī only gave away some of his wealth.[49] Simnānī continued to use his financial resources for religious purposes, and in 709/1309-10 he sent five thousand dirhams to Isfarā'inī's *khānaqāh*.[50]

After several months of following the directions of Sharaf ad-dīn al-Ḥanawayh, Simnānī felt the need to see Isfarā'inī in person. His autobiographical writings incorrectly give the date he set out to visit Isfarā'inī in Baghdad as Muḥarram 686/February 1287.[51] The correct date is most probably Muḥarram of the following year since in Muḥarram of 686/February 1287 Simnānī was in Simnān and had not yet heard of Isfarā'inī from Sharaf ad-dīn.[52] News of his intentions reached Arghūn who sent troops to intercept him in Hamadān and

---

47. *'Urwa*, 299. This is the only context in which Simnānī mentions his wife. As is common in self-narratives of this period, he never mentions his wife and mother by name. The son referred to is probably Nūḥ, who turned four shortly after Simnānī moved to Simnān and adopted Sufi dress. Nothing more is known about him, or about his other son, Abu'ṣ-Ṣafā' (*Chihil majlis*, 178–79).

48. Ṣafadī, *al-Wāfī bi'l-wafayāt*, 7:357; *A'yān al-'aṣr*, 48b.

49. Ibn Ḥajar al-'Asqalānī, 1:266.

50. Landolt, *Révélateur*, 29.

51. *Fatḥ al-mubīn*, 4a; *'Urwa*, 320.

52. Khwāfī gives the date of Simnānī's journey as 687/1288 (2:360).

bring him, by force if necessary, to Sharūyāz (near Tabriz) where the
Ilkhanid ruler was busy constructing the new capital of Sulṭāniyya.
Simnānī was held at the court for eighty days and forced to engage
in theological debates with Buddhist monks from India, Kashmir and
Tibet. At this time Jalāl ad-dīn-i Simnānī and Rukn ad-dīn-i Ṣā'in were
respectively Arghūn's *wazīr* and *nadīm* (royal companion).[53]

Although the reasons underlying his kidnapping are not mentioned, the *Chihil majlis* provides some details which suggest that
Arghūn's personal affection for Simnānī played a part in these events.[54]
When he was first brought back from Hamadān, Arghūn tried to
engage him in light conversation but Simnānī sat there in silence. His
uncle Jalāl ad-dīn and the other courtiers reminded him that he was
one of them, and scolded him for being rude to the Sultan. Arghūn
then called for a Buddhist monk and ordered him to engage Simnānī
in a debate, but Simnānī defeated the Buddhist by demonstrating that
he was ignorant of the true meaning of the Buddha's teachings. Pleased
with Simnānī's performance, Arghūn asked him to stay at the court
but Simnānī refused. Later Arghūn took him into a garden and, after
trying to convince Simnānī that Islam was a false religion, asked him
to remain, even with the status of a Sufi if he wished, for the sake
of the love which Arghūn bore him.[55] Simnānī did so reluctantly, but
when he was denied permission to go to Baghdad he returned to
Simnān without leave, sending Ḥanawayh to Baghdad to see Isfarā'inī.

When his uncle Jalāl ad-dīn learnt of his abrupt departure, with
Arghūn's consent he despatched a mystic named Ḥājjī-yi Āmulī after
Simnānī to distract him from the influence of Isfarā'inī and ensure
that he did not change his itinerary and go to Baghdad. Simnānī states
that he disliked this man from the very start, and saw him in a dream
as a venomous serpent entering his uncle's tent. Over the course of
their journey Simnānī ascertained the true nature of Āmulī's heterodox
and pantheistic beliefs, and tried to convince his Turkish attendant
to kill him. Under threat of death, Āmulī renounced his beliefs and

---

53. *Chihil majlis*, 206.

54. Much of the property that Simnānī gave away after his mystical
conversion was not inherited from his father, but had been given to him by
Arghūn (*Chihil majlis*, 243). Despite Arghūn's affection for him, Simnānī
clearly indicates that he was persecuted at the court. If anyone found out that
he was fasting, they would forcibly put food in his mouth, and even force him
to drink wine. The solution was for Simnānī to dissimulate when he was
fasting (*Chihil majlis*, 178).

55. *Chihil majlis*, 150ff.

burned all the books given to him by his teacher, a certain ʻAfīf ad-dīn al-Miṣrī.[56]

Sharaf ad-dīn al-Ḥanawayh returned from Baghdad towards the end of Shaʻbān, several months after ʻAlāʼ ad-dawla had reached Simnān. He brought with him a message from Isfarāʼinī stating that it was not necessary for them to meet in person, and that Simnānī could continue his mystical exercises under Isfarāʼinī's guidance while remaining in Simnān, using Sharaf ad-dīn al-Ḥanawayh as an intermediary. Isfarāʼinī sent Simnānī an authorization (ijāza) to enter solitary meditation (khalwa) and a reply to a letter containing explanations of mystical experiences, visions and unveilings (mukāshafāt) experienced by Simnānī.[57] As a sign of encouragement he also sent Simnānī a variegated Sufi robe (khirqa-yi mulammaʻa).[58]

Simnānī succeeded in journeying to Baghdad and meeting Isfarāʼinī for the first time in Ramaḍān 688/September 1289. He remained in solitary meditation in the Masjid-i khalīfa until the 26th of Ramaḍān/13 October, when he embarked upon a pilgrimage to Mecca by order of Isfarāʼinī. Following the Ḥajj, he returned to Baghdad towards the end of Muḥarram 689/January 1290 and entered the Shūnīziyya on a two-week solitary retreat according to the principles of Sarī as-Saqaṭī (d. ca. 251/865).[59] It was only after returning from Mecca that Simnānī learned about the execution of his paternal uncle, Malik Jalāl ad-dīn, in 688/1289. In all, he spent approximately one

------

56. *Chihil majlis*, 207ff. This teacher may have been ʻAfīf ad-dīn Sulaymān b. ʻAlī at-Tilimsānī (d. 690/1291), who was accused of being a heretic (zindīq) by some strict religious scholars (Jāmī, 570–71; Landolt, *Correspondence*, 41, note 45). Simnānī claims Āmulī stated that Islamic law was intended only for the ignorant, and that anyone who understood the true nature of the world had no need for it. He also stated that the two main divine mysteries were *kān Allāhu wa-lam yakun maʻahu shay'un* ("There was God and there was nothing besides Him") and *al-ān kamā kān* ("He is today as He always was"). Taken together, these statements are normally understood to imply an ontological identity between God and the universe.

Simnānī appears to have been deeply concerned about the possible negative impact of these teachings, and attempted to gather more information on this Shaykh ʻAfīf ad-dīn al-Miṣrī during his travels (*Chihil majlis*, 211). If this is true, it is a foreshadowing of his later opposition to more pantheistic forms of Sufism which, in Simnānī's mind, compromised God's transcendence and undermined the importance of normative Islamic beliefs and practices.

57. *ʻUrwa*, 322.

58. Khwāfī, 2:360.

59. *ʻUrwa*, 323–24.

additional month with his *shaykh* before Simnānī was given a second Sufi robe and authorized to accept disciples of his own. Isfarā'inī then commanded him to return to Simnān out of piety towards his mother.[60]

The circumstances surrounding Simnānī's first meeting with his *shaykh* suggest a degree of political turmoil involving both Isfarā'inī and the Simnānī family which is not mentioned in Simnānī's writings. Isfarā'inī's instructing Simnānī to go on the Hajj at the same time that his father was imprisoned in Baghdad and his uncle was disgraced and executed seems too propitious to have been coincidental.[61] Furthermore, Isfarā'inī insisted that Simnānī visit Medina and then return with the Iraqi pilgrims' caravan, thus adding more time to his journey.[62] Finally there is Isfarā'inī's insistence that Simnānī return to Simnān, ostensibly to care for his mother, after an all too brief sojourn in Baghdad. At this time Ghazan was actively engaged in campaigns against the Mamluks and, although they briefly held Syria in 698/1299, the Ilkhanids were proving to be the weaker party.[63] Like a number of other Sunnī figures in the Mongol administration, Simnānī's father and uncle appear to have been implicated in conspiracies with the Mamluks. It is likely that Isfarā'inī was eager to get Simnānī out of Baghdad, a city which was a focal point of political unrest during this period.

Life in Simnān

Upon returning to Simnān, 'Alā' ad-dawla as-Simnānī established himself at the Khānaqāh-i Sakkākiyya which he had constructed. At some point he also built a large *khānaqāh* (convent) of his own called Ṣūfīyābād-i Khudādād outside his ancestral home of Biyābānak.[64] He

---

60. *R. fī-dhikr asāmī mashāyikhī*, 74b; *al-Wārid ash-shārid*, 30a; Khwāfī, 2:362–63; cf. Dār al-kutub, untitled (146b); Khwānd Amīr, *Ḥabīb as-siyar* (3:220); and Jāmī (439), which do not mention his stay in Baghdad preceding the journey to Mecca.

61. Rashīd ad-dīn, 2:819–20.

62. *'Urwa*, 324. Simnānī posits that he was instructed to travel with the Iraqi pilgrims' caravan and not informed of his uncle's death for fear that, hearing of the execution, he would go to Syria and cause trouble, thus placing his Sufi associates in Baghdad in a difficult situation.

63. Rashīd ad-dīn, 2:938.

64. No date for the construction of this convent can be found. Also, it is not absolutely certain that Simnānī had Ṣūfīyābād-i Khudādād built himself. An ambiguous reference in Ṣafadī's *Kitāb al-wāfī bi'l-wafayāt* (7:357) and *A'yān al-'aṣr* (48b), which most probably refers to the construction of this

devoted himself in solitary mystical exercises under the guidance of
Isfara'ini, with whom he continued to maintain active correspondence
through the agency of Akhi Sharaf ad-din al-Hanawayh. At this time
Simnani also began to guide disciples, until he had forty people prac-
tising under his direction.[65] However, he was distressed by the worldly
ways of his immediate family, particularly by their allegiance to the
Ilkhanid ruler. He entertained the idea of emigrating to Syria, but
Isfara'ini forbade him to do so.[66]

Simnani excelled in engaging in forty-day meditational exercises
(arba'inat) and, over the course of his life time, allegedly completed
one hundred and forty such retreats at the Khanaqah-i Sakkakiyya
and one hundred and thirty at other locations.[67] He continued his
policy of avoiding contact with the Ilkhanid court which, in turn, was
not sympathetic to his attempts at maintaining close contacts with
Isfara'ini. Simnani nevertheless continued his regular correspondence
with his Sufi guide. In addition to containing the mystical instructions
of Isfara'ini and his answers to questions posed by Simnani, thus
shedding light on the master-disciple relationship in Sufism, these
letters also provide information about Isfara'ini and Simnani's associates and disciples, the organization of Isfara'ini's Sufi circle in
Baghdad, and some hints about the political atmosphere of the time.

Until the reign of Abu Sa'id (716/1316 – 735/1335) Simnani's
relationship with the Ilkhanid court remained strained. His uncle,
Khwaja Rukn ad-din-i Sa'in, was executed by order of Ghazan in
700/1301.[68] There was a temporary amelioration of the situation in
705/1305 when Uljaytu (reigned 704/1304 – 716/1316) accepted
Simnani's religious position and allowed him to continue in a life of
asceticism and mysticism, and invited him to Sultaniyya to participate

---

khanaqah, suggests that the Ilkhan Abu Sa'id might have had it built: "King
Bu Sa'id visited him, and he built a khanaqah for the Sufis, and endowed
it with a waqf."

65. Dar al-kutub, untitled, 146b.

66. al-Warid ash-sharid, 30b.

67. Jami, 439–40; Khwand Amir, Habib as-siyar, 3:220; Shushtari, 2:134;
Mir 'Ali Shir Nawa'i, Majalis an-nafa'is, ed. A.A. Hikmet (N.p.: 1945) 30;
Dihkhuda, Lughatnama, s.v. "'Ala' ad-dawla as-Simnani." For this to be true,
Simnani would have spent almost thirty years of his life in meditation. In
light of the fact that he began his retreats after he met Akhi Sharaf ad-din
in 686/1287, Simnani's two hundred and seventy forty-day retreats account
for sixty percent of the rest of his life.

68. Khwafi, 2:382.

in the inauguration of Uljāytū's own religious center called Abwāb al-birr.[69] For two years before this Uljāytū had obstructed Simnānī's mystical endeavors and had prevented him from visiting Isfarā'inī. The situation worsened again, however, when Uljāytū converted to Shī'ism in 710/1310, at which time Simnānī did not hesitate to voice his displeasure to members of the court.

He was restored to favor under Abū Sa'īd with whom he appears to have wielded a significant amount of religious and political influence. According to one account, the Ilkhan Abū Sa'īd even visited Simnānī at his *khānaqāh*.[70] During this period Simnānī visited Baghdad a number of times and also made at least one, and perhaps two, pilgrimages to Mecca.[71] He was held in very high regard by the Amīrs Chūbān (Abū Sa'īd's chamberlain until 727/1327) and Nawrūz, for both of whom he harbored great affection primarily because they were Sunnīs unlike Ghāzān.[72] He was visited by them in Simnān, and himself visited Mashhad while Nawrūz was governing that city (683/1284 – 696/1296–97).[73] Simnānī made a special trip to Sulṭāniyya to intercede before Abū Sa'īd on behalf of Chūbān after the latter's fall from favor and the execution of his son, Dimashq Khwāja, in 727/1327.[74] He was also held in high regard by the ministers Rashīd ad-dīn Faḍl Allāh-i Hamadānī and Ghiyāth ad-dīn Muḥammad Kart.[75]

Simnānī lived out his last days surrounded by an increasingly large group of disciples. He died in the 'Tower of the Liberated' (*burj-i*

---

69. Ibid., 3:14. Abwāb al-bararā in the text.

70. Ṣafadī, *al-Wāfī bi'l-wafayāt*, 7:357; *A'yān al-'aṣr*, 48b. Abū Sa'īd may have constructed the *khānaqāh* called Ṣūfīyābād-i Khudādād at Biyābānak (see above, note 64).

71. Ṣafadī, *al-Wāfī bi'l-wafayāt* 7:356; Ibn Ḥajar al-'Asqalānī, 1:266; Sadr, 48.

72. Simnānī states that when the Ilkhan adopted Shī'ism, all his courtiers followed suit with the sole exception of Chūbān (*Chihil majlis*, 149).

73. *Chihil majlis*, 158; Sadr, 49.

74. Ḥāfiẓ-i Ābrū Shihāb ad-dīn al-Khwāfī, *Dhayl-i jāmi' at-tawārīkh-i rashīdī*, ed. M. Biyānī (Tehran: Shirkat-i taḍāmunī-yi 'ilmī, 1939), 129–30; Khwānd Amīr, *Ḥabīb as-siyār*, 3:212; cf. the anecdote concerning Chūbān's visit to Simnān and attempt to present Simnānī with gifts (*Chihil majlis*, 149–50; Jāmī, 439–40; Shushtarī, 2:135). For more information on Chūbān's problems with Abū Sa'īd, see Anne K.S. Lambton, *Continuity and Change in Medieval Persia: Aspects of Administrative, Economic and Social History, 11th–14th Century*, Columbia Lectures on Iranian Studies, no. 2 (Albany: Bibliotheca Persica, 1988), 321–22.

75. Khwāfī, 3:23; Sadr, 46.

aḥrār) of Ṣūfīyābād-i Khudādād on the 22nd of Rajab 736/6 March 1336, and was buried in the cemetery of 'Imād ad-dīn 'Abd al-Wahhāb.[76] His grave stands to this day outside the abandoned *khānaqāh*, exposed to the elements except for a meagre rain-shelter.

---

76. Ṣafadī, *al-Wāfī bi'l-wafayāt*, 7:357; Ibn Ḥajar al-'Asqalānī, 1:266; Jāmī, 439; Khwānd Amīr, *Ḥabīb as-siyar*, 3:220; Qāshānī, 50; Dārā Shikūh, 107. Cf. 21 Rajab in Khwāfī (3:45); 2 Rajab in Shushtarī (2:135).

No account describing his move from the Khānaqāh-i Sakkākiyya to Ṣūfīyābād-i Khudādād can be found. The identity of 'Imād ad-dīn remains unknown. An anecdote attributed to Simnānī identifies him as 'Imād ad-dīn 'Abd al-Wahhāb al-Bārsīnī (Pārsānī), who was elevated to the status of *quṭb* after the death of 'Abd Allāh ash-Shāmī in Rabī' II 716/June 1316 (Ibn al-Karbalā'ī, 2:590-91); cf. also the 'Imād ad-dīn 'Abd al-Wahhāb who died at Isfarā'in in 518/1124 (Khwāfī, 2:223).

3

SIMNĀNĪ'S MASTERS AND DISCIPLES

In his writings, Simnānī provides detailed descriptions of why he chose to become a Sunnī Sufi and a disciple of Isfarā'inī. The explanation of his thought process is presented as a didactic means to guide future mystics. His autobiographical writings appear to have been streamlined for this reason, and the names of some of the companions and teachers of his youth are omitted. These were associations which contradicted the self-image Simnānī wished to project: that of a secular youth, ignorant of religion who, through divine grace, comes to a realization of the only true religious path, that of a Sunnī Sufi, devoted to the most excellent mystical guide of the day, the *shaykh* Nūr ad-dīn al-Isfarā'inī of Baghdad.

Simnānī claims that he came about the realization of the nature of the best religious path in a moment of mystical inspiration in Muḥarram 686/February 1287.[1]

> I realized that the religion favored by God is that of the prophets, upon them be peace, because I knew that the leaders of the various tribes of the descendants of Adam agreed that it is necessary for the attainment of a person's perfection to pay attention to three conditions. These are punishment (*siyāsa*) for the sake of order in the world; purification (*ṭahāra*), in this world rather than the next, of one's human nature on account of its blameworthy existence; and worship (*'ibāda*) of God who is the Creator of all things.[2]

This first stage of Simnānī's religious awakening involves the discovery of the laws of nature. His journey of realization begins at

---

1. *Hadiyyat al-muhtadī*, 81b; cf. *'Urwa*, where this thought process is presented in the form of a dialogue with Satan (301–12).
2. Ibid., 82a.

a stage later than that of the birth of self-awareness when individuals become conscious of their own existence, and from this self-awareness infer the existence of a Necessary Being. Such deductive argumentation was unnecessary for a man who had undergone noetic mystical states and therefore possessed experiential knowledge of God's existence and His relationship to human beings. Simnānī begins with the demonstration of the universal acceptance of a need for social law and punishment, self-purification, and the recognition through worship of the Being which causes everything else to exist. Yet Simnānī did not need to derive these conclusions logically, but simply presented them as facts which he had come to know through a process of instantaneous mystical realization. Despite the inspired nature of his knowledge however, Simnānī's three principles of universally accepted natural law are remarkably similar to ideas presented in Islamic philosophical writings.[3]

> He [God] called my attention to the fact that some of the sects observed these conditions only in their outward sense; some of them complied with them in their inner sense; and some of them combined the outer and the inner in their compliance with these conditions. So I approached [the last group's] path submissively, certain that they were the possessors of the truth (*ahl al-ḥaqq*) among the [various] sects.[4]

The people who follow Simnānī's universally accepted conditions only outwardly or merely inwardly are either deficient or hypocritical in their faith. To accept them only in their outward or literal sense is to be lacking in belief and thus to be guilty of idolatry in the manner of people who worship in temples and adore idols such as the Indians, Turks and pre-Islamic Arabs. To adopt them inwardly or in the abstract but not apply them in a practical, exoteric sense is to be guilty of sophistry or hypocrisy. Examples of this second group are the spiritualists (*aṣḥāb al-arwāḥ*) and the Greek philosophers.[5] For Simnānī the ideal was to combine inner belief with outer observance.

---

3. It is clear from Simnānī's works that he was familiar with Islamic philosophical thought. He was almost certainly acquainted with Ibn Sīnā's *Ḥayy ibn Yaqẓān*, in which the hero uses logic to reach certain deductions very similar to the ones presented here by Simnānī (cf. *al-Wārid ash-shārid* [14b–17a], where Simnānī criticizes Ibn Sīnā's philosophical ideas).

4. *Hadiyyat al-muhtadī*, 82a

5. Ibid., 82a–82b.

This combination was to be found only among the followers of the prophets. Thus Simnānī arrives at a second stage of realization, that true compliance with the universal conditions of the laws of nature is through submission to and faith in a divinely ordained system of belief (inward compliance) and religious practise (outward compliance) which is presented to humanity by a series of prophets.

He learned that the prophets who summon people to faith are limited to seven: Adam, Noah, Abraham, Moses, David, Jesus and Muḥammad. Each of them called people to God in compliance with a system of law and with the aid of religious scholars. Of these religions, Simnānī found the legal system of Muḥammad to be the most comprehensive, its ritual purity (*ṭahāra*) the best, and its religious practise (*'ibāda*) the most perfect. Yet, despite this, it was also the simplest, and for this reason he chose to follow Islam.[6]

This conclusion represents the third stage of Simnānī's religious awakening in which he realizes the superiority of Islam over other prophetic, monotheistic religions. It is worth noting that according to this somewhat contrived description of a process of religious realization, Simnānī does not select Islam on the basis of any inherent spiritual superiority. Rather, it is the religion's practicality, comprehensiveness, applicability to Simnānī's time, and (most importantly) simplicity that he finds appealing.

> [God] inspired me that the sects of Islam were also limited to seven: Jabrī, Qadarī, Mu'aṭṭilī, Mushabbihī, Rāfiḍī, Khārijī, and Sunnī, and I succeeded in distinguishing between the truth and falsehood of each sect. I found the Jabrī to be excessive (*ṣāḥib al-ifrāṭ*) in attributing acts to God and thus avoiding responsibility for his actions. . . . The Qadarī is defective (*ṣāḥib at-tafrīṭ*) because he assigns actions to himself and [claims to be] the author of his acts, thus negating the covenant of divine unity. The Mushabbihī is an extremist in likening God to His creation, and in the assertion of a [divine] form (*ṣūra*) like that asserted for His creation. The Mu'aṭṭilī is an extremist for denying the attributes of God that are contained in the Holy Book. . . . The Rāfiḍī is extreme in his love for the Shī'ī *Imāms* (*a'imma ahl al-bayt*) and deficient in his liking for most of the early Muslims

---

6. He states that he has described aspects found in Muḥammad's religion that are not found in others in a treatise entitled *Ādāb sufrat as-safra* (*Hadiyyat al-muhtadī*, 83a).

with whom God was pleased and who were pleased with Him. The Khārijī is extreme in his hatred for the Shī'ī *Imāms* who are lamps of truth for human beings and their summoners to Him, through Him, and for Him.[7]

With the exception of Sunnism, all Islamic sects and theological positions appeared defective to Simnānī. They are all described as being extreme or guilty of excess. For Simnānī the Qur'an provided proof of the shortcomings of these sects, vanquishing each of them with relevant verses:

> And I learnt that God (may He be exalted) says: "Do not be extreme in your religion" (Qur'ān, 4:171; 5:77); and He says: "Good is in Your hand" (3:26) in order to refute the Jabrī; and He says: "Indeed, You are Powerful over all things" (3:26; 66:8) in order to refute the Qadarī; and He says: "There is no like unto Him" (42:11) in order to refute the Mushabbihī; and He says: "He is the Hearer, the Seer" (17:1; 40:20, 56; 42:11) in order to refute the Mu'attilī; and He says: "Say: I ask of you no fee for it, except affection among relatives" (42:23) in order to refute the Khārijī; and He says: "And the first leaders of the Muhājirūn and the Anṣār, and those who followed them in goodness—God is pleased with them and they are pleased with Him" (9:100) in order to refute the Rāfiḍī. And I found the Sunnī standing firmly on the straight path (*aṣ-ṣirāṭ al-mustaqīm*).[8]

For Simnānī the Sunnī sect represented the straight path. As such, it was also the middle course that avoided excesses, a concept resembling the Buddhism Simnānī had rejected as an imperfect religious system. For him Islam was the only true religion, and Sunnism was to other Islamic sects what Islam was to other religions. Yet he noticed that not even the Sunnīs agreed amongst themselves and were divided into various schools, each one denying the leaders of the other. While he was anguishing over the divisiveness of the Sunnīs and wondering about the true identity of the sect which would receive

---

7. *Hadiyyat al-muhtadī*, 83b–84a. Only three of the groups mentioned by Simnānī can accurately be referred to as sects: the Sunnī, Khārijī and Rāfiḍī, the last being a derogatory term for Shī'ī. The other four groups—Jabrī, Qadarī, Mushabbihī, and Mu'attilī—are more akin to theological schools of thought.

8. Ibid., 84a.

salvation, Simnānī was once again blessed with divine intervention. God sent His representative, which was the supportive spirit (*ar-rūḥ al-muttakī'a*), to Simnānī in the spiritual realm. It guided him to a small group of beings. The spirit told Simnānī that God had revealed the truth to them; Simnānī was to surrender his self (*nafs*) to them and follow their practice, for indeed theirs was the straight path. When Simnānī approached this group, he saw the mark of God (*sīmā' al-ḥaqq*) in their faces and noticed that they spoke nothing but the truth.

The spirit had guided Simnānī to none other than the Sufis. He learned that only a small number of such people existed at any time and that they were organized in a hierarchy of seven levels: the people of the mystical quest (*ahl aṭ-ṭalab*), of discipleship (*irāda*), of the mystical path (*sulūk*), of the journey (*sayr*), of mystical flight (*ṭayarān*), of attainment (*wuṣūl*), and the final level of those who had attained the end (*martabat al-mawṣil*), which is the level of 'Alī b. Abī Ṭālib.[9]

It was through this process of reasoning, which Simnānī presents as coming to him in two flashes of mystical insight, that he decided to pursue a Sufi path towards enlightenment. On yet another occasion, when he was transported into the spiritual realm during one of his many forty-day retreats, Simnānī learned that the only path to mystical fulfillment was through Nūr ad-dīn al-Isfarā'inī:

> I witnessed the way in which the rope of discipleship was tied to the pole of sainthood, and the manner in which he controlled my being. I became certain that the path of reaching God was [Isfarā'inī's] path.[10]

Isfarā'inī was indubitably the most influential mystical guide in Simnānī's life. In fact, in his later writings Simnānī consciously de-emphasized his dealings with other mystics and referred to Isfarā'inī as the Pole of Guidance in his time (*quṭb al-irshād fī-zamānihi*).[11] It was not that Simnānī denied the existence of other mystical guides. He was simply convinced that Isfarā'inī was the only true master for

---

9. This hierarchy is that of the *abdāl*, described by Simnānī at other times with some variations. In this instance it is followed by a discussion of the theory of *badal* and the nature of the *quṭb* (*Hadiyyat al-muhtadī*, 85–86).

10. *R. fī-dhikr asāmī mashāyikhī*, 72b–73a.

11. Ibid., 74a.

him.[12] Isfarā'inī, in turn, was equally drawn to Simnānī and extolled his example to government figures[13] as well as to his own disciples at Baghdad among whom Simnānī was ranked highest, taking charge of the *khānaqāh* in Isfarā'inī's absence.[14]

It was through Isfarā'inī that Simnānī derived his chain of mystical affiliation in the following manner:

Nūr ad-dīn al-Isfarā'inī—Ahmad-i Gūrpānī—Radī ad-dīn 'Alī-yi Lālā (d. 642/1244)—Majd ad-dīn al-Baghdādī (d. 616/1219)—Najm ad-dīn al-Khīwaqī al-Kubrā (d. 617/1220)— 'Ammār b. Yāsir al-Bidlīsī (d. between 590 and 604/1194 and 1207)—Abu'n-Najīb as-Suhrawardī (d. 563/1168)—Ahmad al-Ghazzālī (d. 520/1126)—Abū Bakr an-Nassāj (d. 487/1094)—Abu'l-Qāsim al-Jurjānī (d. 469/1076–77)—Abū 'Uthmān al-Maghribī (d. 373/983–84)—Abū 'Alī al-Kātib (d. ca. 340/951) —Abū 'Alī ar-Rūdhabārī (d. 322/934)—Junayd al-Baghdādī (d. 297/910)—Sarī as-Saqatī—Ma'rūf al-Karkhī (d. 200/ 815–16)—Dāwūd at-Tā'ī (d. 165/781–2)—Habīb al-'Ajamī (d. 156/773)—Hasan al-Basrī (d. 110/728)—'Alī b. Abī Tālib (d. 40/661)—Muhammad.[15]

Simnānī mentioned two other chains of authority which he inherited from Isfarā'inī. The first is that of discipleship (*tarīq-i suhbat*) and is identical to the chain mentioned above except that the name of a certain Mansūr-i Khilāf (dates unknown) is inserted between that of Abu'l-Qāsim al-Jurjānī and Abū 'Uthmān al-Maghribī.[16] The second is the path of isolation and seclusion (*tarīqa-yi inziwā wa khalwat*). Its chain of authority is from Abū Sa'īd b. Abi'l-Khayr (d. 440/1049) and represents a line independent from the well-known one of Najm ad-dīn al-Kubrā:

---

12. In a conversation with his father, Sharaf ad-dīn-i Simnānī, who asked him why he chose to become a disciple of Isfarā'inī when there were other mystical guides available, Simnānī mentioned the names of Ibn 'Ajīl, Shams ad-dīn-i Sāwajī, and Khwāja-yi Hājjī (*Chihil majlis*, 255). These names are also mentioned in R. *fī-dhikr asāmī mashāyikhī* (75b–76a).

13. In a letter to Sadr ad-dīn (executed 697/1298), the *sāhib-i dīwān* under Gaykhātū and *wazīr* under Ghāzān, Isfarā'inī praised Simnānī as the model of someone who had quit his worldly life to become a mystic (Landolt, *Révélateur*, 94, note 86).

14. Landolt, *Révélateur*, 28.

15. R. *fī-dhikr asāmī mashāyikhī*, 73b.

16. Dānishpazhūh, 154.

Isfarā'inī—Aḥmad-i Gūrpānī—Raḍī ad-dīn 'Alī-yi Lālā, before whom it is referred to as a Sufi robe (*khirqa*) from—Majd ad-dīn-i Shaykhān, the great grandson of Abū Sa'īd—his father Nūr ad-dīn al-Munawwar—his father Abū Ṭāhir (d. 479/1086)—Abū Sa'īd b. Abi'l-Khayr—Abu'l-Faḍl Ḥasan-i Sarakhsī—Sarrāj—Muḥammad Murta'ish (d. 328/940)—Junayd.[17]

Investiture with Sufi Robes (Khirqas)

Several of these chains were formalized through a number of robes which Simnānī received from Isfarā'inī in recognition of his spiritual affiliation and progress on the mystical path. The first of these was the variegated robe (*khirqa-yi mulamma'a*) mentioned above, which Akhī Sharaf ad-dīn brought from Isfarā'inī in Sha'bān 687/September 1288. This first robe represented Simnānī's formal attachment to Isfarā'inī as a disciple. Approximately ten years after this event, in 697/1298 Isfarā'inī sent him his own robe, which Isfarā'inī had worn for ten years while performing the *dhikr*.[18] This robe is called *al-khirqa adh-dhākira* by Simnānī and was traced back to Najm ad-dīn al-Kubrā.

Simnānī mentions a robe of affiliation called *khirqat al-aṣl* connecting Kubrā with earlier generations of mystics. The chain of transmission of this investiture is as follows:

Najm ad-dn al-Kubrā—Ismā'īl b. Ḥusayn al-Qayṣarī (al-Qaṣrī, d. 589/1193)—Muḥammad b. Mankīl—Dāwūd b. Muḥammad, known as 'Servant of the Mystics' (*khādim al-fuqarā*')—Abu'l-'Abbās b. Idrīs—Abu'l-Qāsim b. Ramaḍān —Abū Ya'qūb aṭ-Ṭabarī—Abū 'Abd Allāh b. 'Uthmān—Abū Ya'qūb an-Nahrajūrī—Abū Ya'qūb as-Sūsī—'Abd al-Wāḥid b. Zayd—Kumayl b. Ziyād—'Alī b. Abī Ṭālib—Muḥammad.[19]

Simnānī also received a *khirqa-yi tabarruk* which was traced back from Isfarā'inī to Najm ad-dīn al-Kubrā—'Ammār al-Bidlīsī—Abu'n-Najīb as-Suhrawardī—his father 'Abd Allāh—his brother Wajīh

---

17. Ibid., 152. Nūr ad-dīn al-Munawwar was not the son of Abū Ṭāhir but of Abū Sa'd As'ad (d. 507/1114) (Meier, *Abū Sa'īd*, appendix 2).

18. Landolt, *Correspondence*, 19.

19. *al-Wārid ash-shārid*, 31a; Dānishpazhūh, 153; *R. fī-dhikr asāmī mashāyikhī*, 73b–74a; Meier, *Fawā'iḥ*, 17.

FIGURE 1

Silsila of 'Alā' ad-dawla as-Simnānī

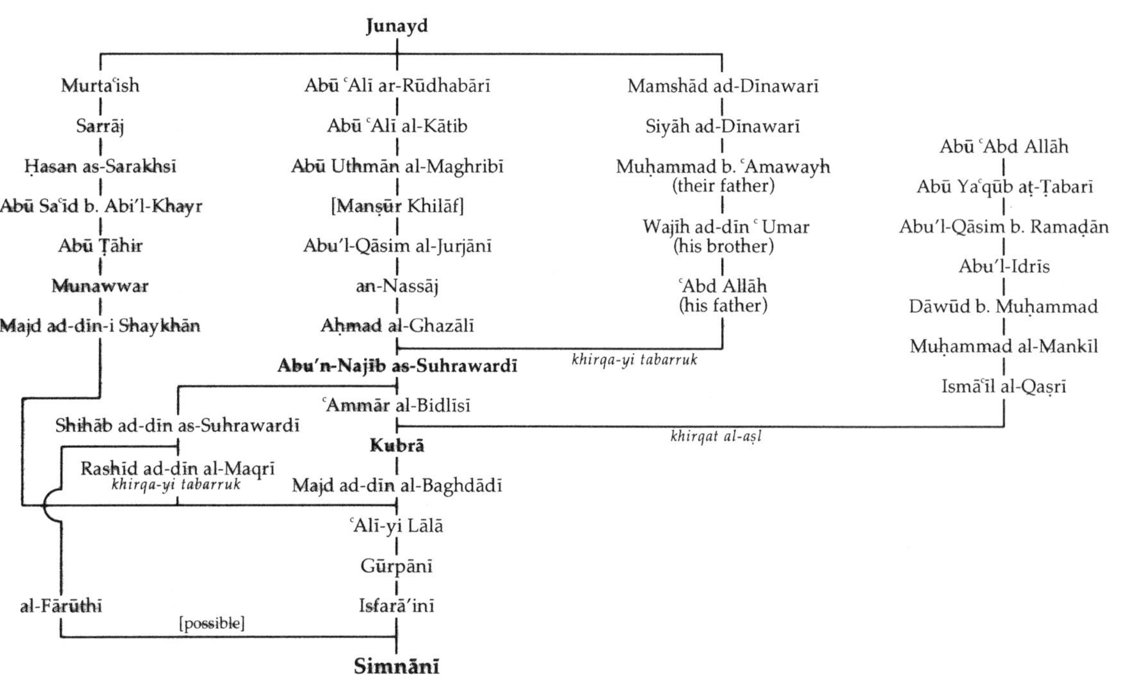

ad-dīn 'Umar—their father Muḥammad b. 'Amawiyya—Aḥmad Siyāh ad-Dīnawarī (with the help of Akhī Faraj az-Zanjānī)—Mamshād ad-Dīnawarī—Junayd—Sarī as-Saqaṭī—Ma'rūf al-Karkhī—Dāwūd aṭ-Ṭā'ī —Ḥabīb al-'Ajamī—Ḥasan al-Baṣrī—Alī b. Abī Ṭālib—Muḥammad.[20]

A secondary line of transmission of the *khirqa-yi tabarruk* was received by Isfarā'inī from Rashīd ad-dīn Abū 'Abd Allāh b. Abu'l-Qāsim al-Maqqarī—Shihāb ad-dīn 'Umar as-Suhrawardī—Abu'n-Najīb as-Suhrawardī.[21] Thus Simnānī received his *khirqa-yi tabarruk* from the Suhrawardī line through two chains of transmission.[22]

In addition to the Sufi robes mentioned above, Simnānī also received from Isfarā'inī a *khirqa-yi hazār mīkhī* (tattered or many-patched robe) which had belonged to Najm ad-dīn al-Kubrā and was given by him to Majd ad-dīn al-Baghdādī who then gave it to 'Alī-yi Lālā.[23] This is perhaps the same as the cap called *kulāh-yi hazār mīkhī*, allegedly belonging to Kubrā and given to Simnānī by Isfarā'inī shortly before Rajab 705/January 1306.[24] A final *khirqa* given to Simnānī by Isfarā'inī allegedly contained a comb belonging to the Prophet which the legendary Indian mystic and contemporary of the Prophet, Abu'r-Riḍā Bābā Ratan, had given to 'Alī-yi Lālā during the latter's visit to India. From 'Alī-yi Lālā the comb was passed to Aḥmad-i Gūrpānī and on to Isfarā'inī.[25]

Simnānī believed in the absolute necessity of a mystical guide on the Sufi path, and regarded most of the famous mystics of earlier

20. *R. fī-dhikr asāmī mashāyikhī*, 74a; Dānishpazhūh, 153.

21. Dānishpazhūh, 154.

22. While at Baghdad, Simnānī also studied with 'Izz ad-dīn al-Fārūthī, who had received a *khirqa* from Shihāb ad-dīn 'Umar as-Suhrawardī (see below, p. 42).

23. Dānishpazhūh, 153.

24. Landolt, *Correspondence*, 19. There is some debate as to whether *hazār mīkhī* refers to a many-patched robe or cap, or whether it in fact represents a form of attire, used in ascetic exercises, which contained small nails sewn into it (cf. Najm ad-dīn al-Kubrā, *Ādāb aṣ-ṣūfiyya*, ed. Mas'ūd Qāsimī (Tehran: Kitābfurūshī-yi Zawwād, 1984), 47–48). For a description of the Sufi rules of dress, including the various kinds of *khirqas*, see G. Böwering, "The *Adab* Literature of Classical Sufism: Anṣārī's Code of Conduct," in *Moral Conduct and Authority*, ed. B.D. Metcalf (Berkeley: University of California Press, 1984), 62–87.

25. Jāmī, 437; Shīrwānī, 505–6. Simnānī allegedly wrapped the comb in the *khirqa* and the *khirqa* in a piece of paper on which he wrote: "This comb is one of the Prophet of God which came to this wretch from the disciple of the Prophet of God, and this *khirqa* came from Abu'r-Riḍā Tan [Bābā Ratan] to this wretch" (Shīrwānī, 506).

generations as his *shaykhs*. His first teacher on the path of spiritual guidance was Abū Yazīd al-Bistāmī, who appeared to him in the spiritual realm over a period of approximately two years. His master on the path of knowledge and the memorizing and practicing of Sufi rules and requirements was the author of the *Qūt al-qulūb*, Abū Ṭālib al-Makkī. In renunciation, abandoning this world and asceticism, he was guided by Ibrāhīm b. Adham (d. ca. 160/776). He learned the way of friendship (*mawadda*) and chivalry (*futuwwa*) from Abū Ḥafs al-Ḥaddād an-Naysābūrī (d. 267/880–81 or 270/883–84).[26]

These figures represent a four-part form of mystical guidance. Bistāmī appears as the spiritual guide of dreams and trances, Abū Ṭālib al-Makkī as the guide in textual matters and ritual action, Ibrāhīm b. Adham as the guide of asceticism, and al-Ḥaddād an-Naysābūrī the model of social behavior. Between them they represent four aspects commonly seen as cornerstones of Sufism. However, the most important influence of earlier mystics was that of Junayd al-Baghdādī, whom Simnānī referred to as the "Master of the Sufi Path" and credited with being his *shaykh* in isolation, solitary meditation and traveling the mystical path.[27]

Among the religious scholars living in his time, Simnānī maintained contact with a number of people other than Isfarā'inī. He paid a great deal of attention to the study of *ḥadīth*, particularly during his stays in Baghdad. Among his teachers in *ḥadīth* were Muḥammad b. 'Abd Allāh ar-Rāshid b. Abu'l-Qāsim al-Baghdādī and 'Izz ad-dīn 'Abd Allāh b. 'Umar b. al-Faraj al-Fārūthī (614/1217 to Dhu'l-Ḥijja 694/October 1295), a Shāfi'ī scholar of Baghdad.[28] Fārūthī was also known as a Sufi, having studied with Abū Ḥafs 'Umar b. Karam b. Abi'l-Ḥasan ad-Dīnawarī and Shihāb ad-dīn as-Suhrawardī (d. 632/1234), from whom he received a Sufi robe (*khirqat at-taṣawwuf*) in 629/1231–32.[29] Even though there is no mention of Simnānī having received any Sufi instruction from him, Fārūthī's relationship with Simnānī provides a third link connecting Simnānī with the Suhrawardī tradition.

---

26. Dār al-kutub, untitled, 145ff.

27. Ibid.

28. Ṣafadī, *al-Wāfī bi'l-wafayāt*, 7:356; Ibn Ḥajar al-'Asqalānī, 1:266.

29. Ibn Rāfi', 18–20; Shams ad-dīn adh-Dhahabī, *Dhayl tadhkirat al-ḥuffāẓ* (Damascus: al-Qudsī, 1928), 85–86; *Ma'rifat al-qurrā' al-kibār*, ed. Muḥammad Jādd al-Ḥaqq ('Ābidīn: Dār al-kutub al-ḥadītha, 1969), 2:552–54; Asnawī, 2:143. Cf. Ibn Rāfi', according to whom Simnānī also studied *ḥadīth* with his maternal uncle, Rukn ad-dīn-i Ṣā'in (162).

Of particular interest is the tenuous relationship between Simnānī and Ṣadr ad-dīn Ibrāhīm Ḥamūya-yi Juwaynī (644/1246 to 722/1322), the son of Kubrā's disciple Sa'd ad-dīn-i Ḥamūya (d. 650/1252). Ṣadr ad-dīn was a scholar of *ḥadīth* and had traveled widely in pursuit of knowledge.[30] Ibn al-Karbalā'ī considers him a respected mystical guide, ranking him as one of the great *shaykhs* of his time along with Ṣafī ad-dīn-i Ardabīlī, 'Abd ar-Razzāq al-Kāshānī and 'Alā' ad-dawla as-Simnānī.[31] His reputation is attested to by the fact that Ghāzān converted to Islam under his direction in Sha'bān 694/June 1295, and along with Ghāzān approximately 80,000 Mongols became Muslims.[32] Ṣadr ad-dīn appears to have had extremely strong ties with the Ilkhanid court,[33] and in 671/1272-73 he married the daughter of the renowned historian 'Aṭā Malik-i Juwaynī (d. 681/1283), whose brother, Shams ad-dīn, served as *ṣāḥib-i dīwān* until his execution in 683/1284.[34]

Ṣadr ad-dīn Ibrāhīm was regarded as a *shaykh* of the Kubrawī order.[35] In addition, Ṣafadī claims that he was a student of Simnānī.[36] It is therefore somewhat surprising that Simnānī would completely avoid mentioning him in his writings, especially since Ṣadr ad-dīn, like Simnānī, was an avid scholar of *ḥadīth* and studied with some of the same teachers. Indeed, they even had students in common.[37] Competition between the Simnānī family and the powerful Juwaynī

---

30. Ibn Ḥajar al-'Asqalānī, 1:69; Junayd-i Shīrāzī, 361, note 111. For a discussion of the origins and correct pronounciation of the Ḥamūya family name, see Sa'īd-i Nafīsī, "Khāndān-i Sa'd ad-dīn-i Ḥamawī," *Kunjkāwīhā-yi 'ilmī wa adabī*, Intishārāt-i dānishgāh-i Tihrān 83 (1950), 8–10, and F. Meier, *Abū Sa'īd*, 322–23, note 22.

31. Ibn al-Karbalā'ī, 1:515.

32. Rashīd ad-dīn Faḍl Allāh, *Tā'rīkh-i mubārak-i ghāzānī*, ed. K. Jahn (London: 1940), 1:76–80; Ibn al-Karbalā'ī, 1:528. For further details on Ghāzān's conversion, see Charles Melville, "Pādishāh-i Islam: The Conversion of Sultan Maḥmūd Ghāzān Khān," *Pembroke Papers*, vol. 1 (Cambridge: Cambridge University Center of Middle Eastern Studies, 1990), 159–77.

33. Rashīd ad-dīn, 2:903.

34. Ibn Ḥajar al-'Asqalānī, 1:69; Junayd-i Shīrāzī, 361, note 111. For further information on Ṣadr ad-dīn Ibrāhīm, see Khwāfī, vols. 2 and 3; Muḥsin al-Amīn, 5:379–82; Dihkhudā, s.v. "Ṣadr ad-dīn;" Nafīsī, "Khāndān-i Ḥamawī," 28–29. His Syrian relatives are dealt with in Dhahabī's *Siyar a'lām an-nubalā'*, vols. 22 and 23. For more information on the Juwaynī family, see Lambton, 305–6.

35. Ibn al-Karbalā'ī, 2:327.

36. Ṣafadī, *A'yān al-'aṣr*, 48b.

37. See below, p. 53.

clan at the Mongol court may have played some part in this, given that Ṣadr ad-dīn was connected to the Juwaynīs both through marriage and by dint of the fact that he came from Baḥrābād, a town in the region of Juwayn. Simnān and Juwayn appear to have vied for status as major Ilkhanid centers of power in Khurāsān and, unlike the Simnānīs, the Juwaynīs were loyal to Aḥmad Takūdār in his conflict with Arghūn.[38] Possibly, the main cause for Simnānī to disown Ṣadr ad-dīn may have had more to do with the latter's father, Saʿd ad-dīn, than with anything else. Saʿd ad-dīn was not completely integrated into the primary chain of succession of the Kubrawī line. Baghdādī, whom Simnānī held in very high regard, disapproved of him and of the entire Ḥamūya family, and Aḥmad-i Gūrpānī had refused to see Saʿd ad-dīn-i Ḥamūya when the latter came to visit him.[39] The primary cause of their antipathy was probably Saʿd ad-dīn's preoccupation with extremely esoteric ideas and with numerology, as displayed in works such as the *Baḥr al-maʿānī* and *Kitāb al-maḥbūb*, and in his veneration of Ibn al-ʿArabī.[40]

Associates and Disciples

The most famous of Simnānī's Sufi contemporaries with whom he maintained contact was ʿAbd ar-Razzāq al-Kāshānī, the important exponent of Ibn al-ʿArabī's thought. The two of them corresponded actively over the ontological relationship of God and the universe, Simnānī being a vocal critic of the concept of oneness of being (*waḥdat*

---

38. Khwānd Amīr, *Dastūr al-wuzarā'*, 288.

39. Dānishpazhūh, 170; Landolt, *Révélateur*, 89, note 42; *Chihil majlis*, 256. It is worth noting that Simnānī did occasionally speak of Saʿd ad-dīn-i Ḥamūya as an authoritative Kubrawī *shaykh* (*Chihil majlis*, 101, 172).

40. Saʿd ad-dīn Ḥamūya mentions Ibn al-ʿArabī, Kubrā and Shihāb ad-dīn as-Suhrawardī as the three most important Sufi figures of the previous generation (Untitled treatise, MS. 3931 Serez, Süleymaniye Kütüphanesi, Istanbul, 33b–43b). The contention that Saʿd ad-dīn was a Shīʿī cannot be taken as the reason for Baghdādī and Simnānī's attitudes towards him (Muḥsin al-Amīn, 5:380; Molé, "Les Kubrawiya," 74ff.). An *ijāza* granted to him by Kubrā in no way suggests that he was regarded as heterodox by his master (MS. 2800, Şehit Ali Paşa, Süleymaniye Kütüphanesi, Istanbul, 29b–30a). There is little evidence of Shīʿī tendencies in his major works, and a treatise of his dealing with eschatological events and the role of Jesus as the Seal of Saints (*khātim al-wilāya*) is thoroughly Sunnī in its outlook (*Risāla fī-ẓuhūr khātim al-wilāya*, MS. 2058, Ayasofya, Süleymaniye Kütüphanesi, Istanbul, 206a–7b; cf. Molé, "Les Kubrawiya," 74–75).

al-wujūd).[41] He was united in this criticism with Ṣafī ad-dīn Abu'l-Fatḥ Isḥāq-i Ardabīlī (d. 12 Muḥarram 735/12 September 1334), the titular founder of the Ṣafawī Sufi order.[42] As is apparent from anecdotes preserved in the *Chihil majlis*, Simnānī considered Ardabīlī a personal friend.[43]

He also corresponded with Ṣalāḥ ad-dīn Ḥasan al-Bulghārī, born in Nakhjiwān in 603/1206–7, who was captured in a raid at the age of seven and taken to Bulghār. After approximately thirty years he returned to Iran and settled in Kirmān, and over time came to be known as a mystical *shaykh* who had received his *khirqa* from Shams ad-dīn at-Tabrīzī (d. 645/1247). He apparently maintained contacts with the Ilkhanid court and journeyed to Tabriz in Jumādā I 698/February 1299, immediately preceding a raid on Kirmān by a group of bandits. He died in Tabriz later that year.[44] Simnānī appears to have considered Bulghārī a teacher and referred to him in their correspondence as "my father" (*pidaram*); Bulghārī in turn called Simnānī his son (*farzand*).[45]

Naqshbandī sources mention Simnānī's correspondence with ʿAlī an-Nassāj-i Rāmtīnī, commonly known as Ḥaḍrat-i ʿazīzān or Khwāja-yi ʿazīzān, the disciple of Khwāja Faghnawī-yi Mawlawī.[46] The main subject of this correspondence was a debate over the comparative merits of vocal and silent *dhikr*, with Simnānī favoring silent recollection.[47]

---

41. This topic has been discussed at some length by H. Landolt in "Der Briefwechsel zwischen Kāshānī und Simnānī über Waḥdat al-Wuǧud," *Der Islam* 50 (1973), 29–81; cf. also S. Waḥīd Ashraf, "Āthwīñ ṣadī hijrī meñ Īrān awr Hindustān meñ Ibn-i ʿArabī ke afkār par radd-i ʿamal," *Dānish* 8 (1986), 104–25.

42. Ibn al-Karbalāʾī, 1:268. A detailed account of Ṣafī ad-dīn-i Ardabīlī's life is contained in Ibn al-Karbalāʾī, 1:222–73.

43. *Chihil majlis*, 6.

44. Khwāfī, 2:282, 287, 343, 379–80; cf. Ibn al-Karbalāʾī, according to whom Ḥasan al-Bulghārī died on 22 Rabīʿ al-awwal 698/28 December 1298 (1:155).

45. Ibn al-Karbalāʾī, 1:151, 146. Ibn al-Karbalāʾī reproduces a letter from Ḥasan al-Bulghārī to Simnānī (1:146–51) and Simnānī's reply (1:151–54). Bulghārī's letter was written just before Simnānī was departing on one of his pilgrimages to Mecca and contains general mystical exhortations with particular reference to the Ḥajj. Note that, like Bulghārī, Simnānī's mother's family also came from Nakhjiwān, although they were originally from Fārs (Lambton, 306).

46. Wāʿiẓ Kāshifī, *Rashaḥāt ʿayn al-ḥayāt*, 2 vols., ed. ʿAlī Asghar Muʿīniyān (Tehran: Bunyād-i nīkūkārī-yi nūriyānī, 1978), 1:63; Riḍā Qūlī Khān, *Tadhkira riyāḍ al-ʿārifīn*, 176.

47. Mehmed Fuad Köprülü, *Türk Edebiyatında İlk Mutasavvıflar* (Ankara: Diyanet İşleri Başkanlığı Yayınları, 1981), 106.

The above-mentioned individuals represent those of his peers with whom Simnānī maintained the greatest contact. However, he also corresponded with Zāhid Ibrāhīm (Ibrāhīm Zāhid-i Gīlānī, d. 700/1300-301), the master of Ṣafī ad-dīn-i Ardabīlī,[48] Shams ad-dīn as-Sāwajī ash-Shushtarī, Aḥmad Mawlānā who was buried at Khwārazm,[49] and with Tāj ad-dīn-i Karkahrī.[50] He also mentions Jamāl ad-dīn ad-Dargazīnī at Dargazīn and Ibn ʿAjīl in Yemen.[51]

Simnānī had a great number of students and disciples over his lifetime, some of whom proved to be important in the course of development of Sufism. He maintained an inner circle of disciples with whom he cultivated a close, almost parental relationship. Many of his works were written at their request, and he refers to a number of them as his sons. Unfortunately, very little is known about the majority of Simnānī's students: there are no entries on them in the biographical dictionaries of the period, and the little that is known is pieced together from Simnānī's writings, the *Chihil majlis* of his student Iqbāl-i Sīstānī, the *Laṭāʾif-i ashrafī* of Ashraf Jahāngīr-i Simnānī and chance references in other Sufi works. The following names appear most frequently as those of his *khalīfas*; several of them bore the title *akhī*, which might denote contacts with *futuwwa* organizations:

1. Akhī Abuʾl-Barakāt Taqī ad-dīn ʿAlī-yi Dūstī-yi Simnānī (d. ca 734/1334) was Simnānī's primary disciple and one of two main teachers of Sayyid ʿAlī-yi Hamadānī, the most famous Kubrawī figure to come after Simnānī. Simnānī granted him a license to guide disciples in Ramaḍān 714/December 1314, and set him up as the *shaykh* of the Khānaqāh-i Rūḍa opposite Simnān's main congregational mosque. Simnānī also gave him control of some of the endowments (*awqāf*) he had established.[52] By 731/1330–31

---

48. For more information on Ibrāhīm Zāhid-i Gīlānī, see Jean Aubin, "Shaykh Ibrāhīm Zāhid Gīlānī," *Turcica* 21–23 (1991), 39–54.

49. *R. fī-dhikr asāmī mashāyikhī*, 76a.

50. Ibn al-Karbalāʾī, 1:340.

51. *R. fī-dhikr asāmī mashāyikhī*, 76b. Jamāl ad-dīn ad-Dargazīnī (Darjazīnī) was the father of Sharaf ad-dīn ad-Dargazīnī (d. 21 Shaʿbān 743/19 January 1343), an important figure in the formation of the Nūrbakhshiyya (Ibn al-Karbalāʾī, 1:397–98). There is no reference or correspondence to link Simnānī to another opponent of non-Muslim Ilkhanid rule, Ibn Taymiyya (661/1263 – 728/1328), nor is there any evidence to suggest that either of them knew of the other's existence.

52. Ibn al-Karbalāʾī, 2:280–81. The *ijāza* is dated Ṣafar 718/April 1318 and is reproduced in its entirety by Ibn al-Karbalāʾī. He also reproduces a letter

he had moved to Hamadān, possibly to a *khānaqāh* built for him by 'Alī-yi Hamadānī.[53] He either died there or in Ṣūfīyābād-i Khudādād, where he was buried.[54]

2. Sharaf ad-dīn Maḥmūd-i Mazdaqanī (d. 766/1364–65) was another teacher of 'Alī-yi Hamadānī who had established himself as a Sufi master in Mazdaqān (between Rayy and Sāwa) by 732/1331–32. The only material on him consists of anecdotal references in the *Chihil majlis* and the *Khulāṣat al-manāqib*, a biography of 'Alī-yi Hamadānī compiled by his disciple Nūr ad-dīn Ja'far-i Badakhshī. Mazdaqānī was apparently more advanced than 'Alī-yi Dūstī and had taught him Simnānī's *dhikr*.[55]

3. Akhī 'Alī-yi Miṣrī was a mystical guide in Syria and Anatolia who learned of Simnānī's reputation and decided to go to Simnān to become his disciple, taking all his students with him.[56] Several anecdotes in the *Chihil majlis* suggest that he was regarded as one of Simnānī's most learned disciples.

4. 'Azīz ad-dīn Muḥammad-i Dahistānī had joined Simnānī at an early age and was one of his closest students who had accompanied him on the Ḥajj.[57] *Farḥat al-'āmilīn wa-furjat al-kāmilīn* (completed Sha'bān 703/March 1304) was written at his request.

5. Najm ad-dīn Muḥammad b. Sharaf ad-dīn Muḥammad al-Adhkānī al-Isfarā'inī had studied *ḥadīth* with Simnānī in addition to being one of his *khalīfas*. He died at a very advanced age in 778/1376 and was buried near Isfarā'in.[58]

6. Akhī Abu'l-Muwāḥid Muḥsin ad-dīn al-Aḥmadī had been a courtier of Shāh Ughūl b. Qā'id in Turkestan, but had a mystical experience which caused him to quit the court. Simnānī was struck by the similarities between his own life and that of Akhī Muḥsin ad-dīn and provided a brief biography of him in the *Bayān al-iḥsān li-ahl al-'irfān* which Simnānī began dictating to him in

of recommendation for 'Alī-yi Dūstī written by Simnānī to a certain Akhī 'Abd al-Ghaffūr al-Abharī (2:278–79). Cf. an anecdote concerning 'Alī-yi Hamadānī at Dūstī's *khānaqāh* which suggests that Dūstī was alive after Simnānī's death (ibid., 2:276).

53. Muḥammad Riyāḍ, *Aḥwāl-u āthār-u ash'ār-i Mīr Sayyid 'Alī-yi Hamadānī* (Islamabad: Markaz-i taḥqīqāt-i fārsī-yi Īrān wa Pākistān, 1985), 16.

54. Ibn al-Karbalā'ī, 1:282.

55. Muḥammad Riyāḍ, 12, 17.

56. *Chihil majlis*, 139; Jāmī, 443–44; Sadr, 58.

57. *Chihil majlis*, 72, 143, 162; Jāmī, 445; Sadr, 62.

58. Jāmī, 444; Sadr, 59.

Baghdad in Dhu'l-qa'da 712/February 1313. He had joined Simnānī not long before this time. Simnānī also dedicated *Risāla ṣadā'if al-laṭā'if* (dated Jumāda II 722/July 1322) to Akhī Muḥsin ad-dīn.

7. Wajīh ad-dīn 'Abd Allāh-i Ghurjistānī became a Sufi master in the region of Ṭūs where he maintained a close relationship with the local ruler. He died in battle and was brought back to Ṭūs to be buried.[59] This is probably the same person as Wajīh ad-dīn Abu'l-Maḥāsin 'Abd Allāh, mentioned in Simnānī's *Farḥat al-'āmilīn*, who asked his master to write a treatise entitled *Ḥadā'iq al-ḥaqā'iq* outlining stages of revelation along the mystical path.[60]

Virtually nothing is known about some of Simnānī's other closest disciples: Muḥammad-i Khurd (or Khirad, at whose request Simnānī wrote the *Risāla-yi nūriyya*), 'Abd Allāh al-Ḥabashī, Akhī 'Alī-yi Rūmī, Akhī 'Alī-yi Sīstānī, Shams ad-dīn-i Gīlānī, Shāh 'Alī-yi Farāhī, and Tāj ad-dīn Muḥammad al-Qushayrī (at whose request *Qawā'id al-'aqā'id*, dated Rajab 699/April 1300, was written).[61]

Several individuals who studied with Simnānī for shorter periods of time have had a profound impact on the development of Sufism and Indo-Iranian culture:

1. Iqbāl Shāh Jalāl ad-dīn b. Sābiq-i Sīstānī (Iqbāl-i Sīstānī, d. ca. 785/1383) was an aristocrat from somewhere in Sijistān who was a frequent visitor to Ṣūfiyābād-i Khudādād. With Simnānī's permission, he began compiling the master's sayings toward the end of 724/1324 and continued in this endeavor until 735/1335.[62] Known variously as the *Chihil majlis*, *Fawā'id*, and *Risāla-yi iqbāliyya*, this work constitutes the most widely circulated source on Simnānī's life and thought. Iqbāl-i Sīstānī also served, along with Ashraf Jahāngīr-i Simnānī, as an intermediary in the correspondence between Simnānī and 'Abd ar-Razzāq al-Kāshānī.

---

59. Ibn al-Karbalā'ī, 2:211, 577; Sadr, 58. cf. there exists an *ijāza* given by Simnānī to a disciple named 'Abd Allāh b. Muḥammad b. Ibn al-Baqī, along with a reply to a letter written by the same individual (N.M. Hirawī, ed., *Muṣannafāt-i fārsī* [Tehran: Shirkat-i intishārāt-i 'ilmī wa farhangī, 1990], xliii–v).

60. See below, p. 180.

61. Shīrwānī, 525; Ma'ṣūm 'Alī Shāh, 2:339; Sadr, 45. Their names appear frequently in the anecdotes preserved in the *Chihil majlis*, many of which are reproduced in Ibn al-Karbalā'ī's *Rawḍat al-janān*.

62. See below, p. 176–78. *Chihil majlis*, 14ff.; Cordt.

2.   Ashraf Jahāngīr b. Sayyid Muḥammad Ibrāhīm-i Simnānī was the ruler of Simnān who abdicated in favor of his younger brother in order to become a disciple of Simnānī. While still a young man, he left Iran for Central Asia where he studied for a period with Bahā' ad-dīn-i Naqshband (d. 791/1389) and met with a number of Naqshbandī figures including Khwāja Muḥammad-i Pārsā (d. 822/1419).[63] From there he went to India and traveled widely before finally settling in Kachawcha.[64] His major works, the *Laṭā'if-i ashrafī* and *Maktūbāt-i ashrafī*, display a substantial impact of Simnānī on his religious thought, although in philosophical matters he was more heavily influenced by his other master, 'Abd ar-Razzāq al-Kāshānī. While in India, Ashraf Jahāngīr met with a number of the most prominent Sufis of the time, including 'Alā' ad-dīn-i Lāhūrī (the master of the Chishtī saint of Pandua, Quṭb-i 'ālam) and Sayyid Muḥammad al-Ḥusaynī-yi Gīsūdarāz (d. 825/1422).[65] Ashraf Jahāngīr maintained a close relationship with the ruler of Jaunpur, Sulṭān Ibrāhīm Shāh-i Sharqī. At Shaykh Quṭb-i 'ālam's behest he wrote a letter to the Sultan asking him to attack Rāja Ganēsha of Dinājpūr in Bengal.[66] He also served as a counsellor in governmental matters to Sulṭān Hūshang of Malwā (r. 809/1406 – 839/1435).[67] He is generally believed to have died on 27 Muḥarram 808/25 July 1405; however, if the incident involving Rāja Ganēsha is taken as true, Ashraf Jahāngīr must still have been alive in 818/1415.[68]

3.   Mīr Sayyid 'Alī b. Shihāb ad-dīn b. Muḥammad-i Hamadānī (Sayyid 'Alī-yi Hamadānī, 12 Rajab 714/22 October 1314 to 6 Dhu'l-Ḥijja 786/19 January 1385) was allegedly Simnānī's nephew by his sister Fāṭima.[69] 'Alī-yi Hamadānī's early education was conducted

---

63. Waḥīd Ashraf Kachawchawī, *Ḥayāt-i Ashraf Jahāngīr-i Simnānī* (Lucknow: Sarfarāz Qawmī Press, 1975), 136ff., with extensive quotations from the *Laṭā'if-i ashrafī*.

64. Waḥīd Ashraf, 41ff.; A.S. Bazmee Ansari, "Ashraf Djahāngīr," *Encyclopaedia of Islam*, new edition, vol. 1 (Leiden: E.J. Brill, 1960), 702b. He left India only once in order to perform the Ḥajj (and visited Simnān on his return journey).

65. Waḥīd Ashraf, 140ff.; S.A.A. Rizvi, *A History of Sufism in India*, 2 vols. !New Delhi: Munshiram Manoharlal, 1978, 1983), 1:266ff.

66. S.A.A. Rizvi, 1:259; Mohammad Habib and K.A. Nizami, eds., *A Comprehensive History of India*, vol. 5 (New Delhi: People's Publishing House, 1970), 717.

67. Rizvi, 1:266.

68. A more probable death date, based on the *Ṭabaqāt-i Shāhjahānī*, is 840/1436–37 (S.A.A. Rizvi, 1:268).

69. Muḥammad Riyāḍ, 11.

under the direction of Simnānī who later sent him to study with his own disciple, Maḥmūd-i Mazdaqānī. Mazdaqānī then sent him to study with Akhī ʿAlī-yi Dūstī, after whose death Hamadānī returned to Mazdaqānī. Although it is unlikely that ʿAlī-yi Hamadānī received much Sufi training from his uncle, he was deeply steeped in Simnānī's tradition and had studied with many of his disciples in addition to the two individuals already mentioned. His master in *futuwwa* was Muḥammad-i Adhkānī.[70] He also studied with Akhī ʿAlī-yi Miṣrī and Akhī Muḥsin (probably Muḥsin ad-dīn al-Aḥmadī).[71] In deference to Simnānī, he signed his poetry with the *nom de plume* "ʿAlāʾī."[72]

After traveling widely in and outside Iran, in 754/1353 ʿAlī-yi Hamadānī settled down in Hamadān, but following Tīmūr's conquest of Khurāsān (772/1370), he left Iran in the company of Ashraf Jahāngīr-i Simnānī and went to Khuttalān in Badakhshān. From there he migrated to Kashmir in 781/1379, where he wielded great influence over Sulṭān Quṭb ad-dīn (r. 780/1378 – 796/1393).[73] Dissatisfied with Quṭb ad-dīn's unwillingness to implement the religious reforms that ʿAlī-yi Hamadānī wanted, he left for Turkestan in 784/1382, and only returned to Kashmir briefly the next year before leaving for Transoxiana. He died at Kūnar in the course of this journey and was buried at Khuttalān. ʿAlī-yi Hamadānī's son, Mīr Muḥammad-i Hamadānī (d. 854/1450) settled in Srinagar around 805/1402 and is largely responsible for the implementation of Sunnī religious reforms during the reign of Sulṭān Sikandar-i Butshikan (The Iconoclast, 796/1394 – 819/1416).[74]

ʿAlī-yi Hamadānī's disciple and son-in-law Isḥāq-i Khuttalānī declared his student, Sayyid Muḥammad-i Nūrbakhsh (d. 869/1464) to be the *Mahdī* and began a rebellion. This was quickly suppressed

---

70. Ibn al-Karbalāʾī, 1:253; Johann Karl Teufel, *Eine Lebensbeschreibung des Scheichs ʿAlī-i Hamadānī* (Leiden: E.J. Brill, 1962), 55, 72.

71. Teufel, 27, 71–72. See also Devin DeWeese, "Sayyid ʿAlī Hamadānī and Kubrawī Hagiographical Traditions," *The Legacy of Medieval Persian Sufism*, edited by Leonard Lewisohn (London: Nimatullahi Publications, 1992), 121–58.

72. G. Böwering, "ʿAlī Hamadānī," *Encyclopaedia Iranica*, edited by Ehsan Yarshater, vol. 1 (London: Routledge and Kegan Paul, 1985), 862b–64a.

73. *Bahāristān-i Shāhī: A Chronicle of Mediaeval Kashmir*, edited and translated by K.N. Pandit (Calcutta: Firma KLM Ltd., 1991), 34; S.A.A. Rizvi, 1:292; Waḥīd Ashraf, 130ff. ʿAlī-yi Hamadānī may have made an earlier visit to Kashmir in 774/1373 during the reign of Shāhmīr Shihāb ad-dīn (Mohammad Habib and K.A. Nizami, *A Comprehensive History of India*, 744; C.E. Bosworth, *The Islamic Dynasties* [Edinburgh: Edinburgh University Press, 1967], 196–98).

74. *Bahāristān-i Shāhī*, 37.

by the Timurid Shāhrukh who had Khuttalānī executed in 826/1423
(possibly 816/1413 or 828/1425). Muḥammad-i Nūrbakhsh, who appears not to have enthusiastically embraced his master's claims regarding him, was pardoned by the Sultan and assumed leadership of
the Hamadānī-Kubrawī line. However, another disciple of Khuttalānī,
Shihāb ad-dīn 'Abd Allāh-i Barzishābādī (d. 872/1468), refused to
recognize the authority of Nūrbakhsh and established a separate line
which came to be called the Dhahabiyya at an unknown date.[75] The
Nūrbakhshiyya and the Dhahabiyya lineages deriving from the
Simnānī tradition constitute two of the major Sufi orders of Iran to
this day.[76]

    4.   Shaykh Khalīfa-yi Māzandarānī, the ideological guide of the
Sarbadār movement, was also a one-time disciple of Simnānī, journeying from Āmul to Simnān to see him.[77] However, their relationship
was neither a close one nor was it enduring. One day, when Simnānī
asked Khalīfa-yi Māzandarānī to which of the four Sunnī *madhāhib*
he belonged, he replied by saying that his quest was to ascertain which
of them was the best. Upon hearing this, Simnānī picked up his ink-
pot and hurled it at Khalīfa-yi Māzandarānī, thus ending their relationship.[78] Khalīfa-yi Māzandarānī went to Baḥrābād to study with the Shī'ī

---

75. Ibn al-Karbalā'ī, 2:207ff, 247–49; Ma'ṣūm 'Alī Shāh, 2:320; Devin
DeWeese, "The Kashf al-Hudā of Kamāl ad-dīn Ḥusayn Khorezmī: A Fifteenth-
century Sufi Commentary on the Qaṣīdat al-burdah in Khorezmian Turkic,"
Ph.D. diss., Indiana University, 1985, 61–62. Cf. L. Massignon, *La passion de
Husayn ibn Mansûr Hallâj* (Paris: Gallimard, 1975), 2:203. Additional factions
of the Hamadānī *silsila* are allegedly those of Qawām ad-dīn-i Badakhshī and
'Abd Allāh-i Shaṭṭārī (d. 832/1428–29), the founder of the Shaṭṭārī order
(Böwering, "'Alī Hamadānī").

76. For further information, see Richard Gramlich, *Die schiitischen
Derwischorden Persiens: Die Affiliationen*, Abhandlungen für die Kunde des
Morgenlandes, no. 36:1 (Wiesbaden: Franz Steiner, 1965).

77. Mīr Khwānd, *Ta'rīkh-i rawḍat aṣ-ṣafā* (Tehran: Kitābfurūshī-yi Pīrūz,
1960), 5:605; Felix Tauer, ed., *Cinq opuscules de Ḥāfiẓ-i Abrū concernant
l'histoire de l'Iran au temps de Tamerlan* (Prague: L'Academie tchécoslovaque
des science, 1959), 15; 'Abd ar-Rafī' Ḥaqīqat Rafī', *Ta'rīkh-i junbish-i
sarbadārān wa dīgar junbishhā-yi īrāniyān* (Tehran: Intishārāt-i āzād andīshān,
1981), 100.

78. Khwānd Amīr, *Ḥabīb as-siyar*, 5:605; A.P. Petrushevsky, *Nahḍat-i
sarbadārān-i khurāsān*, tr. Karīm Kishāwarz (Tehran: Intishārāt-i payām, 1972),
34–35. Simnānī's extreme rage was probably caused by a number of factors.
He might have suspected that Khalīfa-yi Māzandarānī was actually a Shī'ī
posing as a Sunnī, and his failure to declare his affiliation to a Sunnī *madhhab*

Ghiyāth ad-dīn Hibat Allāh al-Maḥmūdī-yi Ḥamūya and then moved on to Sabzawār where he succeeded in rousing the large number of Shīʿī inhabitants.[79]

5.   ʿUbayd Allāh-i Bāybādī is listed as a disciple of Simnānī in the *Shajara-yi ṭabaqāt-i mashāyikh*, a Sufi biographical work dealing with the Hamadānī-Kubrawī line written by ʿAlī-yi Kashmīrī. Bāybādī was the teacher of a certain Abū Ṭāhir-i Khwārazmī, who was one of the masters of Zayn ad-dīn Abū Bakr ʿAlī-yi Tāʾibābādī (d. 791/1389), a prominent religious figure of Timurid times.[80] According to Jāmī, Tāʾibābādī had also studied with Bābā Muḥammad-i Ṭūsī (a student of Simnānī's disciple ʿAbd Allāh-i Ghurjistānī), as well as with the Naqshbandī master, Khwāja Muḥammad-i Pārsā.[81]

6.   Khājū Kamāl ad-dīn Abuʾl-ʿAṭāʾ Maḥmūd b. ʿAlī-yi Kirmānī (Khājū-yi Kirmānī d. 742/1341–42 or 753/1352), the famous Persian poet whose influence Ḥāfiẓ acknowledged, became a disciple of Simnānī after completing his early education in Kirmān. He later settled in Shīrāz under the patronage of Abū Isḥāq-i Injū (r. 742/1341 – 754/1353). He also wrote panegyrics for Sulṭān Abū Saʿīd and the Muẓaffarid Mubāriz ad-dīn Muḥammad (r. 713/1313 – 759/1358) and his ministers. He allegedly collected and organized some of Simnānī's poetry.[82]

Other sometime disciples of Simnānī include Salmān-i Sawajī (d. 769/1367–68), a famous Persian poet attached to the court of Amīr Ḥasan Nuyān and his son Sulṭān Uways-i Īlkānī;[83] the compiler of Simnānī's *dīwān*, Minhāj b. Muḥammad as-Sarāyī; Khwāja Abuʾl-Faḍl Quṭb ad-dīn Yaḥyā (d. 21 Jumāda II 748/28 September 1347), an associate of Malik Muʿizz ad-dīn Ḥusayn-i Kart;[84] Mawlānā Jalāl ad-dīn ʿAtīqī;[85] Majd ad-dīn Ismāʿīl-i Sīsī;[86] and the minister of Uljāytū,

---

only confirmed this in Simnānī's mind. On the other hand, it is conceivable that Simnānī was showing his disgust for someone who misunderstood an essential aspect of the Sunni system, that no *madhhab* is inherently superior to the others.

79. Khwānd Amīr, *Ḥabīb as-siyar*, 3:359.

80. DeWeese, *Kashf al-Hudā*, 57.

81. Jāmī, 499; DeWeese, *Kashf al-Hudā* 57–58.

82. Dawlatshāh, 249–50; Iraj Dehghan, "Khwādjū," *Encyclopaedia of Islam*, new edition, vol. 4 (Leiden: E.J. Brill, 1978), 909b–10a; Sadr, 65.

83. Dawlatshāh, 257–8; Sadr, 68.

84. Khwānd Amīr, *Ḥabīb as-siyar*, 3:385. He also studied with Ṣafī ad-dīn-i Ardabīlī.

85. Ibn al-Karbalāʾī, 1:357.

86. Ibid., 2:95–97.

Khwāja ʿAlāʾ ad-dīn-i Hindū.[87] A letter from Ḥasan al-Bulghārī to Simnānī mentions the names of two individuals named Badr ad-dīn-i Barāʾī and Amīn ad-dīn-i ʿAlī who came to Bulghārī from Simnān.[88] Amīr Sharaf ad-dīn Ibrāhīm b. Ṣadr ad-dīn Muḥammad and the Shīʿī Rukn ad-dīn al-Qazwīnī (d. 799/1396–97) studied with both Simnānī and Ṣadr ad-dīn Ibrāhīm-i Ḥamūya.[89]

The individuals mentioned above were Simnānī's Sufi disciples. In addition to them he had students of *ḥadīth*, among them his *khalīfa* Muḥammad-i Adhkānī.[90] Ṣafadī mentions two students named Sirāj ad-dīn al-Qazwīnī and Imām ad-dīn ʿAlī b. al-Mubārak al-Bakrī.[91] Sirāj ad-dīn ʿUmar b. ʿAlī b. ʿUmar (683/1284 to ca. 750/1349), a *ḥadīth* scholar of Iraq, also studied with Rashīd b. Abuʾl-Qāsim.[92] Imām ad-dīn al-Bakrī is most probably Imām ad-dīn ʿAlī b. Abū Bakr an-Nasawī ash-Shīrāzī, born in 709/1309–10, who studied in Damascus, Cairo and Jerusalem.[93]

Conclusion

Simnānī appears to have been a man of great spiritual sensitivity and awareness of his identity as a Muslim. His religious identity matured during his years of service under the Buddhist Arghūn, at a time when he saw the subjugation of Islamic Iran to an alien, idol-worshipping presence, the fiscal collapse of the country, the religious compromise practiced by the indigenous Persian administrators serving the Ilkhanids, and the humiliation of Muslim religious figures at the hands of Buddhist monks and their Mongol patrons. This inner conflict finally reached a climax in his emotionally heightened state on a battlefield, where he saw the irony of defending the interests of

---

87. Qāshānī, 154. An episode in the *Chihil majlis* describes how one of Simnānī's disciples complained to him that ʿAlāʾ ad-dīn was a cruel man, and asked how Simnānī could have him as a disciple. He replied by saying that ʿAlāʾ ad-dīn was still a Muslim. Even if he had been a Jew or a Christian Simnānī would have accepted him as a student because in so doing Simnānī would be able to show him the nature of the perfect religion which is Islam (*Chihil majlis*, 131).

88. Ibn al-Karbalāʾī, 1:147.

89. Junayd-i Shīrāzī, 361–62; Ibn Rāfiʿ, 98.

90. Shushtarī, 2:135.

91. *al-Wāfī biʾl-wafayāt*, 7:356.

92. Ibn Ḥajar al-ʿAsqalānī, 3:256; Jalāl ad-dīn as-Suyūṭī, *Dhayl ṭabaqāt al-ḥuffāẓ* (Damascus: al-Qudsī, 1928), 358.

93. Ibn Ḥajar al-ʿAsqalānī, 3:170. No date is given for his death.

Arghūn against his Muslim relative, Aḥmad Takūdār: "[Arghūn] served idols and I served him."[94] Thus Simnānī's decision to leave the court and subsequently become a critic of the Ilkhanids constitutes an Islamic reaction to non-Muslim rule.

Simnānī's withdrawal from court life and attempts at self-discovery heightened his feeling of alienation from the political status quo in Iran, an awareness furthered by the successful attempts of his family and the Ilkhanid ruler to place obstacles in his way. The Kubrawī order was intimately connected with the rulers of Iran at this time, and Kubrawī *shaykhs* appear to have functioned as highly valued Islamic clerical figures under the Ilkhanids. Ṣadr ad-dīn Ibrāhīm and Simnānī's connections with the court have already been mentioned. Perhaps Arghūn and Ghāzān's opposition to Simnānī's retirement from the court was based in their fear of losing their ties with and control over a powerful religious figure. Furthermore, Ghāzān's position may also have constituted a reaction to Simnānī's vocal criticism of Shī'ism. This demonstrates that Simnānī's religious opinion was valued by the Ilkhanid ruler.

Like Ṣadr ad-dīn Ibrāhīm and Simnānī after him, Isfarā'inī also maintained ties with the Ilkhanid court and was held in high esteem by the ruler and *amīrs*.[95] At Baghdad, Isfarā'inī was in contact with Jamāl ad-dīn-i Dastirjānī, the inspector of *awqāf* in Iraq who also served as *wazīr* for two months after the execution of Simnānī's father, Sharaf ad-dīn.[96] Isfarā'inī wrote five letters to Ṣadr ad-dīn (d. 697/1298), the *ṣāḥib-i dīwān* under Gaykhātū and *wazīr* under Ghāzān. Ṣadr ad-dīn's successor, Saʻd ad-dīn-i Sāwajī (d. 711/1311), was a disciple of Isfarā'inī.[97] Isfarā'inī also wrote at least one letter to either Uljāytū or Ghāzān.[98]

Isfarā'inī disapproved of the involvement of the Simnānī family with the Ilkhanid court. A letter entitled *Maktūb fī-ḥaqīqat al-ʻaql wa'l-junūn*, from Isfarā'inī to the brothers Sharaf ad-dīn and Jalāl ad-dīn-i Simnānī, admonishes them and invites them to take a more reasonable attitude towards religion.[99] They, in turn, disliked Isfarā'inī and tried to dissuade Simnānī from associating with him. Thus in opposing Simnānī's relationship with Isfarā'inī, the Ilkhanid ruler might have been acting as much on requests put to him by his Simnānī

---

94. *al-Wārid ash-shārid*, 27a.
95. Sadr, 36.
96. Landolt, *Révélateur*, 32.
97. Ibid., 33.
98. Reproduced by Sadr (36–40).
99. Landolt, *Correspondence*, 41, note 44; *Révélateur*, 81, note 1.

ministers as upon personal motives. The wholesale conversion to Islam of the Mongols in Iran roughly coincides with the execution of 'Alā' ad-dawla's maternal uncle Qāḍī Rukn ad-dīn-i Ṣā'in, the last member of the Simnānī family to occupy a high post under the Ilkhanids. The final removal of obstacles placed in Simnānī's path by the court could therefore have resulted from a combination of factors.

Simnānī's description of the process by which he chose to adopt the Sunnī creed shows systematic reflection on a variety of Islamic sects and theological schools. His criticism of the groups he refers to as extreme might be as much a result of his identifying some of their beliefs with those of the Buddhist monks as of a heartfelt loathing for antinomianism and heterodoxy. He was a firm supporter of *jihād* in its exoteric sense and, even when he was well into old age, toyed with the idea of going to Syria to fight for Islam.[100]

He was conscious of the pitfalls of extremism, a characteristic which determined his choice of Sunnism as a religion, and of a moderate form of Sufism based on the beliefs of Junayd al-Baghdādī. Despite being a Sunnī, he held the Shī'ī *imāms*, particularly the immediate family of the Prophet, in very high esteem, a characteristic fairly typical of the Kubrawī order and of Indo-Iranian Sunnism in general.[101]

As a mystic, Simnānī fashioned himself after Ibrāhīm b. Adham, a wealthy prince who abandoned his place in society for a life of asceticism and pious devotion. He appears to have had an almost pathological propensity for visionary experiences, and describes himself as having almost instantaneously attained mystical states that others experienced only after years of practice. He entered these states frequently, both as a result of conscious preparation and of high anxiety and illness. These visionary experiences are crucial in analyzing Simnānī's thought and the role of mystical states in Sufism since, despite emphasizing their ineffable character, he wrote extensively to describe them to his disciples and give instructions on the manner of their attainment.

Despite Simnānī's fame during his life time and the stature he acquired posthumously, no surviving Sufi order lists him as its eponymous founder. The dissemination of Simnānī's mystical thought and *dhikr* practices in Iran, Central Asia and India immediately after his death can largely be credited to Iqbāl-i Sīstānī's *Chihil majlis*, and the

---

100. Cf. above, p. 29.

101. Molé, "Les Kubrawiya." Shushtarī exaggerates Simnānī's devotion to the *Imāms*; his hatred for the Umayyads was not as visceral as is described in the *Majālis al-mu'minīn* (2:137–38).

activities of Ashraf Jahāngīr and ʿAlī-yi Hamadānī. However, the commonly held notion that they were directly responsible for the critical influence that Simnānī's philosophical thought played in the debate over the ontological relationship of God to the world, leading to the eventual exposition of the doctrine known as the oneness of witnessing (*wahdat ash-shuhūd*) described by Ahmad-i Sirhindī (d. 1033/1624) and adopted by the Naqshbandī Sufi order, cannot be taken as accurate.[102] There is no evidence to suggest that any of Simnānī's works were widely distributed in the years immediately following his death. Furthermore, both ʿAlī-yi Hamadānī and Ashraf Jahāngīr disagreed with Simnānī on this philosophical issue, and were more inclined towards the doctrine of *wahdat al-wujūd*. Nor is there any merit to the assertion that Gīsūdarāz adopted Simnānī's philosophical position.[103] Gīsūdarāz's only contact with the Simnānī tradition was through Ashraf Jahāngīr who was not only opposed to Simnānī on this issue, but also saw himself in the role of student rather than master in his single meeting with Gīsūdarāz.[104]

The lack of evidence supporting any direct impact of Simnānī upon the philosophical thought of individuals who are generally accepted as having been influenced by him presents us with two questions: where does this idealogical similarity arise, and why is Simnānī not accorded the stature he clearly enjoyed during his lifetime. I can think of two reasons contributing to this phenomenon. As I will demonstrate in later chapters, one of the primary teachings which Simnānī attempted to inculcate in his disciples was the importance of direct contact between master and disciple. In many of his works the dynamics of this relationship are given primacy over the mystical and metaphysical ideas which have been emphasized by most scholarship on Simnānī. It appears that his closest disciples took this advice to heart: they are all remembered as mystical guides and instructors rather than authors of Sufi texts. This value system, though necessary for the promulgation of a contemplative religious life, would not help in perpetuating Simnānī's intellectual legacy.

The second probable cause for the disappearance of a clear Simnānī tradition lies in the political and religious developments in Iran and

---

102. Wahīd Ashraf; Y. Friedmann, *Shaykh Ahmad Sirhindī* (London: McGill–Queen's University Press, 1971); see below, pp. 97–99, for further discussion.

103. S.A.A. Rizvi, 1:248ff., 266.

104. S. Shah Khusro Hussaini, *Sayyid Muhammad al-Husaynī-i Gīsūdarād on Sufism* (Delhi: Idarah-i Adabiyat-i Delli, 1983), 17–18.

Central Asia in the late fourteenth and early fifteenth centuries. As is seen from his correspondence with 'Alī-yi Rāmtīnī, the spiritual affiliations of some of his students, and the fact that a number of them have Central Asian *nisbas*, there appears to have been substantial contact between Simnānī and the Sufi circles of Transoxiana in which the Naqshbandī order emerged. His two most productive students, 'Alī-yi Hamadānī and Ashraf Jahāngīr-i Simnānī, spent a considerable amount of time in Central Asia. It was here that the Hamadānī-Kubrawī line originated and developed in what appears to have been an atmosphere of mutual respect and cooperation with the Naqshbandiyya. The turn of the Nūrbakhshiyya and Dhahabiyya lines to Shī'ism caused them to be viewed much less favorably by the Uzbek khans than the avowedly Sunnī Naqshbandiyya. A simultaneous shift towards Shī'ism in Iran would have caused the Sunnī doctrinal and philosophical ideas of Simnānī to have an ever-diminishing audience in his native land.[105] As a result of these factors, Simnānī's philosophical and metaphysical ideas appear to have been temporarily ignored both in Iran and in Central Asia where, though he himself was considered both venerable and authoritative, the Shī'ī tendencies of the preservers of his spiritual lineage delegitimized him. It was only several centuries later, in socio-political and religious circumstances similar to those of Ilkhanid Iran, that Aḥmad-i Sirhindī turned to Simnānī's writings and found inspiration for his own ideas which were to become the normative thought of the Naqshbandiyya.

Much of the existing confusion over the impact of Simnānī on the Naqshbandiyya and Central Asian and Indian Sufism in general derives from a misreading of the Naqshbandiyya's and Simnānī's stances on Ibn al-'Arabī and the notion of *waḥdat al-wujūd*. As demonstrated in later chapters, Simnānī was opposed to any doctrine which compromised divine unity and transcendence, and it was in this context that he initially criticized Ibn al-'Arabī. On the other hand, the Naqshbandiyya has traditionally shown interest in the ontological teachings of Ibn al-'Arabī, and it is only as a result of the stance taken by Sirhindī that the order effectively adopted a stance doctrinally opposed to that of *waḥdat al-wujūd*. It is therefore wrong to view

---

105. Cf. DeWeese, whose statement that the Kubrawī order was eclipsed by the Naqshbandiyya because the former was characterized by a "penchant for withdrawal from the world and . . . reluctance to intervene in political affairs" (*Kashf al-Hudā*, 68) cannot be taken as true in the case of important Kubrawī figures such as Kubrā, Baghdādī, Sayf ad-dīn-i Bākharzī, Isfarā'inī, Ṣadr ad-dīn-i Ḥamūya, Simnānī, and 'Alī-yi Hamadānī.

Simnānī as somehow influencing the Naqshbandiyya in the adoption
of an attitude antithetical to that of Ibn al-ʿArabī. Such influence as
he did exert during the early development of the Naqshbandiyya most
probably deals with the practise of *dhikr* and the emphasis placed
upon the fundamental accord between Sufism and *sharīʿa*.[106]

---

106. See below, p. 129. For further discussion, see H. Algar, "Reflections
of Ibn ʿArabî in Early Naqshbandî Tradition," *Journal of the Muhyiddin Ibn
ʿArabi Society* 10 (1991), 45–66.

PART II

4

The Divine and Its Manifestation

Simnānī's understanding of the nature of existence is based upon a complex and hierarchical system connecting God to the universe in general, and to human beings in particular. His scheme, though clearly grounded in the Islamic neoplatonic cosmological tradition, is unique. It combines a static view of God's reality consisting of the divine essence (*dhāt*), attributes (*ṣifāt*), acts (*af'āl*) and effects (*āthār*), with a dynamic view in which God unfolds through the emanation of the universe and manifests Himself within it. This emanation occurs through ten subtle substances (*laṭā'if*) and results in the creation of the human being. The human being then begins an interior ascent through seven subtle substances culminating in the attainment of the subtle substance of I-ness (*al-laṭīfa al-anā'iyya*). Simnānī's scheme of ten subtle substances is therefore cosmological, while that of seven substances is psychological.

In order to maintain the absolute transcendence and oneness of God, Simnānī incorporates a system of mirror imagery within his scheme of emanation. According to this scheme, a subsequent emanation is the locus of manifestation (*maẓhar*) of the object from which it emanates, the word *maẓhar* implying a place of appearance or manifestation in which there is an immediate correspondence between the mirror image (or outward manifestation) and the object reflected or manifested therein. This concept endeavors to remove any possibility of divine indwelling (*ḥulūl*) in a created entity.

In order to emphasize the strong relationship, and show an even greater delineation, between human existence and the transcendent and inscrutable divine essence, Simnānī places two realms between the human and the divine realm, creating a fourfold hierarchy: "Realm of Divinity" ('*ālam al-lāhūt*), "Realm of Omnipotence" ('*ālam al-jabarūt*), "Realm of Sovereignty" ('*ālam al-malakūt*), and the "Human Realm" ('*ālam an-nāsūt*). The mystical journey involves a process of self-perfection which corresponds to an ascent through these realms.[1]

---

1. The terms *lāhūt, jabarūt, malakūt* and *nāsūt* are found in Islamic mystical and philosophical writings prior to Simnānī, although he appears

The Structure of God and the World

"His is the mastery of the heavens and the earth," an absolute mastery (57:2). "He gives life and gives death." Through His wisdom He gives life to the elements at the moment of their composition, and through His glory He gives death to the compound beings by annihilating their forms after having composed them. "And He is Powerful over all things": over giving life to the dead and giving death to the living. "He is the First and the Last and the Apparent and the Hidden and He is Knowledgeable of all things." That is, He is the First in the realm of His divinity, the Last in the realm of His sovereignty, the Manifest in His realm of humanity and the Hidden in the realm of His omnipotence. And the word "He" is a reference to the unicity of His essence which encompasses everything. This is why He commences with it and concludes with the word "He" in His saying: "He is Knowledgeable of all things," that is, He knows all things, the divine realities (*al-ḥaqā'iq al-lāhūtiyya*), fine substances of omnipotence (*ar-raqā'iq al-jabarūtiyya*), particulars of sovereignty (*ad-daqā'iq al-malakūtiyya*), and divisions of humanity (*ash-shaqā'iq an-nāsūtiyya*).[2]

For Simnānī, God is the only being which exists of necessity (*wājib al-wujūd*). He is utterly transcendent, possessing a divine essence which is singular, unique and self-subsistent. This essence contains within itself attributes of perfection, and is absolutely exalted above any attributes of imperfection.[3] God exists eternally, without having any need for praise or recognition by others, unaffected by the faith of the believer or the unbelief of the disbeliever.[4] The nature of the divine essence is such that it is utterly transcendent, beyond the comprehension and imagination of the intellect.[5] Thus descriptions of the essence can only be figurative, not definitive (*'alā-sabīl ar-rasm lā 'alā-sabīl al-ḥadd*).[6]

---

to have been the first thinker to apply them consistently in a hierarchical fashion. See chapter 8 for a brief discussion of the background of these concepts.

2. *Tafsīr najm al-qur'ān*, MS. 165/1, Şehit Ali Paşa, Süleymaniye Kütüphanesi, Istanbul, 43b.

3. *Farḥat al-'āmilīn, wa-furjat al-kāmilīn*, ed. N.M. Hirawī in "Chahār guftār-i shaykh 'Alā' ad-dawla-yi Simnānī," *Dānish* 3 (1985), 34.

4. *Najm*, 63a; 78a.

5. Ibid., 59b.

6. *Farḥat al-'āmilīn*, 34.

Nothing in the invisible and visible realms (*'ālam al-ghayb wa'sh-shahāda*) possesses real existence except the divine essence, attributes, actions and effects.[7] Simnānī sees this concept reflected in the statement "Nothing exists except Allāh" which is ascribed to Junayd al-Baghdādī.[8] Simnānī also believes that the formula *bi'sm Allāh ar-rahmān ar-rahīm* (In the name of Allāh, the Merciful, the Compassionate) refers to this fact: the word *ism* (name) refers to the effect; the word *Allāh* is a reference to the inscrutable divine essence; *ar-rahmān* (the Merciful) refers to the attribute and *ar-rahīm* (the Compassionate) to the act.[9] The divine essence, attributes, acts and effects each occupy a separate realm. Since nothing possesses true existence except these four, all entities fall within these realms which are the Realms of Divinity, Omnipotence, Sovereignty and the Human Realm. The effects belong to the Human Realm, the acts to the Realm of Sovereignty, the attributes to the Realm of Omnipotence, and the essence to the Realm of Divinity. The effect is caused by the act, the act comes from the attribute, and the attribute is based on the essence, the divine essence being that upon which all perfections are based.[10]

First, the progression from the Realm of Divinity to the Human Realm is one of vertical descent, in which each subsequent realm is a mirror (*mazhar*) for the previous one, in the sense that it is the point at which the image of the previous one is manifested. Thus the divine attributes are manifested in the Realm of Omnipotence: phenomena

---

7. "Existence (*al-wujūd*) has four aspects: [God's] perception of His being and its eternal nature, which is called 'life'; His perception of the eternal perfection of His being and the majesty of His being, which is called 'hearing'; His perception of the eternal beauty of His being, which is called 'sight'; and His perception that His being and essence are eternally deserving of praise and glory, which is called 'speech'. " (*Matla' an-nuqat* [extract], MS. 11-mīm, Majāmī' fārsiyya, Dār al-kutub, Cairo, 150a).

8. *Najm*, 52a. This idea—if not in these precise words—is central to Junayd's notion of divine unity (*tawhīd*), particularly with regard to its underlying concepts of divinity (*ulūhiyya*) and the preeternal covenant (*mīthāq*); cf. Ali Hassan Abdel-Kader, *The Life, Personality and Writings of al-Junayd* (London: Luzac, 1962), treatises 6,7,8,11. This phrase does not appear in the major works that record the most famous sayings of Junayd: Abū Nasr as-Sarrāj at-Tūsī, *Kitāb al-luma'*, ed. Abd al-Halīm Mahmūd (Cairo: Dār al-kutub al-hadītha, 1960); Abū Bakr al-Kalābādhī, *at-Ta'arruf li-madhhab ahl at-tasawwuf*, ed. A.J. Arberry (Cairo: Maktabat al-Khānjī, 1933); Abu'l-Qāsim al-Qushayrī, *ar-Risāla al-Qushayriyya* (Cairo: 1940); 'Alī b. 'Uthmān al-Hujwīrī, *Kashf al-mahjūb*, ed. 'Alī Qawīm (Islamabad: Markaz-i tahqīqāt-i fārsī, 1978).

9. *Matla' an-nuqat*, 150a.

10. Ibid.

mentioned in the Qur'ān, such as the Keys of the Unseen (*mafātiḥ al-ghayb* [6:59]), the Seat of Sincerity (*maq'ad aṣ-ṣidq* [54:55]), and the Primordial Book (*umm al-kitāb* [3:7]), exist in the Realm of Omnipotence and are majestic mirrors for the Realm of Divinity. Similarly, the substance (*jawhar*) of the four archangels and the four elements (*mufradāt*) in the Realm of Sovereignty are mirror images of the attributes of omnipotence. The human body is a mirror image of the attributes of sovereignty which are mirrors for the mirrors of the attributes of omnipotence, which in turn are mirrors for the divine attributes.[11]

Second, the progression from the Realm of Divinity to the Human Realm is one of movement from oneness to plurality. This involves divine unfolding and diversification, and can be described as occurring in the horizontal plane in contrast to the vertical series of reflections mentioned above. The Realm of Divinity is given a rank that is described as singular, while the Realm of Omnipotence is tenfold, the Realm of Sovereignty hundredfold and the Human Realm thousandfold. This is the reason for the appearance of a multiplicity of manifest entities in the universe, and the basis of the scheme of emanation which Simnānī describes and which I shall discuss shortly. The multiplicity apparent in the Realms of Omnipotence and Sovereignty and in the Human Realm in no way compromises the oneness of God. God's essence remains unique, maintaining singularity in multiplicity, beyond any possibility of indwelling in another or unification and union with another; exalted above having any partner or peer.[12]

The Realm of Divinity is the abode of the greatest name of God, "Allāh." Simnānī attempts to prove its greatness by dividing the word into the four letters that compose it and demonstrating that, even if the individual letters of the word *allāh* in Arabic orthography are removed one by one, it retains its nature as a name of God. For example, the greatest name of God is used in the verse *"Allāhu lā ilāha illā-huwa"* (Allāh, there is no God but Him [2:255]). If the letter *alif* is removed the word retains its meaning, as in the verse *"li'llāhi mā fi's-samāwāt wa'l-arḍ"* (to Allāh belongs all that is in the heavens and the earth [2:284]). When the first *lām* is removed the verse means the same thing, as in *"lahu mā fi's-samāwāt wa'l-arḍ"* (to Him belongs what lies in the heavens and the earth [2:116]). When the second *lām* is removed, it becomes *huwa* (He), another one of the

---

11. *Najm*, 31a.
12. Ibid., 52a.

divine names as used in the verse: *"huwa'l-ḥayy lā ilāha illā-huwa"*
(He is the Living; there is no god but Him [40:65]).[13]

Since the Realm of Divinity is inscrutable, God can only be
understood by the human intellect through His attributes which reside
in the Realm of Omnipotence. These divine attributes are of two types:
attributes of essence and attributes of action. There are eight attributes
of essence: the Living (*ḥayy*), the Hearer (*samī'*), the Seer (*baṣīr*), the
Speaker (*mutakallim*), the Decreer (*murīd*), the Powerful (*qādir*), the
Knower (*'alīm*) and the Wise (*ḥakīm*). Attributes of essence are
epithets, and are adjectival in that they describe an aspect of God. It
is therefore possible to say that God has life, hearing, sight, speech,
will, power, knowledge and wisdom. Denial of the uncreated nature
of these attributes of essence negates an individual's faith.[14]

The remaining attributes of God are those of action and cannot
be precisely enumerated. Attributes of action are transitive and serve
as sources for the divine effects. They are not, however, descriptive
of the divine essence. Thus even though it is correct to say that God
is the Creator (*khāliq*), Fashioner (*ṣāni'*), Sustainer (*rāziq*) and so on,
this does not imply that God possesses creation, design and
sustenance. Attributes of action are nonessential, and even though
belief in their having been created is inappropriate, it does not negate
one's faith.[15]

Divine Manifestation

God manifests Himself through these non-essential attributes
of action. Divine manifestation occurs simultaneously at a visible and
invisible level through His apparent attribute and His hidden
attribute.[16] Divine self-manifestation is a result of God's need to be
known, lending truth to the *ḥadīth qudsī* favored by the Sufis: "I was
a hidden treasure wanting to be known, and I created creation in order
to be known." God therefore created the earth and the heavens and
what is in them so that the sublime celestial forces may glorify Him
in the spiritual heavens and the sublunar terrestrial forces may praise
Him on the earth.[17] Similarly, He created the human soul as a

---

13. *Farḥat al-'āmilīn*, 46.

14. *Shaqā'iq al-ḥadā'iq wa-ḥadā'iq al-ḥaqā'iq*, MS. 821/7, Halet Efendi,
Süleymaniye Kütüphanesi, Istanbul, 76b.

15. Ibid.

16. *Risāla sirr bāl al-bāl li-dhawi'l-ḥāl*, MS. 11-mīm, Majāmī' fārsiyya, Dār
al-kutub, Cairo, 241b: *ṣifat-i ẓāhirī* and *ṣifat-i bāṭinī*.

17. *Najm*, 65a.

companion for His jealousy (*ghayra*), so that something other than Himself should know Him.[18]

The simultaneous apparent and hidden manifestation of God gives rise to secondary sub-manifestations.[19] Everything that is visible in the visible realm is a mirror of the manifestation of the apparent attribute of God. This includes the celestial elements (*mufradāt*), the heavenly spheres, stars and the 'progeny' (*mutawalladāt*) that are generated from these celestial elements and exist in the sublunar realm.

The manifestation of the hidden attributes of God is of two kinds, a general and a special manifestation, each of these subdivided into two kinds. The general manifestation is simultaneously one of divine grace and power. The manifestation of divine power is through Satan and is of two types: deceit and oppression. The loci of the manifestation of divine power through deceit are rationalist scholars of religion and ascetic heretics, while those through violence are ignorant people and unbelievers. The first group is punished by God through their self-deception in matters of religion, while the latter are punished through violence and affliction. Both groups constitute the inhabitants of hell and they, along with hell itself, constitute loci for the manifestation of divine power.

The manifestation of grace occurs through the angels and is of two kinds, peace and censure. The manifestation of divine grace through censure cleanses an individual of base qualities which are then replaced with praiseworthy ones. The manifestation through peace creates love and longing within individuals compelling them to be drawn towards God. Both these categories of individuals are blessed with divine grace and are the denizens of Paradise and, along with Paradise itself, they constitute loci for the manifestation of divine grace. "Whosoever was a Muslim believer is the mirror (*maẓhar*) of divine grace, blessed for all eternity, and whosoever was a sinful polytheist is the mirror of divine power, afflicted for all eternity."[20]

The special hidden manifestation of God is also of two kinds, divine majesty and beauty. The manifestation of majesty causes the subtle substance of I-ness (*laṭīfa-yi anā'iyyat*) to be purified of the impurities of the temporal physical realm, as a result of which the divine presence becomes established in the heart.[21] The manifestation

---

18. Ibid., 68b.
19. *Sirr bāl al-bāl*, 242a–b. Cf. figure 2.
20. *Najm*, 95a.
21. *Sirr bāl al-bāl*, 242b.

FIGURE 2

Divine Manifestation

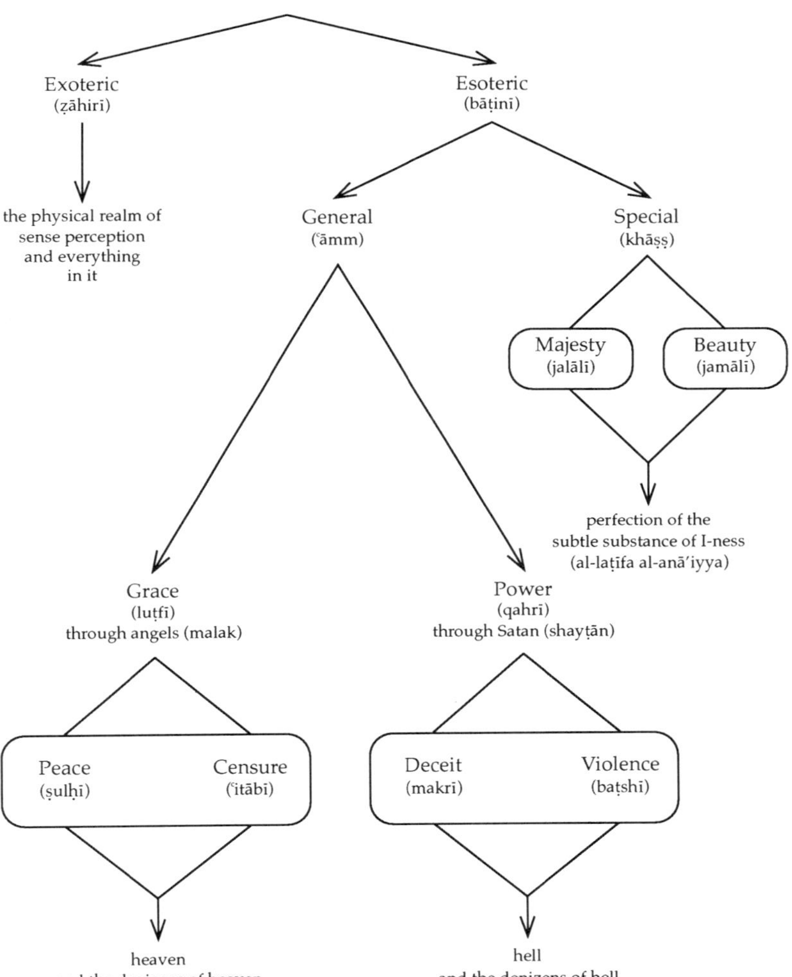

of divine beauty is what causes the subtle substance of I-ness to be given eternal life, as a result of which the heart is drawn to the eternal presence of God. The combination of these two manifestations ultimately results in the perfection of the subtle substance of I-ness. This realization and perfection of the subtle substance of I-ness (*al-laṭīfa al-anā'iyya*) is the ideal goal and ultimate result of all mystical endeavors. It is a central feature of Simnānī's thought and shall be discussed at some length later in this chapter.

The Spiritual and Physical Realms

The duality displayed in Simnānī's understanding of divine manifestation as apparent and hidden permeates his thought. This carries over into a notion of two realms, one finite and the other infinite. The finite realm, called the realm of horizons (*'ālam al-āfāq*) or the physical world, contains the realms of sense perception and temporality. The infinite realm, called the realm of the souls (*'ālam al-anfus*) or the spiritual world, lies beyond the confines of time and finite space.[22] Both these realms are mirrors for attributes of God, the spiritual realm being a mirror for His hidden attribute and the physical realm a mirror of His apparent attribute.[23]

Although the physical realm appears to be larger than the spiritual one, the reverse is true. The physical world, with its visible and invisible dimensions, souls and horizons, and everything else that is within it, is a microcosmic human being, while the human being is a macrocosmic world.[24] The spiritual realm, which is the world that lies within the body, is the macrocosm of the physical world, and the physical world, which appears to be larger than the body, is a microcosm. Since we view the relationship of the body and soul from the point of view of human perception, the breast appears to be larger than the heart and to encompass it. However, at a metaphysical level, it is the heart that is larger. The spiritual realm, of which the mystical heart is a part, exists beyond the confines of the temporal realm and structures such as the human breast, which exist within it.[25]

This theory concerning the correspondence of the physical and spiritual realms propounded by Simnānī is extremely unusual, and

---

22. There is a Qur'ānic basis to the notion of *āfāq* and *anfus*: "We shall show them Our portents on the horizons (*al-āfāq*) and within themselves (*anfusihim*) until it will be manifest unto them that it is the truth" (41:53).

23. *Najm*, 13b.

24. Ibid., 31a.

25. Ibid., 89a.

directly contradicts the dominant Sufi concept which sees the Perfect Human Being (*al-insān al-kāmil*) as a microcosm of the universe.[26] The more common theory is very clearly presented by Simnānī's contemporary 'Azīz ad-dīn-i Nasafī in many of his works, especially the *Zubdat al-ḥaqā'iq*.[27] Nasafī, a student of the Kubrawī master Sa'd ad-dīn-i Ḥamūya, emphasizes a complete correspondence between the microcosmic and macrocosmic realms, so much so that he sees the seven heavens as the seven viscera, the seven planets as the seven organs, the four elements as the four humors, the twelve stations of the zodiac as the twelve senses (five inner, five outer and two motive) and so on.[28]

In Simnānī's writings the two realms of the horizons and souls exist side by side in a state of perfect correspondence, in much the same way as they appear in Nasafī's scheme. For every entity found in the physical realm there is a corresponding entity in the spiritual realm. This complementarity includes the parallel existence of invisible and visible (*ghayb wa-shahāda*) in both realms.

> Know that in the physical realm there is an invisible and a visible and in the spiritual realm there is an invisible and a visible. The invisible of the spiritual realm is finer and greater than the invisible of the physical realm. The garden and the fire [heaven and hell] are present in the invisible of the spiritual realm and are greater than what they are in the invisible of the physical realm.... The visible of the spiritual realm is coarser and smaller than the visible of the physical realm.[29]

It is clear from Simnānī's writings that the difference between the physical and spiritual realms is not that one is visible and the other invisible. On the contrary, both the physical and spiritual realms contain within themselves a visible and invisible dimension. Since

---

26. A similar scheme appears in the *Rawḥ al-arwāḥ fī-sharḥ asmā' al-malik al-fattāḥ* of Aḥmad as-Sam'ānī (d. ca. 489/1096), ed. N.M. Hirawī (Tehran: Intishārāt-i 'ilmī wa farhangī, 1989), 180.

27. *Zubdat al-ḥaqā'iq*, ed. Ḥaqq-Wardī Nāṣirī (Tehran: Kitābkhāna-yi Ṭahūrī, 1985).

28. F. Meier, "The Problem of Nature in the Esoteric Monism of Islam," *Spirit and Nature: Papers from the Eranos Yearbooks*, Bollingen Series, no. 30, vol. 1 (Princeton: Princeton University Press, 1954; rpt. 1972), 188; Nasafī, 105, 135.

29. *al-Wārid ash-shārid*, 19b.

the spiritual realm is the macrocosm of the physical realm, the things
found in it are qualitatively greater than those in the physical realm.
Furthermore, the emphasis in the spiritual realm is upon the metaphysical; therefore the invisible of the spiritual realm is finer (or less
substantive) than the extrasensory in the physical realm of sense
perception. On the other hand, the visible of the spiritual realm is
smaller than that of the physical realm, since very little is beyond
the form of perception utilized in the spiritual realm. For this reason,
even though the visible of the spiritual realm is quantitatively smaller,
it is coarser (or more substantive), in that its bodily existence is of
a qualitatively greater kind than the bodily existence of things in the
physical realm.

The dual spiritual and physical realms and everything that is
within them are brought into being by God through a process which
Simnānī alternatively describes as creation (*khalq*) and emanation
(*fayḍ*). The first entity in the order of creation appears in different
aspects but is one and the same thing:

Although the visible and invisible dimensions of the spiritual
and physical worlds differ in their degree of subtlety and substantiality,
there are corresponding entities in these realms. The visible dimension
of the physical realm consists of the heavens and the earth and all
the celestial bodies, animals and plants that are within them. These
correspond to the visible dimension of the spiritual realm which is
the human body and what it contains by way of faculties, humors,
veins, nerves and organs. In a similar fashion, just as the invisible
dimension of the physical realm contains the spirits of the Jinn and
angels, the invisible of the spiritual realm consists of the human soul
(*nafs*), heart (*qalb*), inmost being (*sirr*), spirit (*rūḥ*) and inner mystery
(*khafī*). The correspondence between the visible and invisible of the
spiritual and physical realms is complete, except that the heart contained in the invisible of the spiritual realm is the potential source
of human perfection, and therefore has a significance unparalleled by
anything in the physical realm.[30]

The dual spiritual and physical realms and everything that is
within them are brought into being by God through a process which
Simnānī alternatively describes as creation (*khalq*) and emanation
(*fayḍ*). The first entity in the order of creation appears in different
aspects but is one and the same thing:

[Muḥammad] said: "The first thing Allāh created was the pen";
and "The first thing Allāh created was my spirit"; and "The first
thing Allāh created was the intellect." He is referring to one
reality in the guise of different metaphors. . . . Allāh taught by
the pen, the first entity created in the aspect of being (*wujūd*);
and "by his [Muḥammad's] spirit," the first entity created in the

---

30. Ibid.

aspect of life (*ḥayā*); and "by his light," the first entity created in the stage of the mystical journey (*sayr*); and "by the intellect," the first entity created within the intelligible elements (*maʿādin al-mufradāt al-maʿnawiyya*).[31]

This is clearly an attempt to allow for a multiplicity of emanations while maintaining the neoplatonic truism that only one can emanate from one. For Simnānī, each of these statements about the nature of the first item in the order of creation refers to a singular reality. The apparent differences are only due to God's use of metaphor and the fact that each of these metaphors is a different aspect of the first created entity. Two of these aspects are the light and spirit of Muḥammad, references to his status as the primordial human being. The other two aspects, the pen and the intellect, are integral to the process of subsequent emanations. The pen is the first creation in the aspect of existence. It is also the first entity brought into being on the plane of action.[32] The "tablet of the intellect," on the other hand, is the first thing created by God on the plane of potentiality.[33] God used this primordial pen of action to write upon the tablet of the intellect everything He wished to express concerning the plan of the world and the appointed time (*al-waqt al-muqaddar*).[34] "He wrote upon it the plan of the world from whose blackness appeared the visible realm and from whose whiteness the invisible realm."[35] In other words, Simnānī likens creation to an act of writing: the pen writes on the tablet thereby dividing creation into the physical and spiritual realms which correspond to the written word and the white background respectively. In so doing, he is also reconciling the seemingly contradictory schemes of creation and emanation into what might be called (for lack of a better term) a Qurʾānic-neoplatonic cosmology.[36]

The visible and invisible realms do not derive directly from the first entity in the order of creation. There are ten consecutive emana-

---

31. Ibid., 21b. Although Simnānī mentions the light of Muḥammad as being the first entity created in the stage of the mystical journey, he does not quote *ḥadīth* in support of his claim. The same traditions are used by Nasafī to show that verbal distinctions which perplex exoteric thinkers have no bearing on the true nature of a thing (Meier, "The Problem of Esoteric Monism," 160–61).

32. *Najm*, 150b.

33. Ibid., 137a–b.

34. Ibid., 137b; *al-Wārid ash-shārid*, 21b.

35. *al-Wārid ash-shārid*, 21b.

36. See chapter 8 for a brief discussion of how Simnānī's cosmology fits within the context of a greater Islamic cosmological tradition.

tions, which Simnānī terms subtle substances (*laṭā'if*), which constitute intermediaries between the first created being, and the physical and spiritual realms with their visible and invisible dimensions.

Emanation and the Compound Human Being

The ten subtle substances emanate from the first created entity in the Realm of Divinity. However, they do not abide in the divine presence, but begin a downward journey, descending to the Realm of Omnipotence where they are distinguished by the attributes of omnipotence. The *laṭā'if* descend from this realm in the form of rare substances (*raqā'iq*) to the 'dwelling places of sovereignty' which are in the Realm of Sovereignty. Here they are distinguished by the divine attributes of action. They descend from here in the form of particulars (*daqā'iq*) to the 'human stations,' which are in the Human Realm which is identical with the physical realm. It is here that they lend expression to the effects placed in the kingly particulars.[38]

The movement of the ten higher substances (*al-laṭā'if al-'ulwiyya*) from the divine presence in the Realm of Divinity to the Human Realm symbolizes the process of emanation. As these substances descend from the divine presence they pass through the intermediate realms of omnipotence and sovereignty. In the process they acquire an increasing degree of differentiation, such that the ten substances are successively transformed first into rare substances by divine attributes and then into particulars by divine acts, until they articulate themselves as the manifest expression of these acts, that is as their effects. This transformation corresponds to the movement from singularity to tenfoldness, to hundredfoldness, and finally to thousandfoldness, as described above in the progression from oneness to multiplicity through the four realms.[39]

The higher, celestial substances result in the emanation of the spheres, which are nine in number and arranged in order of descent. The first sphere and highest heaven is the 'divine footstool,' known to non-mystics as the sphere of Atlas or the heaven of heavens. The next is the sphere holding the constellations, otherwise known as the sphere of the fixed stars. This is followed by the spheres of Saturn, Jupiter, Mars, the Sun, Venus and Mercury. The last sphere is that of

---

37. *Kitāb al-qudsiyyāt*, MS. 165/2, Şehit Ali Paşa, Süleymaniye Kütüphanesi, Istanbul, 204b.

38. Ibid; cf. figure 3.

39. See above, pp. 63–65; *Najm*, 44a.

FIGURE 3

The Fourfold Scheme of Emanation

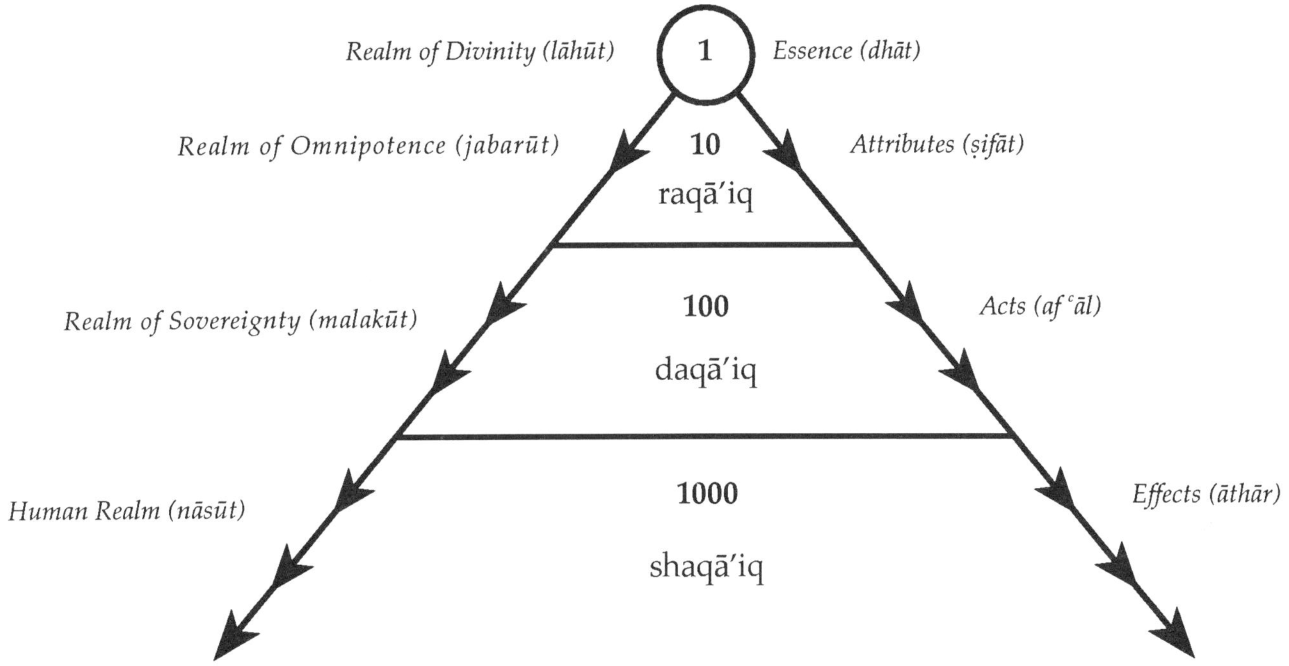

the moon, after which the sublunar terrestrial realm begins. These heavens embody souls and intellects which, combined with the ordered motion of the nine spheres occurring in the best of forms, cause the emanation of the sublunar realm. As a result of this these spheres are considered active agents (*fā'il*), and are called the 'higher fathers' (*ābā-yi 'ulwā*).[40]

The nine heavens are followed by the four sublunar spheres of the elements. These are—in order of their appearance—the sphere of ether which is manifested by fire, then the sphere of air of which wind is a sign, then that of water and finally that of earth. These four spheres are brought into existence through the movement of the spheres and the agency of these 'higher fathers,' as a result of which they are called the 'lower mothers' (*ummahāt-i suflā*). The lower mothers possess ability or potentiality (*qābiliyyat*) while the higher fathers embody action (*fi'liyyat*). The combination of this action and potentiality causes the emanation, in the form of 'progeny' (*mawālīd*), of all substances seen existing on the terrestrial plane.[41]

The first of these terrestrial emanations produced by the combination of the active, higher fathers and potential, lower mothers is inanimate matter. This inanimate matter is an articulation of the ascent of the emanations of the celestial bodies which have settled on the ground. Having descended to the terrestrial plane inanimate matter cannot attain union with its origin yet wishes to return to it by the path of ascent. However, it cannot accomplish this because of its inherent weakness and the lack of celestial properties within it.[42]

The second category of terrestrial emanations is composed of plants, which are obtained from the subordinate emanations of the fixed stars and planets that have settled on the ground.

The third category consists of animals, which are obtained from the steadfast attachment to the ground of the dominant emanations of the planets and the fixed stars, and the subordinate emanations of the footstool, otherwise known as the heaven of Atlas.

The perfect form of the category of animals is the human being, who is the last of the "progeny" (*khātim-i mawālīd*), bearer of

---

40. *Fatḥ al-mubīn*, 8a; cf. figure 4. A similar description of the heavens is contained in the *'Urwa* (463ff.). In order to be faithful to the Arabic, I have translated the term *'aql* as *intellect* in all contexts, ignoring the convention, originating in the Latin Middle Ages, of applying the term *intelligence* to celestial entities and *intellect* to others.

41. Ibid., 8a–b.

42. Ibid., 8b.

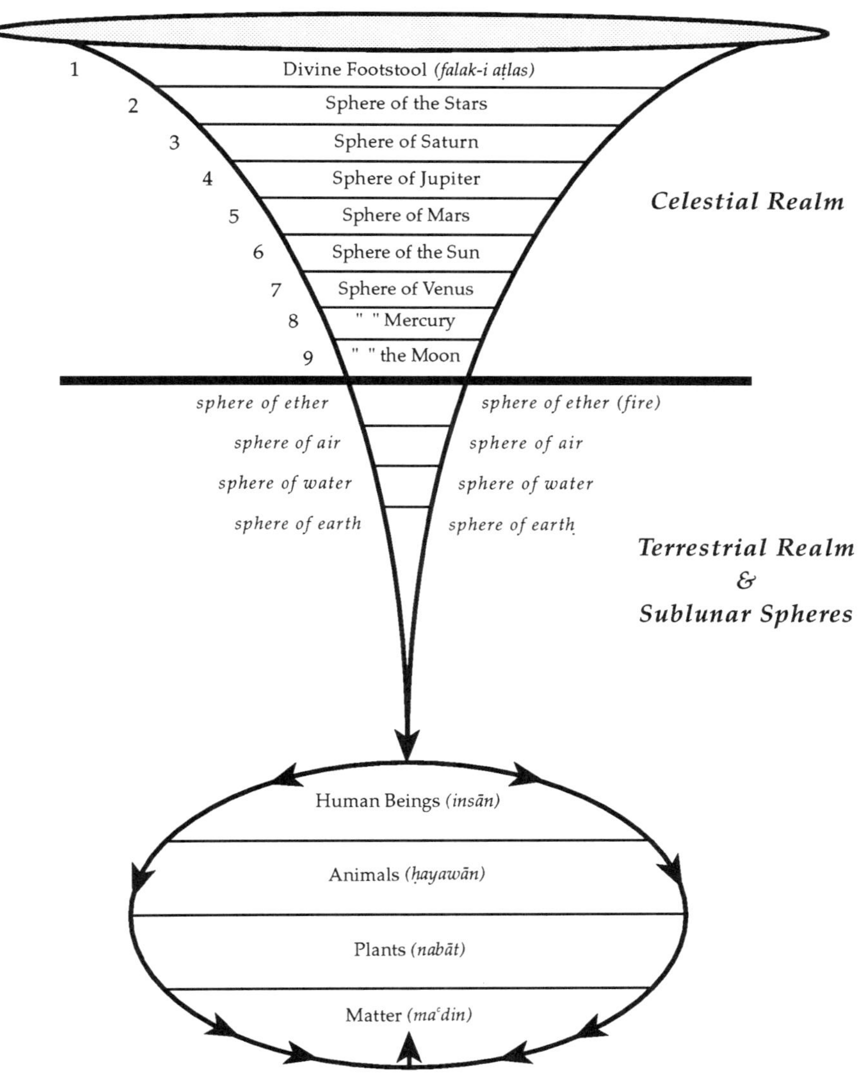

FIGURE 4

Emanation of Celestial and Sublunar Realms

the sacred trust of the knowledge of the divine names, attributes
and essence, deserving of the vicegerency (*khilāfat*) of God, may
He be exalted.[43]

All existent beings contain within themselves faculties or forces
(*quwā*) with which they act upon and influence other things. However,
these forces are not of their own creation but are placed within entities
by God. These forces do not possess being independent of the things
they inhabit, and it is incorrect to think that they exist alone or possess
attributes such as gender or sentience.[44] All celestial and sublunar
entities are divine creations which God nourishes from the heavens
and the earth.[45] All these creations are perishable, as referred to in
the Qur'ānic verse: "Everyone that is thereon will pass away; there
remains but the countenance of your Lord of Might and Glory" (55:26).
Passing away (*fanā'*) refers to the destruction of compounds (*murakkabāt*) and is a manifestation of divine attributes, while destruction
(*halāk*) refers to elements, the obliteration of which is a manifestation
of the essence.[46] By this Simnānī seems to imply that when celestial
compounds and earthly particulars are obliterated, nothing remains
apart from the divine essence. In other words, their existence is
contingent.

The celestial and sublunar emanations serve as loci of manifestation for certain attributes of God and reflect God's act of creation
under different aspects. The celestial elements are mirrors for the
beauty of His bringing them into being; the terrestrial matter or
minerals are mirrors for the beauty of His act of situating them in
time; plants are mirrors for the beauty of His creating them in space,
while animals are mirrors for the beauty of His act of giving form
to them.[47]

Each entity in the sublunar plane has a foundation or a governor
(*qā'im maqām*) in the celestial planes: the intellect is the governor

---

43. Ibid.

44. *Najm*, 21a. " 'Those who believe not in the Hereafter, name the angels
with female names' (53:27): because their vision is limited to their outward
appearance and their intellects are too small to grasp their true meaning, they
believe that the forces (*quwā*) and subtle substances (*latā'if*) are the daughters
of Allāh."

45. Ibid., 73b.

46. Ibid., 33a.

47. *Kitāb qawāṭi' as-sawāṭi'*, MS. 11-mīm, Majāmī' fārsiyya, Dār al-kutub,
Cairo, 155b. *Mūjidiyya, mubdi'iyya, khāliqiyya* and *muṣawwiriyya* respectively.

of the minerals, the angels of the plants, and the Jinn of the animals. Each of the nine heavens, the four sublunar spheres, and the terrestrial emanations are mirrors of the exoteric and esoteric attributes of God, and glorify and exalt Him, each to the best of its own ability.[48]

None of them, however, is capable of being a perfect mirror for God in a form that would carry within itself the sacred trust (*amāna*) consisting of knowledge of the divine essence. This is because those entities which are composed of the lower elements are lacking in the higher ones, and those of them composed of the higher elements are devoid of the lower ones. Only human beings combine within themselves elements from both the higher and lower spheres:

> At the daybreak between the darkness of creation and the light of the divine command, God kneaded the clay of the human being with the two hands of His grace and power and, taking from the higher and lower spheres of matter, He united in it the subtle substance of creation and the divine command in forty levels in four realms: the Realm of Divinity, the Realm of Omnipotence, the Realm of Sovereignty, and the Human Realm.[49]

---

48. *Najm*, 75a; *Qawāṭiʿ as-sawāṭiʿ*, 155b.

49. *Qawāṭiʿ as-sawāṭiʿ*, 155b; cf. "Muqaddima tafsīr al-qurʾān li-ʿAlāʾ ad-dawla as-Simnānī," ed. P. Nwyia in *al-Abḥāth* 26 (1973–77), 146–47; *Najm*, 75b.

5

THE SPIRITUAL BODY AND THE MIRROR OF GOD

The human being is seen as superior to all other created entities. Both the lower compounds (*al-murakkabāt as-sufliyya*) such as the animals and plants, and the higher compounds (*al-murakkabāt al-'ulwiyya*) such as the angels and Jinn are imperfect because they fail to combine within themselves elements of both the higher and lower spheres of existence. The human being's exalted status derives from its composition of elements from both realms. The implication of this is that the human being is a composite of all levels of divine manifestation in this world, and is therefore created in God's image as mentioned in the canonical prophetic saying: "Indeed Allāh, may He be exalted, created Adam in His image."[1]

In agreement with the vast majority of Sufi thinkers, Simnānī maintains that the creation of Adam in the perfect image of God does not imbue human existence with divine attributes, but simply confers upon it the status of the 'seal of created entities' (*khātim at-tarākīb*), capable of carrying within itself the sacred trust which consists of knowledge of the divine essence. The human body serves as the barrier (*barzakh*) by which the nature of the higher, luminescent forces is differentiated from that of the lower, dark ones. At the same time, the human body also serves a purpose in the unification of these two categories of forces, since it is finer than the lower forces and coarser than the higher ones. In this capacity, it functions like cartilage or tendons separating yet joining muscle and bone, without which a physical body cannot be completed.[2]

At the time of the human body's creation, the exalted status as bearer of the divine trust is placed within it only as a potentiality that may be actualized through a process of mystical practice. In its exoteric form, the human body is simply a member of the category of the animals, albeit the highest member of this category. The physical

---

1. *Najm*, 76b.
2. Ibid., 32b.

human body is composed of four elements: the soul of earth, the heart of water, the inmost being of air, and the spirit of fire. In terms of its constitution, the human body is similar to all animals, and as a result behaves like animals who are ruled by their appetites and desires. Lacking any light of spirituality, the four component parts of the human being incline to their own natures: the soul to baseness and indolence, the heart to worldly concerns and desires, the inmost being to passion and self-love, and the spirit to arrogance and anger. It is only after this physical human body is imbued with the light of spirituality that these components reform themselves into a form consistent with the characteristics of a pious human being: the soul acquires purity in exchange for baseness, and replaces indolence with perseverance; the heart concerns itself with the hereafter and its blessings; the inmost being becomes a lover of God and engages in divine worship; and the spirit replaces arrogance with mercy and anger with zeal.[3]

---

3. *Risāla-yi sirr-i samā'*, ed. by N.M. Hirawī in "Chahār guftār-i shaykh 'Alā' ad-dawla-yi Simnānī," *Dānish* 3 (1985), 11. The light of spirituality (*nūr-i rūḥāniyyat*) is a concept which does not appear frequently in Simnānī's thought. It is a poorly defined term which implies the establishment of a mystic soul in the human being. "Of all the lights (*anwār*) in the human body, that of spirituality is closest to the divine realm ('*ālam-i ulūhiyyat*)" (*Sirr-i samā'*, 12–13).

According to Simnānī, 'light' has many meanings and the term is applied to many things, such as the light of the intellect, light of certitude, of the eyes, the sun and so on. These are all lights in relation to their opposites which are darknesses (*ẓulmāt*). The first level of light is that by which God sees Himself; the second by which He sees others; the third by which He sees Himself and others. The fourth is that with which He sees Himself and others with intermediaries and causes (*bi'l-wasā'iṭ wa'l-asbāb*); the fifth is that with which He sees Himself and another without intermediaries and causes. The sixth is the light which He gives to all luminescent things (*nayyirāt*) and which is maintained through Him. Seen in reverse order, the sixth is particular to the singular divine reality (*al-ḥaqīqa al-wāḥida adh-dhātiyya al-lāhūtiyya*); the fifth to the rare substances of the Realm of Omnipotence (*ar-raqā'iq al-jabarūtiyya*), such as the light of divine attributes; the fourth to the particulars of the Realm of Sovereignty (*ad-daqā'iq al-malakūtiyya*) such as the light of the intellect. The third is specific to the particles of the human realm (*ash-shaqā'iq an-nāsūtiyya*), connected to the particulars of the Realm of Sovereignty and benefiting others with its light (such as the light of the sun). The second is also specific to the particles of the human realm, but does not benefit others (such as the light of eyesight). The first level of light is particular to God, and is similar to a likeness which He sees of Himself. The only real light is this light of God, and all other uses of the word are figurative (*Qawāṭi' as-sawāṭi'*, 180a–b).

This transformation occurs through developments in the spiritual human body, the creation of which in the spiritual realm corresponds to the creation of the physical human body in the physical realm. This spiritual human body is the result of the combination of celestial elements, and consists of seven levels called *lata'if* which exist in the physical realm and survive the destruction of the physical body.[4] Each of these subtle substances is progressively more perfect than the previous one, and together they represent the process of actualizing the highest state a human being can possibly attain.

Composition of the Spiritual Body

The first of these resultants is the subtle bodily substance (*al-latīfa al-qālabiyya*) which arises from the combination of the dominant emanations of the divine throne (*'arsh*) and subordinate emanations of the divine footstool (*kursī*), after the completion of the physical created body as an emanation of the ten higher, celestial substances and the lower, elemental ones. This subtle bodily substance dominates the physical body, as a result of which a human being is distinguishable from the category of animals. This human being is the savage, or the "horizonal" human being (*insān-i āfāqī*), who resides in the wilderness, unfamiliar with the habits and customs of civilized people, differentiated from the animals through his faculty of articulated speech.[5] This subtle bodily substance also serves as the womb in which the fetus of the acquired body (*al-badan al-muktasab*) appears, which persists after the destruction of the perishable physical body.[6]

The second resultant is the subtle substance of the soul (*al-latīfa an-nafsiyya*), arising from the dominant emanations of the divine footstool and subordinate emanations of the tablet of the intellect

---

4. *Kitāb al-qudsiyyāt*, 204b.

5. *Fath al-mubīn*, 8b; *'Urwa*, 463. The description of these seven resultant subtle substances and their composition found in *Fath al-mubīn* and the *'Urwa* differs from the version in Simnānī's commentary on the Qur'ān. For the sake of simplicity, I have combined the three in order to present a standardized scheme utilizing terminology which appears most frequently in Simnānī's writings. This standardized version is also presented in figure 5. The higher entities from which the subtle substances emerge are not clearly explained by Simnānī. They might be the inner counterparts to the nine celestial spheres instrumental in the emanation of existents in the visible, sublunar realm.

6. "Muqaddima tafsīr al-qur'ān," 151; *Fath al-mubīn*, 8b ff.

FIGURE 5

Emanation of the Compound Human Being

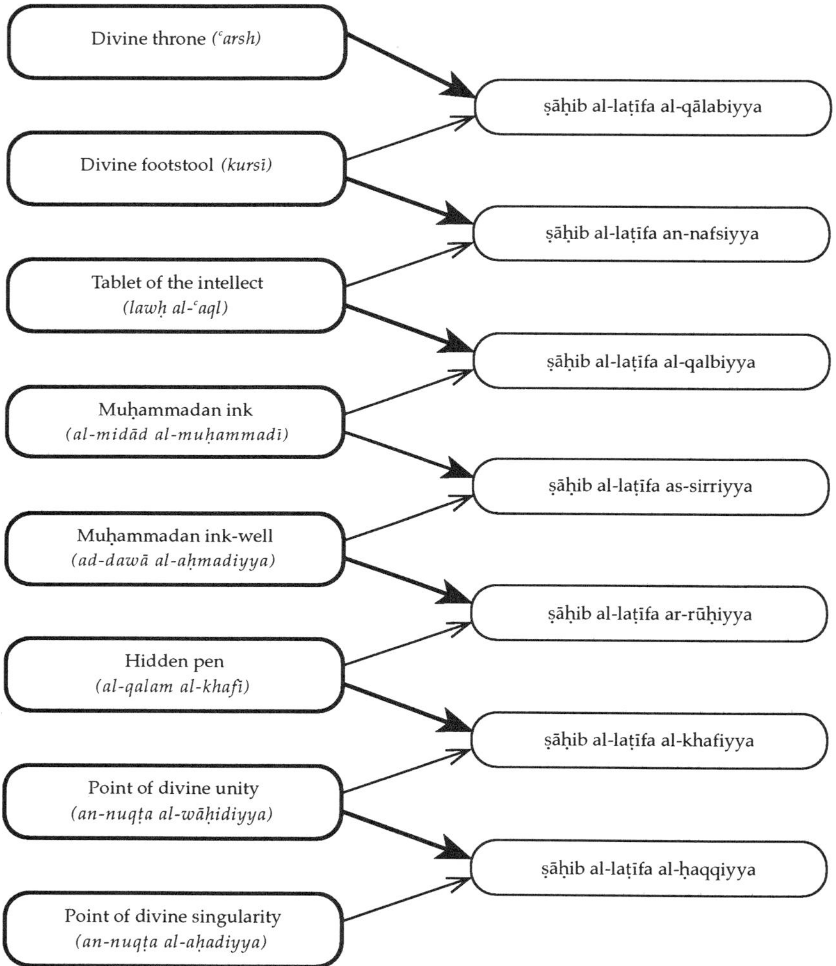

(*lawḥ*). As a result of this subtle substance the human being receives a subtle, perceptive faculty and becomes the nonbelieving human being (*al-insān al-kāfir*), capable of maintaining social and political laws to regulate society, but persisting in his disbelief and polytheism, as a result of which his perceptive faculty remains dark.[7]

The third is the subtle substance of the heart (*al-laṭīfa al-qalbiyya*), arising from the emanations of the tablet of the intellect (*lawḥ al-ʿaql*) as dominant and the celestial Muḥammadan ink (*al-midād al-muḥammadī*) as subordinate. The possessor of this subtle substance is cleansed of the darkness of his acquired body, which departs from the darkness of his nature. Instead of this darkness of unbelief, he is filled with the light of faith and becomes a Muslim as distinguished from a non-Muslim civilized human being.

The subsequent four subtle substances refer to levels of spiritual perfection which are attained as a result of mystical advancement. The fourth is the subtle substance of the inmost being (*al-laṭīfa as-sirriyya*), resulting from the emanations of the tablet of the intellect and the Muḥammadan ink as dominant and the Muḥammadan ink-well (*ad-dawā al-aḥmadiyya*) as subordinate. This substance distinguishes the faithful Muslim (*muʾmin*) who is decorated with the adornment of the light of faith, and whose acquired body has found deliverance from inconstancy.

The fifth is the subtle substance of the spirit (*al-laṭīfa ar-rūḥiyya*), resulting from the dominant emanations of the tablet of the intellect, Muḥammadan ink, and Muḥammadan ink-well, and the subordinate emanations of the mysterious pen (*al-qalam al-khafī*). This substance distinguishes the accomplished mystic (*walī*) from the faithful Muslim.

The sixth resultant is the subtle substance of the mystery (*al-laṭīfa al-khafiyya*), arising from the dominant emanations of the mysterious pen and the higher substances preceding it, and the subordinate emanations of a light which radiates from the locus of divine unity (*an-nuqṭa al-wāḥidiyya*). By this substance the prophet is distinguished from the mystic saint.

The final resultant is the subtle substance of the "real" (*al-laṭīfa al-ḥaqqiyya*) which is brought forth from the emanations of the locus of divine unity as dominant, and those of the locus of divine singularity (*an-nuqṭa al-aḥadiyya*) as subordinate. The possessor of this substance has realized the true nature of Muḥammad, the seal of the prophets, which is the highest status a human being can possibly attain.

---

7. *ʿUrwa*, 463.

The hierarchy of seven subtle substances in the spiritual realm within the human being corresponds to seven prophets in the realm of sense perception. These prophets of one's being are the typification of each successive level in the hierarchy. Just as the successive appearance of prophets in the physical realm signifies the progress of human society towards communal religious perfection, similarly the subtle substances of the spiritual body connote the progress of the human being towards individual mystical perfection.

The first is the subtle bodily substance. This is the human physical form which is the final result of the creative process. This subtle substance is the mold of an individual's acquired, spiritual body. Due to its initial position in the hierarchy of *laṭā'if*, this formal subtle substance is "the Adam of your being."[8]

The second level is the subtle substance of the soul. Here the soul does not imply the concupiscent or appetitive soul which incites to evil, but something which simultaneously undergoes calamities in the physical world (or the "abode of affliction") and also controls the body and curbs its natural disorder by confronting it, just as Noah confronted his people. For this reason it is considered "the Noah of your being."

The third is the subtle substance of the heart. This is the shell or oyster in which forms the rare pearl of the perfect human existence (*durrat al-laṭīfa al-anā'iyya*). As such, it is the parent in whose loins is nurtured an atom of progeny comprising the later subtle substances. Corresponding to the position of Abraham, the ancestor of the later prophets, it is called "the Abraham of your being."[9]

The fourth level is the subtle substance of the inmost being which represents direct communication with God (*munājāt*), and is therefore "the Moses of your being."

The fifth subtle substance is that of the spirit. Since the human spirit is the caliph of God in the kingdom of the human body, this subtle substance is distinguished by the robe of caliphal authority and corresponds to "the David of your being."[10]

---

8. "Muqaddima tafsīr al-qur'ān," 146. The hierarchy of subtle substances in the spiritual body has been described at length by Henry Corbin in *En Islam iranien*, 3:275–355.

9. Ibid., 147.

10. *Najm*, 126b, "Muqaddima tafsīr al-qur'ān," 147. This is a reference to the Qur'ānic verse (38:26): "O David! Indeed We have created you as a representative (*khalīfa*) in the earth; therefore judge among the people with justice, and do not follow desire lest it mislead you from the path of Allāh."

The sixth is that of the subtle substance of the mystery. Supported by the Holy Spirit, it announces the arrival of the seventh and final subtle substance to all the forces which comprise the "nations" (*umam*) of one's subtle substances. In this capacity it functions as "the Jesus of your being."[11]

The final level is the subtle substance of the "real." It is the last of the subtle substances, just as Muḥammad is the seal of the prophets. The attainment of this subtle substance is accompanied by a complete revelation of the true nature of reality:

> the appearance to the one real truth which is "the Muḥammad of your being," of its clear signs which make apparent all the truths (*ḥaqā'iq*) concealed in the higher and lower elements, combined in the subtle bodily substance and its compounds of creation and the divine command placed in the subtle substances of the soul, heart, inmost being, spirit, and mystery.[12]

The Seven Climes of the Spiritual Realm

Simnānī describes the seven subtle substances as kingdoms or climes (*aqālīm*) which constitute the 'garden of existence.'[13] Each of these seven climes of the subtle substances possesses a veil or curtain which conceals it from the preceding and subsequent climes. Furthermore, it has a king ruling over its inhabitants. The first curtain is that of the human body which conceals the realm of the Jinn ruled by Satan. The second is the chest, concealing a kingdom ruled by the soul; the third is the heart, veiling the realm of the mystical heart; the fourth curtain is the garden of the heart (*jannat al-qalb*) behind which is a world ruled by the inmost being; the fifth is the innermost self (*muhja*) concealing the world of the spirit; the sixth is the deepest core of the self (*suwaydā'*), concealing a world wherein the mystery (*khafī*) is manifested. The seventh and last curtain is the Hiddenmost Hidden (*ghayb al-ghuyūb*), which is the abode of eternity to which is manifested the "king of kings." This is the kingdom of the subtle substance of the "real" which cannot be attained without a mystical experience bestowed upon a person by God.[14]

---

11. "Muqaddima tafsīr al-qur'ān," 147. "And remember, Jesus, the son of Mary, said: 'O Children of Israel! I am the messenger of Allāh to you, confirming the law before me, and giving glad tidings of a messenger to come after me whose name shall be Aḥmad' " (61:6).

12. Ibid.

13. *Shaqā'iq al-ḥadā'iq.* 77a.

14. Ibid.

Each of these climes is populated by a community consisting of forces (*quwā*) which correspond to human beings collectively forming the communities of the seven climes in the physical realm. Just as human communities are made up of righteous and impious people, similarly the communities of the seven subtle substances also consist of good and evil forces. Forces which are steadfastly balanced constitute the pious community; forces which are consistently unbalanced constitute the disbelieving community; and forces which vacillate between being balanced and unbalanced make up the hypocritical community.[15] At first, even the faithful forces are inclined towards appetitive preoccupations and are drawn towards the disbelieving forces of the body and lower self which are their kinsfolk. However, even though they are ignorant of the meaning of the divine command, they scrupulously follow the subtle substance (corresponding to a prophet in the finite world) whose community they form.[16]

Certain forces among these communities inhabiting the seven kingdoms come closest to the true nature of the particular subtle substance to which they belong. Each of these constitutes a prophet who calls that community's forces to the religion of the personification of that particular subtle substance. This corresponds to the situation in the physical realm, in which Adam established a religious system which was promulgated by subsequent prophets until the time of Noah. Once the cycle of prophecy reached him, Noah established a new set of principles and laws in accordance with the level of religious development and preparedness of the people of his time.[17]

The prophets after Noah called out to their communities in accordance with his religious law until the arrival of Abraham. Similarly, those who followed him preached in accordance with his law until the prophetic mission of Moses, at which time the Torah was revealed. Subsequent prophets preached Mosaic law until the time of David, who was himself a recipient of revelation in the form of the *Zabūr* (Psalter). Henceforth the general mass of humanity was addressed in accordance with the Torah, and the elect with what is in the *Zabūr*. The distinction between the ideal subtle substances of each level and the righteous ones which subsequently guide their communities in accordance with their laws corresponds to the situation in the temporal realm, where messenger prophets (*rusul*) establish

---

15. "Muqaddima tafsīr al-qur'ān," 149.
16. *Najm*, 61b.
17. "Muqaddima tafsīr al-qur'ān," 149.

a tradition based on a revealed scripture, and are then followed by lesser prophets (*anbiyā'*) who continue to guide the community in a custodial fashion on the basis of these scriptures.

The prophets following David taught his tradition (*sunna*) until the arrival of Jesus who announced the coming of Muḥammad. In the manner of previous generations, the apostles who followed Jesus preached to their community on the basis of Jesus' laws and teachings as contained in his revelation, the *Injīl*. This continued until the arrival of Muḥammad, whose law abrogated all previous laws, and his revelation earlier revelations. Prophecy came to an end with him, so that the learned members (*'ulamā'*) of his community functioned in the capacity of the prophets of old, using his law to call their followers to the straight path.[19]

The progression of prophets in the physical realm corresponds to the seven prophetic figures of the *laṭā'if* in the spiritual realm. Just as the prophets in the physical world guide their communities with laws and revelation, so too do the inner prophets of the spiritual world.

So everything you have heard in the Book addressed to Adam, hear it with your subtle bodily substance. Employ your subtle bodily substance in what the soul has been commanded or forbidden to do; and take example from what has been given as a model for it. Believe that the esoteric level of this Book concerns you in the spiritual realm the way its exoteric level concerns Adam in the temporal realm.[20]

In a corresponding fashion, the verses of the Qur'ān addressed to Noah, Abraham, Moses, David and Jesus, should be heard with the subtle substances of the soul, heart, inmost being, spirit and mystery respectively. Through the references to these prophets in the Qur'ān, these subtle substances guide the human being towards higher levels of mystical development. The final substance is that of the "real" (*al-laṭīfa al-ḥaqqiyya*) which, being the Muḥammad of one's spiritual being, leads all the previous subtle substances and the forces which comprise their communities.[21]

---

18. Ibid., 150.
19. Ibid.
20. Ibid., 147.
21. *Najm*, 18b.

The progression from the basic level of the bodily subtle substance corresponding to Adam, to that of the subtle substance of the "real" corresponding to Muḥammad, is one of increasing mystical enlightenment which takes the form of the removal of veils covering the realm of each substance. Each of these seven realms is greater than the previous one, and one cannot comprehend a particular one until one has transcended it and views it with the vision (*'ayn*) of the subsequent realm. Thus it is not possible to see the nature of the bodily realm of Satan except with the sight of the soul, nor the realm of the soul except with the vision of the heart.[22] Just as in the physical realm, human beings in the spiritual realm progress from one of these levels to the next on the basis of their capacity and degree of readiness to receive mystical knowledge. This is necessary because if absolute realities were made apparent to a person before he was ready to receive them, they would overwhelm him, God knows the degree to which all individuals are capable of grasping mystical enlightenment, and reveals the truth to them on the basis of this level of readiness.[23]

Interior Ascent of the Subtle Substances

The subtle substances represent the seven final stages in the long process through which a human being reaches the highest level of mystical perfection. This scheme begins with the process of emanation from the ten higher substances, through that of the lower substances and spheres, and continues through the creation of matter, plants, and animals, concluding in the actualization of the human form complete with its inner hierarchy of subtle substances.

In actual fact, there are only five hierarchical levels within the spiritual realm: those of the soul, heart, inmost being, spirit, and mystery. The subtle bodily substance represents the point of departure or ascent for these substances, and the subtle substance of the "real" their culmination, marking the completion of the interior mystical journey towards human perfection. It is only these five substances of the soul, heart, inmost being, spirit and mystery which are mentioned in Simnānī's earliest writings; the sevenfold structure of *laṭā'if* appears later on. It can be surmised, therefore, that Simnānī developed his characteristic hierarchy of seven substances on the basis of a fivefold scheme which was prevalent in the writings of earlier thinkers.[24]

----

22. *Shaqā'iq al-ḥadā'iq*, 77a.

23. *Najm*, 140b.

24. Cf. Hermann Landolt, ed., "Deux opuscules de Semnānī sur le moi théophanique," *Mélanges Henry Corbin* (Tehran: 1977), 290; Najm ad-dīn Dāya

For Simnānī, the distinction between the bodily substance and the subsequent five subtle substances is one of degree and of kind. The subtle bodily substance is the foundation upon which the hierarchy of organs in the spiritual body is established. This substance is the acquired body which constitutes the human form in the realm of the spirit, just as the created, physical body constitutes the human form in the physical realm. It is within this acquired body that the process of mystic ascent through the remaining subtle substances occurs.

The seventh and last substance is that of the "real":

The subtle substance of the "real" signifies a capacity obtained from the combination of the four elements, and the commands residing in the bodies along with the realities (*ḥaqā'iq*) placed in the substances. These are perceived through the light of the intellect and of prophecy in harmonious forms, ennobled with the honor of the emanation of the manifestation of the attribute of oneness as dominant, ready to accept the manifestation of the attribute of singularity through the contingent beings and their kin. These kin are the first things perceived with the light of prophecy by the holy divine pen (*al-qalam al-qudsī al-ḥaqqī*) from the letter '*ayn* of the intellect (*al-'aql*), the spiritual ink-well of the letter *nūn*, and the ink of light, as has been referred to in the Qur'ān and Sunna: "*Nūn*, and the pen and that which they write" (68:1).[25]

The subtle substance of the "real" is the final stage in the seven-fold hierarchical development of the mystical human being. It is the result of a combination of emanations which lie closest to the divine essence. As such, it combines celestial and terrestrial properties within itself in a manner unmatched by any other subtle substance. Lying at the pinnacle of the mystical journey, it inhabits an abode called the Hiddenmost Hidden (*ghayb al-ghuyūb*). Not only does this realm lie above the lower substances, but it also encompasses them. Thus the invisible realm of the subtle substance of the "real," which is this Hiddenmost Hidden, encompasses the five invisible realms of

<hr>

ar-Rāzī, *The Path of God's Bondsmen from Origin to Return (Mirṣād al-'ibād min al-mabdā' ilā'l-ma'ād)*, translated by Hamid Algar (Delmar: Caravan, 1982), 18, 134–35, note 9.

25. *Risāla ṣadā'if al-laṭā'if*, MS. 1, Fiqh ḥanafī fārsī, Dār al-kutub, Cairo, 85a.

the spirit, inmost being, heart, soul and body, as well as the invisible realm of the mystery.[26]

Its status as the final subtle substance implies that the subtle substance of the "real" exists at the boundary between the created and divine realms. As such, no intermediaries lie between this substance and God. Whereas the other subtle substances are removed from the divine and must therefore look to intermediate causes as effecting them and having power over them, the subtle substance of the "real" need look only to the divine. Thus, while all the other substances must ask for divine protection from secondary causes, the subtle substance of the "real" seeks divine protection only from God Himself by saying: "My Lord! I seek refuge with You from You!"[27]

The subtle substance of the "real" is separated from God by a boundary called the clear horizon (*al-ufuq al-mubīn*).[28] In fact, it is itself the clear horizon of the Real (*al-ḥaqq*) which cannot be traversed by any human being or other created entity.[29] All subtle substances and other entities are separated from each other by a boundary or horizon. Thus mineral elements have a horizon separating them from plants, plants have a horizon separating them from animals, and animals have a horizon separating them from human beings.[30]

Within the human being there are horizons separating one subtle substance from the next, just as each successive prophet has a boundary delineating his status and function from the next prophet. Each of these prophets and corresponding subtle substances therefore has two horizons: one separating it from the previous one and the other from what lies above. In the case of Muḥammad and the subtle substance of the "real," the upper boundary is the clear horizon which separates the subtle substance from God (*al-ḥaqq*). The lower boundary directed towards the created realm is the highest horizon, so named because it is the limit of attainment for the other subtle substances.[31]

---

26. "Muqaddima tafsīr al-qur'ān," 148.

27. *Najm*, 167a. This is a reference to *Sūrat al-falaq* (113), wherein Muslims are enjoined to seek protection from things apart from God: "Say: I seek refuge with the Lord of the Dawn, From the mischief of created things; From the mischief of Darkness as it overspreads; From the mischief of those who blow on knots; And from the mischief of the envious one as he practises envy."

28. Ibid., 18b–19a.

29. "Muqaddima tafsīr al-qur'ān," 150.

30. *Najm*, 131b.

31. Ibid., 18b–19a; 131b.

Simnānī uses Qur'ānic symbols to name these boundaries. The highest horizon is the boundary separating the subtle substance of the "real" from that of the mystery. It is the point at which Muḥammad stood when Gabriel came to him with the first revelation.[32] The horizon which separates the subtle substance of the mystery from the subtle substance of the spirit lying below it is called the Lote-tree of the Boundary (*sidrat al-muntahā*), while the one separating the subtle substance of the spirit from that of the inmost being is the Garden of Abode (*jannat al-ma'wā*).[33] The Garden of Abode represents a heavenly garden lying within a human being, in which a person might reside forever if he or she were to manage it properly and sow good seeds (of action) in it. However, if one were to despoil it and plant bad seeds in it, it would become hell, and that too exists within each person. Similarly, each person has a Lote-tree of the Boundary which symbolizes the limit of mystical attainment through the human intellect which only possesses created knowledge. This boundary, which represents the horizon between the Realm of Sovereignty and the Realm of Omnipotence, cannot be traversed without God's knowledge, mediation and attraction (*jadhba*).[34]

Preeminence of the Subtle Substance of the "Real"

According to this scheme, the subtle substance of the "real" is not just superior to the other substances because it is the highest and lies closest to God. It is also categorically distinct because it is the only one which lies just beneath the Realm of Divinity in the Realm of Omnipotence, beyond the boundary of the Lote-tree which cannot be traversed without God's intercession. Although in Simnānī's scheme of mystical progress this represents the final stage of attainment, the subtle substance of the "real" is simultaneously the first of the subtle substances, residing with God before the appearance of the other substances. As such, it represents an archetypal substance, an idea similar to the notion of Muḥammad as an archetypal being found in the writings of earlier mystics.[35]

---

32. Ibid., 18b. "He was taught by one mighty in power, imbued with wisdom: for he appeared while he was at the highest horizon" (53:5-7).

33. Ibid., 19b. "By the Lote-tree of the utmost boundary, nigh unto which is the Garden of Abode" (53:14–15).

34. Ibid.

35. Cf. Michel Chodkiewicz, *Le sceau des saints: prophétie et sainteté dans la doctrine d'Ibn Arabî* (Paris: Editions Gallimard, 1986); Henry Corbin, *The*

Simnānī states that the subtle substance of the "real" was near unto God, then it descended from the Clear Horizon to the highest horizon so that the two horizons came together as one, as is referred to in the Qur'ān by the verse "Two bows' length or nearer" (53:9).[36] God then placed the subtle substance of the "real" in all things, but it was covered by curtains and veils and was therefore not apparent. He then nurtured these things until they attained the best of forms which is the mystical heart. It is within the subtle substance of the heart that God then nurtured the seed consisting of the subtle substance of the "real" until it reached the divine presence. God then commanded the subtle substance of the "real" to return to the lower realms in order to warn their denizens and bring them good tidings. For this reason the subtle substance of the "real" is the seal of the subtle substances (*khātim al-laṭā'if*) and the purpose of all creation.[37]

The pre-eternal nature of the Muḥammadan subtle substance changes the status of the Abrahamic substance from being the ancestor of later prophets to that of a patriarch. The subtle substance of the heart is not the first entity to contain within it the seed of the Muḥammadan substance of the "real," but is simply the best vessel within which to nurture the embryonic Muḥammadan substance. This explanation lends greater meaning to Simnānī's assertion that the Abrahamic subtle substance is the oyster in which the Muḥammadan substance of the "real" is nurtured.[38] Oysters do not represent the only receptacles capable of holding within themselves a grain of sand, but rather they are the only vessels in which this grain of sand can be properly nurtured so as to transform it into a pearl.

And everything you have heard addressed to His beloved and the signs that refer to him [Muḥammad], hear them with your subtle substance of the "real" assigned to the bodily emanation. This is the emanation which emanates from the end of the presence of the locus of divine unity (*nihāya ḥaḍrat an-nuqṭa al-wāḥidiyya*)

Man of Light in Iranian Sufism, trans. Nancy Pearson (Boulder: Shambala, 1978); R.A. Nicholson, *Studies in Islamic Mysticism* (Cambridge: Cambridge University Press, 1921; rpt. 1985).

36. *Najm*, 19a. In this context Simnānī refers to the two horizons of the subtle substance of the "real" as the horizon of preeternity (*ufuq al-azal*) and the horizon of posteternity (*ufuq al-abad*), emphasizing the primordial status of the Muḥammadan subtle substance of the "real."

37. Ibid., 62a.

38. See above, p. 84.

instead of the presence of the locus of the divine essence, after the admixture of the realities with each other in all the [other] subtle substances, brought together in a physique constructed by God in the best of forms. It is the last of the compound structures and the seal of the progeny (*mawālīd*) for the completion of the acquired body which is the embryo in the womb of the temporal created body and the embryo in the womb of the real heart from which the disbeliever is isolated. It is the oyster of the pearl of the subtle substance of I-ness (*al-laṭīfa al-anā'iyya*), cast in the sea of the Human Realm which is deserving of being a mirror. . . .[39]

The subtle substance of the "real" is sent by God from His presence to the created realms of the mystical body to act as a warner and bringer of glad tidings to mystics and their subtle substances. This subtle substance of the "real" emanates from the locus of divine unity which, together with the locus of divine singularity (*an-nuqṭa al-aḥadiyya*, which Simnānī also refers to as "the locus of the essence"), constitutes the highest source of emanation for any subtle substance. It is through this process of successively higher emanations that the complete human being attains and finally culminates in the subtle substance of the "real." Through combining within itself the higher and lower elements in a balanced fashion, the compound human being obtains the capacity by which the veil of dust is removed from the face of the divine tablets. Once cleansed, the forms drawn upon these tablets are revealed so that their meaning becomes apparent as is hinted at in the Qur'ān: "He created the human being and taught him the clear expression" (55:3–4). It was in this manner that the secrets of the Qur'ān embodied in the tablets were revealed to Muḥammad, who was capable of understanding them in their entirety.[40]

Since the meaning of the Qur'ān is apparent to the Muḥammadan subtle substance of the "real," it is necessary for a mystic to understand all Qur'ānic references to Muḥammad through the agency of this subtle substance. It is through the perfection of the subtle substance of the "real" that the mystic can then acquire the subtle substance of I-ness, which is nurtured like a rare pearl within the subtle sub-

---

39. "Muqaddima tafsīr al-qur''ān," 149.

40. *Najm*, 31b. Simnānī understands this to be the meaning of the Qur'ānic verse: "And when We have promulgated it, follow thou its reading, then upon Us rests the explanation thereof" (75:18–19).

stance of the "real," just as this latter substance is nurtured within the oyster of the subtle substance of the heart.[41]

The Subtle Substance of I-ness

The subtle substance of I-ness is the end result of the entire process of mystical perfection. In every minute effect (*shaqīqa*) in the Human Realm there is an active particle (*daqīqa*) of the Realm of Sovereignty which is the subtle substance of the divine command, sometimes also referred to as "life." Similarly, in every active particle of the Realm of Sovereignty there is a rare substance (*raqīqa*) of the divine attributes from the Realm of Omnipotence, which is the "life of life." Each of these rare substances contains realities and truths from the attributes of the essence in the Realm of Divinity which are referred to as "the inside of the life of life." Just as one absorbs into oneself the emanations of the rational soul through the agency of the subtle substance of the divine command which resides in all creation, similarly the mystic absorbs the realities of the Realm of Divinity. The subtle substance of I-ness is the result of this absorption of elements from the Realm of Divinity, which are themselves the very life of the particles of the Realm of Omnipotence.[42]

As has already been mentioned, the subtle substance of I-ness is nurtured within the oyster of the subtle substance of the "real." This occurs within the acquired body which serves as the cover (or container) of the subtle substance of I-ness.[43] The relationship of the subtle substance of I-ness to the acquired body is similar to that of the acquired body to the created mortal body, since the created body functions as the womb for the embryo of the acquired body in the belly consisting of the realm of sense perception.[44] Just as the mortal body serves as the shell from which the acquired body is released at death, similarly— through a form of mystical death—the subtle substance of I-ness is released from the acquired body once the latter has been perfected so as to become subtle and illuminated. Removed from this covering, the subtle substance of I-ness comes into its own as a mirror worthy of reflecting the divine essence.[45]

----

41. "Muqaddima tafsīr al-qur'ān," 152.

42. *Khitām al-misk*, MS. 11-mīm, Majāmī' fārsiyya, Dār al-kutub, Cairo, 143b.

43. *Ṣadā'if al-laṭā'if*, 85b.

44. *Kitāb al-qudsiyyāt*, 204b; *Ṣadā'if al-laṭā'if*, 85b.

45. *Ṣadā'if al-laṭā'if*, 85b.

Simnānī lays great emphasis upon the fact that the subtle substance of I-ness is the only entity capable of carrying the sacred trust of gnosis and knowledge of the divine names, and of taking its rightful place opposite the face of God.[46] Neither the higher substances which inhabit the heavens, nor the lower substances which inhabit the sublunar realm are capable of carrying this sacred trust. All elements are temporal and all compound beings ephemeral. The only possible exception is something which combines within itself elements of both the higher and the lower realms. This is the rational human being (*al-insān an-nāṭiq*). The subtle substance of I-ness abides eternally in the human being and is a mirror of God's attributes of grace and power, as well as for His beauty and majesty.[47] This subtle substance resides in all entities, but it is unperfected except in a composite being (*tarkīb*) which combines within itself higher and lower elements from both the visible and invisible dimensions. This compound being is the accomplished mystic who has attained the status of the subtle substance of the "real" and has realized his or her subtle, luminescent acquired body.[48]

When the perfected subtle substance of I-ness first takes its place opposite the face of God it is simply a passive instrument. At this stage it is God who is glorifying Himself by observing His reflection as reflected in the mirror. However, the reflection of His essence is simultaneously glorifying God by bearing witness to His essence. "The Observer is the Glorified and the Observed is the Glorifier, and He is the Observer and the Observed, the Recollector and the Recollected."[49]

The mirror composed of the subtle substance of I-ness is incapable of reflecting God passively for very long. It becomes excited by the experience (*dhawq*) of reflecting divine beauty. It therefore becomes active and is itself a witness (*shāhida*), making God the object that is witnessed.[50] God now manifests Himself to the subtle substance of I-ness by saying:

"Indeed I am Allāh! There is no god but Me! I am the First and the Last and the Apparent and the Hidden, encompassing all things. The life of all living things is from Me, and everything

---

46. *Qawāṭiʿ as-sawāṭiʿ*, 156a; *Khitām al-misk*, 143b; "Muqaddima tafsīr al-qur'ān," 149, 152; *Najm*, 31b, 137b.

47. *Qawāṭiʿ as-sawāṭiʿ*, 156a; *Ṣadā'if al-laṭā'if*, 85b.

48. *Qawāṭiʿ as-sawāṭiʿ*, 156b.

49. *Najm*, 65a-b.

50. Ibid., 137b.

is sustained through Me, and everything is perishable except My face." Then whosoever has reached the subtle substance of I-ness and has seen it, has witnessed this secret, and whosoever has witnessed this secret has seen it, and whosoever has seen it knows the essence of Allāh, may He be exalted.[51]

It is unclear whether God makes this declaration in Himself or in the subtle substance of I-ness. It is no longer possible to differentiate God as He witnesses Himself in the mirror from the mirror as it bears witness to God. They are like two bright lights reflecting back at each other. The beauty of God is reflected and witnessed by the mirror, which then reflects this beauty back to God Who witnesses the perfect reflection of His own beauty as identical to His beauty. In other words, God witnesses the same image of Himself in the mirror as the mirror witnesses in God.

In the instant that the subtle substance of I-ness is transformed from a passive mirror to an active witness, the possessor of this subtle substance acquires permission to enter the divine presence and sees things as they really are.

Permission to enter the divine presence refers to witnessing, in one instant, the many parts of the thousandfold Human Realm in the hundredfold particles of the Realm of Sovereignty, and these in the tenfold rare substances of the Realm of Omnipotence, and these in the singular realities of the singular Realm of Divinity. [And it refers to] seeing them all as one which is the manifestation of the One, and knowing what he has seen, and experiencing what he has known.[52]

Having been admitted to the divine presence and become an active witness to God, the subtle substance of the "real" glorifies the essence of the Lord with a truthful tongue.[53] At this stage proper glorification takes the form of stating: "Glory be to Allāh, the One, the Unique, the Singular, the Eternal, Who neither begets nor is begotten, nor is there any like unto Him! Glory be to Him, how great is His majesty!"[54] However, if any subtle force of the body or lower soul remains in the subtle substance, it says: "Glory be to me, how

---

51. *Qawāṭi' as-sawāṭi'*, 156b.
52. *Khitām al-misk*, 144a.
53. *Najm*, 65a.
54. Ibid., 164b.

great is my majesty!" and "I am the 'real' (*ana'l-ḥaqq*)!" And when
it recovers from the state of ecstasy that had overcome it and caused
such utterances, it cries: "Kill me, Oh my confidants! Because only
through my murder is my life!"[55]

Conclusion

There is great significance to Simnānī's implied criticism of
ecstatic and theophanic utterances, because it reflects the central
message of his thought. Simnānī was writing at a time when many
mystical thinkers were intrigued by the possibility of an ontological
union between the human being and God. He perceived the systemati-
zation of this idea in the writings of Ibn al-'Arabī and his followers
as categorically wrong and potentially harmful to Islam.

Existing scholarship has made much of Simnānī's opposition
towards Ibn al-'Arabī. It is clear that Simnānī's criticism was less
vitriolic and more specific in its intellectual focus than is sometimes
implied. Simnānī did not accuse Ibn al-'Arabī of heresy or antinomianism. On the contrary, he referred to Ibn al-'Arabī with respect.[56]
His criticism was limited to ontological questions, and was based in
Simnānī's deep-seated opposition to any doctrine which compromised
divine unity and transcendence. His early critiques of Ibn al-'Arabī
and his followers must be seen in this context and probably are related
to his extreme antipathy towards Ḥājjī-yi Āmulī, the antinomian Sufi
he tried to have killed, and towards the latter's teacher, 'Afīf ad-dīn
al-Miṣrī.[57] After his lengthy correspondence with Kāshānī (and possibly
further reading of Ibn al-'Arabī's thought), Simnānī appears to have
developed a greater appreciation for Ibn al-'Arabī and lauded his

---

55. Ibid. These are famous theophanic utterances (*shaṭhiyyāt*) attributed
to Abū Yazīd al-Bisṭāmī and Abū Manṣūr al-Ḥallāj. For a discussion of Sufi
ecstatic utterances, see Carl W. Ernst, *Words of Ecstasy in Sufism* (Albany:
SUNY Press, 1985).

56. *Chihil majlis*, 163. Like most Sufi masters, Ibn al-'Arabī shared
Simnānī's belief that Sufis must conform not only to the letter of the law,
but also observe supererogatory religious acts attributed to the Prophet; cf.
William C. Chittick, "Ibn 'Arabī and His School," *Islamic Spirituality:
Manifestations*, edited by S.H. Nasr (New York: Cross Roads, 1991), 49–79.
On at least one occasion, Simnānī actively defends Ibn al-'Arabī, stating that
those who accuse him of granting mystical sainthood (*walāya*) preeminence
over prophethood (*nubuwwa*) misunderstand his teachings (*Chihil majlis*,
175).

57. See above, p. 27.

intentions, if not his methods. In an anecdote preserved in the *Chihil majlis*, Simnānī states that Ibn al-ʿArabī maintained the doctrine of "He is today as He always was" (*al-ān kamā kān*) and the concept of God as absolute being (*wujūd-i muṭlaq*) to prove that the multiplicity of creation in no way compromises the unity of God. Although this concept makes sense to Simnānī, he declares it to be ultimately detrimental.[58]

Simnānī maintained that it is impossible for a contingent being to be transformed into necessary being.[59] Thus a human being can never hope to attain any form of union with God Who constitutes the only necessary being. As a result, any sensation of union with God or annihilation in God (*fanāʾ fiʾllāh*) is a delusion, and theophanic utterances are evidence of this delusion. This occurs when the mystic has realized his subtle substance of mystery, but has not been admitted to the divine presence in the Realm of Omnipotence. Poised at the threshold but not yet completely cleansed of all earthly characteristics, at the moment of the manifestation of the subtle substance of the "real" the mystic mistakenly believes that he is now entering into the essence of God.[60]

For Simnānī there is no possibility of union with the divine, and individuals such as Bisṭāmī, Ḥallāj and Ibn al-ʿArabī are accomplished mystics who, unfortunately, have reached the second to last stage of the mystical path but have stumbled at that point and fallen into the trap of self-delusion. In Simnānī's writings, attainment of the subtle substance of the mystery relates to the subsequent realization of the subtle substances of the "real" and of I-ness the way annihilation (*fanāʾ*) relates to eternal abiding with God (*baqāʾ*) in general Sufi terms. His vision of this relationship closely parallels that of Junayd, for

---

58. *Chihil majlis*, 191–92. In defense of Ibn al-ʿArabī, Simnānī maintains that the former was ignorant of this doctrine's inherent dangers; and since he was intent on affirming the unity of God, Ibn al-ʿArabī would be forgiven any mistakes.

For a detailed analysis of his debate with ʿAbd ar-Razzāq al-Kāshānī over the possibility of divine indwelling (*ḥulūl*) and the doctrine of the oneness of being, see Hermann Landolt, "Der Briefwechsel zwischen Kāshānī und Simnānī über Waḥdat al-Wuǧud," *Der Islam* 50 (1973), 29–81; "Simnānī on waḥdat al-wujud," *Wisdom of Persia: Collected Papers on Islamic Philosophy and Mysticism*, ed. H. Landolt and M. Mohaghegh (Tehran: La branche de Téhéran de l'institut des études islamiques de l'Université McGill, 1971).

59. "Muqaddima tafsīr al-qurʾān," 150.

60. *Najm*, 164b.

whom eternal abiding with God is identified with a state of complete sobriety (*sahw*).[61]

The impossibility of union does not generate any disappointment in Simnānī, for he sees it as the highest triumph of human existence. To him a final dissolution has nihilistic implications: the negation of human existence in this world and a consequent removal of responsibility (and reward) for human action.

Contrary to this nihilistic end, Simnānī sees the human being as the pinnacle of all creation. As the only entity which combines within itself celestial and terrestrial forces in perfect equilibrium, it is the sole creation capable of being an active witness to God's nature and of possessing divine knowledge. The "seal of creations" and the "bearer of divine mysteries," it is granted complete freedom in the pursuit of self-perfection, and is rightly deserving of being God's only caliph, or representative, in the cosmos.[62]

---

61. Abdel-Kader, 88–95.
62. *Khitām al-misk*, 143a.

6

TRAVELING THE SUFI PATH

In the two previous chapters I have discussed the ultimate existential and ontological truths as envisioned by Simnānī. The hierarchy of existence described therein enables a mystic to attain the ultimate state of human perfection which is the perfected subtle substance of I-ness (*al-laṭīfa al-anā'iyya*), the active witness of the divine essence. This order of existence perfected in the subtle substance of I-ness is neither self-evident nor intuitively known. It must be acquired in a manner which is cognitive in its outset and experiential in its conclusion. The process of acquisition is difficult but not impossible, since God has chosen the human being to be the only creature capable of attaining knowledge of the divine. He has accomplished this by placing Adam as His caliph on the earth, and distinguishing Adam's descendants with the honor of being God's caliphs.[1] God created the temporal world to serve a purpose in the perfection of the human being. Since it is an effect derived from divine acts, this world contains within it evidence of the active attributes of God. Knowledge of these attributes enables the human being to become the mirror reflecting knowledge of the essential attributes of God.[2]

> God has given you the greater garden of this world and the lesser garden of your own existence so that you may cultivate them both. And know that your sustenance (*rizq*) is from Allāh, may He be exalted, and not from this garden. If you are not heedless of God who is your Lord, and occupy yourself with cultivating the greater and lesser gardens, and if you know yourself to be His servant, and know that this garden is to be cultivated by you, and that your nearness to the presence of your Lord requires that you occupy yourself with repentance through serving Him, then you shall be among those who are near unto the divine presence

---

1. *Ṣadā'if al-laṭā'if*, 86b.
2. *Najm*, 32a.

and this world will become praiseworthy, blessed and auspicious for you.[3]

This is a result of God's bounty:

"And Allāh is of infinite bounty," (57:21), because He created us out of nothingness and guided us to belief. He sent to us the subtle substances, and taught us how to traverse the path of righteousness and gave us strength in the journey on the traveled path. Then He gave us the reward for the works we did by His power. By His guidance we learnt right from wrong. He gave us more of the light of His essence than was our due so that we may walk by His light among creation. And this is nothing if not infinite bounty.[4]

Human existence has the potential for attaining perfection in this world. However, one cannot attain it except after overcoming the vanity of one's own corporeal existence which only occurs after an act of realization (*'irfān*). After this one comprehends the nature and origin of this vanity, and then learns how to lift the veils of vanity from the beautiful reality of one's own existence.[5]

Simnānī uses an allegorical story to explain why all human beings possess the potentiality for perfecting themselves. If a seed is planted it grows into a tree from which ten thousand seeds are gained, from which, in turn, ten thousand trees grow. From each of these trees ten thousand more seeds are produced, yet each of the subsequent seeds and trees contains an atom from the first seed. Similarly, atoms from the forces of the emanations of the cosmic soul (*qābilāt-i fuyūḍ-i nafs-i kullī*) were present in the seed of Adam, and this atom is in each and every one of his descendants.[6] In the same fashion, the mystic heart, which is created in layers, contains a particular bit of divine wisdom in each of these layers.[7] Yet not everyone will attain their potential for perfection because some people fall short in the correct nurturing of their human nature.[8] This is why some people are raised above others in terms of their devotion and adherence to the correct path.

---

3. *Ṣadā'if al-laṭā'if*, 86b.
4. *Najm*, 49a.
5. *Qawāṭi' as-sawāṭi'*, 169b–170a.
6. *Ṣadā'if al-laṭā'if*, 86a.
7. *Najm*, 88a.
8. *Ṣadā'if al-laṭā'if*, 86a.

Forces of unbelief that incite to evil (*al-quwā al-ammāra al-kāfira*) are united in the human soul with forces of belief which rebuke the soul (*al-lawwāma al-mu'mina*). A soul becomes eternally steadfast and blessed if it redeems itself through the informing substances which are the prophets; cleanses its faculties of the vices of dark, earthly characteristics, evil attributes of water, misleading qualities of air, and the destructive pretensions of fire; then purifies its actions of the collective defilement caused by these impure elements, and washes its insides of the impurity of love for the lower world. Any soul that proves deficient in this process of purification is condemned to eternal torment.[9]

The process of self-perfection involves ridding oneself of attachments to this-worldly pleasures which Simnānī considers worthless on the basis of scriptural evidence: "Know that the life of this world is but play and amusement, pomp, mutual boasting and accumulation of wealth and children. Like the rain, the growth which it brings forth delights the disbelievers; soon it withers. You will see it grow yellow and then become dry chaff. In the End is a severe torment" (57:20).[10] This world is not a permanent abode but a temporal one, with no reality or existence of its own, and is recognized as such by people with mystical insight and understanding. In contrast, the afterlife is true life because it has neither past nor future and is therefore eternal and unchanging.[11]

Individuals are recompensed by their Lord on the basis of their actions in this world. A person concerned solely with pursuing his base desires is given his just punishment, whereas a person concerned with the sincere service of God is blessed with the vision of divine beauty.[12]

Some people believe that they can do without the forces, instruments and tools God has given them for their own advancement. Instead, they disobey God, using these implements improperly in the pursuit of sensuous delights.[13] Those who believe that they can follow their own desires and still enjoy rewards in the afterlife are mistaken, because both this world and the next belong to God.[14] All they have accumulated is the fire of arrogance and disobedience, and they will

---

9. *Najm*, 71b.
10. Ibid., 47a.
11. *Qawāṭiʿ as-sawāṭiʿ*, 158a.
12. *Najm*, 45a.
13. Ibid., 151a.
14. Ibid., 60b.

be punished by God in this world and in the next.[15] Not all who are pious and rightly guided necessarily attain enlightenment in this world, because many people cannot rid themselves of possessions and worldly concerns on account of their familial responsibilities.

Simnānī envisions a three-tiered spiritual order composed of lay adherents, their mystical guides, termed Sufis (*ṣūfiyya*), who divest themselves of all possessions and turn away from this world, and true mystics (*mutaṣawwifa*) who have gone beyond divestment (*tajrīd*) and have attained inner isolation (*tafrīd al-bāṭin*).[16] The *mutaṣawwifa* number 347 in the entire world. Three hundred of them are called 'the brave' (*abṭāl*) and are the beginners among the true mystics. Forty of them are 'substitutes' (*abdāl*), occupying the intermediate rank. Seven are travelers (*sayyāḥūn*) and constitute the highest rank of the true mystics, having been favored by God's intimacy. They act under God's command as His representatives, and guide people in their capacity of successors to the Prophet.[17] This is the rank of the mystical saint (*walī*), because once the door of prophecy had been closed shut that of sainthood opened, so that those of the Muslim religious scholars who are mystical saints lead their community to the light of God like the prophets did before them.[18]

These travelers or saints acquire cosmic significance and form an integral part of the creative process. The very word *kawn* (existence) is composed of the letters *kāf* of the word of the divine command "Be!", the *wāw* of *walāyat* (sainthood), and the *nūn* of *nubuwwat* (prophecy).[19] It is through these saints that all of humanity is sustained and gains success. If they did not exist, the world would be destroyed.[20]

The Sufi saints appear to possess higher status than the prophets in Simnānī's eyes. There are more prophets than saints,[21] and whereas prophets are simply God's messengers in the physical and spiritual

---

15. Ibid., 54a; 56a.

16. *al-Wārid ash-shārid*, 31b-32a.

17. Ibid., 32a.

18. "Muqaddima tafsīr al-qur'ān," 150; see above, p. 87. "Muḥammad said to 'Alī: 'Oh 'Alī! Allāh said to me: "Oh Muḥammad! I have sent 'Alī with the prophets at the esoteric level and with you at the exoteric."' And the meaning of this is explained in his saying to 'Alī: 'You are to me in the status of Hārūn to Mūsā, except there is no prophet after me.'" (Bukhārī, Tirmidhī, Ibn Māja, Ibn Ḥanbal).

19. *Farḥat al-'āmilīn*, 37.

20. *al-Wārid ash-shārid*, 32a–b.

21. *Najm*, 39a.

realms (as *anbiyā'* and *laṭā'if*), the saints constitute the very foundation of the created realm. In this capacity the *walī* functions in the same manner as the 'mystical pole' (*quṭb*) who is the pillar supporting the higher and lower realms without whom these realms could not exist.[22] It is not clear whether or not Simnānī considers the saint and the 'mystical pole' to be identical. Although their function is the same, they differ in number, there being seven *walīs* as compared to four *quṭbs*.[23] In their function, each represents the highest mystical rank attainable by a human being through the long process of spiritual self-realization.

Islamic Foundations of the Path

The process of spiritual self-realization culminates in the attainment of enlightenment (*ma'rifa*), a noetic, life-giving level of understanding which is qualitatively and quantitatively different from all previous levels. In order to reach this level of enlightenment, the individual must first immerse himself in a mystical curriculum which begins with the intellectual and religious recognition of the Islamic foundations upon which Sufism stands: the recognition of God's nature and of His use of revelation, prophecy and other means of guidance to lead human beings to knowledge of Him. This is followed by adherence to the outward and inward articles of faith and religious practice which prepare the mystic for the requirements of the mystical quest itself.

The mystic must first comprehend the nature of God as outlined in the previous chapter. She must understand God as the necessary being who is eternal, then comprehend His oneness, His transcendence of all imperfections, flaws, and possibilities of error, and that He is the Fashioner of everything and the Founder of the world.[24] Then one has to understand His active attributes, and how divine acts are generated from them, just as the act of writing is the cause of the written word. Creation is generated from these attributes and acts. It appears in an ordered fashion and is produced (procreated) out of the higher fathers and lower mothers (*ābā-yi 'ulwī wa ummahāt-i suflī*) in the form of various offspring. Mystical aspirants should then

---

22. Ibid., 29a.

23. Ibid.

24. *Bayān al-iḥsān li-ahl al-'irfān*, MS. 11-mīm, Majāmi' fārsiyya, Dār al-kutub, Cairo, 80b; '*Urwa*, 390ff; *Fuṣūl al-uṣūl*, MS. 1, Fiqh ḥanafī fārsī, Dār al-kutub, Cairo, 47a.

comprehend the distinctiveness of the human being who is a special kind of living being and the seal of compound beings, deserving of being the perfect mirror of God. The status of the crown of creation is a sacred trust which must be honored in a prescribed manner.[25]

Once a person has understood this, he is transformed into a true gnostic (*'ārif*) and attains the status of a peer of the prophets: a mystical saint who possesses the right to guide other seekers of truth.[26]

According to this scheme, the human being must know God through His attributes of Lordship, Holiness, Glory and Justice. Knowledge of the attribute of Lordship cannot be obtained as long as one turns to something other than God and thinks that there is any deity besides Him. Were one deluded in this manner, the individual would fail to abide by God's commands and prohibitions, and be led by his own physical desires.[27]

Knowledge of His attribute of Holiness is not obtained until one has learned that God is the Creator of all notions that occur to one's heart, senses and mind, and until one believes that Allāh is the Designer of all forms in which His attributes appear in the invisible and visible realms. Knowledge of the attribute of His Glory is dependent upon one's knowing that God is Master of His actions.[28] In this capacity He admonishes the person who is deficient in the rectification of the body, in the purification of the heart, and in placing the mirror opposite the face of the Lord. Yet He is forgiving to the person who rectifies the body in accordance with the outward requirements of law, and purifies the heart in accordance with the wisdom of the Sufi path and holds the rectified, purified mirror opposite the face of the Lord in worship.[29]

God has control over all matters: He strikes hard, takes, grants, forbids, gives life and death. He lifts up one group of people and debases another. He does what He wishes and commands what He pleases.[30] It is His role as the Giver of life which enables human beings to attain their perfected state:

"You were dead and He gave you life" (2:28), that is, you were ignorant and He gave you life through knowledge; you were dead

---

25. *Bayān al-iḥsān*, 80b–81a.
26. Ibid., 81a.
27. *Najm*, 68a.
28. Ibid., 68a–b.
29. Ibid., 88a.
30. Ibid., 133b.

in your mothers' wombs and He gave you life through the breath of the spirit; you were dead in the body and He gave you life through the light of faith; you were dead in limbo (*barzakh*) and He gave you life on the Day of Resurrection; you were dead in ignorance and He gave you life through enlightenment; you were dead, unable to behold the face of the Lord, and He gave you life through its sight.[31]

God created the human being using the higher and lower substances as intermediate agents.[32] He created sensual desire and delight so as to put human bodily forces (*al-quwā al-qālabiyya*) to the test.[33] But since God wants all human beings to succeed in perfecting themselves, He has also sent clear signs in the form of the Qur'ān and the institution of prophecy. Through their use He guides people out of the darkness of bodily veils into the spiritual light, and from the darkness of the spiritual veils which derives from the darkness of the body, into the light of God.[34]

Simnānī's Understanding of the Qur'ān

In keeping with the dominant Sunnī belief of his day, Simnānī sees the Qur'ān as the eternal speech of God, and regards anyone who does not consider it divine speech as a heretic, while one who maintains that the physical materials (paper, etc.) which make up the holy book are eternal is simply deluded and ignorant.[35] He considers speech (*kalām*) an essential divine attribute, so that contemplation of the Qur'ān turns the human being into a mirror for God's essential attributes.[36]

O seeker of the inner meaning of the Qur'ān! You should first study the literal level of the Qur'ān and bring your body into harmony with its commands and prohibitions. Secondly, you should occupy yourself with purifying your inner being so that you may comprehend the hidden meaning (*baṭn*) of the Qur'ān according to the instruction of the Merciful One and the inspira-

---

31. Ibid., 87b.
32. Ibid., 39b.
33. Ibid., 28a.
34. Ibid., 44b.
35. *Fuṣūl al-uṣūl*, 48b.
36. *Najm*, 41a.

tion of the Holy Angel. Thirdly, you should contemplate the gnosis of its limit (*ḥadd*) in the realm of hearts. [Only then] will you be distinguished with witnessing its point of ascent (*muṭṭalaʿ*) without thought or reckoning.[37]

According to this scheme the Qur'ān has four levels of meaning corresponding to the four realms of existence. The exoteric dimension of the Qur'ān relates to the Human Realm, the esoteric level to the secrets of the Realm of Sovereignty, the limit of the Qur'ān to the Realm of Omnipotence, and the point of ascent to the Realm of Divinity.[38] Denial of the existence of any of these levels constitutes a break from Islamic belief. According to Simnānī, anyone who denies the literal explanation of the Qur'ān in the physical, human realm is an obstinate heretic. One who denies the esoteric explanation in the spiritual Realm of Sovereignty is a rigid and idiotic anthropomorphist. One who combines the exoteric and the esoteric is a fortunate Sunnī Muslim, whereas one who knows the absolute limit of the Qur'ān in the Realm of Omnipotence is a rightly-guided, knowing believer (*mu'min*). Finally, whosoever attains the point of ascent of the Qur'ānic verses in the Realm of Divinity is a perfect and rightly acting individual (*muḥsin*), witness of the people and privy to the mysteries.[39]

Each of these four levels of the Qur'ān must be interpreted in a different way. The commentator on the exoteric dimension of the Qur'ān should rely exclusively upon his external sense of hearing through which he learned the verses himself. The mystic should rely on inspiration (*ilhām*) to comment on the esoteric dimension, while the accomplished Sufi who has truly declared the unity of God (*muwaḥḥid*) should only comment on the limit with divine permission. The individual who has attained the secret of the essence should not comment at all, but proceed in a faltering manner into the point of ascent of the Qur'ān.[40]

God made the Qur'ān easy to read and a remembrance, warning, and instruction for God-fearing believers.[41] At the same time, He made

---

37. Ibid., 96b–97a. There is a precedent to this idea in a non-canonical tradition of Muḥammad: "Not a verse of the Qur'ān is revealed but it has an exoteric dimension (*ẓahr*) and an esoteric dimension (*baṭn*), and every word has a limit (*ḥadd*), and every limit has a point of ascent (*muṭṭalaʿ*)."

38. Ibid., 18a. Cf. table 1.

39. "Muqaddima tafsīr al-qur'ān," 151.

40. *Najm*, 18b.

41. Ibid., 28a, 100b.

TABLE 1

The Four Dimensions of the Qur'ān

Realm	Qur'ānic Dimension	Rank of Reader	Rank of Commentator	Means of Commentary
Divinity (*lāhūt*)	Point of Ascent (*maṭla'*)	Witness (*shāhid*)	Attainer of the Secret of the Essence (*muṭṭali' 'alā-sirr adh-dhāt*)	Should not comment at all
Omnipotence (*jabarūt*)	Limit (*ḥadd*)	Righteous Mystic (*muḥsin*)	Declarer of the Unity of God (*muwaḥḥid*)	Divine Permission (*idhn*)
Sovereignty (*malakūt*)	Esoteric Dimension (*bāṭin*)	Mystic (*mu'min*)	Mystic (*muḥaqqiq*)	Inspiration (*ilhām*)
Human Realm (*nāsūt*)	Exoteric Dimension (*ẓāhir*)	Believer (*muslim*)	Exoteric Scholar (*mufassir*)	Hearing or Instruction (*sam'*)

every verse of the text a treasure containing innumerable jewels of gnosis, and used allegories to hide the meaning of each verse.[42] The reader should attempt to understand what underlies these allegories, and know that God's purpose in revelation is the cleansing of the heart and purification of the soul.[43] God sends prophets in order to accomplish this goal:

> Allāh, may He be exalted, sent all the prophets to creation to teach them rectification through governance, and refinement through purification, and attention through worship, so that He may see His essence, attributes, acts and effects in the mirror.[44]

Pious individuals believe in the messengers and occupy themselves with their commandments, whereas corrupt individuals deny the messengers and concern themselves with the desires of their own turbid natures.[45] In keeping with the complementarity of the spiritual and physical realms that pervades Simnānī's thought, these prophets also exist within every individual. The subtle substances which

42. Ibid., 110a.
43. Ibid., 59b.
44. Ibid., 88a.
45. Ibid, 76a.

function as inner messengers exist within all higher and lower forces—
they are the so-called "foremost" chosen by God.[46] The forces of the
body, the soul, the heart, the inmost being, the spirit, the mystery
and the "real" which believe in these messengers constitute the
"people of the right hand" who are favored by God, whereas those that
disbelieve in the messenger substances are the "people of the left hand"
and witnesses of God's displeasure.

Simnānī's Understanding of Prophecy

Simnānī places great importance on adherence to what he
considers to be the divinely revealed prophetic tradition, and firmly
believes that it is impossible to attain enlightenment unless one
belongs to this form of religion. In his opinion, the reason why most
of the ancient Greek, Christian and Buddhist mystics failed was
because they pursued the path according to their own personal opinions
and not the guidance of a prophet.[47]

The foremost among these prophets is Muḥammad, and the
subtle substance of the "real" (*al-laṭīfa al-ḥaqqiyya*) corresponds to
him. True believers become distinguished by the light of glory of the
Muḥammadan subtle substance, just as Muḥammad received distinction through the light of God's glory.[48] A subtle Muḥammadan
substance and faculty is created within the body of every individual.
It acts as a warner and announces rewards in the hereafter to the other
faculties if they follow God's teachings.[49]

Simnānī lays great stress on the importance of belief in
Muḥammad and his role as the last of the prophets. He repeatedly
states the necessity of belief in the fundamental doctrines of
normative Islam, and the superiority of Islam over all other religions:

"Believe in Allāh, His messenger, and the light which We have
sent down" (64:8). That is, O forces of the body and soul! Believe
in God who created and fashioned you in the best of forms, and
believe in the subtle substance sent to you, and in the light of
revelation which we have sent down upon it.[50]

---

46. Ibid, 42a. "The companions of the right hand—what will be the
companions of the right hand? And the companions of the left hand—what
will be the companions of the left hand? And those foremost will be foremost"
(56:8–10).

47. Ibid., 107a.

48. Ibid., 148a.

49. Ibid., 142a.

50. Ibid., 77a.

Rejoice, O Muḥammadan [al-muḥammadī], that you certainly are not among the "people of the left hand" if you have entered into the abode of faith, which is your bearing witness that there is no god but God and Muḥammad is the messenger of God. And whosoever bears witness in this manner with sincerity and faith is among the "people of the right hand," and meets with success. It is not possible for Satan to obstruct him from the path.[51]

It is imperative that all individuals who believe in God, His prophet, and the Day of Resurrection, should not incline themselves to the higher forces, nor to the knowledge which results from their own thoughts and intellects, nor to their desires.[52] Rather, they should attach themselves to the Muḥammadan subtle substance of the "real." This constitutes the only way for them to be rewarded by God for their actions and intentions, and to escape the torments of the hereafter.[53]

Despite the fact that Simnānī repeatedly states that one of the major purposes of following the tradition of Muḥammad is to escape punishment from God in this world and the next, he also maintains that true believers do not act out of the fear of punishment, but out of love for God.[54] Rather than perform virtuous acts out of a sense of compulsion, these individuals worship out of zeal and longing for God.[55]

Although all believers will be rewarded by God with enlightenment (maʿrifa) after death, and the true nature of God will become apparent at this time even to those who disbelieve, the greatest reward is reserved for those who believe in His commandments before the lifting of the veil at the moment of death.[56] The best way to attain

---

51. Ibid., 42b; cf. *Najm*, 66b.

52. Ibid., 55a.

53. Ibid., 62a.

54. Ibid., 120a.

55. He relates a story, attributed to Abu'l-Ḥasan al-Kharaqānī (d. 425/1033) and common in Sufi circles, of a mystic who is circumambulating the throne of God along with a host of other beings. He notices that, whereas he is rushing around with enthusiasm, the others are unemotional and listless in their circumambulations. Finally he stops one of the creatures and asks him the reason for their lack of zeal. The latter replies that he is an angel. Whereas the human being is performing the act with enthusiasm and of his own volition, angels have no choice in the matter since it is their nature to circumambulate the throne of God (*Najm*, 101a–b; cf. Meier, *Fawāʾiḥ*, 13).

56. *Najm*, 77b. Evil-doers will not see their Lord in heaven because they are obstructed by the veil (ḥijāb) which they acquired in this world (*Najm*, 135a).

enlightenment in this life is by following the Sufi path, which Simnānī
compares to a tree:

> Sin and repentance are its roots; divestment and isolation are
> its bark; the profession of divine oneness is its fruit; patience,
> purity, sincerity and piety are its leaves; prayer (*wird*), dignity,
> affection and fidelity are its blossoms; poverty, annihilation,
> success and salvation are its branches.[57]

Progress along the mystical path entails a change in the nature
of knowledge possessed by the mystic and in the mystic's vision of
the world. The most elementary form of comprehension is thought
that comes to mind (*zann*). Lying above thought is correct, informed
knowledge which is acquired through instruction. This is succeeded
by the discovered certitude of knowledge, followed by the essence of
certitude which is the same as observed knowledge. Following this
is the reality of certitude which relates to mystical attainment, beyond
which lies the essence of the reality of certitude which relates to
experiential knowledge, otherwise known as mystical "taste" (*dhawq*).[58]
Simnānī explains the various forms of knowledge using the
metaphor of a pomegranate tree. A farmer might inform you that there
is a tree which bears pomegranates within which are seeds like rubies,
each seed in a setting and possessing a sweet taste. Your belief in what
you have heard from him would be based upon correct knowledge.
When you witness the tree turn green and blossom, correct knowledge
is transformed into the discovered certitude of knowledge. When
pomegranates emerge from the blossoms, discovered knowledge is
transformed into the essence of certitude. When the fruit ripens and
you pick it and tear it open and see its seeds and their individual
settings just as the farmer had described, the essence of certitude is
replaced by the reality of certitude. Finally, when you taste the fruit
and its juice enters your body, mingling with your own essence, you
attain the essence of the reality of certitude.[59]
Thought and informed knowledge are both cognitive levels of
understanding and can be attained without engaging in any mystical
exercises. The subsequent levels concern certitude, and cannot be
attained by any means except through adherence to the mystical path
and the recollection (*dhikr*) of God.[60]

---

57. *Shaqā'iq al-ḥadā'iq*, 77b.
58. *Najm*, 21a.
59. Ibid.
60. Ibid., 21b.

Rules for the Novice

The beginning of the Sufi path entails complete adherence to all the exoteric requirements of Islam. However, this is to be preceded by sincere intention, because God looks neither to one's acts nor to appearances, but to the heart and the intention contained therein.[61] In accordance with these conditions, the mystic must believe in God's prophets, books, the existence of angels and Jinn, all eschatological things such as the place of assembly, the path, balance, judgment, and in the witnessing of the beauty of God in heaven.[62] This is followed by strict compliance with the pillars of the faith, bearing in mind that for each of the outer, visible articles there is a corresponding inner, unseen article. Whereas the acts of worship in the visible realm are the five pillars of prayer, struggle (*jihād*), alms-giving, fasting and pilgrimage, the acts of worship in the unseen realm are intention, presence (*ḥudūr*), sincerity and truthfulness.[63] Acts of worship in the unseen realm are of greater significance than ones in the visible realm:

> Spiritual action has greater rewards than physical action. So strive after the easing of physical exertion with spiritual exertion. This is sincere action and true intention and banishing of ruinous thoughts.[64]

True prayer consists of the abstinence of the limbs from inclining towards anything other than Allāh; patience of the soul in fulfilling the sacred trust of God; purity of the heart with the remembrance of God, and the purity of the inmost being in God; and the pre-eminence (*ṣadāra*) of the spirit with the caliphate of God and its complete absorption in Him.[65] True fasting is patience in the face of

---

61. Ibid., 59a.

62. *Fuṣūl al-uṣūl*, 48b.

63. *Najm*, 92a. There is not an exact correspondence in this passage between the number of inner and outer pillars (*arkān*). Absolute correspondence does not appear to have been Simnānī's intention, since he gives nine exoteric acts, having subdivided prayer into four composite parts of kneeling, prostration, standing and sitting. A possible fifth esoteric act would be patience (*ṣabr*), which Simnānī has emphasized elsewhere as one of the fundamental requirements of Sufism (cf. *Risāla fī-tafsīr āyāt qur'āniyya fī-mawḍū' aṣ-ṣabr wa'l-iḥsān*, MS. 11–mīm, Majamī' fārsiyya, Dār al-kutub, Cairo, 136b–141a).

64. Ibid., 112b.

65. *Shaqā'iq al-ḥadā'iq*, 78a.

adversities and the fulfillment of the divine covenant, whereas true struggle is combating passions through perpetual uprightness in all matters.[66] Simnānī emphasizes the dual nature of *jihād*. The lesser struggle is against the enemies of the true religion of Islam in the visible realm, while the greater struggle is against the soul, passions and Satan, all of which are the inner enemies in the invisible realm.[67]

Simnānī considers ritual prayer to be the most important pillar of the faith. It constitutes the combination of all other religious practices: in addition to the various postures of supplication, it involves the glorification and praise of God, as well as recitation of the Qur'ān and of the profession of faith. It gives expression to the fear of and need for God, as well as to personal prayer, humility and self-deprecation.[68]

The prayer remains incomplete if it does not have certain specific effects upon the worshipper's person. Ten signs demonstrating that prayers have been successful are as follows: (i) witnessing divine beauty close to the eye; (ii) smelling the subtle fragrances of divine lordship; (iii) opening up of the breast; (iv) tenderness of the skin; (v) contentment of the heart; (vi) delight of the inmost being; (vii) appearance of the spirit; (viii) ecstasy; (ix) intimate conversation with God (*munājāt*); and (x) listening to the greetings of the divine presence.[69] The mystic should not be saddened or discouraged even if these experiences do not occur. Instead, she should continue religious practices because the goal is not the experiences themselves, but servitude and conformity to the divine command. Great mystical "taste" (*dhawq*) and magnificent sweetness such as have been described above will appear eventually.[70]

Rules for Sufi Practice

Simnānī places a great deal of importance on the spiritual guidance of novice mystics, going so far as to stipulate the correct manner in which they should organize their religious exercises on a daily basis. He provides ten conditions for fulfilling requirements of religious practice in isolation:

---

66. Ibid.

67. *Fuṣūl al-uṣūl*, 68b.

68. *Najm*, 152b–153a.

69. *Fuṣūl al-uṣūl*, 57b.

70. *Kitāb al-waṣāya*, MS. A1588 (Catalog no. 5226), Topkapı Sarayı Müzesi Kütüphanesi, Istanbul, 38a.

1. Before embarking upon the mystical path, the novices should know the basic tenets of the religious sciences.
2. They must perform their prayers with the congregation.
3. They must study a portion of the works of earlier Sufi masters everyday.
4. Their state of seclusion should consist mainly of silent acts of worship, bearing in mind the saying "worship is nine parts silence and one part isolation."[71]
5. They should not read less than one section (*juz'*) of the Qur'ān each day, and contemplate what they read.
6. They should practice remembering God at all times, and not be heedless of Him.
7. They should spend most of their time repeating the formula "there is no god but God" to obtain contentment of the heart.
8. They should perform the supererogatory prayers, because the Prophet said that these have great benefit.
9. They should not engage in religious practices when they are weary.
10. They should organize their time so as to perform their assigned exercises everyday.

This daily routine involves performing customary (*sunan*) dawn prayers, then recollection (*dhikr*) until the time of the obligatory morning prayers performed in the congregation. This is followed by engaging in recollection until sunrise. After this the mystics should say four prayer cycles (*rak'āt*), and then read the Qur'ān until the time of the prayer at midmorning. The midmorning prayer should be followed by a midday nap, after which they should perform a ritual ablution followed by two prayer cycles in gratitude for the ablutions as well as the cycles recommended by prophetic custom. After praying the obligatory midday prayers with the congregation, they should pray two more cycles, then read one section of the Qur'ān, and review the lives and sayings of previous Sufi masters so that this might stimulate them in religious practice. When the time for the afternoon prayer arrives, they should offer four cycles before praying the required number in congregation.[72] The remainder of the afternoon should be spent in

---

71. Ibid., 36a. Similar lists have been compiled by many mystical writers including Abū Saʿīd b. Abi'l-Khayr, ʿAbd Allāh al-Anṣārī, Najm ad-dīn al-Kubrā, and ʿAlī-yi Hamadānī. Despite some similarities, Simnānī's list of requirements is not identical to earlier ones.

72. "Allāh, may He be exalted, has combined the distinguishing features of all other times in the middle prayer which is the *ʿaṣr* prayer. If a human

recollection until the time of the evening prayer, which should be performed with the congregation along with the customary cycles, after which they should perform two supererogatory ones. After completing this evening prayer, for which Simnānī provides a very detailed set of instructions regarding the specific verses of the Qur'ān to be recited, the mystics should resume their *dhikr* until the night prayer. The obligatory prayer should be preceded by four supererogatory cycles and followed by six. After completing the night prayer, the mystics should then sleep for one-third (at the most half) of the night before resuming their mystical exercises the next day.[73]

Progress from this beginning step along the mystical path is clearly divided into a series of stages (*maqāmāt*) and states (*aḥwāl*), where a stage constitutes a way-station or level of attainment on the path, and a state implies a mystical experience occurring within a stage. Whereas stages have a concrete implication of progress and achievement, states are temporary and do not necessarily build upon each other as the mystic progresses in the quest for self-perfection.

Simnānī further categorizes the stages and states in three classes, those of the novice (*mubtadi'*), the intermediate or one in the middle of the Sufi path (*mutawassiṭ*), and the accomplished mystic or one at the end of the path (*muntahī*). He justifies this belief upon the basis of a Qur'ānic verse: "And among them are those who are cruel to their own souls, and those who follow the middle course, and those who are, by Allāh's leave, foremost in good deeds" (35:32).[74] Each stage has nine states, three in the beginning, three in the middle, and three at the end so that, in all, there are one hundred stages encompassing nine hundred states.[75] The axis (*quṭb*) of each stage is the fifth state because the states preceding it are connected to the previous stage, and those after it to the following one. In each of the one hundred stages, the level of the novice is connected with faith, that of the intermediate with patience, that of the advanced with piety, and that of the axis or accomplished (*wāṣil*) with beneficence.[76]

---

being performs his duty at this hour, it is as if he benefits from the distinguishing features of all the other times" (*Najm*, 158a).

73. *Kitāb al-waṣāya*, 36a–37a.

74. *Najm*, 72a. On occasion Simnānī also adds a fourth category signifying the mystic who has attained the goal (*wāṣil*).

75. *Qawāṭiʿ as-sawāṭiʿ*, 175b–76a.

76. *Risāla fī-tafsīr āyāt qur'āniyya*, 139b. Simnānī systematically outlined these one hundred stages and their accompanying states in a treatise entitled *Tabyīn al-maqāmāt wa-taʿyīn ad-darajāt*. Unfortunately, the only surviving manuscript of the work is incomplete (see below, p. 169).

Although the visionary experiences and states which are characteristic of Simnānī's thought apply to all three levels, his didactic
writings on the method of progress along the Sufi path are geared
towards the novice. Simnānī wrote extensively to teach novices the
correct manner of seeking mystical enlightenment, and warned them
of the dangers of wordly preoccupation. The emphasis on elementary
levels of instruction is one of the most distinctive features of Simnānī's
mystical teachings.

Seek the treasure of everlasting knowledge in the corners of dusty
convents. Know for certain that this treasure is inherent to them.
Do not look at the darkness and dirtiness, because these have
been fashioned as a spell (*ṭilasm*) over the treasure so that everyone is not able to find it. When they see it in this form they abhor
it, and thus the treasure does not fall into the hands of strangers.
However if you, the seeker of this treasure, turn your face towards
the presence (*dargāh*) of Muḥammad, and take the key to this
treasure which is the creed "There is no god but God and
Muḥammad is the messenger of God," and obtain the mystery
of opening this treasure from teachers of the path, then opening
this treasure will become easy for you. And when you have
attained the treasure, be not proud. . . . because it is not the final
goal.[77]

---

77. *Farḥat al-ʿāmilīn*, 47–48.

7

SECLUSION AND RECOLLECTION

The pursuit of self-perfection is best undertaken in seclusion (*khalwa*) after withdrawal from society. This form of seclusion, in which Simnānī himself engaged many times during his life, involves isolation of the heart from what is other than the Lord, and attachment to Him, thereby reaching Him and being near unto Him.[1] An individual succeeds in attaining progress through the various stages mentioned above through the pursuit of mystical exercises in seclusion, and refines the subtle substance of I-ness to the point of being a perfect mirror for God. "No one can reach the stage of beauty of submission except in seclusion."[2] This seclusion is particularly difficult when one first practices it, because at this stage the mystic wages a war against the lower soul and Satan.[3] In light of the importance of seclusion in his mystical vision, it is not surprising that Simnānī devoted much attention to its nature and requirements. Similar emphasis is also found in the works of other Kubrawī mystics, in particular Kubrā and Baghdādī, who have listed the conditions of seclusion and elaborated on each one. These are normally the eight principles of seclusion attributed to Junayd al-Baghdādī although, on occasion, two items are added to the list.[4] Simnānī adheres strictly

---

1. *Shaqā'iq al-ḥadā'iq*, 77b.

2. *al-Wārid ash-shārid*, 34a.

3. *Najm*, 73b.

4. An expanded version of Junayd's list is discussed in Kubrā's *Risāla ila'l-hā'im al-khā'if min-lawmat al-lā'im*, edited in M, Molé "Traité mineurs de Naǧm al-dīn Kubrà," *Annales islamologiques* 4 (1963), 23–37. See also Kubrā's *al-Uṣūl al-ʻashara* (pp. 15–22 of the same article), and ʻAbd al-Ghafūr-i Lārī's Persian translation, edited by Najīb Māyil-i Hirawī (Tehran: Intishārāt-i Mawlā, 1984)). Cf. Majd ad-dīn al-Baghdādī, *Tuḥfat al-barara*, tr. M.B. Sāʻidī-yi Khurāsānī (Tehran: Intishārāt-i marwī, 1989), 134ff.); Meier, *Fawā'iḥ*, 2–3; Muhammad Isa Waley, "Najm al-Dīn Kubrā and the Central Asian School of Sufism (The Kubrawiyyah)," *Islamic Spirituality: Manifestations*, edited by S.H. Nasr (New York: Crossroads, 1991), 80–104.

to the principles of Junayd and believes that, at the most elementary level, seclusion is useless without these conditions. It is within the parameters of these eight conditions that his teachings regarding mystical experience can best be described:[5]

1.   Controlling the external senses.
2.   Maintaining a continual state of ritual purity.
3.   Continual fasting.
4.   Continual silence.
5.   Continual repetition of the formula "There is no god but God."
6.   Continual banishing of distracting thoughts.
7.   Fixing the heart totally on the mystical guide.
8.   Ceasing to raise objections to God.

These conditions and the concepts underlying them merit further elaboration. Although seclusion is ultimately an interior process through which one isolates oneself from everything except God, it also consists of physical withdrawal from society. This must occur in a cell (*bayt al-khalwa*) which should only be large enough for one person to pray in, and should possess no windows so as to prevent sunlight from entering it.[6] This form of isolation helps achieve the desired goal of controlling the external senses. In order to maximize the effects of seclusion, the mystic should not exit the cell except to perform bodily functions, renew the state of ritual purity, and perform ritual prayers.[7]

Maintaining a continual state of ritual purity, fasting and silence also serves to control the external senses with the ultimate goal of subduing the soul. This is the lower soul, identical with the subtle substance of the animal spirit (*laṭīfa-yi rūḥ-i ḥayawānī*), which is the source of evil and the cause of base characteristics.[8] The lower soul which incites to evil is a companion of Satan and does his bidding in the physical and spiritual realms. This soul continually combats the noble forces of the heart and spirit, wishing to subjugate them and employ them in its own service and that of its faculties.[9] Even

---

5. *al-Wārid ash-shārid*, 34a ff.; *Fatḥ al-mubīn*, 4a ff.; *Fuṣūl al-uṣūl*, 49b ff.; *Salwat al-ʿāshiqīn*, in *Muṣannafāt-i fārsī*, ed. N.M. Hirawī (Tehran: Shirkat-i intishārāt-i ʿilmī wa farhangī, 1990), 279ff. The eight conditions do not appear in the same order in all four texts.

6. *al-Wārid ash-shārid*, 34a.

7. *Fatḥ al-mubīn*, 4b.

8. *Sirr bāl al-bāl*, 239b.

9. *Najm*, 157a.

after the individual has advanced along the Sufi path, this appetitive soul retains its hereditary disposition derived from the lower forces which have not been purified of base characteristics.[10] The appetitive soul is not destroyed by voluntary death (*al-mawt al-ikhtiyārī*), otherwise known as annihilation (*fanā'*), but is simply fragmented so that its virulence remains. It is only in the ultimate death of the physical body that it can be exterminated. Mystics must guard against the soul for this reason, and beware of inclining towards the desires of this ruler of the mortal realm as long as they are alive.[11]

For the novice, the best way to combat the soul is to engage in ascetic practices such as abstaining from food, speech and sleep.[12] Simnānī refers to this as being cruel to one's soul, denying the soul its due and satisfaction except for the minimal amount needed to sustain the body.[13] Any other sustenance that reaches it from the physical world only increases its eagerness to persist in its base nature.[14] However, one should be wary of forbidding to one's soul what God has made permissible. The only exception to this is when, at the commencement of the mystical quest, the mystic is deprived of the guidance of a *shaykh* and, out of ignorance, abstains from what has been made lawful. But once she knows the path properly or learns it from a guide, the novice Sufi should repent for previous actions and eat just enough of what she had forbidden to herself as to symbolically end the abstention.[15]

Ritual purity also serves to combat the lower soul. Maintaining a continual state of ritual purity serves as armor in the stage of war against the lower soul and Satan.[16] "Ablution is a great light which illuminates the darkness of seclusion."[17] Whereas external ablutions

10. Ibid., 72a.

11. Ibid., 72b; 164a.

12. Ibid., 69b.

13. Ibid., 72a. This is referred to in the *ḥadīth*: "Indeed your soul has a right upon you" (*Najm*, 110b; Bukhārī, Muslim, Abū Dāwūd, Tirmidhī, Nasā'ī, Ibn Māja, Ibn Ḥanbal). The attitude of the mystic with regard to the soul changes at later stages along the path. The intermediate (*mutawassiṭ*) should befriend the soul because at this level it becomes the mount of the mystic, serving a purpose in mystical advancement. The advanced mystic should make sure the soul accords God His due, and guide it in the direction of piety and righteousness (*Najm*, 72a).

14. Ibid.

15. Ibid., 76a.

16. *Fatḥ al-mubīn*, 4b.

17. *Risāla-yi nūriyya*, MS. 1105, Carullah Efendi, Süleymaniye Kütüphanesi, Istanbul, 48a.

serve to cleanse the body of physical impurities, inner ablutions
consist of having an attentive heart and a tongue busy with recollection, both of which serve to purify the mystic and combat the lower
nature.[18] The entire mystical quest can be seen as a process of inner
purification, called the greater cleansing, which parallels the attainment of levels along the path. The novice attains the purification
specific to physical manifestation or theophany in the physical realm
(*at-tajallī aṣ-ṣuwarī*), the intermediate that of the manifestation of
light, the advanced that of spiritual manifestation or theophany in
the unseen realm (*at-tajallī al-ma'nawī*). The pole (*quṭb*) is subjected
to experiential manifestation of the divine (*at-tajallī adh-dhawqī*) only
after the destruction of the created body.[19]

> So strive, O heedless ones, to cleanse the tablet of your inner
> selves of the dust of the created world that settles on its face
> as a result of the wind of passion. [Strive] in noble recollection
> so that you may read all the revealed and nonrevealed books and
> ascend to the primordial book which is stored in the Realm of
> Omnipotence near the Lord.[20]

A major purpose of seclusion is to engage in recollection, thereby
cleansing oneself to the point of being the perfect witness of God.
Continual silence is one of the conditions of seclusion, and is useful
in negating the outer senses and combating the lower soul. The only
mitigating circumstance in which the mystic may break this silence
and exit the cell is to consult the *shaykh* for the explanation of a
mystical experience which cannot be understood on one's own. Even
so, it is better to try and seek the master's guidance mystically within
the spiritual state. One should only speak face to face with the guide
as a last resort when one is incapable of benefiting from him in the
unseen realm.[21]

This notable exception to the requirement of perpetual silence
underscores the importance of the mystical guide in Simnānī's ideas.
Simnānī did not trivialize the importance of studying books. In fact,
he exhorted mystics to study the writings of earlier masters, and

----

18. *Fatḥ al-mubīn*, 4b.

19. *Khitām al-misk*, 142a. In this instance Simnānī is using the term
'purification' (*ṭahāra*) with the connotation of the annihilation of the self
(*fanā'*) which is a desired goal of all mystical exercises (see below, p. 141ff.).

20. *Najm*, 30b.

21. *Fatḥ al-mubīn*, 4b.

instructed them to consult Abu'n-Najīb as-Suhrawardī's *Ādāb al-murīdīn* for the etiquette of the Sufi path, and to study the *Tuhfat al-barara fi'l-masā'il al-ʿashara* of Majd ad-dīn al-Baghdādī for details regarding the path itself.[22] However, knowledge acquired from these books cannot replace the teachings of a living guide.

The guide must be living in the mortal realm in order to lead the mystic on the straight path and explain distracting thoughts and their causes as they are encountered along the path.[23] It is because of this necessity of having a living master that God created Muhammad, the first mystical guide, as a mortal, and commanded him to say: "I am a mortal like you" (18:110).[24] All later mystical guides derive their spiritual authority from Muhammad through ʿAlī b. Abī Ṭālib. ʿAlī is the saint (*walī*) whom Muhammad entrusted with spiritual secrets, and whom he taught the nature of attaining the spiritual realm of light and took to the presence of God.[25]

Simnānī claims that it is not possible to become a Sufi without attaching oneself to a *shaykh*.[26] Those who do not attach themselves to a guide but instead pursue the mystical path according to their own wishes and ideas derive absolutely no benefit from their exercises.[27] Only if one surrenders oneself to the master and abandons personal volition is it possible to traverse the path to God.[28] The tutelage of a guide thus acquires paramount importance in the mystical quest. "The treatment of the sick heart is not possible without a skillful and sympathetic doctor."[29]

Surrendering oneself to the master implies complete trust in his instructions. The mystic should never question his instructions openly or secretly. That would be tantamount to letting the soul converse secretly with Satan, allowing Satan to enter the soul and fill it with doubt concerning the divine essence and attributes.[30] Trust in the *shaykh* should be such that even if the master were to command the

---

22. *al-Wārid ash-shārid*, 33b.

23. *Najm*, 107b. Though the guide must be living, he need not be living at the same location as the disciple, as Simnānī knew from his own experience with Isfarā'inī (*Salwat al-ʿāshiqīn*, 280).

24. Ibid., 133b.

25. Ibid., 107b–108a.

26. Ibid., 64b.

27. Ibid., 99a.

28. Ibid., 108a; 133a–b.

29. Ibid., 46b.

30. Ibid., 52b.

mystic to engage in activities which seemed to contradict the correct practices of the path, he should perform them without question. The abandonment of supererogatory religious practices at the command of the *shaykh* is better than their performance of one's own volition. Similarly, acts of asceticism are to be abandoned if one is so instructed by the guide: "If the disciple eats a basted chicken and a sweet dessert everyday at the command of his *shaykh*, it is better than eating nothing for an entire week except a scrap of barley bread of his own volition."[31]

Complete and absolute attachment of the heart to the master in this manner is more difficult than the earlier conditions of seclusion mentioned above, but its benefits are greater. If the mystic is weak in this attachment, weakness also appears in attachment to the tradition of the Prophet Muḥammad. "The mystical aspirant should know that one cannot reach one's goal except through the master, in accordance with the verse: 'Each group knew its own drinking place' (2:60). The mystic's drinking place is the sainthood of the *shaykh*."[32]

The next condition of seclusion is the continued banishing of all thoughts, be they good or bad. Control of the inner senses, which is a desired result along the mystical path, cannot be accomplished without the banishing of thought. The mystic must recognize the *shaykh* as the explainer of visions and mystical events and should not attempt to understand them on his own. God will ennoble him later on with the light of intellect and justice so that from the light of the intellect he will obtain the ability to discern, and from the light of justice the power of differentiation.[33]

The method through which one succeeds in banishing all thought and controlling the inner senses is the recollection of God (*dhikr*). This is the main mystical practice prescribed by Simnānī, and consequently he describes its method and meaning in great detail.

The Rules of Recollection

Simnānī often uses the metaphor of light to explain the function of recollection along the mystical path. Through recollection a light

---

31. Ibid., 67a.

32. *Fatḥ al-mubīn*, 5a–b. Despite the centrality of the *shaykh* in Simnānī's teachings, he is careful to emphasize that the Sufi should not immitate his master or earlier mystics, but should model his behavior on the Prophet, because what earlier *shaykhs* achieved was a direct result of their following in Muḥammad's footsteps (*Salwat al-ʿāshiqīn*, 288).

33. Ibid., 5a.

known as the light of love appears. However, if elements of physical human existence remain in the individual, smoke accompanies this light and obstructs the mystic from it. The only way to dissipate this smoke is with the light of Muḥammad. Through following him and performing the fundamental ritual requirements of prayer, fasting, and so forth, the divine secrets which are in the treasure house of the heart are revealed to the mystic.[34]

According to Simnānī, God commands Muslims to recollect Him: "And remember the name of your Lord by morning and by evening" (76:25). The remembrance of God in the evening of the body (*al-aṣīl al-jismānī*) and the morning of the spirit (*al-bukra ar-rūḥāniyya*) diminishes the power of disbelieving and evil forces.[35] On another occasion they are commanded: "And remember the name of your Lord and devote yourself with complete devotion" (73:8).[36]

People who intentionally do not engage in divine recollection are the party of Satan. "Truly it is the party of Satan that will perish" (58:19).[37] In contrast, righteous people are constantly engaged in the recollection of God and cannot be distracted from it by any worldly concerns, being mindful of the verse: "Remember Me and I will remember you" (2:152).[38] Such a mystic abandons everything at the command of his guide, and through his constant occupation with the remembrance of God attempts to negate all the blessings bestowed upon him, seeking nothing from God but God Himself.[39]

"And the places of worship are for Allāh, so invoke no one along with Allāh" (72:18). That is, the mosques of the hearts were built

---

34. *Sirr-i samā'*, 11. Simnānī justifies the centrality of divine recollection on the basis of several Qur'ānic verses (the imperative form from the root *dh-k-r* appears at least seven times in the Qur'ān): "Everything that is in the heavens and the earth glorifies God" (57:1; 59:1; 61:1) refers to the heavens of the mind and the earth of the body, implying that all the forces stored in the mind and buried in the body glorify God (*Najm*, 56a).

35. Ibid., 122a.

36. Ibid., 111a. Other frequently cited Qur'ānic references to *dhikr* are: "O You who believe! Remember Allāh with much remembrance" (33:41); "Remember your Lord much and praise Him in the early hours of night and morning" (3:41); "So when you have completed the prayers then remember Allāh standing and sitting and lying down" (4:103); "And remember your Lord within yourself humbly and with awe and under your breath by morning and evening" (7:205); "And remember your Lord when you have forgotten" (18:24).

37. Ibid., 54b.

38. Ibid., 119b.

39. Ibid., 53a.

in the spiritual realm for Allāh, so do not invoke the name of anyone else along with the recollection of God in these mosques. Do not permit harmful thoughts to enter into your heart. Most of the arrogance in *dhikr* occurs because the recollector allows thought to enter during recollection, so guard against extraneous thoughts in the *dhikr* of the heart.[40]

Simnānī began his mystical quest without the guidance of a *shaykh* and designed his mystical exercises on his own. He claimed that, until the arrival of Akhī Sharaf ad-dīn, his *dhikr* consisted of performing three hundred prayer cycles (*rak'āt*) a day and repeating the formula "There is no god but God" 200,000 times.[41] However, he claims to have learnt a more elaborate exercise from his master Nūr ad-dīn al-Isfarā'inī who had received it in an unbroken chain of transmission from Ma'rūf al-Karkhī (d. 200/815–16). From him it was traced back to 'Alī b. Abī Ṭālib through 'Alī b. Mūsā ar-Riḍā.[42]

Although the *dhikr* formula used by Simnānī is certainly the same one used by Isfarā'inī, the ritual itself is markedly different from Simnānī's description of the *dhikr* practice Akhī Sharaf ad-dīn engaged in at their first meeting. It is possible that Isfarā'inī had instructed Simnānī in a different—and possibly more advanced or efficacious— *dhikr* exercise than the one he had taught Akhī Sharaf ad-dīn. It is also possible that Simnānī modified Isfarā'inī's *dhikr*, retaining his *shaykh*'s formula but adding his own breathing exercises and bodily movements.

According to Simnānī's *dhikr* practice, the mystic should sit cross-legged facing the *qibla* and start by reciting a prayer:

Allāh! There is no god but Him! On Him do I rely, and He is the Lord of the majestic throne. O my Lord! I seek refuge with you from the goadings of the demons, and seek refuge from the lord whom they attend.[43]

After this he must say the credal formula three times, then envision his *shaykh* in his heart as if the master were present before him. Then the *dhikr* itself can commence. The ideal formula for

---

40. Ibid., 108b.

41. Dār al-kutub, untitled, 145a ff.; cf. above, p. 22; *R. fī-dhikr asāmī mashāyikhī*, 73a–b; *'Urwa*, pp. 314–15.

42. *al-Wārid ash-shārid*, 34b.

43. Ibid., 34a.

recollection is the credal statement: "There is no god but God (*lā ilāha illā Allāh*)." This formula should be uttered in four beats: (i) With all his strength, the mystic should exhale the *lā* from above the navel. (ii) He should then inhale the *ilāha* to the right side of the breast, (iii) then exhale the *illā* from the right side to the left, (iv) and then inhale the *Allāh* to the physical, pineal heart (*dil-i ṣanūbarī-i shakal*) which is on the left side of the breast. This causes the energy of the word *Allāh* to reach the heart and burn all desires contained therein. From this pineal heart, which is simply a piece of flesh and the abode of the animal spirit, a window is opened to the real mystical heart. From here the light of faith shines forth. The inner spiritual realm is illuminated by this light and the mystic obtains information about the true nature of the composite parts of the body and which among the bodily forces are benign and which malignant.[44]

While engaging in *dhikr* the mystic must draw his eyes upward toward the eyebrows so that he can observe the manner in which the daily *dhikr* practice ascends from the level of the stomach to that of the liver, from there to the physical, pineal heart, and onward to the head. From here it ascends to the real, mystical heart, after it has been granted light by the physical eyes.[45] It is in the ascent to this mystical heart that colors and visions are manifested to the person engaged in recollection.

It is imperative that the mystic attempt to control his breath and observe its tempo so that he is engaged in recollection in each moment and with every breath. He acquires a new level of enlightenment with each new breath, because every breath has a right over him just as he has a share from each breath. His share from breath is life, whereas the right of the breath over him is the recollection of God through which he acquires gnosis of the divine attributes and essence.[46]

If the mystic fails to engage in recollection at one of the prescribed times, he should make up for it in the morning or late afternoon. However, it is abominable (*makrūh*) to engage in recollection when it is time for ritual prayer.[47] It is forbidden for a mystic to pass a single day without occupying himself with *dhikr* from after the morning prayer until sunrise, and from sunset until darkness falls.

---

44. *Fatḥ al-mubīn*, 4b. Cf. R. Gramlich, *Die Schiitischen Derwischorden Persiens, Section 2: Glaube und Lehre* (Wiesbaden: Franz Steiner, 1976), 401ff., where a *dhikr* practice attributed to Simnānī is described.

45. Ibid., 5a.

46. *Najm*, 74a–b.

47. *Fuṣūl al-uṣūl*, 74a.

FIGURE 6

Simnānī's *dhikr*

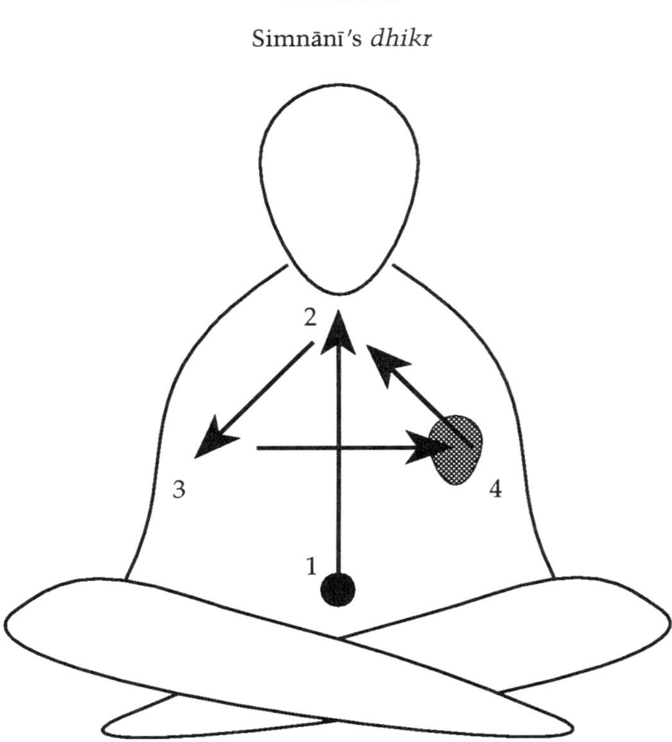

Simnānī states that whosoever does not engage in recollection at these
two times, yet claims to be a Sufi, is an impostor who cannot become
a true Sufi even if he were to complete a thousand retreats.[48]

> Do not be conceited about your seclusion and gnosis. . . .
> Recollect God at all times and combat your soul so that it is
> not occupied with worldly desires. Call [your soul] to accounts
> five times every day and night, and be critical in your examina-
> tion. Persevere in recollection, especially from the time of the
> morning prayer until sunrise, and from sunset until nightfall,
> lest you be heedless of the recollection of God at these two times.
> You will then be written into the register of the mystics who

---

48. *Najm,* 74b.

strive for the good and recollect God, not [the register] of those who are lazy, indolent and heedless.[49]

The mystic's tongue cannot be purified except through recollecting God's name, as is stated in the Qur'ān: "Glorify the name of your Lord, most high" (87:1). The highest name of God is "Allāh." But, according to Simnānī, the credal formula "There is no god but Allāh" is a better *dhikr* formula than "Allāh," because the latter is contained in the former which has the additional advantage of negating plurality and affirming divine unity.[50] Simnānī declares that it is for this reason that the most knowledgeable masters of the Sufi path, all of whom belong to the school (*ṭabaqa*) of Junayd al-Baghdādī, chose this credal statement as the ideal *dhikr* formula for individuals who embarked on the Sufi path and strove to purify their hearts so that the power of recollection of God would descend upon them.[51]

God has collected all blessings and benefits in this credal formula,[52] and whosoever recites it with sincerity and true belief will be among the companions of the right hand. Such people will be successful in their endeavors and Satan will be unable to obstruct them from the path. Simnānī quotes a tradition of Muḥammad in order to emphasize the importance of this formula: "Whosoever says 'There is no god but God' with sincerity enters paradise."[53]

The weight Simnānī gives to the credal statement as the ideal form of *dhikr* underscores the importance he attaches to adherence to normative Islamic belief on the Sufi path. This importance in no way diminishes as one progresses along the esoteric stages towards the final goal:

Blessings upon whoever follows him [Muḥammad] in the law; and blessings upon blessings for whoever follows him in the law and the path; and blessings upon blessings upon blessings for whoever follows him in the law and reaches knowledge of certitude in the form of *dhikr*, then follows him in the path and reaches the essence of certitude in the meaning of *dhikr*; then follows him in reality and reaches the reality of certitude with

49. Ibid., 74b–75a.
50. *Salwat al-'āshiqīn*, 288.
51. Ibid., 140a.
52. Ibid., 36a.
53. Ibid., 42b. The heavenly garden to which such a mystic is admitted is the one nearest the Lord (*al-janna al-muḍāfa ila'r-rabb*) (36a).

the reality of recollection; then exalts the course of his hidden recollection above the outward form of recollection, its meaning and its reality so that he deserves to have true recollection flow over him.[54]

If one says the credal profession of faith just once with sincerity, one steps from the circle of disbelief into the sphere of Islam, and vanquishes the physical icons of disbelief. However, there are other inner, metaphorical icons which are the idols of one's own desire to which the Qur'ān refers in verse 45:23: "Do you see one who takes as his god his own desire?" These idols cannot be defeated except through constant *dhikr* with perfect concentration and complete understanding and observance of the statement "I wish for nothing except God." Such a mystic must strive so that no thought remains within him after the long vowel (*madd*) of the word *lā* has been pronounced. Under no circumstances should any distracting thoughts be harbored when the end of the formula is uttered, because nothing can be associated with the name of God.[55]

Simnānī differentiates between audible (*adh-dhikr al-jahrī*) and silent recollection (*adh-dhikr al-khafī*), and firmly maintains the superiority of the latter, going so far as to state that audible, outward *dhikr* is forbidden both on religious and intellectual grounds.[56] To support his position on religious grounds Simnānī provides several quotations from the Qur'ān: "Recollect you Lord in your soul with humility and in reverence, and without loudness of words, in the mornings and evenings" (7:205); "Call on your Lord with humility and in private, for Allāh loves not those who trespass beyond bounds" (7:55); "Neither say your prayer aloud, nor say it in a low tone, but seek a middle course" (17:110). In addition, he also provides several quotations from prophetic tradition such as this one related by Abū 'Abd ar-Raḥmān as-Sulamī (d. 412/1021): "The best recollection is the silent one, and the best sustenance is that which just suffices."[57]

---

54. Ibid., 42b.
55. *Fatḥ al-mubīn*, 5a.
56. *Mawārid ash-shawārid*, MS. 11-mīm, Majāmī' fārsiyya, Dār al-kutub, Cairo, 147b.
57. Ibid. Another relevant tradition quoted by Simnānī is from the day at Khaybar when Muḥammad came upon a group of Muslims who were raising their voices in prayer. Upon seeing them the Prophet said: "Control yourselves, because you are not calling the deaf nor someone who is absent, but He is listening and near; indeed, He is with you" (Bukhārī, Ibn Ḥanbal, Ibn Māja). Simnānī also quotes from the *Manfa'at as-sālik* of 'Ammār al-Bidlīsī and the *Tuḥfat al-barara* of Majd ad-dīn al-Baghdādī in support of silent recollection.

In addition to these religious reasons, there are ten intellectual proofs supporting the superiority of silent *dhikr*.

1. One of the benefits of seclusion is controlling the external senses so that the inner senses might develop. Audible *dhikr* does not aid in repressing the external sense of hearing.
2. Breath control is primarily obtained through inner light; this cannot be attained through audible recollection.
3. Sincerity is required in all religious practices. Audible recollection results in showmanship which overshadows sincerity.
4. Complete obliteration of desire is necessary on the mystical path for the *dhikr* to reach the heart. This desire cannot be destroyed except with the heat of strong, silent *dhikr* which reaches the real, mystical heart. On the other hand, when a mystic continues to engage in audible recollection, his breath ascends and most of the heat escapes from his mouth, preventing him from reaching the esoteric level.
5. Audible recollection confounds the brain and confuses the intellect.
6. Audible recollection contains the wine of the soul and causes the desire of the soul to overwhelm audition of the recollection.
7. Audible recollection confuses the heart during divine conversation, prayer, and the mystics' presence with their Lord.
8. Unlike audible recollection, silent recollection is the opening of the door to the unseen.
9. Audible *dhikr* constitutes the abandonment of appropriate behavior in the presence of God, and makes the mystic deserving of punishment.
10. Through audible recollection, mystics are deprived of listening to the recollection of the Recollected Who is the goal of the recollector.[58]

I have translated *adh-dhikr al-jahrī* as audible rather than vocal recollection in order to avoid confusion regarding the various levels of *dhikr* which are mentioned by Simnānī. In addition to audible recollection, he refers to a form of silent *dhikr*, generally called the strong, silent recollection of the tongue (*adh-dhikr al-lisānī al-qawī al-khafī*), but occasionally also referred to as the bodily recollection of the tongue (*adh-dhikr al-lisānī al-qālabī*). This form of recollection is similar to audible *dhikr* in that it is external and requires the

____

58. Ibid., 148b–49a.

conscious attention of the recollector as it flows over the tongue. However, unlike audible *dhikr*, the silent recollection of the tongue is inaudible, and does not distract the mystic from the quest in the manner mentioned above with regard to audible *dhikr*.[59]

Vocal *dhikr*, or recollection of the tongue (*adh-dhikr al-lisānī*), is best for mystics at early stages of the quest because it gets rid of impurities obtained through preoccupation with acquisition in the temporal realm. Deliverance from this preoccupation is obtained through purification which cannot be achieved except through the strong, silent, and vocal recollection of the credal profession of faith.[60]

Although this form of recollection is to be practiced silently, great care should be taken in its repetition. The formula should be said forcefully and all syllables must be pronounced properly, because the strength of the heart derives from correct pronunciation.[61] "When [the mystic] takes the breath of the bodily recollection of the tongue, the mortal earth and physical mountains are raised from their places."[62]

In the early stages of the mystical quest, when the mystic is still easily distracted by his desires, he must observe the occurrence of recollection. At this stage he must consciously occupy himself with the banishing of passions. This is not possible except through the negation of all volition and the affirmation of God as the Master of volition in this world and the next.[63] One purpose of consciously

---

59. Cf. an untitled treatise by Saʿd ad-dīn-i Ḥamūya in which he states that *dhikr* has seven stages: (i) *dhikr* of the tongue; (ii) *dhikr* of the tongue along with the heart; (iii) *dhikr* of the heart without the tongue; (iv) *dhikr* of the heart with the spirit; (v) *dhikr* of the spirit without the heart; (vi) *dhikr* of the spirit with the inmost being (*sirr*); (vii) *dhikr* of the inmost being without the spirit (MS. 706, Köprülü Kütüphanesi, Istanbul, 120a).

Simnānī also refers to audition (*samāʿ*), or listening to music, in the context of his discussions on *dhikr*. He considers audition to be not without merit, but maintains that it contains serious pitfalls which render it dangerous for most mystics. "Audition is a drug which, if eaten by itself without being prepared together with other good medicines, becomes a deadly poison" (*Fuṣūl al-uṣūl*, 80b). To support his argument, Simnānī refers to the positions of Abū Ḥanīfa and ash-Shāfiʿī regarding audition, Abū Ḥanīfa having said that it was forbidden whereas ash-Shāfiʿī that is was permissible. In explaining the latter position, Simnānī states that ash-Shāfiʿī was thinking of the elite among the mystics for whom it does not constitute a danger (*Sirr-i samāʿ*, 14).

60. *Najm*, 71a.

61. *Fuṣūl al-uṣūl*, 74a.

62. *Najm*, 98a.

63. *al-Wārid ash-shārid*, 34b.

engaging in *dhikr* is to avoid making religion an automatic or habitual act since true worship consists of the abandonment of habit.[64] To affirm one's faith and then ignore the true nature of religion by turning it into something that is habitual or inherited is as reprehensible as being a disbeliever.[65]

> Strive so that you are present in recollection, humble in recitation, submissive in your obedience to Him, as if you were listening to the Qur'ān from God and recollecting Him as if you were sitting in His presence.[66]

Although such constant attention is necessary at the early stages of recollection, eventually the mystic should attain a stage in which he loses awareness both of the recollection and of himself. It is through this loss of his own existence that the mystic attains the essence of the reality of certitude (*ḥaqīqa ḥaqq al-yaqīn*).[67]

> Have you ever had a time in recollection when your were not a thing remembered? If this is not the case, then you will never perfect true recollection (*adh-dhikr al-ḥaqīqī*), because one of the characteristics of *dhikr* is the forgetting of everything besides God as He says in His book: "And remember your Lord when you have forgotten" (18:24), that is, forgotten everything but the Lord. So read the Lord's Word when He says: "Was there not a time in the life of man when he was not even a mentionable thing" (76:1). This is the state (*ḥāl*) which appears to the recollector who has travelled to the level (*martaba*) of Adam whereupon the power of the recollection of God overwhelms the clay of his body. The clay vanishes from his clayness, and the light of true recollection penetrates all parts of his body.[68]

Simnānī mentions three kinds of recollection which are hierarchical in nature such that a mystic progresses from one to the next over the course of the mystical quest. The first is the repetition of the formula *lā ilāha illā Allāh* in the manner outlined above. This

---

64. *Najm*, 66b.
65. Ibid., 59a, 46b.
66. Ibid., 46b.
67. Ibid., 100b.
68. Ibid., 119a.

form of recollection is of the human realm (*nāsūtī*), because inhabitants of this realm believe in the existence of a multitude of deities and are veiled from the "God of gods and Lord of lords." The negation of deities and the affirmation of the sole existence of Allāh contained in this *dhikr* formula helps deliver novice mystics from polytheism.[69] The second form of recollection is of the Realm of Sovereignty and consists solely of the name "Allāh," as God commanded Muḥammad: "Say 'Allāh!' Then leave them to plunge in vain discourse and trifling" (6:91). The name of God is sufficient at this stage because in the Realm of Sovereignty—in the absence of plurality—there is no need for the negation of other deities.[70] The third formula of recollection in the Realm of Omnipotence is simply the word *huwa* (He), because God gives it precedence over the name "Allāh" in describing divinity (*bayān at-tawḥīd*). Simnānī supports the primacy of this formula on the basis of a prophetic saying: "When the servant is established in the quiddity of the Lord, he knows oneness with his heart."[71]

While engaging in recollection the mystic undergoes a series of experiences which constitute a systematic annihilation of the self, and sees a progression of colors and visions which function as signs or milestones marking advancement on the path. Simnānī describes these mystical visionary experiences in such vivid detail that they constitute one of his major contributions to Sufi thought. However, before describing these visions, Simnānī gives two points of warning to those engaged in mystical exercises. The first is that, while engrossed in *dhikr*, the mystic must never enter among ordinary people because his speech in the mystical state is based on knowledge which is not commonly known, its real meaning lying beyond the comprehension of most human beings who would most likely consider him mad.[72] The second is that all experiences and visions must comply with Islamic orthodoxy. Any mystical experience which is not in accordance with the Qur'ān and the Prophet's tradition is deception and temptation thrown in the mystic's path by Satan.[73]

---

69. *Qawāṭi' as-sawāṭi'*, 176b.

70. Ibid.

71. Ibid., 177a. There is a fourth formula which relates to the Realm of Divinity. This is the supreme name of God which is unpronounceable, exalted above any form which would be comprehensible in the Human Realm and the Realm of Sovereignty.

72. *al-Wārid ash-shārid*, 35a; *Najm*, 156a; *Salwat al-'āshiqīn*, 281.

73. *Farḥat al-'āmilīn*, 53ff. To underscore this point Simnānī reproduces a non-canonical *ḥadīth* tradition: "Any action not in accordance with my

The Hierarchy of Visions and Colors

When the mystic strives towards God she produces the light of recollection within herself, and sees various colors according to her degree of advancement. As she progresses through the hierarchy of seven subtle substances, the flow of light increases as does the purity of its colors.[74] These colors and visions are displayed to her by God in accordance with His saying: "Out of them come pearls and corral" (55:22). The pearls are the lights of the mysteries of the inmost being (al-asrār as-sirrī) which are extracted from the celestial ocean, while the corral, which is brought forth from the lower sea, constitutes the fires of the love of the heart.[75]

The colors that appear to the mystic in the beginning are from the Realm of Sovereignty, constituting the colors of the mystical states. The lights that shine in the heart of the mystic in the intermediate stage are the lights of the Realm of Omnipotence. The secrets which descend upon the subtle substance of I-ness and manifest themselves to the inmost being are from the Realm of Divinity.[76] In light of the nature of these manifestations, it must be understood that the visions witnessed in the mystical state are not outside the human being but exist within the kingdom of the soul.[77]

The mystic must traverse the climes of the seven hierarchical subtle substances of the mystical body as part of the journey culminating in the attainment of divine knowledge. In this journey the mystic must remove a succession of curtains, each of the seven climes having a curtain consisting of ten thousand veils, and having a color specific to it. In describing these curtains and veils and the means of their removal, Simnānī emphasizes the fact that it is the

---

tradition is disobedience before Allāh, Most Majestic." He also quotes extensively from the sayings of earlier mystics, among them Junayd al-Baghdādī, Shiblī, Abū Bakr [probably Abū 'Alī] ad-Daqqāq, Abū Sulaymān ad-Dārānī, Sahl at-Tustarī, Sarī as-Saqatī, Abū Yazīd al-Bistāmī, Abū 'Uthmān al-Maghribī, Ahmad b. Abi'l-Hawārī and Majd ad-dīn al-Baghdādī. The quotation from Junayd is as follows: "No one has ever reached Allāh, may He be exalted, except through Allāh; and whosoever makes his path to God, Most Majestic, other than through following the tradition of the Prophet (al-Mustafā) goes astray."

74. *Qawātiʿ as-sawātiʿ*, 179b.
75. *Najm*, 33a.
76. *Qawātiʿ as-sawātiʿ*, 160a.
77. *Farhat al-ʿāmilīn*, 41.

mystic who is veiled by them, not God, since nothing can veil God.[78] The first curtain is that of the physical realm or of Satan and is dark and turbid. The second is that of the soul and is blue on the outside and green on the inside. The third curtain is of the unseen of the heart and is red or ruby colored. After this comes the white and very fine curtain of the unseen of the inmost being and then the yellow one of the spirit. These are followed by the veil of the unseen of the mystery, which is of a luminescent black of the utmost clarity. The final curtain is of the Hiddenmost Hidden, corresponding to the realm of the subtle substance of the "real." This curtain is described either as being green, or else as being pure light and having no color on account of its extreme purity, brilliance, subtlety, grandeur and majesty.[79] After the removal of these seven curtains consisting of seventy thousand veils, the mystic reaches the greatest veil (*ḥijāb-i kibriyā'*). At this stage one must "place one's head in humility on the threshold of supplication" so that one may be overcome by a mystical experience (*jadhba*) from the divine realm and be transported to the divine presence.[80]

Simnānī devoted an entire treatise to the description of the colors and visionary experiences which the mystics undergo in their quest for perfection. Known as the *Risāla-yi nūriyya* or *Risālat al-anwār*, this treatise is both poetic and allegorical. However, despite its somewhat flowery style, the *Risāla-yi nūriyya* systematically and exhaustively conveys the most salient features of visionary mystical experiences encountered along the Sufi path. In light of this, I have closely followed Simnānī's argument as presented in this treatise in the description of these visions given below.[81]

When the mystic turns his face from the visible dimension of the physical realm he should also turn away from the visible dimension of the spiritual realm and face the invisible of the spiritual realm. The first curtain that appears before him is turbid until he strikes the stone of his heart with the flint of the credal formula "*lā ilāha illā Allāh.*" Suddenly, the hidden fire which is placed in him becomes apparent, and he stands in the fireship of the soul (*ḥarrāqa-yi nafs*). He feeds this hidden fire with the firewood of the body until it becomes ignited and that turbid curtain is transformed to dark blue.

---

78. *Risāla-yi nūriyya*, 48b.

79. *Shaqā'iq al-ḥadā'iq*, 77a; *Risāla-yi nūriyya*, 48a–b.

80. *Risāla-yi nūriyya*, 48b.

81. I have translated this treatise in its entirety in "A Kubrawī Treatise on Mystical Visions: The Risāla-yi nūriyya of 'Alā' ad-dawla as-Simnānī," *Muslim World* 83:1 (1993), 68–80.

As he dries the firewood of existence and the remaining pieces or morsels of delight, the colors become purer and the smoke decreases. When the morsels are purified so as to be composed entirely of that which is just, then no smoke remains and a pleasant odor reaches the nose. In addition, colorful lights appear, and one has visions of spiritual people. All of the above experiences result from the blessing of the strength of recollection and from guarding the morsel from the moisture of sensual delight.[82] The novice mystic witnesses these visions as a result of the subtle substance of beauty which is placed in his breast after his escape from the darkness of the body.[83]

The differences between the colors red, white, yellow, black and blue in this stage are a result of the strength of the fire of *dhikr*. It is possible that the essence of the fire of recollection may come out from behind the curtain and shout: "I am everything" (*hama manam*). It is imperative that the person not be arrogant at this point since this is the stage of the beginners in recollection. If he were to be arrogant he would be forbidden entry into higher stages of the path.[84]

The second fire which appears to the mystic on the path is undefined, but insofar as it can be described it is the fire of reality, of recollection, love, longing, desire, anger, deviltry (*shayṭanat*), and of the physical body. It is possible to differentiate between all these fires with signs that occur along the path, but the novice should not attempt to differentiate between them without the guidance of the *shaykh* because, tricked by Satan, the mystic may grow arrogant and leave the path. It is therefore necessary that the disciple report everything to the *shaykh* so that he may explain the mystical experiences and visions.[85] If the guide commands the mystic to repel these thoughts at this stage, he must do so regardless of how difficult it proves to be. The guide's command to repel these thoughts serves to counteract the mystic's excessive attachment to experiences. If one were not to obey the *shaykh* in this matter one would not ascend any further on the path, but rather meet with the gravest of consequences.[86]

After this, when the existence soiled by the morsels of sensual delight and tarnished by the filth of disobedience is completely burned, and annihilation has been obtained as a result of the fire of recollection, then the light of the soul becomes apparent, the curtain of which is a pleasing dark blue.

---

82. Ibid., 44b.
83. *Najm*, 114b.
84. Ibid., 103a; *Risāla-yi nūriyya*, 44b.
85. *Risāla-yi nūriyya*, 44b–45a.
86. *Najm*, 57a.

Subsequently the light of the heart appears, the curtain of which is ruby red. Upon seeing this light the individual experiences a great mystical 'taste' in his heart and obtains permanence on the path.[87] Sometimes, in the early stages of purifying the heart, the mystic sees the tablet of his heart blackened with different patterns (*nuqūsh*); then he sees that it has been wiped clean and purified of these images. After this he observes it completely covered with the word "Allāh"; then the tablet is polished clean and only the singular name of God—"Allāh"—remains. After this he sees that this name is written with an ink of red light, then with white light, and then with green. Finally he sees a tablet of light which has neither color nor images upon it. At that very instant, the images (*nuqūsh*) of direct knowledge of the divine (*al-'ilm al-ladunī*) appear upon it. This constitutes the stage of the unveiling of secret knowledge.[88]

After this stage the light of the inmost being shines forth, the curtain of which is white. In this stage he acquires knowledge of the delight of unveiling. This is followed by the light of the spirit which shines forth with an extremely pleasing yellow color. The lower soul is weakened and the heart strengthened by seeing it. After this the light of the mystery, to which the holy spirit is a reference, is manifested. Its curtain is of such a pure and awesome blackness that the mystic is annihilated by the fear of seeing it.[89]

The water of eternal life is arrayed in this darkness. Whoever gives himself a cup in the luminescence of the light of the Prophet...and remains in the shadow of obedience to him, like Khiḍr that person reaches the spring of the water of life which is the source of the lights of the attributes. There he drinks a cupful of love from the heavenly river of grace, and becomes deserving of that which the Lord, Most High, manifests to him through the attributes of beauty and majesty.[90]

When the subtle substance of mystery announces the coming of the subtle substance of the "real," the forces of the body and soul disbelieve it. This state appears to the mystic after he has traversed the veils of the substances of the body, soul, heart, inmost being and spirit, and has abided in their abodes (*mawāṭin*) until God sends to

87. *Risāla-yi nūriyya,* 45a.
88. *Najm,* 55a.
89. *Risāla-yi nūriyya,* 45a.
90. Ibid.

him the subtle substance of mystery in order to lift him up from this
stage and admit him into the realm of mystery. The mystic must
abandon all his supererogatory religious practices at the command
of his guide in order to make transcending this level easier.[91] The
mystic should abandon physical activity and vocal recollection at this
point, because physical activity is simply a means for reaching this
state.[92]

In addition to abandoning nonessential religious practices, the
mystic must not incline himself towards the jewels that are placed
in this darkness, but should travel with sincere steps and a strong
heart. He must not fear any of the dreadful forms and sounds he experiences, so that the light of the mystery might become apparent
from its potentiality in the invisible dimension. If this occurs, then
fear is transformed into intimacy. And when he has fulfilled the
requirements of this stage, absolute light, which is a particular attribute of God, is manifested.[93] It is green in color, this greenness being
a sign of the life of the tree of existence.

The manifestation of absolute light (*nūr-i muṭlaq*) is not possible
except in paradise, when it is accompanied by certain effects. First
the mystic experiences her own annihilation. After that she experiences visions of eschatological events, such as standing on the boundary (*barzakh*); splitting of the sky; transformation of the earth; flying
of the mountains; dispersal of the fixed stars; the changed rising of
the sun and the moon; the dimming of the planets; judgement of
accounts on the balance; traversing the path; being thrown into the
abyss; and being lifted up by levels. When the mystic sees these signs,
she should know herself to be in the eternal garden. Then she should
pay complete attention to the beauty of God's presence, not inclining
to anything else, so that the holy essence (*dhāt-i muqaddas*) may be
manifested, illuminating the nature of everything that the mystic has
seen before.[94]

The manifestation of the light of God is exalted above everything
and has no similitude. The light of the mystery is manifested above
the head and has no similitude in the visible realm and is such that
it annihilates the mystic at the very onset of its manifestation. The

---

91. *Najm*, 66b.

92. Ibid, 70b.

93. *Risāla-yi nūriyya*, 45a.

94. Ibid., 45b; *Najm*, 132b. The visions described by Simnānī at this stage
correspond to eschatological events which are referred to in the Qur'ān and
widely elaborated upon by Islamic theologians.

light of the spirit is greater than that of the sun, and is generally manifested behind the back, although sometimes it appears from the left and right. The light of the inmost being resembles that of the spirit, but is brighter and subtler. Its manifestation occurs opposite the mystic and strikes his eyes, enters his body and annihilates him. When the mystic returns from that state of annihilation, he finds much knowledge within himself which he did not possess before. When this light falls on his eyes it permeates all parts of his body and he sees himself like illuminated, limpid water, since both his skin and clothes are illuminated.

The light of the heart resembles that of the moon. This light is manifested on the left side of the mystic and annihilates him. In this state, effort in the heart is decreased, and strange lights and states appear to the mystic.

The light of the soul surrounds the individual. It resembles a polished door or window on which the sun is shining and from which the reflection is falling on the wall. This light of the soul does not possess the power to annihilate (*quwwat-i ifnā'*), but simply helps to illuminate visible things. The mystic also sees other lights at this stage, such as that of a candle, lamp or lantern, which represent the lights of the spirits of classes (*ṭabaqāt*) of humans and Jinn, according to their differing levels of attainment.[95]

The sparks of fire that the mystic sees in the beginning are signs of having traversed the element of the fire of one's own existence. Traveling through the air is a sign of passing the element of air. Swimming in the sea or in rivers, and walking on water are signs of the mystic's passing the element of water. Levitating above streets, houses and walls is a sign of the mystic having traversed the earthy portion of himself which is the fourth and final element in the physical composition of a person. Each time the various parts of the mystic's body are purified of the darkness of the morsels of sensual delight, pure, swiftly moving and beautifully colored fires become visible, as do clean, bright air, crystal clear waters, wide streets, clean and majestic palaces, beautiful carpets and wonderful feasts.[96]

If parts of the mystic's body are sullied by morsels of sensual delight and soiled by selfish desires, he sees the opposite of this, such as frightening, smoldering fires, swirling with smoke, into which he falls and is burned. In addition, he may see a crucible into which he is hurled, or turbid winds, lightning, frightening predicaments, and

---

95. *Risāla-yi nūriyya*, 45b–46a.
96. Ibid., 46a.

terrifying darkness in which he is imprisoned. Other awful visions may be manifested, such as turbid, filthy waters in which he drowns, or narrow, dark streets, and ruined, waste-filled palaces. Whenever the mystic tries to escape this desolation he is surrounded on all sides by high walls. He sees hills of sand on which he walks with great difficulty, and deep, dark pits into which he falls. In this stage dangerous beasts such as the snake, scorpion, lion, leopard, bear and boar become apparent and torment him.[97]

Escape from this state is dependent upon transcending the attributes of the soul which incites to evil. To the degree that the mystic exchanges the darkness of the morsels of sensual delight for the purity of the morsels of truth, blameworthy attributes are transformed into praiseworthy ones, and the fearsome, detestable images described above are transformed into noble or pleasing ones, such as deer, and colorful, melodious birds. In order to realize this transformation the mystic must comprehend the reality underlying the frightening visions such as the scorpion, fire and rubble. Within these frightening, worldly forms there lie beautiful and positive things such as the reality of the heavenly nymph and of eternal life (*ḥaqā'iq al-ḥūriyya wa'l-khuldiyya*), as well as eternal blessings.[98]

After the mystic progresses further along the path, there comes a time when the animal forms are discarded and the human form is assumed. The seeker then sees himself as the mystical traveler that he is, and suddenly the purity of the morsel of reality is greater, as is its beauty. The outward sign of the beauty of the invisible form in the visible realm is the good conduct of the mystic. After transcending this state, the dark, hidden personality of the human being becomes illuminated, and the mystic becomes light personified. At this stage the mystic ascends to the reality of the subtle substance of I-ness (*laṭīfa-yi anā'iyyat*) and the acquired body (*badan-i muktasab*) abides with him eternally.[99]

Annihilation and Resurrection

A significant feature of the mystical visionary journey described above is the experience wherein the individual is annihilated and is subsequently resurrected. Simnānī uses the terms 'annihilation' (*fanā'*)

---

97. Ibid.
98. *Najm*, 37b; *Risāla-yi nūriyya*, 46b.
99. *Risāla-yi nūriyya*, 46b.

and 'resurrection' (*qiyāma*) interchangeably in this context. Nevertheless, the phenomena which they describe are not always identical.

He uses the term *fanā'* to connote annihilation of the self in a manner consistent with its meaning in Sufi thought in general. This loss of self occurs at four levels: (a) at the beginning of the path as a result of recollection; (b) in the middle of the path as annihilation *from* the recollection; (c) annihilation *in* recollection which occurs at the end of the path; and (d) annihilation in the object of recollection which is the beginning of attainment of the divine realm. After this the mystic abides with God (*baqā'*), having attained the stage of servitude which is the noblest of stages and most splendid of levels.[100]

This particular description of the varieties of annihilation is in the context of *dhikr* practice. In all other references to the destruction and subsequent resurrection of the individual, Simnānī uses the term *qiyāma* to the virtual exclusion of *fanā'*. Occasionally he also defines this experience as death (*mawt*), especially when referring to the three primary forms of annihilation in human experience, these being voluntary death (*al-mawt al-ikhtiyārī*), compulsory death (*al-mawt al-iḍṭirārī*), and the great and awesome promised day (*al-yawm al-maw'ūd al-kabīr al-'aẓīm*) marking the collective death of all human beings. These forms of annihilation are accompanied by resurrections. The first of these is the lesser resurrection obtained through voluntary death, as referred to in a saying attributed to the Prophet: "Die before you die." The second is the intermediate resurrection which is also mentioned in a non-canonical *ḥadīth*: "Whoever dies, his resurrection has occurred."[101] The third is the greater resurrection which is the collective or general one. The nature of reality and of the mystical endeavor will be made apparent to everyone after physical death and resurrection, be it the individual intermediate one or the final one. However, truly virtuous individuals seek this state before they die, and engage in mystical and ascetic exercises in this life in order to annihilate themselves. This is what is known as voluntary death, and is greatly rewarded by God both in this world and in the next.[102]

The attainment of voluntary death, or annihilation before the occurrence of physical death, is the immediate goal of all mystical exercises. It is only once this has been attained that the ultimate goal of true knowledge and admittance into the divine presence can be achieved. According to Simnānī, voluntary death is attained through

---

100. *Shaqā'iq al-ḥadā'iq*, 77b.
101. *Najm*, 103b; cf. 157a–b.
102. Ibid., 45a, 47b. Cf. figure 7.

FIGURE 7

Levels of Death and Resurrection

Kind of Death	Corresponding Resurrection
The Promised Day *(al-yawm al-mawᶜūd)*	Collective Resurrection *(al-qiyāma al-ᶜāmma* or *al-kubra)*
Compulsory Death *(al-mawt al-idṭirārī)*	Intermediate Resurrection *(al-qiyāma al-wusṭā)*
Voluntary Death *(al-mawt al-ikhtiyārī)*	Lesser Resurrection *(al-qiyāma aṣ-ṣughrā)*

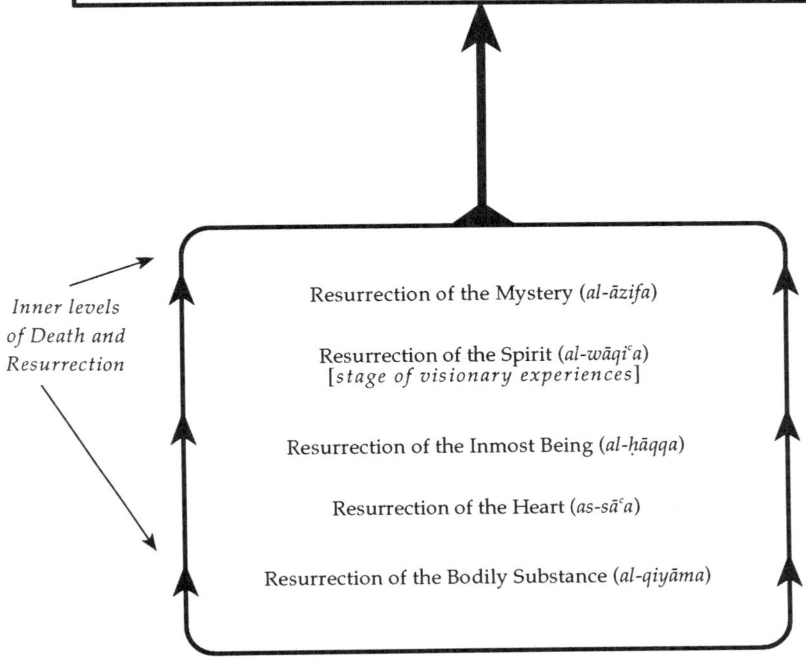

Inner levels of Death and Resurrection

Resurrection of the Mystery (*al-āzifa*)

Resurrection of the Spirit (*al-wāqiᶜa*)
[*stage of visionary experiences*]

Resurrection of the Inmost Being (*al-ḥāqqa*)

Resurrection of the Heart (*as-sāᶜa*)

Resurrection of the Bodily Substance (*al-qiyāma*)

a series of annihilations and resurrections. The Qur'ān refers to this plurality of resurrections through multiple terms such as *al-qiyāma, aṭ-ṭāmma, aṣ-ṣākhkha, al-ḥāqqa, al-ghāshiya, as-sā'a,* and *al-wāqi'a.*[103] These resurrections correspond to the hierarchic levels of the spiritual body.

The first resurrection is that of the body which is referred to by the term *al-qiyāma.*[104] This is followed by the resurrection of the heart (*as-sā'a*) and of the inmost being (*al-ḥāqqa*).[105] The next resurrection is that of the spirit and is known as *al-wāqi'a* (the event). This is the level at which the most dramatic visionary experiences occur, as have been described above in some detail. Due to the power of this resurrection the mountains move and the earth shakes, and the gale winds of grace fan the fires of longing and love, making the waters of wisdom sink into the earth and thereby admitting the mystic to previously unknown knowledge.[106]

The final resurrection is that of the mystery and is known as *al-āzifa.* The intensity and dread of this experience are such that none other than God can reveal it.[107] This is the resurrection which lies closest to the divine presence. The mystic attains the level of the subtle substance of the "real" after its occurrence and abides eternally in the divine presence.

Conclusion

Simnānī was highly aware of the difficulties involved in following the mystical path. Not only did he warn his readers about the pitfalls they might encounter, but he also discussed the very real possibility that many people might lack the ability or resolve to complete this perilous journey. The difficulties one might encounter stem from two main sources, the overpowering nature of mystical experience, and the physical and spiritual demands of the path.

In this chapter I have described at length both the pleasant and fearsome visions encountered on the path as discussed by Simnānī.

---

103. Ibid., 154a.

104. Ibid.

105. Ibid., 98b, 36b. There is no resurrection of the soul because the lights and visions manifested at that level are not powerful enough to cause annihilation (see above, p. 137). The resurrection of the inmost being is further divided into three levels which Simnānī names but does not explain (*Najm,* 97a).

106. Ibid., 36b–37a.

107. Ibid., 23a.

These constitute the complementary facets of mystical experience which are generally described in Sufism as expansion (*bast*) and contraction (*qabd*). The former connotes the state of ease or expansion in which the mystic is released from the overpowering aspects of mystical experience, while the latter constitutes the sense of overpowering and constriction which frightens the mystic and tempts him to abandon the quest.

Simnānī lays great emphasis on the importance of giving equal weight to these two states. The mystic should not be pleased with one of them and discouraged by the other, but rather should remain steadfast in his recollection of God in either event.[108] At such times as he is contracted he should recall the non-canonical *hadīth*: "The heart of the believer is held between two of God's fingers."[109] He should realize that the state of contraction, like that of expansion, is from God and should put complete trust in Him. This constitutes the eighth and final condition of seclusion, that of ceasing to raise objections to God in *qabd* and *bast*, and being content with whatever happens.[110]

The second major source of difficulty on the mystical path is the lack of aptitude or resolve. If, for some reason, the individual does not attain the experience of mystical "taste" through recollection, he should attempt to reaffirm his commitment to the purpose of the exercise by declaring: "Indeed, I recollect God for God's sake, not for mystical experience." He should also take comfort in the fact that even if he does not attain this taste in this world he will surely do so in the afterlife.[111] However, if he lacks the opportunity or capacity for proper recollection, he should know that God is forgiving and has mercy on the mystic's weakness, just as He has mercy upon him for his inability to abandon his physical activities. If he is unable to persist on the mystical path, he should at least continue with his external acts of obedience which are the five pillars of the faith, and abide by all the commandments of God and His prophet.[112] In this manner,

---

108. Ibid., 144a, 47a.

109. Ibid., 41b.

110. *al-Wārid ash-shārid*, 34a.

111. *Najm*, 66a. Simnānī provides a list, attributed to Abū Saʿīd b. Abiʾl-Khayr, of ten qualities to look for in a potential disciple: he must be intelligent, obedient, keen of hearing, spiritually perceptive, truthful, trustworthy, young, capable of guarding the confidence of his *shaykh*, receptive to advice and criticism, and artful (*Salwat al-ʿāshiqīn*, 286).

112. Ibid., 53b.

he will be able to follow the path of righteousness, even though he will never be among the possessors of direct knowledge of the divine (*al-ʿilm al-ladunī*) since the only manner of its attainment is through perseverance on the mystical path and fulfillment of all its requirements:

> If you rid yourself of the world and its bondage in the stage of divestment, then following the path is possible for you. However, you cannot attain your subtle substance of the "real" as long as there remains within you any false content of the subtle substances of the body, soul, heart, inmost being, spirit or mystery. When you have isolated your soul in the stage of isolation, you will be able to attain your subtle substance of the "real", but you will not witness God. . . . Once you have declared God to be one in the stage of unification (*maqām at-tawḥīd*) you will be able to witness Him, but you will not be informed of the secrets of the singular essence as it deserves to be known so long as there remains within you the awareness of unification (*tawḥīd*). But when you have rid yourself of the awareness of unification and established divine unity in the stage of oneness (*maqām al-waḥda*), firmly in the stage of servitude, then God. . .informs you of the secrets of His holy essence, His glorified attributes, and His exact, perfect and harmonious effects, and makes you honor His secrets, treasure His lights, and mirror His effects.[113]

---

113. Ibid., 168a.

8

CONCLUSION

A prolific author, Simnānī has left a wealth of sources providing information on his life and thought. One hundred and fifty-four titles are ascribed to him; these refer to 104 separate works of which 79 are known to exist today (not including his considerable correspondence). The emphasis in his writings is upon instruction, covering theoretical aspects of mystical, theological, philosophical and legal thought, as well as the minute and seemingly prosaic points of everyday religious practice and conduct.

The self-image that is presented in Simnānī's autobiographical writings sheds much light upon the form and purpose of his religious career. Simnānī wished to present himself as a secular youth, ignorant of religion, who, through divine grace, came to a realization of the only true religious path, that of Sunnī Sufism. Despite Simnānī's repeated statements to the contrary, however, it is clear that he had substantial contacts with Sufi figures in his youth, and continued communicating with them after his employment at the Ilkhanid court. There are no indications that he contemplated accepting any form of Shī'ism or considered adopting the Buddhist faith which served as the court religion during his years of civil service.

His purpose in presenting such a personal history appears to be threefold. First, Simnānī wished to create a sharp contrast between his youth and later years in order to emphasize the salvific role of religion in his life, and of divine intervention on the occasion of his first mystical experience on the battlefield in 683/1284 and on several occasions thereafter. Second, he wanted to distance himself from more pantheistic forms of Sufism which he found unacceptable at both an intellectual and spiritual level, as well as from other heterodoxies such as Shī'ism and the neoplatonic school of philosophy prominently represented by Ibn Sīnā. Various forms of Shī'ism were widely prevalent in his day and were influential at the Ilkhanid court. Similarly, the school of mystical thought which emphasized the possibility of some form of union between human beings and God—best addressed by Ibn al-'Arabī—was growing increasingly popular to the point of threatening to become the only major school of Sufi philosophy.

The third and final reason for Simnānī's emphasis upon his conversion experience and subsequent process of discovery which led him to Sunnī Sufism was his admiration for Sunnī mystical figures such as Junayd al-Baghdādī and Majd ad-dīn al-Baghdādī. Simnānī firmly believed in the accuracy and efficacy of their teachings and wished to follow squarely in their footsteps.

His debt to Majd ad-dīn al-Baghdādī is readily obvious when Simnānī's writings are compared with the *Tuḥfat al-barara*. Simnānī considered this work to be a required text for everyone who wished to travel the mystical path.[1] In none of his major treatises does Simnānī contradict any idea presented in Majd ad-dīn al-Baghdādī's work.

The impact of Junayd al-Baghdādī is equally obvious. Simnānī referred to his ideas and sayings frequently, and Junayd's influence on Simnānī's thought appears second only to that of Majd ad-dīn and Simnānī's teacher, Nūr ad-dīn al-Isfarā'inī. Simnānī's disapproval of ecstatic utterances *(shaṭḥiyyāt)* in favor of continual obedience and worship of God resembles Junayd's doctrine of sobriety. He also attributed the requirements of meditation in seclusion *(sharā'iṭ al-khalwa)* to Junayd, whom he considered the preeminent master of the Sufi path.

The high regard in which Simnānī held Junayd al-Baghdādī is in perfect harmony with Simnānī's emphasis on Sunnī belief and the necessity of absolute adherence to all its tenets. At no stage along the mystical path did he believe it was permissible to suspend any of the exoteric requirements of religion. Thus he forbade his disciples from engaging in *dhikr* during the time periods stipulated for ritual prayer. He also maintained that any mystical experience or vision which was not in accordance with the exoteric requirements of Sunnism was invalid and the devil's delusion.

One of Simnānī's major goals was to prove that Sufism is not only fully compatible with normative Islam, but that it is, in fact, the highest form of normative Islamic belief. He maintained that it was not possible for human beings to attain any form of union with or annihilation in God since human beings are contingent beings and God exists of necessity, and it is impossible for a contingent being to be transformed into a necessary one. Instead, at the end of the mystical path, the mystic completes the process of inner purification

---

1. *al-Wārid ash-shārid*, 33b. I am currently preparing a critical edition and translation of this work for publication.

by reaching the perfection of the subtle substance of I-ness (*al-laṭīfa al-anā'iyya*) which constitutes the ultimate human state. This subtle substance of I-ness is the perfect mirror of God, the only thing in the celestial and sublunar realms capable of reflecting the divine essence, attributes, acts and effects. The human mirror of God cannot reflect His beauty and majesty passively, but instead becomes excited by the reflection and is transformed into an active witness of God. In this capacity the human being comprehends that the ultimate state is that of servitude to God, eternally and perfectly bearing witness to His beauty and majesty. "The stage of servitude is more splendid than the stage of unity (*tawḥīd*), because every servant attests to unity but not all who attest to unity are servants."[2]

Simnānī wrote in great detail describing the path leading to enlightenment, and his instructions on the Sufi path are some of the most descriptive and valuable writings of their kind. He firmly believed that the appetitive soul, which is the source of evil, cannot be destroyed by voluntary death, otherwise known as annihilation (*fanā'*) on the mystical path. It is only in physical death that this soul is exterminated. For this reason, the mystic must guard against the soul as long as he is alive.[3]

Guarding against the soul and weakening its power involves a series of outer and inner requirements specified by Simnānī. In the process of fulfilling these requirements of the path, the mystic undergoes a variety of visionary experiences involving a hierarchy of colors and lights. The emphasis on mystical visions is a hallmark of the Kubrawī school. Simnānī's detailed accounts of these visions, which are similar to, though not identical with, Kubra's visions described in his *Fawā'iḥ al-jamāl wa-fawātiḥ al-jalāl*, constitute a substantial contribution to this facet of Kubrawī mysticism.

Another major contribution of Simnānī to Sufi thought is in the realm of theories concerning the mystical human body. He developed the five-tiered structure of earlier thinkers into a hierarchy of seven subtle substances. In describing these substances, Simnānī maintained a complementarity between the physical and the spiritual realms. According to this scheme the spiritual human body, which is infinite, constitutes a macrocosmic universe containing the same things found in the finite realm and in much the same proportion. Like the physical world, the spiritual realm consists of seven climes, each inhabited by a people who are guided to the truth by a prophet. The inhabitants

---

2. *Shaqā'iq al-ḥadā'iq*, 77b.
3. *Najm*, 72b.

of the spiritual realm are faculties or forces (*quwā*), and the prophets that guide them are the subtle substances (*laṭā'if*). The one exception to the correspondence of the two realms is in the existence of the mystical heart in the spiritual realm which has no equivalent in the physical universe. This heart is the source of spiritual perfection and progress along the mystical path.

The complementary structure of the spiritual and physical realms, as well as the hierarchy of seven subtle substances, exist within a more fundamental, all-encompassing structure of divine self-manifestation occurring in four levels. It is within the framework of these four levels that Simnānī sees not only the process of emanation and creation, but also the spiritual journey to human perfection. Accordingly, the mystical path has four main levels with a *dhikr* formula specific to each one. Each of these levels results in a particular kind of annihilation which leads to a specific form of divine self-manifestation.[4] Simnānī's method of thinking is extremely visual and diagrammatic, and this fourfold structure, clearly derived from neoplatonic metaphysics as developed in an Islamic context, forms the structural basis of his thought.

Though Simnānī is unique in his systematized and hierarchic presentation of the interior subtle substances and their correspondence to entities in the physical realm, his ideas belong squarely within a greater tradition of speculative thought in the Islamic world. Concepts such as subtle substances and divine and human realms were widely used in philosophical circles centuries before he was born. Similarly, his image of the origin and structure of the cosmos as well as the terminology he uses while discussing it belongs to a tradition of philosophical inquiry which includes such luminaries as al-Fārābī and Ibn Sīnā, as well as lesser known yet highly influential Ismā'īlī thinkers.

Divine Emanation and the Islamic Philosophical Tradition

Greek cosmological ideas, in particular the Ptolemaic structure of the universe, had been translated into Arabic during the second/ninth century, and a hundred years after that had spread throughout the Islamic world. It was on this foundation that later Islamic cosmological thought was developed, most notably by al-Fārābī and Ibn Sīnā. Though distinct not only in many of their ideas but also in their approach, these two philosophers propagated certain concepts

---

4. Cf. table 2.

TABLE 2

Mystical Advancement and Divine Manifestation

Level along the Mystical Path	Key Practice	Dhikr Formula	Form of Annihilation	Level of Manifestation	Realm
One who has attained the goal (*wāṣil*) A mystical pole (*quṭb*)	Beneficence (*iḥsān*)	The Greatest Name (*al-ism al-ʿaẓīm*)	Annihilation in the object of recollection (*fanāʾ fiʾl-madhkūr*)	Experiential or intuitive manifestation (*at-tajallī adh-dhawqī*)	Realm of Divinity (*ʿālam al-lāhūt*)
Accomplished mystic (*muntahi*)	Piety (*taqwā*)	*hūwa*	Annihilation in recollection (*fanāʾ fiʾdh-dhikr*)	Spiritual manifestation (*at-tajallī al-maʿnawī*)	Realm of Omnipotence (*ʿālam al-jabarūt*)
Intermediate (*mutawassiṭ*)	Patience (*ṣabr*)	*Allāh*	Annihilation from recollection (*fanāʾ ʿan adh-dhikr*)	Manifestation of light (*at-tajallī an-nūrī*)	Realm of Sovereignty (*ʿālam al-malakūt*)
Novice (*mubtadiʾ*)	Faith (*imān*)	*lā ilāha illā Allāh*	Annihilation through recollection (*fanāʾ biʾdh-dhikr*)	Physical Manifesation (*at-tajallī aṣ-ṣuwarī*)	Human Realm (*ʿālam an-nāsūt*)

which set them and the Islamic thinkers who followed them apart from their Aristotelian precursors: their distinctive scheme of emanation, the notion that the celestial forces or intellects are ensouled, and the idea that the last of the incorporeal, celestial intellects performs functions relating to both the human intellect and the physical world.[5]

al-Fārābī is the first known philosopher to describe a scheme of emanation comprising ten celestial intellects which was adopted by Ibn Sīnā, the Ismā'īlī cosmographers, al-Ghazzālī, Ibn al-'Arabī and Simnānī, among others. This cosmography is set apart from the structures proposed by Ptolemy, Galen and Aristotle by the idea that there is something which lies beyond the sphere of the fixed stars. al-Fārābī called this highest sphere the "First Heaven" (*as-samā' al-ūlā*). It is produced by the First Intellect when it comprehends its own essence, and corresponds to the Second Intellect which is produced by the First Intellect when it comprehends God.

> The hierarchy of being then descends through a series of eight further emanated intellects together with which are generated the Fixed Stars, Saturn, Jupiter, Mars, the Sun, Venus, Mercury, and the Moon. The Tenth Intellect is the last of those separate or transcendent entities (lit. separate things, *al-ashyā' al-mufāriqa*) that are both intellects and intelligibles (*'uqūl wa ma'qūlāt*) in their essence, and that require for their existence neither matter nor substrate (*mawḍū'*).[6]

The Tenth Intellect is called the Active Intellect (*al-'aql al-fa''āl*) by al-Fārābī. It serves as an intermediate cause through which the sublunar realm comes into being, both directly from the Active Intellect, as in the case of the human intellect, and indirectly from its corresponding sphere, as in the case of matter.[7] This view of the cosmos is adopted by Ibn Sīnā for whom, as for al-Fārābī, the impetus

---

5. Herbert A. Davidson, *Alfarabi, Avicenna, and Averroes on Intellect* (New York: Oxford University Press, 1992), 128; Daniel C. Peterson, "Cosmology and the Separated Intellects in the 'Rāḥat al-'aql' of Ḥamīd al-dīn al-Kirmānī," (Ph.D. diss., University of California, Los Angeles, 1990), 301.

6. Ian R. Netton, *Allāh Transcendent: Studies in the Structure and Semiotics of Islamic Philosophy, Theology and Cosmology* (London: Routledge, 1989), 115.

7. See Netton, p. 116ff. for a discussion of the centrality of the Active Intellect in al-Fārābī's conception of God's relationship to the created world.

behind the unfolding of the cosmos is the concept of entelechy, founded on the tension between potentiality and actuality.

> Entelechic instincts motivate the unfolding of the universe. Each Intelligence actualizes its inherent creative potential by emanating a lesser Intelligence, a celestial Soul, and a heavenly body. . . . Each stage of emanation, starting with the Necessary Existent and ending with the sublunary realm, results from the internal need of its agent, which Avicenna calls love or passion ('ishq), to fulfill its innate potential.[8]

It is, in fact, Ibn Sīnā whose cosmological ideas found currency in Sufi philosophical circles and, even though Simnānī criticizes him, it is to him that Simnānī is directly indebted not only for his own understanding of the emanation of the cosmos but also for the separation between essential and non-essential attributes and the notion that there is a correspondence between the celestial and human souls and bodies. However, since he is first and foremost a theistic Sufi who only resorts to philosophical paradigms to articulate that which he knows experientially, Simnānī faces none of the major problems dealt with by Ibn Sīnā, namely, how to reconcile the emanation of multiplicity from a singular and transcendent diety.[9] Even so, Simnānī echoes Ibn Sīnā's tripartite scheme of emanation wherein the ten celestial intellects are accompanied by a sphere and a soul, and are identified with archangels.[10]

The figures who come closest to prefiguring Simnānī's cosmological scheme are the Ismā'īlī philosophers, Abū Ya'qūb as-Sijistānī (d. between 386/996 and 393/1003) and Ḥamīd ad-dīn al-Kirmānī (d. after 411/1020). This does not imply an Ismā'īlī influence on Simnānī's thought, but rather demonstrates that cosmological concepts and terms used by Simnānī were debated in Islamic intellectual circles three centuries before he was born, and were therefore used by Simnānī

---

8. Peter Heath, *Allegory and Philosophy in Avicenna* (Philadelphia: University of Pennsylvania Press, 1992), 38–39.

9. There is some disagreement over whether Ibn Sīnā's cosmology and scheme of emanation are Islamic, in the sense that they reflect the Qur'ānic doctrine of creation *ex nihilo*. For further discussion, see P. Morewedge, *The "Metaphysics" of Avicenna (ibn Sīnā)* (New York: Columbia University Press, 1973), 271ff.

10. For a clear outline of emanation according to Ibn Sīnā, see Heath, 37–38.

as the commonly accepted philosophical explanation for the existence of the universe.

Like those of other Ismāʿīlī writers, as-Sijistānī's cosmology is both complicated and very hierarchical. He appears to be the first thinker to refer to the celestial spheres as "fathers," the four elements as "mothers," and the existents in the sublunar realm (minerals, plants and animals) as "progeny."[11] However, he differs markedly from Simnānī not only in the number of spheres, but also in his conceptualization of the relationship of the hierarchical physical universe to the spiritual one.

al-Kirmānī modified this hierarchical scheme by introducing the doctrine of ten intellects into Ismāʿīlī cosmological speculation. He also made significant changes in the Ismāʿīlī numerological study of the cosmos, and proposed a fourfold hierarchy in which there is a progression from one to ten, to one hundred, and finally to one thousand.[12] In al-Kirmānī's case, however, this hierarchy exists within the context of a highly numerological concept of four cosmic orders which bear no resemblance to Simnānī's conception of the four realms of divine manifestation.[13]

The Four Realms

The terms *lāhūt, jabarūt, malakūt and nāsūt* are found in Islamic mystical and philosophical writings prior to Simnānī, although he appears to have been the first thinker to apply them consistently in a hierarchical fashion. The term *lāhūt* coupled and contrasted with *nāsūt* is found neither in the Qurʾān nor in canonical *ḥadīth. Nāsūt* is not even discussed in early Arabic dictionaries, and it is quite possible that the use of these terms was borrowed from Arabic

---

11. Abū Yaʿqūb as-Sijistānī, *Kitāb ithbāt an-nubuwāt*, ed. ʿĀrif Tāmr (Beirut: Imprimerie catholique, 1966), 13ff., with a diagram on page 23; J.B. Harley and D. Woodward, editors, *The History of Cartography*, vol. 2, book 1: Cartography in the Traditional Islamic and South Asian Societies (Chicago: University of Chicago Press, 1992), 82.

12. Ḥamīd ad-dīn al-Kirmānī, *Rāḥat al-ʿaql*, ed. Muṣṭafā Ghālib (Beirut: Dār al-Andalus, 1967), 236ff. For a summary of al-Kirmānī's system of emanation, see Peterson, 327ff.

13. al-Kirmānī's four cosmic realms are those of creation (*ibdāʾ*), matter (*jism*), religion (*dīn*) and the second emanation (*al-inbiʿāth ath-thānī*). Two diagrammatizations of this structure are reproduced along with an English translation in *The History of Cartography*, 84–85.

Christian writings derived from Syriac sources.[14] al-Ḥallāj uses these two words frequently in his writings to signify the polarity between the divine and human natures,[15] making a formal distinction between *lāhūt* as "imparticipable divinity" and *nāsūt* as "deified humanity" or "the form assumed by the divine word prior to all creation."[16] Abū Ḥafṣ 'Umar as-Suhrawardī (d. 632/1234) was aware of the Christian origins of these terms and consequently rejected their use.[17]

The term *'ālam al-mulk* (the realm of kingdom or possession) or simply *al-mulk* (kingdom) is used far more frequently in Islamic sources than *nāsūt* to designate the human or physical realm as the realm over which God is king. In the writings of al-Ghazzālī, *'ālam al-mulk* constitutes the lowest in a series of three created realms. It is often paired with *'ālam al-malakūt*, which has the same meaning but, perhaps because of its assimilation from Aramaic into Arabic (making it sound more impressive), is used exclusively to designate the royalty or sovereignty of God.[18] To *mulk* and *malakūt* al-Ghazzālī adds the concept of *'ālam al-jabarūt* (Realm of Omnipotence), although the mutual relationship between these terms is not constant in his writings nor does *jabarūt* occupy a prominent place in his thought. He normally sees *'ālam al-jabarūt* as a boundary between two created realms, the human realm of *mulk* and the heavenly realm of *malakūt*.[19] This is the inverse of the arrangement of the Realms of Sovereignty (*malakūt*) and Omnipotence (*jabarūt*) in Simnānī's hierarchy. On other occasions, however, al-Ghazzālī sees both *malakūt* and *jabarūt* as realms of angels, *jabarūt* being the higher of the two.[20]

---

14. Louis Gardet, " 'Ālam," *Encyclopaedia of Islam*, new edition (Leiden: E.J. Brill, 1960), 1:349b–52a; also R. Arnaldez, *"Lāhūt and Nāsūt,"* 5:611b–14b.

15. Louis Massignon, *The Passion of al-Ḥallāj*, trans. Herbert Mason, Bollingen Series, no. 98 (Princeton: Princeton University Press, 1982).

16. Ibid.

17. "[P]eople who teach *ḥulūl* (divine indwelling) and maintain *ḥulūl*, and teach that God dwells in select bodies. In explaining this they have some of the Christian doctrine of *lāhūt* and *nāsūt* in mind" (Abū Ḥafṣ 'Umar as-Suhrawardī, *'Awārif al-ma'ārif*, ed. 'Abd al-Ḥalīm Maḥmūd and Maḥmūd b. ash-Sharīf (Cairo: Dār al-kutub al-ḥadītha, n.d.), 1:233.

18. A.J. Wensinck, *La pensée de Ghazzālī* (Paris: Adrien-Masonneuve, 1940), 83. The term *malakūt* appears a number of times in the Qur'ān (6:75; 7:185; 23:88; 36:83). *Jabarūt* appears for the first time in *ḥadīth*.

19. Ibid., 84–85.

20. A.J. Wensinck, *On the Relationship Between Ghazali's Cosmology and His Mysticism*, Mededeelingen der Koninkliike Akademie van Wetenschappen,

From the time of al-Ḥallāj and al-Ghazzālī, these terms continue to be used extensively in Islamic mystical writings, although they are not applied consistently. The polarity between *lāhūt* and *nāsūt* is maintained in the writings of Rūzbihān Baqlī-yi Shīrāzī (d. 606/1209). This is also the case in the writings of Ibn al-ʿArabī, although for him *lāhūt* and *nāsūt* imply the inward and outward aspects of reality rather than two different realms.[21]

The use of *mulk, malakūt* and *jabarūt* is not as well-defined. Rūzbihān Baqlī presents *malakūt* and *jabarūt* as two mystical realms which can be spiritually experienced by human beings. However it is not clear if he considers them as distinct hierarchical elements.[22] Ibn al-ʿArabī mentions these terms as the corporeal realm, spiritual realm and imaginal realm, respectively, but he does not use them extensively or systematically.[23] Kāshānī provides definitions for all three terms yet they fail to form a hierarchy in his explanations. For him the pair *mulk* and *malakūt* are identical with the visible and invisible realms.[24] *Malakūt* is identical with the realm of the divine command and that of the spirits. *Mulk* is identical with the created realm and that of physical bodies, while *jabarūt* is the realm of the divine names and attributes.[25]

The Kubrawī mystics prior to Simnānī do not order these terms in a more elaborate and formal hierarchy. Saʿd ad-dīn-i Ḥamūya (with whom Simnānī had little contact) comes closest to prefiguring Simnānī's characteristic hierarchy of four realms. Like his Sufi predecessors, he too seems to be working with two complementary structures, one of *lāhūt* and *nāsūt*, and the other of the four hierarchical realms. However, he appears to be the first Kubrawī writer to use the term *nāsūt* along with *malakūt, jabarūt* and *lāhūt*, and to arrange the realms in the same order of ascendence as is found in Simnānī's

---

Afdeeling Letterkunde, vol. 75, series A, no. 6 (Amsterdam: N.V. Noord-Hollandsche Uitgevers-Maatschappij, 1933), 11.

21. A.E. Affifi, *The Mystical Philosophy of Muhyid din-Ibnul Arabi* (Lahore: Sh. Muhammad Ashraf, n.d.), 14.

22. Rūzbihān Baqlī-yi Shīrāzī, *Kitāb ʿabhar al-ʿāshiqīn*, ed. H. Corbin and M. Moin (Tehran: Institut français d'iranologie de Téhéran, 1958; rpt. 1981), 5, 25, 126.

23. William C. Chittick, *The Sufi Path of Knowledge* (Albany: SUNY Press, 1989), 282.

24. ʿAbd ar-Razzāq al-Kāshānī, *Kitāb iṣṭilāḥāt aṣ-ṣūfiyya*, ed. A. Spenger (Lahore: al-Irshad, rpt. 1974), 67.

25. Ibid., 89.

writings. Ḥamūya claims that the manifestation of divine perfection takes its origin from the Realm of Divinity, that of beauty appears from the Realm of Sovereignty (*mulk* as opposed to *malakūt*), and that of majesty occurs in the Realm of Omnipotence, while all three manifestations can be seen in the mysteries of the Human Realm (*nāsūt*).[26] Ḥamūya applies neither these terms nor this system consistently. He uses *mulk* and *malakūt* interchangeably, occasionally refers to *malakūt* in the plural,[27] and at other times collapses *jabarūt* and *malakūt* into each other, creating a vague spiritual realm separating *nāsūt* from *lāhūt*.[28]

It appears that by the time of Ḥamūya's writing *nāsūt* had replaced *mulk* in designating the Human Realm. This was probably more due to assonance with the other three terms than to anything else. Despite Ḥamūya's use of these terms, however, Simnānī appears to have been the earliest writer to have applied them consistently to refer to a fourfold structure of existence.

The Concept of *Laṭā'if*

The term *laṭīfa* (plural *laṭā'if*) has been variously translated as "spiritual substance,"[29] "mystical subtleties,"[30] "subtle centers of perception,"[31] "centres subtils,"[32] "organes subtils,"[33] and "Feinstoff" or "Feinstoffwesen."[34] In the context of Simnānī's thought, the most accurate translation is "subtle substance," identical with the German "Feinstoff."

---

26. Sa'd ad-dīn-i Ḥamūya, *al-Miṣbāḥ fi't-taṣawwuf*, ed. N. Māyil-i Hirawī (Tehran: Intishārāt-i mawlā, 1983), 72.

27. Ibid., 101.

28. Ibid., 66, 123.

29. R. A. Nicholson, *Studies in Islamic Mysticism* (Cambridge: Cambridge University Press, 1921; rpt. 1980), 51.

30. Gerhard Böwering, *The Mystical Vision of Existence in Classical Islam*, Studien zur Sprache, Geschichte und Kultur des islamischen Orients, no. 9, ed. Bertold Spuler (Berlin: Walter de Gruyter, 1980), 141.

31. Hamid Algar tr., *The Path of God's Bondsmen from Origin to Return (Mirṣād al-'ibād min al-mabdā' ila'l-ma'ād)*, by Najm ad-dīn ad-Dāyā ar-Rāzī (Delmar: Caravan, 1982), 18.

32. Landolt, *Révélateur*, 54.

33. Henry Corbin, *En Islam iranien*, 3:278.

34. Richard Gramlich, *Die Schiitischen Derwischorden Persiens*, no. 36:2–4 (Wiesbaden: Franz Steiner, 1976), 63 note 287.

The word *laṭīfa* is not treated as part of a technical lexicon in Arabic dictionaries. The early work of Ibn al-Anbārī (d. 577/1181) does not have an entry for it and the *Lisān al-ʿarab* of Ibn Manẓūr (d. 711/1311) and *al-Qāmūs al-muḥīṭ* of al-Fīrūzābādī (d. 816/1413) treat it simply as the feminine of *laṭīf*. Not surprisingly, since it is a much later work than the Arabic lexicons cited above, Dikhuda's Persian *Lughatnāma* refers to *laṭīfa* as a technical term. He states that in the understanding of the mystics it is a subtle reference, the conceptualization of which cannot be explained.[35] He goes on to define the term *laṭīfa-yi insāniyya* as something which the philosophers call the rational soul and the mystics refer to as the heart, but which is in reality the spirit.

In the context of Sufism, the notion of subtle substances acquires a technical sense as early as the classical period of Islamic mysticism. Sahl at-Tustarī (d. 283/896) expresses a concept of subtle (*laṭīf*) substances while expounding his theory of the natural self and the spiritual self:

> When man dies, He [God] will extract from him (*yanziʿu ʿanhu*) the subtle substance (*laṭīf*) of the luminous spiritual self (*nafs ar-rūḥ an-nūrī*) out of the subtle substance (*laṭīf*) of the dense natural self (*nafs aṭ-ṭabʿ al-kathīf*), by which man comprehends the things (*ashyā'*) and has the vision (*ru'ya*) in the heavenly kingdom (*malakūt*). . . . the dense natural self (*nafs aṭ-ṭabʿ al-kathīf*) has its subtle substance (*laṭīf*) and the spiritual self (*nafs ar-rūḥ*) has its subtle substance (*laṭīf*).[36]

A more detailed understanding of the term emerges in the writings of Abū Manṣūr al-Ḥallāj (d. 309/992), for whom the *laṭā'if* are substances which are distinct entities attached in some manner

---

35. Dikhudā, 21:215a-b. This definition appears to be a Persian rendition of an Arabic original which appears in the *Iṣṭilāḥāt* of ʿAbd ar-Razzāq al-Kāshānī and is repeated in the *Kitāb at-taʿrīfāt* of ʿAlī al-Jurjānī. Dikhudā also states that the term *laṭīfa* is used on several occasions by Saʿdī and Ḥāfiẓ but there appears to be no apparent consciousness of a technical sense on their part.

The word appears neither in the Qur'ān nor in *ḥadīth* literature. However, the root *l-ṭ-f* is represented in the Qur'ān by the word *laṭīf* which is one of the attributes of God. It appears in this capacity on seven occasions (6:104; 12:160; 22:63; 31:16; 33:34; 42:19; 67:14), and in all but two of these (12:160; 42:19) it is paired with *khabīr* (the Informed), another divine attribute.

36. Böwering, *Mystical Vision*, 244–45.

to the physical body. Yet it is not clear from his writings as to whether these *laṭā'if* are within the body or encasing it, or if they are essential components of the physical human form. It is stated that on his ascension to heaven Muḥammad cast off one of his concentric coverings (*laṭā'if*).[37] This would imply that the *laṭā'if* exist as a series of concentric veils, distinct in form and of differing origins. These veils of the soul, heart, spirit and inmost being (*sirr*) separate the individual from the divine center and must be lifted successively by acts of divine grace.[38] It is also stated that the *laṭā'if* are encased within the human body. They are bestowed upon the body by God and function as the source of human beings' autonomy during their lifetime, residing in their physical bodies like a star in its sphere. Upon death *laṭā'if* survive in individual human beings and transform them into their resurrection bodies.[39]

It was left to Abū Ḥāmid al-Ghazzālī to provide what appears to be one of the earliest systematic treatments of the term *laṭīfa* in Islamic mystical thought. Ghazzālī makes a sharp distinction between materiality and spirituality and explains the difference between the material, outer body and the spiritual, inner body by comparing material bodily elements in the form of heart, spirit, soul and intellect to their spiritual counterparts.

As opposed to the outer heart which is simply a piece of flesh found in the bodies of beasts and humans, both alive and dead, the inner heart is a divine, spiritual, subtle substance. This *laṭīfa* is the essential reality of the human being and is the possessor of divine knowledge. The relationship of this subtle substance to the bodily heart resembles the relationship of the limbs to the body or that of a user of an instrument to the instrument itself.[40] Ghazzālī calls upon the word *laṭīfa* to explain the terms *qalb* (heart) and *rūḥ* (spirit). The inner heart is the divine subtle substance (*laṭīfa rabbāniyya rūḥāniyya*); the inner spirit is defined as the knowledgeable perceptive substance (*al-laṭīfa al-'ālima al-mudrika min-al-insān*).

The writings of Ibn al-'Arabī and his school continue to develop the concept of *laṭīfa* as a subtle substance, and two disciples of his thought, 'Abd ar-Razzāq al-Kāshānī and Sharīf 'Alī al-Jurjānī (d. 816/1413), have provided definitions for the word. Kāshānī refers to

---

37. Massignon, *Passion of al-Hallāj*, 1:14, note 78.

38. Ibid., 3:17.

39. Ibid., 16.

40. Abū Ḥāmid Muḥammad b. Muḥammad al-Ghazzālī, *Iḥyā' 'ulūm ad-dīn*, 4 vols. (Cairo: Maṭba'at al-istiqāma, n.d.), 3:1:3ff.

a *laṭīfa* as a subtle allusion, the meaning of which cannot be expressed adequately in writing.[41] He provides a lengthier definition for the subtle human substance (*al-laṭīfa al-insāniyya*), reflecting the importance of this concept in Ibn al-ʿArabī's school of thought:

> [*al-laṭīfa al-insāniyya*] is the rational soul, called by [the mystics] the heart, and in fact it causes the spirit to descend to a rank close to that of the soul. It is related to the soul in one form and related to the spirit in another. The first form is called the breast and the second the heart.[42]

It is clear from Simnānī's works that he was familiar with the language of his Sufi predecessors and adopted the concept of subtle substances (*laṭāʾif*) from their technical vocabulary. For him, a *laṭīfa* is a subtle substance, non-corporeal in form and imperceptible to the natural senses. As such, one variety of these subtle substances belongs to the spiritual realm and constitutes an integral part of the mystical body. Another variety of these subtle substances are the ten higher substances (*al-laṭāʾif al-ʿulwiyya*) which are the direct emanations of the first entity in the order of creation, and from which all remaining emanations appear.

Simnānī's Legacy

Simnānī has left a lasting impression upon the development of Islamic mysticism. His teachings concerning the requirements of the path and the visions encountered therein served as a distinguishing feature of the Rukniyya, a subbranch of the Kubrawiyya named after him. Through ʿAlī-yi Hamadānī these ideas also influenced Sayyid Muḥammad-i Nūrbakhsh and subsequently the Nūrbakhshī order.

In addition to his philosophical and visionary ideas, Simnānī has also had a great deal of impact on Sufi theories of social and political action, or what has been called the "lesser mystic way."[43] There is much evidence to support the theory that Simnānī was deeply involved in the political movements of his day. It may be of some significance

---

41. Kāshānī, 46. Jurjānī gives a virtually exact quotation of Kāshānī's definition (ʿAlī al-Jurjānī, *Kitāb at-taʿrīfāt* [Istanbul: Maṭbaʿa Aḥmad Kāmil, 1909], no page numbers).

42. Ibid.

43. F.C. Happold, *Mysticism: A Study and an Anthology* (London: Penguin Books, 1963; rpt. 1988), 100ff.

that his first religious experience occurred on a battlefield when he was fighting on behalf of the Buddhist ruler Arghūn against Arghūn's Muslim relative, Aḥmad Takūdār. Even after his retirement from courtly life, he continued to maintain contacts with the Ilkhanid court, and sided with Sunnī princes such as Amīr Chūbān and Amīr Nawrūz in their intrigues. During the reign of Abū Saʿīd, Simnānī appears to have been the foremost Sufi figure in the Ilkhanid empire. Abū Saʿīd may even have constructed a *khānaqāh* in recognition of Simnānī's authority as a *shaykh*.[44]

His mystical life also suggests an interest in political and social movements. Najm ad-dīn al-Kubrā is believed to have died defending his city against the Mongols. In his biographical writings, Simnānī states on several occasions that he had considered going to Syria to engage in *jihād*. Furthermore, Simnānī was a one-time teacher of Khalīfa-yi Māzandarānī, the spiritual leader of the Sarbadār movement, and was also well-acquainted with Ṣafī ad-dīn al-Ardabīlī. Both these major Sufi leaders figure prominently in the developmental stages of religio-political movements in Iran.

The development of a theory concerning the mysticism of action and the politicization of religion are logical outcomes of Simnānī's thought. In refuting the popular pantheistic idea that human beings do not possess any existence apart from God, he negated the development of social apathy and nihilism. According to his own mystical philosophy, the ultimate human state is one of servitude, wherein the mystic becomes a perfect and eternal witness to God. This implies not only that human existence is separate from, albeit dependent upon, God, but also that human beings bear a great responsibility because they alone are capable of carrying the sacred trust of divine gnosis. Through this gnosis the mystic realizes that ultimate mystical truths are perfectly compatible with the exoteric teachings of Islam, and that, as the most perfect of God's creations and His representative (*khalīfa*) in the created realm, the human being must function in a custodial capacity in this world. This belief accords cosmic importance to human action, and can easily lead to a strictly normative Sunnī form of mystical activism. This very aspect of Sufism is a hallmark of the Naqshbandī order—especially in its Mujaddidī form—that seems to have been derived from Simnānī's writings.

Simnānī's contacts with the Naqshbandiyya began during his life time when he corresponded with Khwāja-yi ʿAzīzān ʿAlī-yi Rāmtīnī. The subject of their debate was the comparative merits of

---

44. See above, p. 28.

vocal versus silent recollection (*dhikr*), and Simnānī favored the silent form. Silent recollection has since become one of the major distinguishing features of the Naqshbandiyya. However, Simnānī's greatest impact on the development of Naqshbandī thought is through Aḥmad-i Sirhindī.

Simnānī's concept that the ultimate mystical state is that of being a witness to God's essence, attributes, acts and effects was further elaborated by Sirhindī in the doctrine of oneness of witnessing (*waḥdat ash-shuhūd*). It has been maintained in the writings of the Mujaddidī branch of the Naqshbandiyya—and subsequently in Sufi hagiographical works—that Sirhindī was originally a believer in the doctrine of oneness of being, and that he later underwent a conversion experience which led him to believe in the oneness of witnessing. However, it seems clear from Sirhindī's *Maktūbāt* that he was in agreement with Simnānī very early on in his spiritual development and that the conversion experience is overstated.[45] It appears, therefore, that Simnānī's influence on Sirhindī must be greater than is usually assumed.

Not coincidentally, Sirhindī advocated an activist form of mysticism which, in the last two centuries, has been emphasized at the expense of other aspects of his thought. This is largely a result of developments in India and Central Asia where the Naqshbandiyya has emphasized normative Sunnī Sufism along with social and political action. Simnānī's influence in this regard has been so far-reaching as to inspire the influential poet and philosopher, Muḥammad Iqbāl (d. 1357/1938), who maintained that Junayd al-Baghdādī and Simnānī were his precursors in the development of the philosophy of the self (*asrār-i khūdī*).[46]

The clear influence of Simnānī's ideas upon Sirhindī and the Naqshbandiyya, as well as their possible impact on Islamic thinkers of this century, may conceal a critical role played by Simnānī in the development of modern Islamic theories of politics and religion. Given

---

45. Friedmann, 24.

46. A.H. Kamali, "The Heritage of Islamic Thought," *Iqbal: Poet-philosopher of Pakistan*, ed. Hafeez Malik (New York: Columbia University Press, 1971), 212. Sanjani should be read Simnānī, since there is no known 'Alā' ad-dawla as-Sanjānī [Sangānī]. The only possible person other than Simnānī that this reference might allude to is Rukn ad-dīn Maḥmūd-i Sanjānī (d. ca. 597/1200), also called Shāh-i Sanjan, a Chishtī figure who is primary known for his poetry (Junayd-i Shīrāzī, 357; Mustawfī al-Qazwīnī, *Tā'rīkh-i guzīda*, 674; *Nuzhat al-qulūb*, 151, Riḍā Qūlī Khān, *Riyāḍ al-'ārifīn*, 158).

the political and religious situation of his time, Simnānī believed that Islamic belief and polity were threatened. This is evident both in the philosophy he espoused and in the sense of urgency which pervades his writings. He sought to reconcile the social and spiritual dimensions of human experience by formulating a cohesive theory of existence. According to this view, the spiritual and social spheres exist in a parallel and complementary relationship. Mystical aspirations and achievements do not diminish the importance of social concerns; on the contrary, they strengthen them.

Appendix A:
The Written Works of Simnānī

Historical sources describe Simnānī as a prolific writer. In his *Kitāb al-wāfī bi'l-wafayāt*, Ṣafadī claims that he wrote more than three hundred works.[1] His many writings are known to have included works of Qur'ān commentary (*tafsīr*), miscellaneous treatises (*risālāt*) and letters (*makātīb*).[2] Dawlatshāh Samarqandī quotes a treatise by Simnānī entitled *Miftāḥ* in which he claims:

> I have blackened [with ink] a thousand sheaves of paper in the way and description of Sufism, and have spent and given in *waqf* a hundred thousand dinars of my father's property and [my] inheritance to the Sufis.[3]

The majority of Simnānī's works were written in Arabic, although he frequently used Persian, which was his native language. The larger treatises, as well as technical ones which he judged to be important, are written in Arabic. Less formal works as well as simplified versions of major treatises are in Persian so as to be accessible to a wider audience than if they were available only in Arabic.

Simnānī's style of writing is typical of his era. He resorted to alliteration and the use of rhymed prose (*saj'*) both in Arabic and in Persian. He clearly had greater facility in Persian, although his penchant for compound sentences and dangling modifiers often makes them difficult to translate. His Arabic treatises display a sound knowledge of the language, and contain frequent citations of Arabic poetry and proverbs.

Information concerning Simnānī's writings can be found in all references to him in biographical and hagiographical works. In addi-

---

1. Ṣafadī, 7:357; Ibn Ḥajar al-ʿAsqalānī, 1:266.
2. Shīrwānī, 523.
3. Dawlatshāh, 251.

tion, incidental references to his works exist in many historical and mystical texts. Simnānī himself wrote an extremely valuable short treatise entitled *Maṭāf al-ashrāf* which provides a partial list of the Arabic works he had composed.[4] Not all of these treatises exist today, nor is this a complete list of the known works which can be attributed to Simnānī with accuracy.

Preliminary bibliographies of Simnānī's works have been compiled by several scholars, most notably 'Abd ar-Rafī' Ḥaqīqat and Nazif Ṣahinoğlu.[5] The following pages represent the most comprehensive list of his writings that can be compiled at this time. Titles of Simnānī's works are arranged in five sections. The first two deal with his major and minor treatises. The third section contains a record of his correspondence. This is followed by a section listing the works that are no longer known to be extant. The fifth section lists the titles of Arabic works that appear only in the *Maṭāf al-ashrāf*. The final part of this chapter gives a detailed description of the existing manuscripts of his commentary on the Qur'ān, entitled *Najm al-qur'ān*, which constitutes the basic text analyzed in this study. In the first two sections, works are listed under their most accurate title along with an English translation and a list of variant titles. This is followed by an inventory of the locations of manuscripts of the work and a brief description of the text, where applicable. With the exception of the first section where works are listed according to their relative degree of importance, treatises are presented in chronological order; undated titles are listed alphabetically. The manuscripts I have consulted are marked by an asterisk.

Major Works

Among the many works of Simnānī, eleven major texts are differentiated from the rest both in terms of their length and their importance for a complete understanding of the author's life and

---

4. See below, p. 184.

5. Earlier, less comprehensive bibliographical information appears in Nafīsī's article, Brockelmann (*Supplement*), Sadr, Landolt (*Correspondence*), Cordt, Kaḥḥāla, Dihkhudā, and the articles on Simnānī in *Encyclopaedia Iranica* and the *Encyclopaedia of Islam*, new edition. Hirawī has included a list of Simnānī's works in his edition of the *'Urwa*, as well as separately in an article ("Kitābshināsī wa nuskhashināsī-yi 'Alā' ad-dawla Simnānī," *Kitābshināsī*, no. 1, ed. Akhtar Rāhī and 'Ārif Nawshāhī (Lahore: Maktaba-yi 'ilmiyya, 1986), 156–98).

thought. Of these, eight are written in Arabic, two in Persian and one in both languages.

1. *Najm al-qur'ān.* Star of the Qur'ān.

This is Simnānī's commentary on the Qur'ān, and is the most important of his works in terms of its value as a summary of his thought. Since this commentary is the primary textual source of this study, I reserve a detailed discussion of this work for the last part of this appendix.

2. *al-'Urwa li-ahl al-khalwa wa'l-jalwa* (Arabic and Persian). The Bond for the People of Seclusion and Splendor.

Variant titles:

(a) *'Urwat al-wuthqā*
(b) *Kitāb al-'urwa*
(c) *al-'Urwa li-ahl al-khalwa wa'l-jalwa fī-mā yajibu al-i'tiqād bihi*
(d) *al-'Urwa al-wuthqā li-ahl at-taqā*
(e) *Ṣafwat al-'urwa*
(f) *Mashāri' abwāb al-quds wa-marāti' aṣḥāb al-uns*

Locations:

1. MS. 482, Aṣir Efendi, Süleymaniye Kütüphanesi, Istanbul, entitled *Kitāb al-'urwa,* dated 725/1325 and allegedly copied from the autograph.*
2. MS. 1432, Lâleli, Süleymaniye Kütüphanesi, Istanbul, entitled *Ṣafwat al-'urwa,* dated 733/1332–33 at Ṣūfīyābād-i Khudādād.*
3. MS. 1347 (No. 905), Oriental Public Library, Bankipore, entitled *al-'Urwa li-ahl al-khalwa,* dated ca. 800/1397–98.[6]
4. MS. Oriental 3649. (Catalog No. 19), British Museum, London, entitled *al-'Urwa li-ahl al-khalwa wa'l-jalwa.* It is incomplete, and probably dates from the tenth/sixteenth century.[7]
5. MS. 1080, Mishkāt, Kitābkhāna-yi markazī-yi dānishgāh, Tehran; an Arabic version entitled *al-'Urwa li-ahl al-khalwa wa'l-jalwa fī-mā yajibu al-i'tiqād bihi,* completed by Kamāl ad-dīn Muḥammad

---

6. Mawlawī 'Abd al-Ḥamīd, *Miftāḥ al-kunūz al-khafiyya, fihrist-i dastī-yi Oriental Public Library, Bankīpūr* (Patna: 1918), 137. *Catalogue of the Arabic and Persian Manuscripts in the Oriental Public Library at Bankipore,* vol. 13 (Patna: 1928), 89. (The first catalog erroneously lists his name as as-Sam'ānī).

7. Charles Rieu, *Supplement to the Catalogue of the Persian Manuscripts in the British Museum* (London: British Museum, 1977), 11.

b. ‘Alā’ ad-dīn Aḥmad b. Jamāl ad-dīn Muḥammad Khafarī on 12 Jumāda I 973/5 December 1565 at Golkonda, Deccan.[8]

6. MS. 2731, Kitābkhāna-yi majlis, Tehran; a Persian version dated 5 Shawwāl 1142/12 April 1730, with the commentary of a certain Zayn ad-dīn in the margins.[9]

7. MS. 1583, Esat Efendi, Süleymaniye Kütüphanesi, Istanbul; in Arabic and bearing the title *al-‘Urwa li-ahl al-khalwa wa’l-jalwa*, copied by ‘Abd ar-Raḥmān Efendīzāda in Ṣafar 1119/April-May 1707.[10]

8. MS. 3047 (14291D), Raza Library, Rampur, entitled *al-‘Urwa li-ahl al-khalwa wa’l-jalwa*, copied by Ghulām Muṣṭafā b. ‘Abd al-Walī b. Muḥammad Aslam-i Sukhānwī in 1143/1730–31.[11]

9. MS. 203, Kitābkhāna-yi āstān-i quds-i riḍawī, Mashhad. This is an inaccurate Persian version entitled *‘Urwat al-wuthqā*. It is undated, but was entered into the catalog of the collection in 1292/1875.[12]

10. MS. 482, Reisülküttâb Mustafa Efendi, Süleymaniye Kütüphanesi, Istanbul, 96ff.* A copy of the final redaction completed in 722/1322. The colophon states that the work was copied from Simnānī’s autograph. Taking into account the script, paper and the fact that Simnānī’s certification (allegedly dated Rabī‘ I 725/February 1325) at the end is in another hand, this claim appears false.

11. Private collection, Sayyid Ḥusayn Shahshahānī, entitled *Mashāri‘ abwāb al-quds wa-marāti‘ aṣḥāb al-uns*.[13]

12. MS. 1378/2, Ṣehit Ali Paşa, Süleymaniye Kütüphanesi, Istanbul, fols. 9a–51b, entitled *Mashāri‘ abwāb al-quds wa-marāti‘ aṣḥāb al-uns*.*

---

8. ‘Alīnaqī Munzawī-yi Tihrānī, *Fihrist-i kitābkhāna-yi ahdā’ī-yi Āqā-yi Sayyid Muḥammad Mishkāt bi kitābkhāna-yi dānishgāh-i Tihrān* (Tehran: Intishārāt-i dānishgāh-i Tihrān, 1951), 3:474–75; cf. *‘Urwa*, 46, where the manuscript is listed as MS. 648, Kitābkhāna-yi markazī-yi dānishgāh, Tehran.

9. *‘Urwa*, 48; cf. Landolt (*Correspondence*, 37, note 33), according to whom it is dated 1144/1732.

10. Süleymaniye Kütüphanesi, card catalog; Landolt, *Correspondence*, 37, note 33.

11. Imtiaz Ali Arshi, *Catalogue of the Arabic Manuscripts in Raza Library, Rampur*, vol. 4 (Rampur: 1971), 118.

12. Sadr erroneously states that this is an autograph (Sadr, 104).

13. Sadr, 102–3.

13.   MS C2315 (Nov. 958, Catalog no. 2459), Oriental Institute, St. Petersburg, 54 folios, entitled *al-'Urwa al-wuthqā li-ahl at-taqā*.[14]

The *'Urwa* is invaluable for the study of Simnānī's biography and thought. The book was originally composed in Arabic. Simnānī began writing it in Ramaḍān 720/October 1320 in Ṣūfīyābād-i Khudādād and finished it on 23 Muḥarram 721/22 February 1321. He supervised the revision of the work in the same year and, in Jumāda II 722/June 1322, completed a third and final version.[15]

A Persian redaction also exists which is believed to have been written by Simnānī himself. Although the style and content are very similar to that of his other Persian works it is possible that the translation was made by a student soon after his death.

Mashāri' abwāb al-quds and *Ṣafwat al-'urwa* are different versions of the same work and can be dated with precision: the *Mashāri'* to 711/1311 (MS. 1378 Ṣehit Ali), and the *Ṣafwat al-'urwa* from Jumāda II 728/April 1328 to 18 Dhu'l-Ḥijja 728/24 October 1328.[16]

An edition providing both the Arabic and Persian versions has been published by Najīb Māyil-i Hirawī.[17]

3. *Tabyīn al-maqāmāt wa-ta'yīn ad-darajāt* (Arabic).[18] The Explanation of Stations and the Appointment of Levels.

Possible variants:

(a) *Faḍl aṭ-ṭarīqa*
(b) *Faḍl ash-sharī'a*

Locations:

1.   MS. 11-mīm, Majāmī' fārsiyya, Dār al-kutub, Cairo, fols. 45a-72a, incomplete copy contained in a collection copied by Muḥammad b. Ibrāhīm b. Muḥammad 'Abd al-Ghafūr as-Simnānī, completed at Qazwīn on 3 Rabī' I, 887/22 April 1482.*

---

14. A.B. Khalidova, *Arabskie Rukopisi Instituta Vöstokovedeniiâ*, (Moscow: Nauka, 1986), 1:136.

15. Hirawī ed., *'Urwa*, 46; Khwāfī, 3:33.

16. F. Meier, "'Alā' al-Dawla al-Simnānī" in *Encyclopaedia of Islam*, new edition; cf. Molé, according to whom an autograph of the *Mashāri'* is dated 16 Ramaḍān 715/14 December 1315 ("Les Kubrawiya," 76, note 58).

17. 'Alā' ad-dawla as-Simnānī, *al-'Urwa li-ahl al-khalwa wa'l-jalwa*, ed. Najīb Māyil-i Hirawī (Tehran: Intishārāt-i Mawlā, 1983).

18. *Maṭāf al-ashrāf*, MS. 353, Karaçelebizade, Süleymaniye Kütüphanesi, Istanbul, 79a; *Fatḥ al-mubīn*, 10a; *Risāla fī-tafsīr āyāt qur'āniyya fī-mawḍū' aṣ-ṣabr wa'l-iḥsān*, 140b; *Khitām al-misk*, 144a; *'Urwa*, 356.

2.   MS. 2135, Feyzullah Efendi, Süleymaniye Kütüphanesi, Istanbul,
     fols. 46a–117b. It bears the title *Faḍl ash-sharī'a* but probably
     should be called *Faḍl aṭ-ṭarīqa.*[19]

The Cairo manuscript lists one hundred mystical stations
(*maqāmāt*) and describes each one in three levels (*darajāt*) for aspirants
on the mystical path and a final one for the mystical axis (*quṭb*). Each
level of the aspirants is further divided into three states (*aḥwāl*): initial,
medial and final. The levels and stations are viewed as progressive.
Accordingly, a mystic cannot proceed from one to the next of these
hundred stations and one thousand states without God's help (*tawfīq*)
and a teacher's guidance.[20] The work is mentioned by Simnānī in *Maṭāf
al-ashrāf* (79a) and therefore was compiled some time before 28 Ṣafar
714/13 June 1314.

4.   *Fuṣūl al-uṣūl* (Persian). Chapters on the Fundamentals [of Religion].
     Variant titles:
                    (a) *Fuṣūl fi'l-uṣūl*[21]
                    (b) *Fuṣūl al-uṣūl al-mashhūr bi-mā lā budda
                         minhu*[22]
                    (c) *Mā lā budda fi'd-dīn*
     Possible variant: *Uṣūl al-islām wa'd-dīn 'alā-zubdat al-'aqā'id
al-ḥaqq wa'l-yaqīn.*
     Locations:
1.   MS. 1 (Catalog No. 2034), Fiqh ḥanafī fārsī, Dār al-kutub, Cairo,
     fols. 47b–84b, entitled *Fuṣūl al-uṣūl.*[23]*
2.   MS. 1431/1, Esat Efendi, Süleymaniye Kütüphanesi, Istanbul, fols.
     1a–64b, entitled *Mā lā budda fi'd-dīn*, dated 6 Rabī' II 776/14
     September 1374, copied for a Shaykh Shams ad-dīn by Nūr ad-
     dīn b. Badr ad-dīn al-Ḥāfiẓ aṭ-Ṭarazī.*
3.   MS. 1189, Manisa İl Halk Kütüphanesi, Manisa, 80 folios,
     entitled *Uṣūl al-islām wa'd-dīn 'alā-zubdat al-'aqā'id al-ḥaqq
     wa'l-yaqīn.*[24]

---

19. Meier, "'Alā' al-Dawla al-Simnānī"; Cordt, bibliography.

20. 71b–72a; this manuscript is missing the first 49 stations.

21. Ismā'īl Pāshā al-Baghdādī, *Hadiyyat al-'ārifīn* (Istanbul: Milli Eğitim
Basımevi, 1951), 108; Nafīsī, 362.

22. Ibid.

23. The catalog erroneously entitles this work *Kanz al-akhbār.*

24. Manisa İl Halk Kütüphanesi proof slips in the Süleymaniye
Kütüphanesi, Istanbul.

The treatise is divided into three parts. The first section is an exoteric exposition on the basic articles of faith. Simnānī states that it is necessary to believe in all the prophets, revealed books, the destination (*manzil*), path (*ṣirāṭ*), balance (*mīzān*), judgement (*ḥashr wa nashr*), the existence of angels and Jinn, and the vision of God's beauty in heaven. This is followed by a section on the fundamentals of religious practice (*uṣūl ad-dīn*) in which Simnānī provides a detailed description of the manner of prayer, fasting, alms-giving, *ḥajj* and *jihād*, with references to the multifarious opinions of significant legal scholars and Sufi masters. Simnānī describes *jihād* in its external and internal aspects as the lesser *jihād* and greater *jihād* respectively. This introduces the third part of the treatise which is concerned with the fundamentals of Sufism which comprise the rules of seclusion (*sharā'iṭ-i khalwat*) and a detailed description of *dhikr* and listening to music (*samā'*).

Fuṣūl al-uṣūl appears to be the title given by Simnānī to a revised version of the work. It is referred to as *Mā lā budda* in a *waṣiyya*, in *Farḥat al-'āmilīn* (Sha'bān 703/March 1304), and in *Ādāb as-sufra*.[25] However, there are references to *Ādāb as-sufra* in the Cairo manuscript of *Fuṣūl al-uṣūl* (60a–b). The work has been published by Hirawī under the title *Mā lā budda minhu fi'd-dīn*.[26]

5. *Kitāb al-qudsiyyāt* (Arabic).[27] The Book of Holy Inspiration.

MS. 165, Ṣehit Ali Paşa, Süleymaniye Kütüphanesi, Istanbul, fols. 168b–231a, copied by Ḍiyā' ad-dīn al-Malaṭī, the grandson of Simnānī's disciple 'Alī-yi Rūmī, in Ṣūfīyābād in Ṣafar 780/June 1378.*

A collection of twenty-four short treatises each bearing the title of *qudsiyya*, which seems to imply an inspired lecture or tract.[28] Each title consists of a place-name which is not exclusive to that *qudsiyya* but can be repeated a number of times. These place-names most probably refer to the *khanaqāhs* in which the treatises were composed. There are seven entitled *Qudsiyya baghdādiyya* (173b–75b; 175b–78a;

---

25. *Waṣiyya*, 11-mīm, Majāmi' fārsiyya, Dār al-kutub, Cairo, 245a; *Farḥat al-'āmilīn*, 58; *Muṣannafāt-i fārsī*, 175; *Ādāb as-sufra*, ed. Hirawī, *Muṣannafāt-i fārsī*, 12.

26. *Muṣannafāt-i fārsī*, 13–125.

27. Mentioned in *Maṭāf al-ashrāf* (79b); cf. the title *Qudsiyya* mentioned by Jāmī in the *Sharḥ qaṣīda-yi 'Aṭṭār* (Sadr, 107).

28. Cf. the *Qudsiyya* in MS. 1796, Veliyüddīn Efendi, Beyazit Kütüphanesi, Istanbul, folio 133a, which clearly states that Simnānī was inspired with it while engaged in ritual prayer (see below, p. 192).

184a–84b; 184b–86a; 193a–93b; 193b–95a; 195a–99b), one entitled *Qudsiyya baghdādiyya hurūliyya* (203b–11b), one *Qudsiyya hurūliyya baghdādiyya* (182a–84a), one *Qudsiyya simnāniyya* (200b–203a), two *Qudsiyya simnāniyya sakkākiyya* (172a–73b; 211b–27a), one *Qudsiyya sakkākiyya simnāniyya* (178b–81b), three *Qudsiyya sakkākiyya* (227b–29b; 229b–30a; 230b), three *Qudsiyya ṣūfīyābādiyya* (181b–82a; 199b–200b; 230b–31a), three *Qudsiyya rāhatābādiyya* (171b–72a; 178a–78b; 186a–87a), one *Qudsiyya sabzavāriyya* (187a–93a), and one entitled *Qudsiyya islāmābādiyya* (168b–71a).

Only four of the titles have any reference to the content of the treatises: describing subtle substances and faculties (*fī-bayān al-laṭā'if wa'l-quwā*, folios 168b–71a), concerning physical existence (*fī'l-wujūd*, folios 187a–93a), concerning the explanation of a station of the prophetic tradition (*fī-sharḥ mawqif min al-mawāqif al-āthāriyya*, folios 203b–11a), and a *Qudsiyya sakkākiyya* called in the spiritual realm the Mosques of Words and Monasteries of Sayings (*musammā fī'l-ghayb bi-jawāmi' al-kalim wa-ṣawāmi' al-ḥikam*, folios 211b–27a).[29]

6. *Bayān al-iḥsān li-ahl al-'irfān* (Arabic). The Exposition of Good Works for the People of Gnosis.

Variant title: *Bayān al-iḥsān li-ahl al-īqān*.

Locations:

1. MS. 11-mīm, Majāmī' fārsiyya, Dār al-kutub, Cairo, 78b–129b; part of a collection copied by Muḥammad b. Ibrāhīm b. Muḥammad 'Abd al-Ghafūr as-Simnānī, who completed the *majmū'a* at Qazwīn on 3 Rabī' I, 887/22 April 1482.*
2. MS. Or. 1925, British Museum, London, 3b–40b; part of a collection dated 894/1489 at Simnān.[30]
3. MS. 1188, Şehit Ali Paşa, Süleymaniye Kütüphanesi, Istanbul, folios 1b–55b, completed by 'Abd al-Muḥsin b. 'Abd al-Mu'min Ḥāfiẓ-i Shīrwānī on 22 Muḥarram 914/23 May 1508.*
4. MS. 2844r7, Kitābkhāna-yi Sipāhsālār, Tehran, 260b–321b.[31]
5. MS. 2914, Kitābkhāna-yi Sipāhsālār, Tehran, part of a collection copied by Muḥammad Ismā'īl-i Isfarajānī in 1234/1818–19.[32]

---

29. Mentioned as an independent treatise under this title in *Maṭāf al-ashrāf* (79b).

30. W. Thackston, ed., *Opera Minora* (Cambridge, MA: Harvard University, Office of the University Publisher, 1988), xiv.

31. Ḥaqīqat, *Khumkhāna*, 52; *Muṣannafāt-i fārsī*, xxxiii.

32. *Muṣannafāt-i fārsī*, xxxiv.

The *Bayān al-iḥsān* has been published (under its variant title of *Bayān al-iḥsān li-ahl al-īqān*) along with a study of Simnānī's life, works and thought by Nazif Şahinoğlu as a doctoral dissertation.[33] It has also been edited by Wheeler Thackston and N.M. Hirawī.[34]

This text was written for Simnānī's disciple, Abu'l-Mawāhib Muḥsin, of whom a brief biography is given in the beginning. It is divided into four chapters:

1. Theological and connected matters (*ilāhiyyāt wa-mā yata'allaqu bihā*).
2. Prophetic and related matters (*nabuwwāt wa-mā yuḍāfu ilayhā*).
3. Election and what is in accordance with it (*walāyat wa-mā yunāsibuhā*).
4. The manner of achieving the level of beneficence and attaining the world of certitude which is a sign of the final hour (*kayfiyyat-i huṣūl-i martaba-yi iḥsān wa wuṣūl bi 'ālam-i īqān ki ishārat-i sā'at ast*).

This treatise very closely resembles the *'Urwa* both in structure and in content and was completed on 19 Ramaḍān 713/7 January 1314 at Ṣūfīyābād-i Khudādād. It could conceivably represent an early draft of the *'Urwa*.

7. *al-Falāḥ li-ahl aṣ-ṣalāḥ* (Arabic). Success for the Righteous.
   Possible variants:
   > (a) *Risāla-yi falāḥ*[35]
   > (b) *Kitāb al-falāḥ*[36]
   MS. 3543, Chester Beatty Library, Dublin. 323 folios.
   Allegedly the first volume of a massive work on Islamic faith and life, this text is said by Sa'īd Nafīsī as being comprised of three volumes.[37] The copyist of the only known manuscript is Muḥammad b. al-Ḥusayn b. al-Ḥasan al-Iṣfahānī as-Simnānī, and the date 29 Sha'bān 735/24 April 1335. The scribe allegedly collated this copy with the autograph.[38] This work is mentioned in *Maṭāf al-ashrāf* (79a) and therefore dates from before 28 Ṣafar 714/13 June 1314.

---

33. See above, p. 11.
34. *Opera Minora*, 7–56; *Muṣannafāt-i fārsī*, 181–249.
35. Shushtarī, 2:137.
36. Nafīsī, 362.
37. Ibid., 363.
38. A.J. Arberry, *A Handlist of the Arabic Manuscripts in the Chester Beatty Library* (Dublin: Hodges, Figgis and Co., 1958), 3:20–21.

8. *al-Wārid ash-shārid aṭ-ṭārid bi-shubhat al-mārid* (Arabic). The Inspiration that refutes the Devil's Sophistry.

Variant titles:

> (a) *al-Wārid aṭ-ṭārid bi-shubhat al-mārid*[39]
> (b) *al-Wārid ash-shārid aṭ-ṭārid li-subhat al-mārid*[40]
> (c) *Madārij al-maʿārij fi'l-wārid aṭ-ṭārid bi-shubhat al-mārid*[41]
> (d) *Madārij al-maʿārij*[42]
> (e) *al-Madārij wa'l-maʿārij*[43]

Locations:

1. MS. A1588 (Catalog No. 5226), Topkapı Sarayı Müzesi Kütüphanesi, Istanbul, folios 13b–35b.*
2. MS. 606/5, Pertev Paşa, Süleymaniye Kütüphanesi, Istanbul, folios 66b–83a.*
3. MS. 933, Hekimoğlu Ali Paşa, Süleymaniye Kütüphanesi, Istanbul, folios 151b–72a, completed by Ibrāhīm al-Kudūshī on 21 Ramaḍān 1119/5 December 1707.*

The treatise is divided into four chapters:

a. A critical discussion of the ideas of Ibn Sīnā.
b. A discussion of the sayings of the philosophers (*muḥaqqiqīn*) concerning the spirit.
c. A discussion of the nature of the subtle human substance (*al-laṭīfa al-insāniyya*).
d. Elucidation of the path of truth (*ṭarīq al-ḥaqq*) from among the various paths.

The first three chapters are philosophical in nature. The fourth describes the events and decisions that lead to Simnānī's resolution to become a disciple of Nūr ad-dīn al-Isfarā'inī, and contains some valuable information on Simnānī's biography. The treatise was completed in 699/1299–1300 (when Simnānī was forty years old),

---

39. *Maṭāf al-ashrāf*, 79b; *Sirr bāl al-bāl li-dhawi'l-ḥāl*, 231b.

40. Brockelman, *Geschichte der Arabischen Litteratur* (Leiden: E.J. Brill, 1949), 2:263.

41. Nafīsī, 362; Sadr, 107.

42. *Fuṣūl al-uṣūl*, 57a; *Maṭāf al-ashrāf*, 79b; *Sirr bāl al-bāl*, 231b; Ṣafadī, 7:357; Ibn Ḥajar al-ʿAsqalānī, 1:266; *Hadiyyat al-ʿārifīn*, 1:108.

43. ʿUmār Riḍā Kaḥḥāla, *Muʿjam al-muʾallifīn*, s.v. "Aḥmad as-Simnānī."

sometime after Rajab of that year since his *Qawā'id al-'aqā'id* is referred to in this work (34b).

9. *Kitāb qawāṭi' as-sawāṭi'* (Arabic). The Screens of Radiance. Variant titles:
        (a) *Risāla fī-qawāṭi' as-sawāṭi'*
        (b) *Sawāṭi' al-qawāṭi'* [44]

Locations:
1. MS. 11-mīm, Majāmī' fārsiyya, Dār al-kutub, Cairo, folios 155b–83a, part of a collection copied by Muḥammad b. Ibrāhīm b. Muḥammad 'Abd al-Ghafūr as-Simnānī and completed at Qazwīn on 3 Rabī' I, 887/22 April 1482.*
2. MS. 1796, Veliyüddin Efendi, Beyazit Devlet Kütüphanesi, Istanbul, folios 97b–103b, dated 27 Ramaḍān 837/7 May 1434.*

Containing crucial elements of Simnānī's mystical thought arranged in twelve chapters (*sawāṭi'*). It is dated 703/1303–304 and has been edited by Thackston.[45]

10. *Kulliyāt-i dīwān-i ash'ār-i fārsī wa 'arabī*. Complete Works of Persian and Arabic Poetry.
Locations:
1. MS. 1554, Persian, Bibliothèque Nationale, Paris, 213 folios. The colophon states that it was completed on Tuesday, 24 Ramaḍān 736/6 May 1336 (two months and two days after Simnānī's death) in Ṣūfiyābād-i Khudādād and was allegedly compiled by a disciple of Simnānī by the name of Minhāj b. Muḥammad as-Sarāyī[46]
2. MS. 112, Elliot Collection, Bodleian Library, Oxford. 178 folios. Dated Shawwāl 864/July 1460. None of Simnānī's Arabic poetry is contained in this copy.*

Simnānī wrote a great deal of poetry, of which specimens appear in almost all his works, including his commentary on the Qur'ān. A collection of his poetical works was written in *dīwān* form by his

---

44. *Maṭāf al-ashrāf*, 79a; *Risālat al-ikhtiyār li-dhawī'l-i'tibār*, MS. 11-mīm, Majāmī' fārsiyya, Dār al-kutub, Cairo, 154a; mentioned by Simnānī in letter B II (p. 72) of his correspondence with Isfarā'inī (Landolt, *Correspondence*, 47–48, note 68); Ibn al-Karbalā'ī, 2:126.

45. *Opera Minora*, 83–110.

46. E. Blochet, *Catalogue des manuscrits persans dans la Bibliothèque Nationale* (Paris: Imprimerie nationale, 1905), 3:205.

student Minhāj b. Muḥammad as-Sarāyī. Excerpts from this *dīwān*
were published in *Khumkhāna-yi waḥdat* by 'Abd ar-Rafī' Ḥaqīqat.
It has since been published as a *dīwān* by the same scholar on the
basis of the Paris manuscript.[47]

The printed edition comprises 3,638 verses of poetry in Persian
and Arabic, more than two-thirds of them being in Persian. These are
in the form of 18 *qaṣīdas*, 255 *ghazals*, 541 *rubā'īs*, 10 *mathnawīs*,
one poem in *tarjī' band*, and the balance comprising shorter poems.
The 1,080 Arabic verses are all arranged in *ghazal* form.

Simnānī's pen-name of 'Alā' ad-dawla appears in many of the
Persian poems but in only one Arabic composition (492). However,
in light of the doctrinal content of these verses and their frequent
references to events, people and places in Simnānī's life, there can be
little doubt as to their authorship.

11. *Chihil majlis-i shaykh 'Alā' ad-dawla-yi Simnānī* (Persian).
Forty Assemblies of Shaykh 'Alā' ad-dawla as-Simnānī.
Variant titles:

(a) *Fawā'id*
(b) *Risāla-yi Iqbāliyya*[48]
(c) *Risāla-yi majālis*
(d) *Majālis-i arba'īn*

Locations:
Under the title of *Risāla-yi majālis*:
1. MS. 3455r281, Majlis-i shūrā-yi millī, Tehran.[49]

Under the title of *Fawā'id*:
2. MS. D.8(6), E.G. Browne, University Library, Cambridge.
    Undated.[50]

---

47. 'Abd ar-Rafī' Ḥaqīqat, editor, *Dīwān-i kāmil-i ash'ār-i fārsī wa 'ārabī-yi
shaykh 'Alā' ad-dawla-yi Simnānī* (Tehran: Shirkat-i mu'allifān wa
mutarjimān-i Īrān, 1985). Some poems by Simnānī are also found in MS. 1015,
Mishkāt, Kitābkhāna-yi dānishgāh, Tehran, folios 41–43, dated Dhu'l-qa'da
913/March 1508 ('Alīnaqī Munzawī-yi Tihrānī, *Fihrist-i kitābkhāna-yi
ahdā'ī-yi Āqā-yi Sayyid Muḥammad Mishkāt bi kitābkhāna-yi dānishgāh-
i Tihrān* (Tehran: Intishārāt-i dānishgāh-i Tihrān, 1951), 1:201–3).

48. Ibn al-Karbalā'ī; al-Khwānsārī al-Iṣbahānī, *Rawḍat al-jannāt* (Tehran:
Maktaba-yi Ismā'īlīyān, 1970), 8:69.

49. Ḥaqīqat, *Khumkhāna*, 54.

50. E.G. Browne and R.A. Nicholson, *A Descriptive Catalogue of the
Oriental Manuscripts belonging to the late E.G. Browne* (Cambridge: 1932).

3. MS. D.21, in the same collection, folios 90b–111b. Undated.
4. MS. 184, Būhār Library, Calcutta.[51]
5. Private collection, Jawād Kamālian.[52]
6. MS. 11-mīm Majāmīʿ fārsiyya, Dār al-kutub, Cairo, folios 248b–315b, part of a collection copied by Muḥammad b. Ibrāhīm b. Muḥammad ʿAbd al-Ghafūr as-Simnānī, who completed the *majmūʿa* at Qazwīn on 3 Rabīʿ I, 887/22 April 1482.*
7. MS. Or.1925, British Museum, London, folios 41b–89a. In a collection dated 894/1489 at Simnān.[53]

Under the title of *Chihil majlis*:
8. MS. 1446, Bodleian Library, Oxford.[54]
9. An uncataloged manuscript in the Kitābkhāna-yi majlis-i shūrā-yi millī, Tehran, preliminary no. 320.[55]
10. MS. 1, Fiqh ḥanafī fārsī, Dār al-kutub, Cairo, folios 11b–47a.*
11. MS. 1031, Islāmiyya College, Peshawar University, Peshawar, 220pp., dated 1005/1596–97.[56]
12. MS. 312/28, Kitābkhāna-yi Muḥammad Shafīʿ, Lahore, including 37 *majālis*.[57]
13. MS. 313/30 in the same collection. The colophon states that this manuscript is the autograph, written by Amīr Iqbāl b. Sābiq-i Sijistānī in 724/1323.[58]
14. MS. 1099/2, Tavşanlı Zeytinoğlu Kütüphanesi, Kütahya, pages 131–333, entitled *Majālis-i arbaʿīn* and dated 1095/1684.[59]

This is a collection of Simnānī's sayings put together by his student Iqbāl b. Sābiq-i Sīstānī (Sijistānī). Its primary importance is for the biography of Simnānī. Sīstānī left behind two collections, one

51. Mawlawī Qāsim Ḥasīr Riḍawī and Mawlawī ʿAbd al-Muqtadir, *Catalogue of the Persian Manuscripts in the Būhār Library* (Calcutta: 1921), no. 184.

52. H. Corbin, *Avicenne et le récit visionnaire* (Teheran-Paris: 1954), 1, 282.

53. *Opera Minora*, xiv.

54. Sachau and Ethé, *Catalogue of the Persian Manuscripts in the Bodleian Library* (Oxford: 1889).

55. Molé, "Les Kubrawiya," 79.

56. *Fihrist-i mushtarak-i nuskhahā-yi khaṭṭī-yi fārsī-yi Pākistān* (Islamabad: Markaz-i taḥqīqāt-i fārsī-yi Īrān wa Pākistān, 1984), entry no. 2527.

57. Ibid.

58. Ibid.

59. Tavşanlı Zeytinoğlu Kütüphanesi proof slips stored in the Süleymaniye Kütüphanesi, Istanbul.

entitled *Chihil majlis* (or *majālis*) and the other *Fawā'id*, which were later fused into a common redaction. The analytical study of H. Cordt sheds some illuminating light upon the stemma of the text.[60]

The *Chihil majlis* exists in three printed versions. The first, by 'Abd ar-Rafī' Ḥaqīqat, is a relatively poor copy based on MS. D.21, Brown, comprises fifty-nine *majālis*, and does not accurately reflect the original.[61] This problem has been discussed at some length by Najīb Māyil-i Hirawī in his introduction to the *'Urwa*.[62] The second edition by Hirawī constitutes the most accurate edition of the text.[63] A third version based upon the British Library and Dār al-kutub manuscripts has been published by Thackston.[64]

Minor Works

12. *Risāla-yi sirr-i samā'* (Persian). The Secret of Listening to Music. Possible variant: *Sirr jawāz as-samā'*.
     Locations:
  1. MS. 11-mīm, Majāmī' fārsiyya, Dār al-kutub, Cairo, folios 189b–93a, in a collection copied by Muḥammad b. Ibrāhīm b. Muḥammad 'Abd al-Ghafūr as-Simnānī, completed at Qazwīn on 3 Rabī' I, 887/22 April 1482.* Published by Hirawī on the basis of this manuscript.[65]
  2. MS. 1592, Bursa Genel Kütüphanesi, Bursa, folios 54a–61b, entitled *Sirr jawāz as-samā'*.

This treatise concerns *dhikr* and the efficacy and legality of listening to music (*samā'*). Simnānī gives his own opinion that *samā'* is dangerous for those not highly advanced on the mystical path, and mentions the legal positions of Abū Ḥanīfa and Shāfi'ī in support of his views. This is the first treatise Simnānī wrote after his formal

---

60. Cordt, 39ff. His analysis and German summary utilizes MSS. 2–5, 7 and 8.

61. Iqbāl-i Sīstānī, *Chihil majlis-i Shaykh 'Alā' ad-dawla-yi Simnānī*, edited by 'Abd ar-Rafī' Ḥaqīqat (Tehran: Shirkat-i mu'allifān wa mutarjimān-i Īrān, 1979).

62. *'Urwa*, 17–25.

63. *Chihil majlis* (Tehran: Intishārāt-i adīb, 1987).

64. *Opera Minora*, 175–244.

65. "Chahār guftār-i shaykh 'Alā' ad-dawla-yi Simnānī," *Dānish* 3 (1985), 3–70; *Muṣannafāt-i fārsī*, 1–6.

conversion to Sufism; it is also the earliest known treatise by him, dated 687/1288 (193a).

13. *Risāla dar taḥqīq-i anā'iyyat* (Persian). Treatise on the Realization of Selfhood.

Possible variant: *Mujmal aṣ-ṣanā'i' al-'alāniyya fī-bayān al-laṭīfa al-anā'iyya.*[66]

MS. Or. 9725, British Museum, London.[67]

Important for the development of concepts of selfhood or "I-ness" (*anā'iyya*) in his thought. Dated by Simnānī in Rajab 699/March–April 1300, and published by H. Landolt.[68]

14. *Qawā'id al-'aqā'id* (Arabic). Principles of the Creed.

Variant title: *Fawā'id al-'aqā'id.*[69]

MS. 11-mīm, Majāmī' fārsiyya, Dār al-kutub, Cairo, 244a, extract only.*

It was written for Tāj ad-dīn Muḥammad b. Abu'l-Qāsim Muḥammad al-Qushayrī in Rajab 699/April 1300.[70]

15. *Mawārid ash-shawārid* (Arabic). Destinations of the Helpless.
Variants: *Maqālāt mawārid ash-shawārid.*[71]
Locations:
  1. MS. 1796, Veliyüddin Efendi, Beyazit Devlet Kütüphanesi, Istanbul, folios 72b–94a.*
  2. MS. 11-mīm, Majāmī' fārsiyya, Dār al-kutub, Cairo, folios 147b–49b. Incomplete.*

A discussion of key mystical and religious concepts arranged in one hundred inspirations (*wārid*). It was completed on 4 Rajab 701/5 March 1302 (94a).

16. *Farḥat al-'āmilīn wa-furjat al-kāmilīn* (Persian). The Joy of the Laborers and Pleasure of Perfect Human Beings.
Locations:
  1. MS. 11-mīm, Majāmī' fārsiyya, Dār al-kutub, Cairo, folios 211b–27a, in a collection copied by Muḥammad b. Ibrāhīm b.

---

66. *Maṭāf al-ashrāf*, 79b.

67. G.M. Meredith-Owens, *Handlist of Persian Manuscripts: 1895–1966*, (London: 1968), 7.

68. Landolt, "Deux opuscules," 279–319.

69. *Maṭāf al-ashrāf*, 79b; *al-Wārid ash-shārid*, 34b; *Najm*, 90a; *Hadiyyat al-'ārifīn*, 108; Kaḥḥāla, s.v. "Aḥmad as-Simnānī."

70. Nafīsī, 362.

71. *Hadiyyat al-'ārifīn*, 1:108.

Muḥammad ʿAbd al-Ghafūr as-Simnānī and completed on 3
Rabīʿ I, 887/22 April 1482 at Qazwīn.*
2.   MS. 1592, Bursa Genel Kütüphanesi, Bursa, folios 123a–56a.
3.   MS. Or.1925, British Museum, London, folios 158b–72a, in a
     collection dated 894/1489 at Simnān.[72]

The work has been published by Hirawī based on the Dār al-
kutub manuscript.[73] A second edition has been prepared by
Thackston.[74]

The treatise was written in Shaʿbān 703/March 1304 at the
request of Simnānī's disciple ʿAzīz ad-dīn-i Dahistānī. It begins with
an outline of Dahistānī's mystical career, followed by a discussion of
the nature of the divine essence. This is followed by a tract on a person
engaged in the mystical quest and an explanation of ecstatic utterances
(*shaṭhiyyāt*), beginning with unacceptable ones and proceeding to
acceptable statements.

Simnānī begins to outline stages of revelation along the mystical
path, saying that he plans to discuss this matter further in a work
entitled *Ḥaqāʾiq ad-daqāʾiq* which his student Wajīh ad-dīn Abuʾl-
Maḥāsin ʿAbd Allāh asked him to write.

This is followed by a discussion of Allāh as the greatest of God's
names, and quotations from earlier Sufis and *ḥadīth* in support of his
view that any reality (*ḥaqīqat*) that is revealed is deception and
temptation if it is not in accordance with the Qurʾān and the Prophet's
tradition. Much of the material in this treatise appears similar to the
early parts of the *ʿUrwa*; this may represent yet another partial draft
of that work.

17.   *Hadiyyat al-mustarshidīn wa-waṣiyyat al-murshidīn* (Persian).
Gift for the Seekers of Guidance and Counsel for the Guides.
      Variant Title: *Risāla dar bāb-i dhikr.*
      Locations:
1.   MS. 11-mīm, Majāmiʿ fārsiyya, Dār al-kutub, Cairo, folios
     245a–48a.*
2.   MS. Or.1925, British Museum, London, folios 144b–47a. In a
     collection dated 894/1489 at Simnān.[75]

---

72. *Opera Minora*, xiv.
73. Hirawī, "Chahār guftār," 30–59; *Muṣannafāt-i fārsī*, 153–75.
74. *Opera Minora*, 135–50.
75. Ibid., xiv.

3. MS. 1796, Veliyüddin Efendi, Beyazit Devlet Kütüphanesi, Istanbul, folios 70b–71b.*

A brief treatise of guidance (*waṣiyya*), dated 705/1305–6. Published by Thackston.[76]

18. *Khitām al-misk* (Persian). The Crowning Touch [The Seal of Musk].

Locations:

1. MS. 11-mīm, Majāmī' fārsiyya, Dār al-kutub, Cairo, folios 141b–44b, in a collection copied by Muḥammad b. Ibrāhīm b. Muḥammad 'Abd al-Ghafūr as-Simnānī, completed at Qazwīn on 3 Rabī' I, 887/22 April 1482.*
2. MS. 1592, Bursa Genel Kütüphanesi, Bursa, folios 62a–69b.
3. MS. Or.1925, British Museum, London, folios 188b–91a, in a collection dated 894/1489 at Simnān.[77]

This work describes the greater spiritual purification (*aṭ-ṭahāra al-kubrā*) and the manner of its attainment. It was completed at Isfarā'inī's house on 9 Dhu'l-qa'da 712/8 March 1313.[78] It has been published by Thackston based upon the Cairo and London manuscripts.[79]

19. *Risāla fī-dhikr asāmī mashāyikhī* (Arabic). Treatise enumerating the Names of my Masters.

MS. 11-mīm, Majāmī' fārsiyya, Dār al-kutub, Cairo, folios 72a–76b.[80]*

This manuscript is allegedly copied from a larger work entitled *Kitāb al-falāḥ li-ahl aṣ-ṣalāḥ* (72a; see above, p. 173). In addition to being an account of Simnānī's Sufi affiliation, this treatise is extremely valuable for its biographical information. It also contains a list of mystics with whom Simnānī had met, and brief biographies of earlier Sufis. The treatise states that Isfarā'inī was born in 639/1241–42 and was seventy-three years old at the time of writing (76a–b); it can therefore be dated to 712/1312–13.

20. *Risāla fatḥ al-mubīn li-ahl al-yaqīn* (Persian). Clear Victory for the People of Certitude.

---

76. Ibid., 169–74.
77. Ibid., xiv.
78. Landolt, *Révélateur*, 92, note 62.
79. *Opera Minora*, 71–74; according to Thackston, the date of its completion is 714/1314.
80. Published by Thackston (*Opera Minora*, 1–5).

Possible variants:

      (a) *Kitābhā wa risālahā-yi miftāḥ*[81]
      (b) *Miftāḥ*[82]

Locations:

1. MS. 11-mīm, Majāmiʿ fārsiyya, Dār al-kutub, Cairo, folios 193b–211a, in a collection copied by Muḥammad b. Ibrāhīm b. Muḥammad ʿAbd al-Ghafūr as-Simnānī, completed at Qazwīn on 3 Rabīʿ I, 887/22 April 1482.*
2. MS. 1, Fiqh ḥanafī fārsī, Dār al-kutub, Cairo, folios 2b–11a.*
3   MS. 1592, Bursa Genel Kütüphanesi, Bursa, folios 70a–101b.
4   MS. 9863, Kitābkhāna-yi markazī-yi dānishgāh, Tehran.[83]

This treatise, written at the request of Akhī ʿIzz ad-dīn, contains a first-hand account of Simnānī's conversion and the experiences which led up to his induction into the Kubrawī order as a disciple of Isfarā'inī. It also contains guidance on the requirements of seclusion and a description of the mystical states (*ghaybāt*) which accompany its stages. The treatise also depicts the structure of the universe and the process of emanation that finds its conclusion in the spiritual human being.

An event that occurred on 11 Shawwāl 712/9 February 1313 is described in the treatise (209a). The work is mentioned in *Bayān al-iḥsān* (122a), and must therefore have been composed some time between Shawwāl 712/February 1313 and 19 Ramaḍān 713/7 January 1314. Published by N.M. Hirawī.[84]

21. *Manāẓir al-maḥāḍir li'n-nāẓir al-ḥāḍir* (Arabic). Views of the Assemblies for the Prepared Observer.

    Variant title:

      Manāẓir al-maḥāḍir li'l-munāẓir al-ḥāḍir.[85]

MS. 3973, Kitābkhāna-yi millī-yi malik, Tehran, dated 1047/1637–38 and collated with an autograph completed at Ṣūfīyābād on 29 Shaʿbān 713/19 December 1313.

Marijan Molé has published this work accompanied by a French translation.[86] The treatise is based in large part on quotations from

---

81. Sadr, 106.

82. Dawlatshāh, 251.

83. *Muṣannafāt-i fārsī*, xxxv.

84. Ibid., 252–75.

85. *Maṭāf al-ashrāf*, 79a.

86. Molé. "Un traité de ʿAlā' al-Dawla Simnānī sur ʿAlī b. Abī Ṭālib," *Bulletin d'études orientales* 16 (1958–60), 61–99. An offprint of this edition has been published (without reference to Molé) as *Manāẓir al-maḥāḍir li'l-munāẓir al-ḥāḍir* (Port Said: Maktabat ath-thiqāfa ad-dīniyya, n.d.).

the *Nahj al-balāgha*. It is similar in style and attitude to Simnānī's other works, combining reverence for the *ahl al-bayt* with condemnation of those who curse 'Ā'isha and the first three caliphs.

22.   *Sharḥ-i ḥadīth-i arwāḥ al-mu'minīn* (Persian). Explanation of the Tradition [beginning] "The Spirits of the Believers."
    Variants:
              Manhaj al-jumaḥ.[87]
    Locations:
1.   MS. 11-mīm, Majāmī' fārsiyya, Dār al-kutub, Cairo, folios 130a–36a.*
2.   MS. 2844, Kitābkhāna-yi sipāhsālār, Tehran, folios 321b–28a.[88]
3.   MS. Or.1925, British Museum, London, folios 280b–85b, in a collection dated 894/1489 at Simnān.[89]
4.   MS. 1796, Veliyüddin Efendi, Beyazit Devlet Kütüphanesi, Istanbul, folios 135a–37a, dated 29 Shawwāl 841/25 April 1438.*
    An incomplete and inaccurately edited version has been published by Hirawī[90] A second edition has been prepared by Thackston.[91] The treatise discusses the following *ḥadīth* dealing with the fate of the spirits of the believers after the destruction of the physical body:

$$\text{إنّ أرواح المؤمنين طير خضر تعلق في شجر الجنّة.}^{92}$$

The work was written at the request of Simnānī's disciple, Abu'l-Mawāhib Muḥsin, who knew this *ḥadīth* from the *Mashāriq al-anwār an-nabawiyya min-ṣiḥāḥ al-akhbār al-muṣṭafawiyya* of Raḍī ad-dīn Ḥasan b. Muḥammad aṣ-Ṣaghānī al-Lāhūrī (d. 650/1252).[93] The *ḥadīth* is listed with several variants, followed by a discussion. It was completed in Ṣūfīyābād-i Khudādād on 3 Dhu'l-Qa'da 713/19 February 1314.[94]

---

87. *Opera Minora.*
88. Hirawī, "Chahār guftār," 7.
89. *Opera Minora,* xiv.
90. "Chahār guftār," 17–21; *Muṣannafāt-i fārsī,* 177–80.
91. *Opera Minora,* 57–64.
92. "Indeed the spirits of the believers are green birds that derive sustenance from the trees of Paradise," (*Ṣaḥīḥ Muslim,* ed. M. Fu'ād 'Abd al-bāqī, 3:1503) (Hirawī, "Chahār guftār," 6).
93. Ḥājjī Khalīfa, *Kashf aẓ-ẓunūn* (Istanbul: Milli Eğitim Basımevi, 1971), 2:1688ff; Ibn al-Athīr, 2:242–43; Hirawī, "Chahār guftār," 6.
94. *Opera Minora,* 64.

23. *Maṭāf al-ashrāf* (Arabic). Circumambulation of the Illustrious.
MS. 353, Karaçelebizade, Süleymaniye Kütüphanesi, Istanbul, folios 78b–80a.*

An autobibliography of Simnānī's Arabic works. Simnānī claims that it occurred to him to compile a list of the titles of his Arabic books and treatises which would serve as guides on the mystical path. The titles are then enumerated within the framework of a series of instructions enjoining disciples which work to study for which purpose. It is dated 28 Ṣafar 714/13 June 1314 at Ṣūfīyābād-i Khudādād.

24. *Risāla fī-tafsīr āyāt qur'āniyya fī-mawḍū' aṣ-ṣabr wa'l-iḥsān* (Arabic and Persian). Treatise commenting upon Qur'ānic Verses concerning Patience and Beneficence.
Variant title:

Risāla fī'l-īmān wa'ṣ-ṣabr wa't-taqwā wa'l-iḥsān.
Locations:
1. MS. 11-mīm, Majāmī' fārsiyya, Dār al-kutub, Cairo, folios 136b–41a, in a collection copied by Muḥammad b. Ibrāhīm b. Muḥammad 'Abd al-Ghafūr as-Simnānī, completed at Qazwīn on 3 Rabī' I, 887/22 April 1482.*
2. MS. Or.1925, British Museum, London, folios 275b–80a, in a collection dated 894/1489 at Simnān.[95]

The work comprises a mystical explanation of the meaning of the terms *ṣabr* and *iḥsān* in the Qur'ānic context, and describes their importance on the mystical path. It was begun in Arabic but completed in Persian at the request of Simnānī's disciple, Abu'l-Mawāhib Muḥsin, who felt that this valuable piece of spiritual guidance would be accessible to a wider audience if written in the vernacular (137a). Simnānī wrote the treatise while in seclusion (*khalwa*) at Ṣūfīyābād-i Khudādād and completed it on 14 Shawwāl 714/21 January 1315. It has been edited by Thackston.[96]

25. *Risāla fī-ḥaṣr al-mawjūdāt* (Arabic). Treatise on the Enumeration of Existent Beings.
MS. 353/5, Karaçelebizade, Süleymaniye Kütüphanesi, Istanbul, folios 92b–93a.*

Arguing that existent beings (*mawjūdāt*) consist of two types: essential (*wājib*) and potential (*mumkin*). It is probably written in

---

95. Ibid., xiv.
96. Ibid., 65–70.

Simnānī's own hand and was completed in the Burj-i aḥrār at Ṣūfīyābād-i Khudādād in Jumāda II 720/July 1320.

26.   *Risāla ṣadā'if* [sic] *al-laṭā'if li-man fī-baḥr ad-dunyā bi-ka'bat al-qalb ṭā'if* (Persian). Seashells of Subtleties for One circumambulating the Ka'ba of the Heart in the Ocean of this World.
    Variant title: *Ḥadā'iq al-laṭā'if.*
    MS. 1, Fiqh ḥanafī farsī, Dār al-kutub, Cairo, folios 84b–87b.*
    This valuable treatise was written at the request of Simnānī's disciple, Abu'l-Mawāhib Muḥsin al-Aḥmadī, and is dated Thursday 20 Jumāda II 722/6 July 1322. It may be an autograph. The work purports to explain to the Persian reader the significance of the seven subtle substances of the spiritual body, and to discuss the subtle substance of I-ness (*laṭīfa-yi anā'iyyat*), the acquired body (*badan-i muktasab*) and the unfettered body (*badan-i maḥlūl*).

27.   *'Iqd durar al-asrār wa-'aqd 'arā'is al-akhbār* (Arabic). Necklace of the Pearls of Secrets and the Contract of the Brides of Tradition.
    MS. 685/1, Kasidecizade Efendi, Süleymaniye Kütüphanesi, Istanbul, folios 1b–10b.*
    A discussion of existence and eschatological symbolism, followed by an explanation of Junayd's conditions of seclusion. The work was completed on 6 Jumāda II 728/18 April 1328, and this manuscript is allegedly copied from the autograph.

28.   *Mathal an-nūr* and *Qudsiyya hurūliyya* (Arabic). The Likeness of Light.
    Locations:
  1. MS. 1796, Veliyüddin Efendi, Beyazit Devlet Kütüphanesi, Istanbul, folios 133b–34a, dated 841/1437-38.*
  2. MS. 2815, Şehit Ali Paşa, Süleymaniye Kütüphanesi, Istanbul, folios 112b–114a.*
    A brief treatise in which Simnānī emphasizes the correspondence between colored lights and the seven subtle substances. It was completed on either 24 Jumāda II 729/25 April 1329 or 14 Jumāda I 729/16 March 1329.

The following works cannot be dated with precision:

29.   *Jawhar al-asrār* (Arabic). The Essence of Secrets.
    Variant titles:
                (a) *Jawāhir al-asrār*
                (b) *Jawhar al-asrār al-murabbā fī-baḥr qulūb al-abrār*

Locations:
1. MS. 1796, Veliyüddin Efendi, Beyazit Devlet Kütüphanesi, Istanbul, folios 94a–95b, dated 8 Ramaḍān 837/18 April 1434.*
2. MS. 896, Gazi Husrev-Begova Biblioteka, Sarajevo, pp. 78–80, completed sometime after 994/1586.[97]

A cosmological treatise discussing the celestial and terrestrial elements (*al-mufradāt al-'ulwiyya wa's-sufliyya*). It is mentioned in *al-Wārid ash-shārid* (25a) and must therefore have been written before 699/1299–1300.

30.   *Risāla sirr bāl al-bāl li-dhawi'l-ḥāl* (Persian). The Secret of the Heart of Hearts for the Possessors of Mystical States.
      Variant titles:

> (a) *Risāla sirr al-bāl li-dhawī ahl al-ḥāl*[98]
> (b) *Sirr bāl al-bāl*[99]
> (c) *Risāla sirr bāl al-bāl fī-aṭwār sulūk ahl al-ḥāl*

      Locations:
1. MS. 11-mīm, Majāmī' fārsiyya, Dār al-kutub, Cairo, folios 227b–43b, entitled *Risāla sirr bāl al-bāl li-dhawi'l-ḥāl*, in a collection copied by Muḥammad b. Ibrāhīm b. Muḥammad 'Abd al-Ghafūr as-Simnānī, completed at Qazwīn on 3 Rabī' I, 887/22 April 1482.*
2. MS. FY564, İstanbul Üniversitesi Kütüphanesi, Istanbul, folios 143a–62b, entitled *Risāla sirr bāl al-bāl fī-aṭwār sulūk ahl al-ḥāl*.*
3. MS. 5863, Kitābkhāna-yi markazī-yi dānishgāh, Tehran.[100]
4. MS. Or.1925, British Museum, London, folios 172b–85a, in a collection completed at Simnān in 894/1489.[101]

This work was composed for 'Umar al-Jājarmī. It comprises a description of a mystical experience which Simnānī underwent during his retreat in Jumāda II 701/February 1302, and an explanation of some mystical technical terminology, including the soul, heart, mystery and various levels of theophany (*tajallī*). Published by Thackston and Hirawī[102]

---

97. Kasim Dobrača, *Katalog Arapskih, Turskih i Perzijskih Rukopisa*, Gazi Husrev-Begova Biblioteka, vol. 2 (Sarajevo: 1979), 90–96.
98. *Hadiyyat al-'ārifīn*, 1:108; Nafīsī, 362.
99. Şahinoğlu, *Türkiye Diyanet Vakfı İslam Ansiklopedisi*, s.v. "Alâuddevle-i Simnânî."
100. *Muṣannafāt-i fārsī*, xxix; cf. Sadr, who claims it is the autograph.
101. *Opera Minora*, xiv.
102. Ibid., 151–68; *Muṣannafāt-i fārsī*, 128–51.

31.   *Shaqā'iq al-ḥadạ'iq wa-ḥadā'iq al-ḥaqā'iq* (Arabic). Flowers of the Gardens and the Gardens of Realities.
     Variant titles:
          (a) *Shaqā'iq al-ḥadā'iq fī-sharḥ ḥadā'iq al-ḥaqā'iq fī-ishtiqāq al-jalāl*[103]
          (b) *Ḥadā'iq al-ḥaqā'iq wa-shaqā'iq ad-daqā'iq*[104]
          (c) *Shaqā'iq ad-daqā'iq wa-ḥadā'iq al-ḥaqā'iq*[105]
     Locations:
   1.   MS. 821/7, Halet Efendi, Süleymaniye Kütüphanesi, Istanbul, folios 76b–78b, possibly dated 5 Rabī' II 1029/29 February 1620.*
   2.   MS. 896, Gazi Husrev-Begova Biblioteka, Sarajevo, completed sometime after 994/1586.[106]
     A short but valuable treatise explaining the meaning of key mystical terms, and referring to each explanation as a *ḥadīqa* (garden). It is mentioned as *Ḥaqā'iq ad-daqā'iq* in *Farḥat al-'āmilīn wa-furjat al-kāmilīn* (220b) and must therefore date from before Sha'bān 703/March 1304.

32.   *Risālat al-ikhtiyār li-dhawi'l-i'tibār* (Arabic). Treatise on Free Will for People who have the Ability of Reflection.
     MS. 11-mīm, Majāmī' fārsiyya, Dār al-kutub, Cairo, folios 151b–54b.*
     On the mystical significance of various letters of the alphabet, with particular emphasis on the letter *alif*. The treatise refers to *Qawāṭi' as-sawāṭi'* (154a) and is mentioned in *Maṭāf al-ashrāf* (79b); it is therefore dated sometime between 703/1303–4 and 28 Ṣafar 714/13 June 1314.

33.   *Badā'i' aṣ-ṣanā'i'* (Arabic). Wonders of Artisanship.
     MS. 1796, Veliyüddin Efendi, Beyazit Devlet Kütüphanesi, Istanbul, folios 1b–44a.*
     A collection of mystical exhortations arranged in one hundred "arrangements" (*ṣan'a*), with frequent quotations from the Qur'ān. The work is mentioned several times in *Najm al-qur'ān* (87b, 152a, 158a) and in *Maṭāf al-ashrāf* (79a), and must therefore date from before 28 Ṣafar 714/13 June 1314.

---

     103. *Hadiyyat al-'ārifīn*, 1:108.
     104. *Maṭāf al-ashrāf*, 79b.
     105. Kasim Dobrača, *Katalog Arapskih, Turskih i Perzijskih Rukopisa*, Gazi Husrev-Begova Biblioteka, vol. 2 (Sarajevo: 1979), 90-96.
     106. Ibid.

34.   *Nuqṭa* (Persian). Point.
    Possible variant: *Nuqṭa dawā'ir al-wujūd li-ahl al-kashf wa'sh-shuhūd.*[107]
    MS. 96r3, Kitābkhāna-yi majlis-i sanāt, Tehran.
    A mystical interpretation of a noncanonical *ḥadīth* beginning *"anā nuqṭa taḥt al-bā'"* (I am the point under the letter *bā'*).[108] Possibly dated prior to 28 Ṣafar 714/13 June 1314.

35.   Untitled (Persian).
    MS. 1796, Veliyüddin Efendi, Beyazit Devlet Kütüphanesi, Istanbul, folios 51b–52a.*
    A lecture on life after death, written after the age of 69, and therefore no earlier than 728/1328.

36.   *Ādāb as-sufra* (Persian). Table Manners.
    Variant titles:
                    (a) *Ādāb sufrat as-safra*[109]
                    (b) *Ādāb-i sufra*[110]
    MS. 254, Majāmī' Ṭal'at, Dār al-kutub, Cairo.[111]
    A treatise outlining the correct manner of cooking, setting a table and washing one's hands. It is mentioned in *Fuṣūl al-uṣūl*, and has been published by Hirawī[112] It has also been translated into Arabic.[113]

37.   *Risāla fi'l-'aql wa'l-'ilm* (Persian). On Rational Thought and Religious Knowledge.
    MS. FY93, İstanbul Üniversitesi Kütüphanesi, Istanbul, folios 18b–19a.*
    A brief tract employing extensive quotations from *ḥadīth* to prove that religious knowledge (*'ilm*) is superior to rational thought (*'aql*).

38.   *Dhikr al-khafī al-mustajlib li'l-ajr al-wafī* (Persian).[114] Recollection of the Mystery which acquires the Perfect Reward.

----

    107. *Maṭāf al-ashrāf*, 79a.
    108. Ḥaqīqat, *Khumkhāna*, 55.
    109. *Hadiyyat al-muhtadī*, 82b.
    110. *Fuṣūl al-uṣūl*, 60a-b.
    111. Ḥaqīqat, *Khumkhāna*, 51.
    112. *Muṣannafāt-i fārsī*, 7–12; an inaccurate edition of this text was printed as an appendix to the *Tadhkira-yi Kajajī* (Shiraz: 1948).
    113. *Risāla ādāb as-sufra*, translated and edited by Sha'bān Rabī' Ṭarṭūr (Cairo: al-Hay'a al-miṣriyya al-'āmma li'l-kitāb, 1987).
    114. Mentioned in *Sirr bāl al-bāl*, 243b.

Variant titles:

> (a) *Risāla bayān dhikr al-khafī li'l-ajr al-wāfī*[115]
> (b) *Bayān adh-dhikr al-khafī al-mustajib al-ajr al-wāfī*[116]
> (c) *Risāla fi's-sulūk*

MS. FY1056, İstanbul Üniversitesi Kütüphanesi, Istanbul, folios 104b–109a, dated Rabī' II, 940/October 1533; missing folio 106.*

Intended as a piece of spiritual counsel (*waṣiyya*) for all mystics (108b), the work consists of an exhortation to *dhikr*, using ten quotations from the Qur'ān and *ḥadīth* to support the arguments presented therein. It also contains advice on the correct attitude towards property, family and the consumption of food.

39.   *Risāla durar ad-dar* (Arabic). On the Pearls of Achievement.

MS. 1796 Veliyüddin Efendi, Beyazit Devlet Kütüphanesi, Istanbul, folios 45b–48b.*

A discussion of the macrocosmic and microcosmic realms (*al-'ālam al-kabīr wa'ṣ-ṣaghīr*).

40.   *Hadiyyat al-muhtadī wa-hidāyat al-mubtadi'* (Arabic). Gift of the Rightly Guided and Guidance for the Beginner.

Variant title: *Hadiyyat al-muntahī wa-hidāyat al-mubtadī.*

MS. 353, Karaçelebizade, Süleymaniye Kütüphanesi, Istanbul, folios 80b–86a.[117]*

Important for Simnānī's biography. It was written at the request of one of his disciples, with the stated goal of explaining the differences between various religious paths. It discusses the shortcomings of different religions, sects and theological schools and explains why Sufism and Sunnism are the best courses. The colophon states that this is an extract from a longer work entitled *Taḥiyyat al-mubtadī wa-hadiyyat al-muntahī*, which is also mentioned in Simnānī's treatise entitled *Maṭāf al-ashrāf* (79a). It bears neither a date nor the name of a scribe, but is written in the same hand as the following treatise which is dated Muḥarram 792/December 1389.

41.   *Ḥall al-'iqāl* (Persian). Explanation of the Ambiguous.

Variant title: *Ḥall al-'iqāl fī-tahdhīb an-nufūs.*

---

115. *Fuṣūl al-uṣūl*, 74a.

116. *Hadiyyat al-'ārifīn*, 1:108.

117. The treatise begins with the variant title but the correct form appears within the text (86a).

MS. 2248, Persian, Bibliothèque Nationale, Paris, 113 folios, prepared in 886/1481–82 for a certain 'Alā' ad-dīn Tülük-Timur.

An explanation of technical vocabulary. It is allegedly Simnānī's own translation of a work by the same title that he had originally written in Arabic. The lengthier title *Ḥall al-'iqāl fī-tahdhīb an-nufūs* has been written on folio 3 at some later point.[118]

42. *Ḥāshiya-yi marmūzāt* (Arabic). Commentary on the Allusions.
MS. 1262/30, Mishkāt, Kitābkhāna-yi dānishgāh, Tehran, folios 120a–22a.

Allegedly a fragmentary commentary on the *Kitāb al-marmūzāt al-'ishrīn* of Ṣadr ad-dīn Abu'l-Ma'ālī al-Muẓaffar al-'Adawī al-Baghnawī (d. 688/1289).[119]

43. *Irshād al-mu'minīn* (Persian). Guidance for the Believers.
MS. 855, Taṣawwuf (catalog no. 1666), Āṣifiyya, Hyderabad, dated 855/1451.[120] It is probably an *ijāza*.

44. *Irshād nāma* (Persian). Letter of Guidance.
MS. 4137r20, Kitābkhāna-yi malik, Tehran.[121] An *ijāzā*.

45. *Risāla fi'l-jam' wa't-tafriqa*. Concerning Union and Separation.
MS. 896, Gazi Husrev-Begova Biblioteka, Sarajevo, pp. 80–82, completed sometime after 994/1586.[122]

A collection of sayings of earlier Sufis concerning the significance of the terms 'union' (*jam'*) and 'separation' (*tafriqa*).

46. *Lama'āt* (Persian). Flashes.
MS. 6096r14, Kitābkhāna-yi malik, Tehran.

----

118. E. Blochet, *Catalogue des manuscrits persans dans la Bibliothèque Nationale* (Paris: Imprimerie nationale, 1905), 4:196.

119. M. Taqī Dānishpazhūh, ed., *Fihrist-i kitābkhāna-yi ihdā'ī-yi āqā-yi Sayyid Muḥammad Mishkāt bi kitābkhāna-yi dānishgāh-i Tihrān* (Tehran: Chāpkhāna-yi dānishgāh, 1959), 3:5:2674; *Kashf aẓ-ẓunnūn*, 2:1658.

120. *Fihrist-i kutub-i 'arabī wa fārsī wa urdū makhzūna-yi kutubkhāna-yi Āṣifiyya-yi Sarkār-i Ilāhī*, vol. 4 (Hyderabad: Maṭbū'a-yi kār-i 'ālī, 1936), 178–79; Ḥaqīqat, *Khumkhāna*, 51.

121. Ḥaqīqat, *Khumkhāna*, 51–52.

122. Kasim Dobrača, *Katalog Arapskih, Turskih i Perzijskih Rukopisa*, Gazi Husrev-Begova Biblioteka, vol. 2 (Sarajevo: 1979), 90–96.

A collection of five short, mystical tracts in prose and poetry, each entitled a *lum'a*. They were allegedly compiled by a Turkish poet named Hakkı Efendi, in a book entitled *al-Majmū'a al-'irfāniyya*, and have been reproduced by Hirawī.[123]

47.   *Risāla miṣbāḥ ahl as-sunna* (Arabic). The Lamp for the People of Tradition.
    Possible variant: *Manhaj al-bālighīn*.[124]
    MS. 896, Gazi Husrev-Begova Biblioteka, Sarajevo, pp. 54–65, completed sometime after 994/1586.[125]
    A selection of sayings from the *Kitāb minhāj al-'ābidīn ila'l-janna* of Aḥmad al-Ghazzālī.

48.   *Risāla-yi nūriyya* (Persian). Treatise on Illumination.
    Variant titles: *Risālat al-anwār*.
    Possible variant: *Nūr an-nūr wa-surūr al-muṭṭali' 'alā-asrār al-mastūr*.[126]
    Locations:
 1.   MS. 1796, Veliyüddin Efendi, Beyazit Devlet Kütüphanesi, Istanbul, folios 109b–12b, possibly dated 841/1437–38.*
 2.   MS. 4409, Kitābkhāna-yi Ganjbakhsh, Islamabad, pages 751–62, in a collection of works by 'Alī-yi Hamadānī, compiled in 851/1447.[127]*
 3.   MS. 1105, Carullah Efendi, Süleymaniye Kütüphanesi, Istanbul, folios 44a–48b, entitled *Risālat al-anwār* and dated Sha'bān 899/May 1494.*
 4.   MS 4274, Kitābkhāna-yi dānishgāh, Tehran.[128]
 5.   Private collection of 'Ārif Nawshāhī. This inaccurate manuscript was copied by Muḥammad Ghanī, a disciple of Akhund Darwīza-yi Nangarhārī (d. 1048/1638–39), and completed on 16 Dhu'l-Ḥijja 1048/10 April 1639.*
A valuable treatise describing the varieties of light and their properties as encountered on the mystical path. It was written at the request of Simnānī's disciple, Muḥammad-i Khurd. This work has

---

123. *Muṣannafāt-i fārsī*, xli–xlii, 419–21.

124. *Maṭāf al-ashrāf*, 79b.

125. Kasim Dobrača, *Katalog Arapskih, Turskih i Perzijskih Rukopisa*, Gazi Husrev-Begova Biblioteka, vol. 2 (Sarajevo: 1979), 90–96.

126. *Maṭāf al-ashrāf*, 79a.

127. The catalog erroneously lists this treatise as ending on p. 756.

128. Hirawī, "Kitābshināsī," 183.

been variously attributed to Shihāb ad-dīn as-Suhrawardī, 'Alī-yi Hamadānī and 'Alā' ad-dawla as-Simnānī.[129] An incomplete and inaccurate edition based on the Tehran and Islamabad manuscripts has been published by Hirawī.[130]

49.   *Qudsiyya* (Arabic). Holy Inspiration.
       MS. 1796, Veliyüddin Efendi, Beyazit Devlet Kütüphanesi, Istanbul, folios 48b–49b.*
       A discussion of things existing in the contingent realm ('*ālam al-imkān*).

50.   *Qudsiyya* (Arabic). Holy Inspiration.
       MS. 1796, Veliyüddin Efendi, Beyazit Devlet Kütüphanesi, Istanbul, folios 52b–53a.*
       Concerning the celestial pen and ink pot.

51.   *Qudsiyya* (Arabic). Holy Inspiration.
       MS. 1796, Veliyüddin Efendi, Beyazit Devlet Kütüphanesi, Istanbul, folio 133a–b.*
       Concerning the inner and outer senses. Revealed to Simnānī while he was performing ritual prayers in the Burj al-aḥrār at Ṣūfīyābādi Khudādād.

52.   *Rijāl al-ghayb*. Men of the Unseen.
       MS. 2964/19, Manisa İl Halk Kütüphanesi, Manisa, folios 103–6.[131]

53.   *Salwat al-'āshiqīn wa-saktat al-mushtāqīn* (Persian). Solace of the Lovers and Silence of the Friends.
       Variant titles:
                    (a) *Salwat al-'āshiqīn*[132]
                    (b) *Salwat al-'āshiqīn wa-sakīnat al-mushtāqīn*

---

129. This issue is discussed at some length by Hirawī in "Chahār naẓar-i pīrāmūn-i chahār athar-i mansūb bi Sayyid 'Alī-yi Hamadānī" (*Dānish* 11 [1988], 90–116). Cf. Muḥammad Riyāḍ, *Aḥwāl-u āthār-u ash'ār-i Mīr Sayyid 'Alī-yi Hamadānī* (Islamabad: Markaz-i taḥqīqāt-i fārsī-yi Īrān wa Pākistan, 1985), 160ff., where this treatise is attributed to 'Alī-yi Hamadānī.
130. *Muṣannafāt-i fārsī*, 301–11. An annotated English translation by the author appears in *Muslim World* 83 (1993), 68–80.
131. Manisa İl Halk Kütüphanesi proof sheets in the Süleymaniye Kütüphanesi, Istanbul.
132. Ḥaqīqat, *Khumkhāna*, 53.

(c) *Salwat al-'āshiqīn wa-sakat al-mushtāqīn*[133]
(d) *Salwat al-'āshiqīn wa-sakīnat al-mushtāqīn*[134]
(e) *Sukūt al-'āshiqīn*

Locations:
1. MS. 1667, Taṣawwuf, Kitābkhāna-yi Āṣifiyya, Hyderabad, dated 855/1451, entitled *Sukūt al-'āshiqīn*.[135]
2. MS. 1592, Bursa Genel Kütüphanesi 1592, Bursa, folios 22a–53a. This copy is preserved under the title *Salwat al-'āshiqīn wa-sakīnat al-mushtāqīn* and dated 21 Shawwāl 877/21 March 1473.
3. MS. 9863, Kitābkhāna-yi markazī-yi dānishgāh, Tehran.[136]

Containing much information on the conditions and practices of *dhikr*, as well as sayings of earlier Sufi figures, in particular 'Alī-yi Lālā, Ahmad-i Gūrpānī, Majd ad-dīn al-Baghdādī and Abū Sa'īd b. Abi'l-Khayr. An edition of this treatise has been published by Hirawī.[137]

54. *Sharḥ ādāb al-baḥth* (Arabic). Commentary on the Art of Discourse.

MS. 616/7, Tavşanlı Zeytinoğlu Kütüphanesi, Kütahya, folios 179–95, copied by Yūsuf 'Alī Astarābādī in 734/1334–35.[138]

55. *Sharḥ fuṣūṣ al-ḥikam*. Commentary on the Bezels of Wisdom. Possible variants:

(a) *Hawāshī bar futūḥāt*[139]
(b) *Maftūḥat al-futūḥāt*[140]

MS. 11:2350, Kitābkhāna-yi dānishgāh, Tehran.[141]

Simnānī's commentary on the *Fuṣūṣ al-ḥikam* of Ibn al-'Arabī is potentially an extremely valuable work. Unfortunately only a fragmentary copy of it is known to exist, with a commentary by an anonymous student of Kāshānī and Dāwūd-i Qayṣarī.[142]

---

133. Sadr, 101; Haqīqat, *Khumkhāna*, 50.

134. Nafīsī, 362.

135. *Fihrist-i kutub-i 'arabī wa fārsī wa urdū makhzūna-yi kutubkhāna-yi Āṣifiyya-yi Sarkār-i Ilāhī*, vol. 4 (Hyderabad: Matbū'a-yi kār-i 'ālī, 1936), 182–83.

136. *Muṣannafāt-i fārsī*, xxxvi.

137. Ibid., 277–300.

138. Tavşanlı Zeytinoğlu Kütüphanesi proof sheets in the Süleymaniye Kütüphanesi, Istanbul.

139. Jāmī, *Nafaḥāt* and *Tafsīr-i qaṣīda-yi 'Attār* (Sadr, 106); Ma'ṣūm 'Alī Shāh, 1:324; al-Khwānsārī al-Isbahānī, 8:55–56.

140. *Maṭāf al-ashrāf*, 79a.

141. Haqīqat, *Khumkhāna*, 54.

142. Ibid.

56.   *Risāla-yi shaṭranjiyya* (Persian). Chess Treatise.
      Variant title: *Risāla dar asrār-i shaṭranj.*
      Locations:
   1. MS. 1796, Veliyüddin Efendi, Beyazit Devlet Kütüphanesi, Istanbul, folios 106b–7b.*
   2. MS. 441, Ḥikmat, Kitābkhāna-yi markazī-yi riḍawī, Mashhad.
   3. MS. Persian 162, Library of the University of Cambridge, Cambridge, folios 232–34.[143]
   4. Private collection of the author. This is an inaccurate copy which bears no date but appears to have been written no earlier than the twelfth/eighteenth century.*
   5. MS. 11-mīm, Majāmī' fārsiyya, Dār al-kutub, Cairo, folios 316b–17b. An incomplete copy.*
      A discussion of mysticism using the symbolism of a chessboard. Published by N.M. Hirawī.[144]

57.   *Shurūṭ-i khalwat* (Persian). Conditions of Seclusion.
      Possible variants:
    (a) *Risāla fī-ādāb al-khalwa*[145]
    (b) *Risālat at-taṣawwuf fī-ādāb al-khalwa*[146]
    (c) *Kitāb ādāb al-khalwa*[147]
      Locations:
   1. MS. 3660r18, Kitābkhāna-yi majlis, Tehran, dated 916/1510–11 and allegedly copied from the autograph.[148]
   2. MS. 151/6, Persian, Bibliothèque Nationale, Paris, folios 19b–49b.

58.   *Risāla fī-ṭabaqāt aṣ-ṣūfiyya* (Persian). Classes of Sufis.
      MS. 1796, Veliyüddin Efendi, Beyazit Devlet Kütüphanesi, Istanbul, folios 108a–109a.*
      Explaining five hierarchical categories of Sufis.

59.   *Tadhkirat awliyā' Allāh taʿālā* (Arabic). Record of the Saints of God.

---

143. C.A. Storey, *Persian Literature: A Bio-bibliographic Survey*, vol. 2, part 3 (Leiden: E.J. Brill, 1977), 388.

144. "Chahār guftār," 22–29; *Muṣannafāt-i fārsī*, 323–28.

145. *Hadiyyat al-ʿarifīn*, 1:108; Kaḥḥāla, s.v. "Aḥmad as-Simnānī"; Nafīsī, 362.

146. E. Blochet, *Catalogue des manuscrits persans dans la Bibliothèque Nationale* (Paris: Imprimerie nationale, 1905), 1:104.

147. *Lughatnāma*, s.v. "'Alā' ad-dawla-yi Simnānī"; *Aʿyān ash-shīʿa*, s.v. "Aḥmad b. Muḥammad as-Simnānī."

148. Ḥaqīqat, *Khumkhāna*, 52.

MS. 896, Gazi Husrev-Begova Biblioteka, Sarajevo, pp. 65–77, completed sometime after 994/1586.[149]

A collection of sayings of earlier Sufis ostensibly compiled by Simnānī.

60. *Tadhkirat al-mashāyikh* (Persian). Record of the Masters.
Ms. 159/10, Bibliothèque Nationale, Paris, 231b–36a.[150]
Valuable for Simnānī's mystical affiliation through the Kubrawī line. Several kinds of chains of investiture are mentioned, including those of seclusion (*inziwā wa khalwat*), discipleship (*ṣuḥbat*) and distinctive kinds of Sufi robes. Edited by Muḥammad Taqī Dānishpazhūh and subsequently revised by N.M. Hirawī[151]

61. *Tanbīh al-murīdīn*. Admonition for the Seekers.
Locations:
 1. MS. A793, Catalog no. 871, Oriental Institute, Tashkent.[152]
 2. MS. C1817, Catalog no. 872, Oriental Institute, Tashkent.[153]

62. *Wārid* (Arabic). Inspiration.
MS. 1796, Veliyüddin Efendi, Beyazit Devlet Kütüphanesi, Istanbul, folios 52a–52b.*
Arguing that the Sufi is better than the begging ascetic (*faqīr*).

63. *Wārid* (Arabic). Inspiration.
MS. 1796, Veliyüddin Efendi, Beyazit Devlet Kütüphanesi, Istanbul, folio 52b.*
Stating that all things have two dimensions.

64. *Risāla-yi wārida-yi qudsiyya* (Persian). Treatise of Holy Inspirations.
MS. 11-mīm, Majāmī' fārsiyya, Dār al-kutub, Cairo, folios 76b–78a.*
A brief philosophical treatise in Arabic enumerating entities in the contingent world ('ālam al-imkān).

---

149. Kasim Dobrača, *Katalog Arapskih, Turskih i Perzijskih Rukopisa*, Gazi Husrev-Begova Biblioteka, vol. 2 (Sarajevo: 1979), 90–96.

150. E. Blochet, *Catalogue des manuscrits persans dans la Bibliothèque Nationale* (Paris: Imprimerie nationale, 1905), 1:125.

151. "Khirqa-yi hazār mīkhī," 147–178; *Muṣannafāt-i fārsī*, 313–22.

152. A.A. Semenov, *Tashkent Academy Catalog* (in Russian), 10 vols. (Moscow: 1952–73), 1:133.

153. Ibid., 134.

A number of minor treatises by Simnānī were written either in Arabic or in Persian as spiritual counsel (*waṣiyya*) for his disciples. The following works are distinct from each other but follow a similar pattern in their content:

65.   *Waṣāya-yi awliyā'* (Persian). Guidance of the Saints.
       MS. 1592, Bursa Genel Kütüphanesi, Bursa, folios 102a–107b.

66.   *Waṣāya* (Arabic). Spiritual Guidance.
       MS. A1588 (Catalog no. 5226), Topkapı Sarayı Müzesi Kütüphanesi, Istanbul, folios 35b–38a.*
       This work is divided into four chapters, each containing ten *waṣiyyas*. The chapters are:
    1.   Concerning employment (*khidma*).
    2.   Concerning isolation ('*uzla*).
    3.   Concerning companionship (*ṣuḥba*)
    4.   Concerning contentment (*riḍā*) and abiding (*baqā'*).
       The tenth *waṣiyya* of the second chapter contains detailed instruction on how mystics should pass each of their waking hours and how long they should sleep.

67.   *Zayn al-mu'taqad li-zayn al-mu'taqid* (Persian). The Beauty of Doctrine for the Adornment of the Believers.
       Locations:
    1.   MS. 290.1706, Mevlânâ Müdesi Kütüphanesi, Konya, 41 fols., copied between 833/1430 and 840/1437, and allegedly collated with the autograph.[154]
    2.   MS. Or. 9725, British Museum, London.[155]

68.   Extract in Arabic entitled *Min al-ma'ārif* in MS. 11-mīm, Majāmī' fārsiyya, Dār al-kutub, Cairo, folio 244.*

69.   Untitled, beginning with the word *laṭīfa* (Arabic).
       MS. 353, Karaçelebizade, Süleymaniye Kütüphanesi, Istanbul, folios 86b–88b, copied by Muḥammad al-Jayrān, and dated the end of Muḥarram 792/January 1390.*
       It discusses key mystical concepts including God (*al-ḥaqq*), His creation of the physical world as a mirror for His essence, attributes

---

154. A. Gölpınarlı, *Mevlânâ Müzesi Yazmalar Kataloğu*, vol. 2 (Ankara: Türk Tarih Kurumu Basımevi, 1971), 15.
155. F. Meier, *Abū Sa'īd-i Abū l-Ḥayr*, 172, note 142, states that this is a Persian version of *al-Wārid ash-shārid*.

and His actions, and His creation of microcosmic finite time (*az-zamān al-āfāqī*) and macrocosmic spiritual time (*az-zamān al-anfusī*).

70.   Untitled (Arabic).
       Possible title: *Risālat at-tawḥīd wa-maʿrifat al-ʿilm al-ludanī*.
       MS. 1796, Veliyüddin Efendi, Beyazit Devlet Kütüphanesi, Istanbul, folios 53b–63a, in a collection of treatises dated Ṣafar 834/October 1430.*

71.   Untitled (Arabic).
       MS. 1796, Veliyüddin Efendi, Beyazit Devlet Kütüphanesi, Istanbul, folios 44b–45b.*
       An explanation of the term *kashf* (unveiling).

72.   Untitled (Arabic).
       MS. 1796, Veliyüddin Efendi, Beyazit Devlet Kütüphanesi, Istanbul, folios 96a–97a, dated 10 Ramaḍān 837/20 April 1434.*
       Concerning the supremacy of the letter *alif*.

73.   Untitled (Arabic).
       MS. 1796, Veliyüddin Efendi, Beyazit Devlet Kütüphanesi, Istanbul, folios 96a–97a, dated 10 Ramaḍān 837/20 April 1434.*
       A disjointed treatise outlining the mystical journey of the heart and soul, emphasizing the concept of love (*maḥabba*) with special reference to the prophet Yūsuf (Joseph).

74.   Untitled (Arabic).
       Locations:
   1. MS. 11-mīm Majāmiʿ fārsiyya, Dār al-kutub, Cairo, folios 145a–47a.*
   2. MS. 1796, Veliyüddin Efendi, Beyazit Devlet Kütüphanesi, Istanbul, folio 113a–b.*
       Information about events in Simnānī's life (147a). In addition to biographical data, it contains a list of Sufis with whom he met or to whom he felt indebted. Published by Thackston.[156]

75.   Untitled (Arabic).
       Possible titles:
                              (a) *Kashf sirr at-tajallī* [157]
                              (b) *at-Tajalliyyāt* [158]

---

156. *Opera Minora*, 75–77.
157. *al-Wārid ash-shārid*, 25b.
158. Sadr, 107.

MS. 2077 Carullah Efendi, Süleymaniye Kütüphanesi, Istanbul, folios 70b–71a.*
Dealing with divine manifestation during *dhikr*.

76.   Untitled (Arabic).
MS. 1796, Veliyüddin Efendi, Beyazit Devlet Kütüphanesi, Istanbul, folio 51b.*
A brief lecture on the physical body.

77.   Untitled (Persian).
MS. 1183/7, Yeni Camii, Süleymaniye Kütüphanesi, Istanbul, folios 225b–226b.*
Deals with the virtues of silent *dhikr*, with reference to the teachings of earlier Kubrawī masters such as 'Ammār al-Bidlīsī, Najm ad-dīn al-Kubrā and Majd ad-dīn al-Baghdādī.

78.   Untitled (Persian).
Private collection of Sa'īd Nafīsī, recently transferred to the Kitābkhāna-yi markazī-yi dānishgāh, Tehran, and as yet uncataloged.[159]
Approximately fifty pages long; Mozaffer Sadr has reproduced the beginning and end of this work in his study on Simnānī.[160]

79.   Untitled.
Majmū'a No. 14, Dānishkada-yi ilāhiyyāt, Tehran, folios 359b–73a.[161]

Correspondence

1.   Correspondence with Nūr ad-dīn al-Isfarā'inī.
Simnānī corresponded with Isfarā'inī without interruption from before their initial meeting until the latter's death in 717/1317. The major portion of the letters exchanged between them has been published along with an introductory study of both individuals by H. Landolt.[162] These letters are contained in two collections entitled

---

159. Ḥaqīqat, *Khumkhāna*, 50.
160. Sadr, 102.
161. Landolt, *Révélateur*, 92, note 62.
162. Hermann Landolt, ed., *Correspondence spirituelle échangée entre Nuroddin Esfarayeni et son disciple 'Alaoddawleh Semnani*, Le departement d'iranologie de l'institut franco-iranien de recherche, no. 21 (Tehran: L'institut franco-iranien de recherche, 1972).

Majmū'a-yi rasā'il an-nūr fī-shamā'il ahl as-surūr and *Kitāb al-maktūbāt.*[163]

Two additional letters which form part of this correspondence are preserved separately in MS. Or. 9725, British Museum, London, and have been published by Landolt.[164] This exchange dates from after Simnānī's trip to Baghdad and initiation into the Kubrawiyya by Isfarā'inī in Ṣafar 689/February 1290, but before the composition of the *Mashāri' abwāb al-quds* (711/1312) and the *'Urwa.*[165]

Some further correspondence between Simnānī and Isfarā'inī is found in the following locations:

1. MS. 1592, Bursa Genel Kütüphanesi, Bursa, folios 108a–22b, dated 717/1317–18.
2. MS. I,4120, İsmail Saib Kütüphanesi, Ankara, folios 145b–48a.
3. MS. 1796, Veliyüddin Efendi, Beyazit Devlet Kütüphanesi, Istanbul, folios 49b–51a.*
4. MS. 11-mīm, Majāmī' fārsiyya, Dār al-kutub, Cairo, 187b.*
5. MS. 1431/3, Esat Efendi, Süleymaniye Kütüphanesi, Istanbul.

2. Correspondence with 'Abd ar-Razzāq al-Kāshānī.

Simnānī's dialogue with one of the most famous proponents of Ibn al-'Arabī's thought is an important subsection of his corpus providing insight into Simnānī's attitudes towards *waḥdat al-wujūd.* Two letters and two replies exchanged with Kāshānī are preserved in MS. 3455r279, Kitābkhāna-yi majlis-i shūrā, Tehran.[166] This exchange has been published in German translation along with an analytical study by Landolt.[167] Other portions of their correspondence are found in MS. 4190r14, Kitābkhāna-yi millī-yi malik, Tehran, and MS. 1835,

163. Landolt, *Révélateur,* 10; Ḥaqīqat, *Khumkhāna,* 56.

164. Hermann Landolt, "Deux opuscules de Semnānī sur le moi théophanique," *Mélanges offerts à Henry Corbin* (Tehran: 1977), 279–319; G.M. Meredith-Owens, *Handlist of Persian Manuscripts, 1895–1966* (London: 1968), 7.

165. Landolt, "Deux opuscules," 279–80.

166. A.H. Haeri, *Fihrist-i kitābkhāna-yi majlis-i shūrā-yi millī* (Tehran: 1969), 10:3:1376ff.

167. Hermann Landolt, "Der Briefwechsel zwischen Kāshānī und Simnānī über Waḥdat al-Wuǧūd," *Der Islam* 50 (1973), 29–81. Landolt has also published a shorter English version of this study minus the translated texts as "Simnânî on Waḥdat al-wujûd," *Wisdom of Persia, Collected Papers on Islamic Philosophy and Mysticism,* edited by H. Landolt and M. Mohaghegh (Tehran: La branche de Téhéran de l'institut des études islamiques de l'Université McGill, 1971), 93–111.

Persian, India Office Library, London,[168] and the *Laṭā'if-i ashrafī* of
Ashraf Jahāngīr-i Simnānī.[169] One exchange of letters from these
sources has been published by Hirawī.[170]

3.   One exchange of letters between Simnānī and Ḥasan al-
Bulghārī.[171] Their correspondence is undated but must necessarily have
taken place before Bulghārī's death in 698/1299.

4.   Simnānī's reply to a letter from a disciple named Shaykh ʿAbd
Allāh, located in MS. 3457, Kitābkhāna-yi majlis-i shūrā, Tehran, pp.
208–11, and printed by Hirawī.[172]

5.   One letter to the religious figure and courtier Tāj ad-dīn-i
Karkahrī (Kahrandī), portions of which are reproduced in the *Rawḍāt
al-janān*.[173]

6.   One exchange of correspondence with ʿAlī-yi Rāmtīnī, an
abstract of which is found in the *Rashaḥāt ʿayn al-ḥayāt*.[174]

Works Attributed to Simnānī Not Known to be Extant

1.   *al-Falāḥ fī-mukhtaṣar sharḥ as-sunna*.[175] Salvation in the Precis
of the Commentary on the Tradition [by al-Baghawī].
	Possible variant: *Mukhtaṣar sharḥ as-sunna-yi Baghawī*.[176]

2.   *Risāla fiʾl-futuwwa*.[177] Treatise on Chivalry.

---

168. Massignon, *The Passion of al-Hallāj*, 4:35.
169. Ḥaqīqat, *Khumkhāna*, 55; Massignon, *The Passion of al-Hallāj*, 4:35.
170. *Muṣannafāt-i fārsī*, 337–46.
171. Ibn al-Karbalāʾī, 1:151ff.
172. *Muṣannafāt-i fārsī*, xliv–xlv, 333–36. This is probably his disciple ʿAbd
Allāh-i Ghurjistānī.
173. Ibn al-Karbalāʾī, 1:340–45. Tāj ad-dīn-i Kahrandī is mentioned by
Mustawfī-yi Qazwīnī as having been a Sufi guide at Tabriz during the reign
of Abū Saʿīd (*Taʾrīkh-i guzīda*, 676).
174. Wāʾiẓ-i Kāshifī, 1:63.
175. *Hadiyyat al-ʿārifīn*, 1:108.
176. Ḥaqīqat, *Khumkhāna*, 57.
177. Nafīsī, 362. The *Futuwwat nāma* found in MS. 1796, Veliyüddin
Efendi, Beyazit Devlet Kütüphanesi, Istanbul, folios 171b–74a could possibly
be this work. It is normally attributed to ʿAlī-yi Hamadānī (cf. Marijan Molé,
"Les Kubrawiya," 98; also "ʿAlī b. Ṣihābaddīn-i Hamadānīʾnin Risāla-i
futuwwatīyaʾsi," *Ṣarkiyat Mecmuası* 4 [1961], 33–72).

3. *Lubb al-qūt li-ṭālib al-wuṣūl ila'l-ḥayy alladhī lā-yamūt.*[178] The Source of Nourishment for the Seeker of Attainment of the Living Who does not Die.
  Variant title: *Lubb al-qūt.*[179]

4. *Mafātīḥ al-jinān wa-maṣābīḥ al-janān.*[180] Keys of the Gardens and Lamps of the Hearts.
  Variant title: *Maṣābīḥ al-janān.*[181]

5. *al-Maqālāt fī't-taṣawwuf.*[182] Essays on Sufism.

6. *Mūḍiḥ maqāṣid al-mukhliṣīn wa-mafḍaḥ 'aqā'id al-mudda'īn.*[183] Elucidator of the Goals of the Sincere and Exposer of the Doctrines of the Pretenders.

7. *Muhjat at-tawḥīd.*[184] The Core of Unity.

8. *al-Mukāshafāt al-munqidh min al-āfāt.*[185] The Revelation which is the Savior from Calamity.

9. *Wāqi'at ar-rāfi'a.*[186] The Occasion of Elevation.

Titles Mentioned Only in Simnānī's *Maṭāf al-ashrāf* (79a–b)

10. *Daqīqa fī-ḥaqīqat as-salṭana.* A Detail in the Nature of Governance.

11. *Faḍīḥ i'tiqād al-mulḥidīn wa-tawḍīḥ rishād al-muwaḥḥidīn* Exposer of the Beliefs of the Nonbelievers and Elucidation of the Integrity of the Monotheists.

---

178. *Maṭāf al-ashrāf*, 79b.
179. *Fuṣūl al-uṣūl*, 55b.
180. *Maṭāf al-ashrāf*, 79a.
181. Ṣafadī, 7:357; Nafīsī, 362.
182. *Hadiyyat al-'ārifīn*, 1:108.
183. Shushtarī, 2:136; Ma'ṣūm 'Alī Shāh, 2:340; *Lughatnāma*, s.v. "'Alā' ad-dawla-yi Simnānī"; Sadr, 106; *A'yān ash-shī'a*, s.v. "Aḥmad b. Muḥammad as-Simnānī."
184. *Hadiyyat al-'ārifīn*, 1:108.
185. *Maṭāf al-ashrāf*, 79b; Khwānd Amīr, *Ḥabīb as-siyar*, 2:220; Kaḥḥāla, s.v. "Aḥmad as-Simnānī"; *Hadiyyat al-'ārifīn*, 1:108; *Lughatnāma*, s.v. "'Alā' ad-dawla-yi Simnānī"; Nafīsī, 362; Sadr, 106.
186. *Farḥat al-'āmilīn*, 47.

12.   *Gharā'ib ar-raghā'ib li'l-ḥāḍir wa'l-ghā'ib.* The Wonders of the Desired for the Present and the Absent.

13.   *Ibtihāj dhawi'l-mi'rāj bi's-sirāj al-waḍḍāḥ.* Delight of Those Who have Ascended with the Luminous Lamp.

14.   *Risālat al-intibāh li'l-āhī 'an Allāh.* Treatise on Awakening to God through God.

15.   *Lubb lubāb dhawi'l-albāb.* The Essence of Essences of those endowed with Hearts.

16.   *Majāmi' al-manāfi'.* Assembly of Benefits.

17.   *Manāhij al-mu'minīn wa-mabāhij al-muḥibbīn.* Methods of the Believers and Delights of the Lovers.

18.   *Muntaqid maṭla' an-nuqaṭ wa-multaqiṭ majma' al-laqaṭ.* The Critic of the Dawn of Points and the Collector of the Assembly of Gleanings.

19.   *Mustashhidāt.* Attestations.
       Variant title: *Mushāhadāt.*

20.   *Nuṣūṣ jard al-iṣṭilāḥāt wa-fuṣūṣ ḥudūd al-maqāmāt.* Texts Revealing Terminology and the Quintessence of the Definitions of Stations.

21.   *Riyāḍ al-afkār al-qudsiyya al-marḍiyya 'an-al-afkār al-insiyya.* Gardens of Holy and Wholesome Meditations about Human Contemplation.

22.   *Taḥdhīr dhawi't-tasakhkhur 'an-al-ishtighāl bi'l-asr dūn-al-amr wa'l-qinā'a bi'l-yasīr 'an-al-kathīr.* Warning to the Jeering against Being Preoccupied with the Whole without Reason and Being Satisfied with Less rather than More.

23.   *Takhlīṣ an-nafs 'an-sijn al-ḥads.* Liberation of the Soul from the Prison of Conjecture.

24.   *Risālat al-wuqūf bayn-yaday ar-rabb ar-ra'ūf al-'aṭūf.* The Treatise on Standing before the Merciful and Compassionate Lord.

25.   *az-Ẓunūn allatī ta'tī min-funūn al-junūn*. The Beliefs coming from the Varieties of Madness.

Simnānī's Commentary on the Qur'ān

The Qur'ānic commentary of 'Alā' ad-dawla as-Simnānī constitutes the most valuable source of information on his thought. Although it is not as systematic or comprehensive as the *'Urwa*, this commentary provides clear and concise descriptions of his worldview alongside lucid examples of mystical instruction. Unlike the *'Urwa*, Simnānī's Qur'ān commentary has not undergone repeated revisions. It dates from the most productive period of his life when he wrote most of his major treatises, and presents ideas and arguments close to the form in which they were originally conceived. In fact, some portions of the work were written as a direct result of visionary experiences.[187]

Twenty-seven manuscripts of the work can be traced in a variety of manuscript libraries. The earliest ones accessible to me, MS. 54, Hekimoğlu Ali Paşa, and MS. 165, Şehit Ali Paşa, Süleymaniye Kütüphanesi, Istanbul, and MS. 13259, Aleppo, Ḥāfiẓ al-Asad Library, Damascus, were completed in 758/1357, 779/1377 and 780/1378, thus dating from about a generation after the author's death. All three copies are in excellent condition. Simnānī's autograph is no longer known to exist, although it appears that MS. 54, Hekimoğlu was copied from it. MS. 165, Şehit Ali was copied directly from MS. 54, Hekimoğlu and, as explicitly stated in its margin, later compared with the autograph.

There can be no doubt as to the authenticity of this work. Simnānī himself mentions it under the title *Maṭla' an-nuqaṭ wa-majma' al-luqaṭ*.[188] Early biographical accounts about Simnānī also credit him with having written exegetical works.[189] The content of the *tafsīr* itself provides clear proof about its authorship: it mentions other works by Simnānī and refers to events in his life; the style and subject matter are clearly his own.

Simnānī's commentary on the Qur'ān cannot be precisely dated nor can its title be unequivocally ascertained. Simnānī states in the commentary that he commenced the work twenty years after he embarked on the mystical path, although it remains unclear as to

---

187. *Najm*, 75a.
188. *Maṭāf al-ashrāf*, 79a; *'Urwa*, 331.
189. Asnawī, 1:349; Dāwūdī, 1:66; Ibn 'Imād, 6:125.

when he felt his mystical career had begun.[190] The three possible dates
could be the occasion of his first mystical experience (683/1284), his
first meeting with Isfarā'inī (Ramaḍān 686/October 1287), or his
investiture with the Sufi mantle of the Kubrawī order (Ṣafar 689/
February 1290). It can safely be assumed, therefore, that Simnānī
commenced his Qur'ānic commentary between 703/1304 and 709/1310.
Regardless of the precise date, the *tafsīr* was clearly compiled after
Simnānī had established definite contact with the Kubrawī tradition
and well after his first contact with Isfarā'inī.

The commentary is known by several titles including *Najm al-
qur'ān, at-Ta'wīlāt an-najmiyya* and *Tafsīr baṭn al-qur'ān,* in addition
to the name *Maṭla' an-nuqaṭ wa-majma' al-luqaṭ* mentioned above.[191]
The title *Najm al-qur'ān,* or *Tafsīr najm al-qur'ān,* appears within
the commentary. The name *Maṭla' an-nuqaṭ wa-majma' al-luqaṭ* was
also used by Simnānī, but appears to refer solely to the introduction
which was written separately from the remainder of the *tafsīr.* The
commentary begins with aṭ-Ṭūr (*sūra* 52) and is ostensibly a continuation of the *tafsīr* conceived by Najm ad-dīn al-Kubrā who died before
he had completed his exegesis of the seventeenth and eighteenth verses
of adh-Dhāriyāt (*sūra* 51). The title *at-Ta'wīlāt an-najmiyya* therefore
refers to the *tafsīr* as begun by Kubrā. The title *Najm al-qur'ān* may
also be derived from his name. The name also carries the connotation
of an "installment," referring to the fact that it is only a partial
commentary. *Najm* may also be used meaning "star," implying that
the commentary concentrates on the most important features or
verses of the Qur'ān. All these ideas may very well be subsumed in
the title *Najm al-qur'ān.*

It is not clear whether the Qur'ānic commentary until *sūra* 51:19
was written exclusively by Kubrā, or part by him and part by Dāya.[192]
Kubrā's commentary on the Qur'ān is known variously as *'Ayn*

---

190. *Najm,* 26a.

191. The title *Najm al-qurrā' fī-ta'wīlāt al-qur'ān* is most probably a
typographical error (Kaḥḥāla, s.v. "Aḥmad as-Simnānī"); cf. the brief discussion
on the correct title in Ateş, *İşârî Tefsîr Okulu,* 152.

192. Problems concerning the authorship of this commentary have been
discussed at length by F. Meier in "Stambuler Handschriften dreier persischer
Mystiker: 'Ain al-quḍāt al-Hamadhānī, Nağm ad-dīn al-Kubrā, Nağm ad-dīn
ad-Dāja," *Der Islam* 24 (1937), 1–42; S. Ateş, " Üç müfessir bir tefsīr," *İlâhiyât
Fakültesi Dergisi* 18 (1970), 85–104. Cf. also W. Shpall, "A Note on Najm al-
dīn al-Rāzī and the *Baḥr al-ḥaqā'iq,*" *Folia Orientalia* 22 (1981–84), 69–80.

al-ḥayāt,[193] *al-ʿAwārif*[194] and *Baḥr al-ḥaqāʾiq*.[195] A commentary with
the same titles is also attributed to Najm ad-dīn ad-Dāya. Elsewhere
it is stated that the *Baḥr al-ḥaqāʾiq* is the name of Kubrā's Qurʾānic
commentary which was completed by his "disciple" (*tilmīdh*) Dāya.[196]

It is possible that there are two different continuations to Kubrā's
commentary, one by Simnānī and the other by Dāya.[197] In light of the
fact that a number of manuscripts claim that the *tafsīr* ending at 51:19
is Dāya's work, it is also conceivable that Dāya revised Kubrā's commentary and was therefore credited with its authorship by later
copyists.

Although it commences with the *sūra* following the last one
dealt with by Kubrā, Simnānī's commentary on the Qurʾān is an independent work differing from the earlier commentary both in style and
content. It was clearly conceived as such by Simnānī. He did not pick
up immediately where Kubrā left off, but proceeded to the beginning
of aṭ-Ṭūr (*sūra* 52). The main text of the commentary is preceded by
a lengthy introduction and an explanation of the first *sūra* (*al-Fātiḥa*).
Simnānī's introduction spells out his purpose and methodology in
writing the *tafsīr* and promises an extremely lengthy work.[198] The
tafsīr that Simnānī actually wrote differs in style and subject matter
from what was outlined in the introduction. It is also substantially
shorter than the grandiose scheme which the introduction presents.[199]
Taking into consideration the stylistic differences between the introduction and the *tafsīr* itself, it is probable that the title *Maṭlaʿ an-
nuqaṭ wa-majmaʿ al-luqaṭ* refers solely to the introduction, and that
the main body of the commentary was written later in his life.

---

193. MS. 153, Damat İbrahim Paşa, Süleymaniye Kütüphanesi, Istanbul.

194. MS. 54, Hekimoğlu Ali Paşa, Süleymaniye Kütüphanesi, Istanbul.

195. MS. 1085, Halet Efendi and MS. 92, Şehit Ali Paşa, Süleymaniye
Kütüphanesi, Istanbul.

196. MS. 1085, Halet Efendi.

197. Meier, "Stambuler Handschriften," 11ff. Dāya and Simnānī are not the
only writers to complete Kubrā's Qurʾānic commentary. Cf. MS. A576, İstanbul
Üniversitesi Kütüphanesi, Istanbul, which consists of the *Baḥr al-ḥaqāʾiq*
followed by a partial *tafsīr* which is probably the work of Najm ad-dīn Bashīr
b. Abū Bakr b. Ḥāmid b. Sulaymān b. Yūsuf az-Zaynabī (d. 646/1248).

198. The introduction has been edited by Paul Nwyia ("Muqaddima tafsīr
al-qurʾān li-ʿAlāʾ ad-dawla as-Simnānī," *al-Abḥāth* 26 [1973–77], 141–57), and
analyzed by Henry Corbin (*The Man of Light in Iranian Sufism*, 121–44).

199. Cf. Ḥājjī Khalīfa, who states that Simnānī's *tafsīr* is in thirteen volumes
(*Kashf aẓ-ẓunūn*, 1:449).

Simnānī's Qur'ānic commentary proceeds verse by verse, discussing each in turn. No verses are omitted, although some of them are dealt with in a perfunctory manner. On such occasions, the author only paraphrases the text, explains the grammar or illustrates a minor point using Persian verse. Other Qur'ānic verses inspire Simnānī to provide lengthy, and often elaborate, expositions on points of philosophy, mysticism, law and religious life. It is obvious from the content of the *tafsīr* that Simnānī did not have any preconceived arguments in mind which he then would have fitted into the framework of a commentary on the Qur'ān. All the same, the intricate explanations he provides for many of the verses accurately reflect his mystical vision. As such, it is a fine example of Sufi exegetical literature.

The *Najm al-qur'ān* is to be found in two formats: either by itself as a monograhical work or else appended to Kubrā's *tafsīr* (henceforth referred to as Type A and Type B respectively). The earliest manuscripts are examples of the former and comprise the introduction and commentaries on the *Fātiha* and *sūras* 52–114. The fact that it was not originally treated as the continuation of the existing Kubrawī commentary further supports the assertion that Simnānī's commentary was viewed as an independent *tafsīr*. The earliest known example of the work to be bound together with Kubrā's commentary is dated 907/1501–2. In this format *Najm al-qur'ān* is sometimes missing the introduction and the commentary on the *Fātiha*. The transition between the Kubrā/Dāya and Simnānī sections is normally marked by the statement:

The author terminated at this point and passed away, may God have mercy upon him. It was completed by 'Alā' ad-dawla, the student of the *shaykh*, may God, Most Exalted, have mercy on them both.

The following manuscripts of Simnānī's commentary on the Qur'ān are known to be extant:[200]

1.   MS. C1447 (Nov. 958, Catalog no. 548), Bukhara Collection, Oriental Institute, St. Petersburg, 224 pages.

---

200. MS. 1305, Şehit Ali, Süleymaniye Kütüphanesi, mentioned by Brockelmann (*Geschichte des Arabischen Litteratur*, 2nd ed. [Leiden: E. J. Brill, 1943–49], Supplement 2:281), does not exist; cf. also the İstanbul Üniversitesi Kütüphanesi card catalog, which erroneously states that MS. A1799, folios 540–53, contain a copy of this *tafsīr*.

The catalog gives the date of completion as 734/1336 [sic]. The manuscript consists of the entire *tafsīr*, including the commentary on the *fātiḥa* (Type A).[201]

2. MS. 54, Hekimoğlu Ali Paşa ve Camii, Süleymaniye Kütüphanesi, Istanbul, 103 folios.*

Twenty-five lines per page. Illuminated title page and covers. Very clear and beautifully written with quotations and key phrases in large red letters. *Sūra* headings are set apart from the text, comprising both the *basmala* and the name of the *sūra*. The first folio is damaged and has been reinforced with the loss of two or three lines.

It is falsely attributed to Kubrā in the catalog. Type A, although the illuminated title page says: ". . . 'Alā' ad-dawla Aḥmad as-Simnānī. . .completed the *tafsīr* of Shaykh Najm ad-dīn al-Kubrā entitled *al-'Awārif*." Completed on 15 Dhu'l-Ḥijja 758/29 November 1357 at Ṣūfīyābād-i Khudādād.

3. MS. 13259, Aleppo, Ḥafiz al-Asad Library, Damascus, 236 folios.

Type A. Beginning is missing. Completed on Sha'bān 779/ December 1377 at az-Zāwiyya al-Bisṭāmiyya in Aleppo by 'Alī b. Muḥammad b. Ḥasan, known as Ibn aṣ-Ṣāyigh.

4. MS. 165/1, Ṣehit Ali Paşa, Süleymaniye Kütüphanesi, Istanbul, folios 1–168.*

Type A. Completed in Ṣafar 780/June 1378 at Ṣūfīyābād by Yūsuf b. As'ad b. 'Alī ar-Rūmī, better known as Ḍiyā' ad-dīn al-Malaṭī, the grandson of Simnānī's disciple 'Alī-yi Rūmī. The margin next to the colophon states that this copy was compared with the original written in Simnānī's hand.

5. MS. 131, Manisa İl Halk Kütüphanesi, Manisa, folios 128b–56a.

Type A. An incomplete copy missing folios 148–55, dated 867/1462–63.

6. MS. 233/2, Carullah Efendi, Süleymaniye Kütüphanesi, Istanbul, folios 465–528.*

The title page identifies it as *Tafsīr 'ayn al-ḥayāt li'sh-shaykh Najm ad-dīn ar-Rāzī tilmīdh Najm ad-dīn al-Kubrā* but erroneously states that he wrote it up to an-Najm (*sūra* 53), after which it was

---

201. A.B. Khalidova, *Arabskie Rukopisi Instituta Vöstokovedeniiâ* (Moscow: Nauka, 1986), 1:61.

completed by 'Alā' ad-dawla as-Simnānī. The Simnānī section begins with aṭ-Ṭūr (*sūra* 52), lacking both the introduction and commentary on the Fātiḥa (Type B). The manuscript is dated 907/1501–2.

7.   MS. 14, Turhan Valide Sultan, Süleymaniye Kütüphanesi, Istanbul, folios 453b–530b.*

Type B. Illuminated title: *Kitāb tafsīr baḥr al-ḥaqā'iq. Najm al-qur'ān* commences on folio 453b and has an illuminated title. The colophon lists several dates for the commencement and completion of the two parts. The date of completion of the Simnānī section is either 23 Shawwāl 923/8 November 1517 or 3 Dhu'l-Ḥijja 927/4 November 1521.

8.   MS. 130, Murat Molla Kütüphanesi, Istanbul, folios 311–57.

Type B. The title *Tafsīr 'ayn al-ḥayāt* appears on folio 1a. There is a table of contents (1b–2a). The Simnānī section begins on folio 311a. The transition is marked by the customary statement announcing the author's death and stating that the work was completed by his student, whose name is incorrectly given as Najm ad-dīn ad-Dāya. No date or scribe is mentioned at the end of Simnānī's *tafsīr*, although the date 3 Dhu'l-qa'da 965/17 August 1558 appears at the end of the previous section (310b). However, the two parts are clearly written in different hands, the first part possibly being considerably older than the second.

9.   MS. 83, Hamidiye, Süleymaniye Kütüphanesi, Istanbul, folios 482b–568a.*

Type B. There is no break between the two parts, Simnānī's *tafsīr* running from 482b to 568a. His introduction is included as is the commentary on the *Fātiḥa*. The colophon states that the manuscript was completed on 11 Rabī' I 1009/10 September 1600.

10.   MS. 206, Gazi Husrev-Begova Biblioteka, Sarajevo, folios 479b–565a, completed on 11 Rabī' I 1009/10 September 1600.[202]

Type B. The Kubrā section ends on folio 479b and the scribe correctly attributes the latter part to 'Alā' ad-dawla as-Simnānī. There is no break between the two parts, Simnānī's *tafsīr* running from 479b to 565a. His introduction is included as is the commentary on the *Fātiḥa*.

---

202. Kasim Dobrača, *Katalog Arabskih, Turskih i Perzijskih Rukopisa*, Gazi Husrev-Begova Biblioteka, vol.1 (Sarajevo: 1963), 198–200.

11.   MS. 1047, Arabic, Kitābkhāna-yi millī, Tehran, 210 folios.*
Type B, the latter portion being attributed to Najm ad-dīn ad-Dāya. It contains Simnānī's entire *tafsīr*, including the lengthy introduction. *Sūra* headings are used inconsistently. Completed in Muḥarram 1010/June 1601 by a Muḥyī ad-dīn Ḥusayn an-Nīkadī.[203]

12.   MS. 18, Halet Efendi ve Eki, Süleymaniye Kütüphanesi, Istanbul, folios 550a–637a.*
Type B. It is called the *Tafsīr baḥr al-ḥaqā'iq* of Najm ad-dīn ad-Dāya on the title page. However, this is followed by a brief biography of Kubrā and a statement to the effect that this work is the *Tafsīr 'ayn al-ḥayāt* of Kubrā which was brought to completion by his student Najm ad-dīn ad-Dāya. The phraseology is exactly the same as that found in MS. 130, Murat Molla. There is no mention of Simnānī at the beginning. The date 1085/1674 appears at the end of the Kubrā portion (549b).
The Simnānī section starts afresh on folio 550a but has no title page. It comprises the introduction and the complete commentary on the *Fātiḥa* and *sūras* 52 to 114. Completed in Dhu'l-Ḥijja 1085/ February–March 1675 by Muḥammad Ḥusayn Kalyāykālī [?] (637a).

13.   MS. 536, Beyazit Devlet Kütüphanesi, Istanbul, folios 333–99, dated 1174/1760–61.

14.   MS. 345, Garrett Collection, Firestone Library, Princeton University, Princeton, folios 1b–109.*
Type A, entitled *Tafsīr najm al-qur'ān*. Completed in Jumāda II 1222/August 1807 at the *madrasa* of Murat Paṣa by Walī ad-dīn b. Muḥammad Qasṭamūnī.

15.   MS 6359, Dār al-kutub, Cairo.
Type B. The work is entitled *at-Ta'wīlāt an-najmiyya*, written by Abu'l-Makārim Aḥmad b. Muḥammad b. al-Biyābānakī [as-Simnānī].[204] The text is in five volumes, the first four being *at-Ta'wīlāt an-najmiyya* of Najm ad-dīn al-Kubrā and possibly Dāya, and the final volume containing Simnānī's *tafsīr*. Copied by Muḥammad Hāshim al-Busnawī in 1286/1869.

---

203. The Kubrā section was completed on 28 Shawwāl 1009/22 April 1601 (133b).
204. *Catalogue des MSS. Arabes de la bibliothèque du Caire* (Fihris al-kutub al-'arabiyya al-makhṭūṭa bi'l-kutubkhāna al-khidawiyya), 1:65; Muḥammad Ḥusayn adh-Dhahabī, *at-Tafsīr wa'l-mufassirūn*, 2:394–95.

16.　MS. 162, Hasan Hayri ve Aptullah Efendi, Süleymaniye Kütüphanesi, Istanbul, folios 1–114.*

Type A. The title page (1a) identifies the work as the *tafsīr* of 'Alā' ad-dawla as-Simnānī entitled *Najm al-qur'ān*, stating that it constitutes an appendix to *at-Tafsīr an-najmī* (presumably that of Najm ad-dīn al-Kubrā).

The colophon is extremely difficult to read. The manuscript is dated a Friday in Rabī' II; the year cannot be discerned. The copyist's name appears to be Muḥammad b. 'Abd Allāh b. Muḥammad al-Bisṭāmī.

17.　MS. 153, Damat İbrahim Paşa, Süleymaniye Kütüphanesi, Istanbul, folios 469–540.*

Type B. It is entitled *Tafsīr 'ayn al-ḥayāt* of Najm ad-dīn al-Kubrā and contains a brief biography of Kubrā. Dāya is credited with seeing the *tafsīr* to its completion. The Kubrā section ends on folio 468b, the Simnānī portion beginning on folio 469b. Neither the date nor the name of the scribe appear anywhere in the manuscript.

18.　MS. 31/2, Hacı Mahmut Efendi (Yahya Efendi Dergahı), Süleymaniye Kütüphanesi, Istanbul, folios 171b–255a.

Type B. The completion is correctly attributed to Simnānī. A short paragraph of prose follows on folio 171b which is not part of Simnānī's commentary. The *Najm al-qur'ān* then commences on the same page. Neither the date nor the name of the scribe appear in the text.

19.　MS. 92, Kılıç Ali Paşa, Süleymaniye Kütüphanesi, Istanbul, folios 482–567.*

Type B. The old title page, giving the name of the work as *Tafsīr ḥaqā'iq an-Najm ad-Dāya*, has been pasted over. The Kubrā section ends on 481b and Simnānī is correctly credited with having completed the work. The Simnānī section begins on folio 482a and is complete, comprising the introduction as well as the commentary on the *Fātiḥa* and *sūras* 52 to 114. Neither a date nor the name of a scribe appears anywhere in the manuscript.

20.　MS. 92, Şehit Ali Paşa, Süleymaniye Kütüphanesi, Istanbul, folios 478b–563a.*

Type B, entitled the *Tafsīr baḥr al-ḥaqā'iq* of Kubrā. The Simnānī section begins on folio 478b, line 18, and is only separated from the preceding section by the statement announcing the author's death and correctly identifying Simnānī as the author of the remainder of the *tafsīr*. The complete text of *Najm al-qur'ān* is reproduced. No date or scribe's name appears anywhere in the manuscript.

21. MS. Orient M II 14, Universitäts-Bibliothek, Basel, 80 folios.*
Type A, entitled *Tafsīr baṭn as-sab'a* and bearing no date or name of a scribe.

22. MS. 874, Königlichen Bibliothek, Berlin, 279 folios.[205]
Type A. Untitled manuscript which is wrongly attributed to 'Abd al-Karīm al-Jīlī (d. ca. 820/1417). It contains the introduction of Simnānī and a commentary on the *Fātiḥa* and *sūras* 52–114. No date or scribe.

23. MS. 53, Dārülmesnevi (Şeyh Mehmed Murad), Süleymaniye Kütüphanesi, Istanbul, folios 1–133.*
Type A. The title appears on 1a: *Tafsīr 'Alā' ad-dīn* [sic] *as-Simnānī min-awsaṭ sūrat al-mujādala ilā-ākhir al-qur'ān*. There are extensive comments in the margins of the introduction. The *tafsīr* does not start until the middle of al-Mujādala (*sūra* 53). There is also a major section of the text missing between folios 9 and 10. No date or scribe is mentioned.

24. MS. 3665/5, Esad Efendi, Süleymaniye Kütüphanesi, Istanbul, folios 15b–24b.*
This manuscript is a *majmū'a* comprising 173 folios which contain several *qaṣīdas* by various poets. The introduction to Simnānī's commentary on the Qur'ān together with his *tafsīr* of the *Fātiḥa* comprise folios 15b–24b. No date or scribe.

25. Private collection, estate of Qāsim Ghanī. This manuscript was originally at Simnān.
No further information is available on it at present.[206]

26. MS. 8562 Ẓāhiriyya, Ḥāfiẓ al-Asad Library, Damascus, pp. 12–16. A fragmentary copy dated 1119/1707.[207]

---

205. W. Ahlwardt, *Verzeichniss der Arabischen Handschriften der Königlichen Bibliothek zu Berlin*, vol. 1, Die Handschriften-Verzeichnisse der Königlichen Bibliothek zu Berlin, vol. 7 (Berlin: A.W. Schade, 1887), 344–45.
206. Sadr, 98–99; Ḥaqīqat, *Khumkhāna*, 49.
207. *Fihrist makhṭūṭat dār al-kutub aẓ-Ẓāhiriyya: Tafsīr*, 3:395.

27. MS. 337, Beyazit Devlet Kütüphanesi, Istanbul, folios 1b–39a.[*]
An incomplete copy consisting of Simnānī's introduction and his commentary on an-Nabā' to an-Nās (*sūras* 78–114). No date or scribe.

Appendix B:
Chronology of Events

Date	Events in Simnānī's life	Political Events
654/1256		Hulākū's reign begins.
656/1258		Conquest of Baghdad and end of the Caliphate.
658/1260		Battle of ʿAyn Jālūt (25 Ramaḍān/3 Sept.).
659/1261	Simnānī's birth (Dhu'l-Ḥijja/November)	
663/1265		Death of Hulākū. Abāqā's reign begins.
673/1275	Simnānī meets two Sufis named Mahdi-yi Ḥājjī and Ḥājjī-yi Abharī.	
674/1275–76	Simnānī joins the court of Arghūn.	
680/1282		Death of Abāqā. Aḥmad Takūdār's reign begins.
683/1284	Simnānī's first mystical experience during the battle at Aqkhwāja (16 Ṣafar/4 May).	Takūdār deposed. Arghūn's reign begins. Simnānī's paternal uncle, Jalāl ad-dīn-i Mukhliṣ, made *wazīr* by Arghūn.
685/1286	Leaves the *urdū* of Uljāytū for Simnān (16 Shaʿbān/7 Oct.). Second mystical experience occurs on this journey.	

Date	Events in Simnānī's life	Political Events
686/1287	Third major mystical experience (Muḥarram/ February–March).	
	Initial contact with Sharaf ad-dīn-i Ḥanawayh (ca. Ramaḍān/October).	
687/1288	Attempts to go to Baghdad to see Isfarā'inī but is stopped at Hamadān and taken to Sharūyāz (Muḥarram/February).	
	Returns to Simnān without the Ilkhan's permission (Rabī' II/April).	
688/1289	Meets Isfarā'inī for the first time in Baghdad (Ramaḍān/ September).	
	Leaves for the Ḥajj (26 Ramaḍān/13 Oct.)	Execution of Jalāl ad-dīn-i Mukhliṣ.
689/1290	Returns to Baghdad from Mecca. Learns of his uncle's execution (Muḥarram/January).	
	Receives *ijāza* from Isfarā'inī and leaves for Simnān (Ṣafar/February).	
690/1291		Death of Arghūn. Gaykhātū's reign begins.
695/1295		Gaykhātū overthrown. Baydū ascends to the throne (Rabī' II/March).
		Ghāzān deposes Baydū (Dhu'l-Ḥijja/November).
		Execution of Simnānī's father, Sharaf ad-dīn.

Date	Events in Simnānī's life	Political Events
700/1301		Execution of Simnānī's maternal uncle, Rukn ad-dīn-i Ṣā'in.
703/1304		Death of Ghāzān. Uljāytū's reign begins.
710/1310		Uljāytū converts to Islam.
716/1316		Death of Uljāytū. Abū Saʿīd's reign begins.
717/1317	Death of Isfarā'inī	
720/1320	Begins writing the *'Urwa* in Ṣūfīyābād (Ramaḍān/October).	
728/1328	Completes third and final version of the *'Urwa* entitled *Ṣafwat al-'urwa* (18 Dhu'l-Ḥijja/24 Oct.).	
736/1335–6	Death of Simnānī (22 Rajab/6 March).	Death of Abū Saʿīd.
756/1355		End of Ilkhanid rule in Iran.

GLOSSARY OF TECHNICAL TERMS

'abd: slave, servant of God [see *'ubūdiyya*].

abdāl (sing. *badal*): substitutes, the intermediate rank of the true mystics (*ahl at-taṣawwuf*).

abṭāl (sing. *baṭal*): heroes, the lowest level of true mystics (*ahl at-taṣawwuf*).

āfāq: horizons [see *ufuq* and *'ālam al-āfāq*].

ahl at-taṣawwuf: true mystics, higher in status than the Sufis (*ṣūfiyya*). They are divided into the categories of *abṭāl, abdāl,* and *sayyāḥūn*.

'ālam: world, realm.

'ālam al-āfāq: the world of horizons, otherwise called the physical or finite realm.

'ālam al-anfus: the spiritual realm.

'ālam al-ghayb wa'sh-shahāda: the invisible and visible realms.

'ālam al-jabarūt (adj. *jabarūtī*): the Realm of (divine) Omnipotence.

'ālam al-kawn wa'l-fasād: the temporal realm.

'ālam al-lāhūt (adj. *lāhūtī*): the Realm of Divinity.

'ālam al-malakūt (adj. *malakūtī*): the Realm of (divine) Sovereignty.

'ālam an-nāsūt (adj. *nāsūtī*): the Human Realm.

'amal (pl. *a'māl*): acts, actions.

amāna: sacred or divine trust.

amthāl: allegories, allegorical instruction by God.

'aql: intellect, also known as the divine tablet [see *lawḥ* and *lawḥ al-'aql*].

arba'īn: a mystical retreat (*khalwa*) lasting for a period of forty days.

arḍ al-bashariyya: the mortal or temporal realm.

'arsh: the divine throne [see *kursī*].

aṣḥāb al-mash'ama: people of the left hand; those cursed by God.

aṣḥāb al-yamīn: people of the right hand; those favored by God.

athar (pl. *āthār*): effect, particularly a divine effect.

ātish-i dhikr: the fire of recollection. This fire is attained along the Sufi path and causes the annihilation of the individual, manifesting visions, colors and lights in the process.

awliyā': see *walī*.

'ayn al-yaqīn: essence of certitude, constituting the second lowest level of mystical knowledge.

badan: body, specifically referring to the human body (*al-badan al-insānī*).

al-badan al-maj'ūl: the created, physical body.

al-badan al-muktasab [*badan-i muktasab*]: the acquired body obtained through a process of spiritual perfection.

bakhshī: Buddhist monk.

banda: servant [see *'abd*].

barzakh: limbo; isthmus; boundary between two realms, or between levels of the soul.

bāṭin: esoteric, hidden, inside; inner dimension [opp. *ẓāhir*].

baṭn: esoteric, hidden or inner dimension [opp. *ẓahr*].

baṭn al-qur'ān: the esoteric dimension of the Qur'ān.

but-parast: idol-worshipper, a term Simnānī applies to Buddhists and Mongols (particularly Arghūn) before their conversion to Islam.

daqīqa (pl. *daqā'iq*): individual particles; particulars, corresponding to the degree of differentiation and multiplicity occurring in the Realm of Sovereignty (*'ālam al-malakūt*).

dhākir: recollector, one engaged in divine recollection [see *dhikr*].

dharra: seed, atom, nucleus.

dhāt: essence, particularly the divine essence.

dhawq: mystical comprehension, "taste".

dhikr: remembrance, recollection of God (normally in a ritualized, formulaic manner).

adh-dhikr al-ḥaqīqī: true recollection; the ideal form of recollection which occurs within the spiritual body of the mystic without his or her awareness.

adh-dhikr al-jahrī: recollection of the tongue which is said out loud; audible recollection.

adh-dhikr al-khafī: silent recollection.

adh-dhikr al-lisānī al-qawī al-khafī: silent recollection of the tongue; the basic form of *dhikr* in which the mystic engages in recollection consciously but does not say it out loud [also known as *adh-dhikr al-lisānī al-qālabī*].

dil: heart [see *fu'ād* and *qalb*].

dil-i ṣanūbarī: the pineal heart; the physical heart so named because of its pineal shape.

dunyā: the lower world; earthly realm [see *'ālam*].

fanā': annihilation of the self, which is then followed by resurrection at a higher mystical level [see *qiyāma*].

fayḍ: emanation, being both the process of emanation and the resultant emanations themselves.

fi'l (pl. *af'āl*): act, particularly a divine act.

fu'ād: the physical, organic heart [see *qalb*].

ghāfil: heedless, ignorant.

ghayb al-ghuyūb: the hiddenmost hidden, representing the realm of the subtle substance of the "real" (*al-laṭīfa al-ḥaqqiyya*).

ḥaḍarat al-ḥaqq: divine presence.

ḥāl (pl. *aḥwāl*): a mystical state [see *maqām*].

ḥaqīqa (pl. *ḥaqā'iq*): truth, reality.

ḥaqīqa ḥaqq al-yaqīn: the essence of the reality of certitude, constituting the highest form of mystical knowledge.

ḥaqq: a divine name, God, reality, truth, right [opp. *bāṭil*].

ḥaqq al-yaqīn: the reality of certitude, constituting the second highest form of mystical knowledge.

hawā: worldly or sensuous desires, passions.

ḥijāb: veil or curtain; there are seventy thousand of these veiling human beings from God.

ḥulūl: indwelling, the presence of God within a created entity.

'ibāda: worship, acts of worship; religious practice.

ijāza: certificate or diploma granted by a *shaykh* authorizing a mystic to teach disciples.

ilhām: inspiration.

'ilm: knowledge, most often rationally or scientifically acquired.

al-'ilm al-ladunī: direct, unmediated knowledge of the divine.

al-'ilm al-majhūl: knowledge that is unknown to ordinary people; mystical knowledge.

al-'ilm aṣ-ṣaḥīḥ as-samā'ī: rational knowledge acquired through hearing or instruction; this constitutes the highest level of non-mystical knowledge.

'ilm al-yaqīn: certitude of knowledge, constituting the lowest form of mystical knowledge.

insān (pl. *nās*): human being.

iqlīm (pl. *aqālīm*): region; clime of the spiritual realm.

'irfān: an act of realization; sometimes a cognate for Sufism.

'izza: divine glory.

jabarūt: divine omnipotence [see *'ālam al-jabarūt*].

jadhba: a sudden mystical experience or trance granted by God, representing the only way to attain the highest state of enlightenment.

jāhil: ignorant, benighted, heedless [see *ghāfil*].

jalāl: divine majesty [see *jamāl*].

jamāl: divine beauty [see *jalāl*].

kāfir: disbeliever, non-Muslim.

kalām: speech; the divine attribute of speech.

kalima: word; most often a reference to the Islamic credal formula (*al-kalima aṭ-ṭayyiba*) [see *tahlīl*].

kamāl: divine perfection, perfection.

kashf: unveiling, uncovering, discovery.

kashf al-ghiṭā' [or *kashf al-ḥijāb*]: lifting of the veil.

kathīf: substantive, corporeal, coarse [opp. *latīf*].

kawn: existence.

khafī: inner mystery.

khalīfa: representative, vicegerent.

khalq: creation, being both the creative process and the results of that process; also refers specifically to human beings.

khalwa: seclusion for the purpose of engaging in mystical exercises [see *'uzla*].

khātim: seal, referring to human beings as the seal of all created entities (*khātim at-tarākīb*), Muḥammad as the seal of prophets (*khātim al-anbiyā'*), and the subtle substance of the "real" as the seal of subtle substances (*khātim al-latā'if*).

khātir (pl. *khawātir*): personal thought devoid of divine inspiration or guidance [see *zann*].

khirqa: a Sufi robe, awarded by a *shaykh* to disciples as a mark of distinction.

kursī: the divine footstool [see *'arsh*].

lāhūt: divinity [see *'ālam al-lāhūt*].

latīf: subtle, nonsubstantive [opp. *kathīf*].

latīfa (pl. *latā'if*): subtle substance, normally associated with the spiritual body.

al-latīfa al-anā'iyya (*latīfa-yi anā'iyyat*): the subtle substance of I-ness which is the end result of the mystical quest.

al-latīfa al-ḥaqqiyya: subtle substance of the "real," corresponding to the status of Muḥammad which represents the final stage on the mystical path and results in the perfection of the subtle substance of I-ness (*al-latīfa al-anā'iyya*).

al-latīfa al-khafiyya: subtle substance of the mystery.

al-latīfa an-nafsiyya: subtle substance of the soul.

al-latīfa al-qālabiyya: subtle substance of the body, constituting the lowest level of the spiritual body.

al-latīfa al-qalbiyya: subtle substance of the heart.

al-latīfa ar-rūḥiyya: subtle substance of the spirit.

al-latīfa as-sirriyya: subtle substance of the inmost being.

lawḥ: divine tablet, equated with the intellect [see *'aql* and *lawḥ al-'aql*].

lawḥ al-'aql: divine tablet of the intellect [see *lawḥ* and *'aql*].

lawn (pl. *alwān*): colors, especially those manifested on the mystical path.

luṭf: divine grace, as opposed to power [opp. *qahr*].

maḥabba: love, normally (but not exclusively) referring to love for this world (*maḥabbat ad-dunyā*).

malakūt: divine sovereignty [see *'ālam al-malakūt*].

ma'nā (adj. *ma'nawī*): ideal, inner meaning or dimension [opp. *ṣūra*].

maqām (pl. *-āt*): Station or stage along the mystical path [see *ḥāl*].

ma'rifa (pl. *ma'ārif*): enlightenment, sometimes translatable as gnosis or knowledge of the divine.

martaba: stage, particularly along the mystical path.

maṭla' al-qur'ān: point of departure or ascent of the Qur'ān, representing the beginning of divine or real knowledge contained in God's word.

al-mawt al-ikhtiyārī: voluntary death; the loss or annihilation of the self which is a goal of mystical exercises [see *fanā'* and *qiyāma*].

maẓhar: locus of manifestation, sometimes translatable as mirror [see *mir'ā*].

mir'ā: mirror [see *maẓhar*].

mubtadi': a beginner or novice on the mystical path.

mufradāt: elements.

mu'min: faithful Muslim, believer.

munājāt: divine conversation; personal conversation with God.

muntahī: an individual at the end of the mystical path.

murakkabāt: compounds, composites.

al-murakkabāt as-sufliyya: lower or sublunar compounds.

al-murakkabāt al-'ulwiyya: higher or celestial compounds.

mushabbihī: anthropomorphist.

mushāhada (*-āt*): witnessing or bearing witness.

mushāhadat al-wajh: witnessing the divine face.

muslik: mystical guide [see *shaykh*].

mutawallad (pl. *-āt*): progeny; matter, plants or animals generated by the combination of the celestial and terrestrial forces (*al-quwā al-ʻulwiyya wa' s-sufliyya*).

mutawassit: an individual in the middle of the mystical path; an "intermediate."

nafs: soul, particularly the appetitive soul, identical with the subtle substance of the animal spirit (*latīfa-yi rūh-i haywānī*).

nār adh-dhikr: fire of recollection [see *ātish-i dhikr*].

nāsūt: pertaining to humanity [see *ʻālam an-nāsūt*].

nazāha: divine transcendence, exaltation.

nūr (pl. *anwār*): light, especially light as manifested along the mystical path.

nūr adh-dhāt: light of the divine essence.

nūr al-īmān: light of faith.

nūr-i mutlaq: absolute light, or light of the divine essence.

qabd and *bast*: contraction and expansion, constituting two complementary yet opposing states on the mystical path.

qadīm: eternal.

qahr: divine power, as opposed to grace [opp. *lutf*].

qalam: pen, particularly the divine pen.

qalb: heart, particularly the inner mystical heart (*al-qalb al-haqīqī*) [see *fuʼ ād*].

qiyāma: resurrection following annihilation [see *fanāʼ*]. Simnānī uses the term *qiyāma* to denote the successive experiences of loss of self and renewal along the mystical path.

qurb: nearness (unto God).

qutb (pl. *aqtāb*): the mystical and cosmic "pole," constituting the highest attainable rank in Islamic mysticism [see *ahl at-tasawwuf*].

al-quwā al-qālabiyya: bodily forces.

al-quwā as-sufliyya: the lower or terrestrial forces which serve as mothers in the generation of matter, plants and animals [see *al-quwā al-ʻulwiyya*].

al-quwā al-ʻulwiyya: the higher or celestial forces which serve as fathers in the generation of matter, plants and animals [see *al-quwā as-sufliyya*].

quwwa (pl. *quwā*): force, faculty.

raqīqa (pl. *raqā'iq*): rare substance, corresponding to the degree of differentiation and multiplicity that occurs in the Realm of Omnipotence (*'ālam al-jabarūt*).

rizq: sustenance.

rūḥ: spirit.

ṣadr: breast, chest.

sālik: mystical traveler, mystic, Sufi.

sayyāḥūn (sing. *sayyāḥ*): travelers; the highest rank of the true mystics (*ahl at-taṣawwuf*) [see *quṭb*].

shāhid: witness [see *mushāhada*].

shakmāniyya: Buddhism and Buddhists; perhaps also Hindus.

shaqīqa (pl. *shaqā'iq*): divisions, sections; parts of a greater whole; the level of differentiation and multiplicity that occurs in the human realm (*'ālam an-nāsūt*).

shaykh: master, teacher, or mystical guide.

sidrat al-muntahā: Lote-tree of the Boundary, representing the border between the Realm of Sovereignty (*'ālam al-malakūt*) and the Realm of Omnipotence (*'ālam al-jabarūt*).

ṣifa (pl. *ṣifāt*): attribute.

ṣifa dhātiyya: essential attribute; attribute of the divine essence.

ṣifa fi'liyya: active attribute; attribute of divine action.

sirr: inmost being.

siyāsa: social laws; punishment; the ordering of society; governance.

ṣūra (adj. *ṣuwarī*): form; apparent, outward dimension [opp. *ma'nā*].

tafrīd: isolation of a mystic from society, preceded by divestment of all worldly possessions [see *tajrīd*].

ṭahāra: cleansing, purification.

tahlīl: the credal formula "There is no god but God."

tajallī: manifestation, particularly manifestation of the divine attributes (*tajallī aṣ-ṣifāt*) or essence (*tajallī adh-dhāt*).

tajrīd: divestment of all worldly possessions.

ṭarīq: see *ṭarīqa*.

ṭarīqa: path, mystical path; Sufi order.

taṭhīr: see *ṭahāra*.

tawakkul: complete reliance upon God in all matters and recognition of God as the sole actor and cause.

tawḥīd: the affirmation of divine unity.

'ubūdiyya: servitude [see *'abd*].

ufuq (pl. *āfāq*): horizon or boundary between two realms [see *barzakh*]; also meaning a limit in the context of the finite realm (*'ālam al-āfāq*).

umm al-kitāb: the primordial book, a reference to the celestial archetype of the Qur'ān.

uns: intimacy; particularly divine intimacy.

'uzla: isolation; withdrawal for the purpose of engaging in mystical practices [see *khalwa* and *tafrīd*].

waḥdāniyya: oneness, unity; particularly divine oneness.

waḥdat al-wujūd: Unity or oneness of being, referring to the ideas of Ibn al-'Arabī and the school which derives its inspiration from him.

wājib al-wujūd: existing of necessity, referring solely to God [opp. *mumkin*].

walī (pl. *awliyā'*): favored by God, mystical saint.

wāqi'a: a mystical experience; also a reference to the annihilation and resurrection of the spirit [see *fanā'* and *qiyāma*].

wuḍū': ritual purification [see *ṭahāra*].

wujūd: being, existence, bodily existence.

wuṣūl: attainment.

ẓāhir: exoteric, outward, apparent [opp. *bāṭin*].

ẓahr: exoteric, apparent or outer dimension [opp. *baṭn*].

ẓann (pl. *ẓunūn*): thought, conjecture, idea, generally negatively connoting the ideas of an individual which are arrived at without divine help [see *khāṭir*].

Bibliography

Works by 'Alā' ad-dawla as-Simnānī

Bayān al-iḥsān li-ahl al-'irfān. MS. 11-mīm, Majāmī' fārsiyya, 78b–129b. Dār al-kutub, Cairo.

Chihil majlis-i shaykh 'Alā' ad-dawla-yi Simnānī. Compiled by Iqbāl-i Sīstānī. Edited by Najīb Māyil-i Hirawī. Tehran: Intishārāt-i adīb, 1987.

"Deux opuscules de Semnānī sur le moi théophanique." Edited by Hermann Landolt in *Mélanges Henry Corbin*. Tehran: 1977, 279–319.

Farḥat al-'āmilīn wa-furjat al-kāmilīn. Edited by Najīb Māyil-i Hirawī in "Chahār guftār-i shaykh 'Alā' ad-dawla-yi Simnānī." *Dānish* 3 (1985), 3–70.

Fuṣūl al-uṣūl. MS. 1, Fiqh ḥanafī fārsī, 47b–84b. Dār al-kutub, Cairo.

Hadiyyat al-muhtadī wa-hidāyat al-mubtadi'. MS. 353, Karaçelebizade, 80b–86a. Süleymaniye Kütüphanesi, Istanbul.

Khitām al-misk. MS. 11-mīm, Majāmī' fārsiyya, 141b–44b. Dār al-kutub, Cairo.

Kitāb qawāṭi' as-sawāṭi'. MS. 11-mīm, Majāmī' fārsiyya, 155b–83a. Dār al-kutub, Cairo.

Kitāb al-qudsiyyāt. MS. 165/2, Şehit Ali Paşa, 168b–231a. Süleymaniye Kütüphanesi, Istanbul.

Kitāb al-waṣāya. MS. A1588 (Catalog 5226), 35b–38a. Topkapı Sarayı Müzesi Kütüphanesi, Istanbul.

Maṭāf al-ashrāf. MS. 353, Karaçelebizade, 78b–80a. Süleymaniye Kütüphanesi, Istanbul.

Maṭla' an-nuqaṭ [extract]. MS. 11-mīm, Majāmī' fārsiyya, 150a–51a. Dār al-kutub, Cairo.

Mawārid ash-shawārid. MS. 11-mīm, Majāmī' fārsiyya, 147b–49b. Dār al-kutub, Cairo.

"Muqaddima tafsīr al-qur'ān li-'Alā' ad-dawla as-Simnānī." Edited by Paul Nwyia in *al-Abḥāth* 26 (1973–77), 141–57.

Muṣannafāt-i fārsī. Edited by Najīb Māyil-i Hirawī. Tehran: Shirkat-i intishārāt-i ʿilmī wa farhangī, 1990.

Opera Minora. Edited by Wheeler Thackston. Sources of Oriental Languages and Literatures, no. 10. Cambridge, MA: Harvard University, Office of the University Publisher, 1988.

Risāla ādāb as-sufra. Translated into Arabic and edited by Shaʿbān Rabīʿ Ṭarṭūr. Cairo: al-Hayʾa al-miṣriyya al-ʿāmma liʾl-kitāb, 1987.

Risāla fī-dhikr asāmī mashāyikhī. MS. 11-mīm, Majāmiʿ fārsiyya, 72a–76b. Dār al-kutub, Cairo.

Risāla fatḥ al-mubīn li-ahl al-yaqīn. MS. 1, Fiqh ḥanafī fārsī, 2b–11a. Dār al-kutub, Cairo.

Risālat al-ikhtiyār li-dhawiʾl-iʿtibār. MS. 11-mīm, Majāmiʿ fārsiyya, 151b–54b. Dār al-kutub, Cairo.

Risāla-yi nūriyya. MS 1105, Carullah Efendi, 44a–48b. Süleymaniye Kütüphanesi, Istanbul.

Risāla ṣadāʾif al-laṭāʾif. MS. 1, Fiqh ḥanafī fārsī, 84b–87b. Dār al-kutub, Cairo.

Risāla sirr bāl al-bāl li-dhawiʾl-ḥāl. MS. 11-mīm, Majāmiʿ fārsiyya, 227b–43b. Dār al-kutub, Cairo.

Risāla-yi sirr-i samāʿ. Edited by Najīb Māyil-i Hirawī in "Chahār guftār-i shaykh ʿAlāʾ ad-dawla-yi Simnānī." *Dānish* 3 (1985), 3–70.

Risāla fī-tafsīr āyāt qurʾāniyya fī-mawḍūʿ aṣ-ṣabr waʾl-iḥsān. MS. 11-mīm, Majāmiʿ fārsiyya, 136b–41a. Dār al-kutub, Cairo.

Shaqāʾiq al-ḥadāʾiq wa-ḥadāʾiq al-ḥaqāʾiq. MS. 821/7, Halet Efendi, 76b–78b. Süleymaniye Kütüphanesi, Istanbul.

Tafsīr najm al-qurʾān. MS. 165/1, Şehit Ali Paşa, 1–168, and MS. 54, Hekimoğlu Ali Paşa ve Camii. Süleymaniye Kütüphanesi, Istanbul.

Untitled treatise. MS. 11-mīm, Majāmiʿ fārsiyya, 145a–47a. Dār al-kutub, Cairo.

al-ʿUrwa li-ahl al-khalwa waʾl-jalwa. Edited by Najīb Māyil-i Hirawī. Tehran: Intishārāt-i Mawlā, 1983.

al-Wārid ash-shārid. MS. A1588 (Catalog no. 5226), 13b–35b. Topkapı Sarayı Müzesi Kütüphanesi, Istanbul.

Secondary Sources

Abd ar-Raḥmān, Mīrzā. *Taʾrīkh-i ʿulamāʾ-yi Khurāsān.* Edited by M. Bāqir-i Khurāsānī. Mashhad: Kitābfurūshī-yi diyānat, 1962.

Abdel-Kader, Ali Hassan. *The Life, Personality and Writings of al-Junayd.* London: Luzac, 1962.

Addas, Claude. *Ibn 'Arabī ou la quête du soufre rouge.* Bibliothèque des sciences humaines. Paris: Gallimard, 1989.

Affifi, A.E. *The Mystical Philosophy of Muhyid din-Ibnul Arabi.* Cambridge: Cambridge University Press; rpt. Lahore: Sh. Muhammad Ashraf, n.d.

Ahmad, Aziz. *Studies in Islamic Culture in the Indian Environment.* Oxford: Oxford University Press, 1964.

————. *An Intellectual History of Islam in India.* Edinburgh: University of Edinburgh Press, 1969.

————. "Religious and political ideas of Shaikh Ahmad Sirhindī." *Rivista degli studi orientali* 36 (1961), 259–70.

Al-Shaibi. Kamil M. *Sufism and Shi'ism.* Surbiton: LAAM, 1991.

Algar, Hamid. "Some Observations on Religion in Safavid Persia." *Iranian Studies* 7:1–2 (1974), 287–90.

————. "Reflections of Ibn 'Arabî in Early Naqshbandî Tradition." *Journal of the Muhyiddin Ibn 'Arabi Society* 10 (1991), 45–66.

————. see also Dāya ar-Rāzī.

al-Amīn, Muḥsin. *A'yān ash-shī'a.* 3rd edition. Beirut: Maṭba'at al-inṣāf, 1961.

Anawati, G.C. and L. Gardet. *Mystique musulmane: aspects et tendances.* Etudes musulmanes, no. 8. Edited by Etienne Gilson and Louis Gardet. Paris: Librairie philosophique J. Vrin, 1968.

Ansari, A.S. Bazmee. "Ashraf Djahāngīr." *Encyclopaedia of Islam,* new edition. Vol. 1. Leiden: E.J. Brill, 1960, 702b.

Arnaldez, R. "Lāhūt and Nāsūt." *Encyclopaedia of Islam,* new edition. Vol. 5. Leiden: E.J. Brill, 1985, 611b–14b.

Ashraf, Sayyid Waḥīd. "Āthwīñ ṣadī hijrī mēñ Īrān awr Hindustān mēñ Ibn-i 'Arabī kē afkār par radd-i 'amal." *Dānish* 8 (1986), 104–25.

al-Asnawī, Jamāl ad-dīn. *Ṭabaqāt ash-shāfi'iyya.* 2 vols. Edited by 'Abd Allāh al-Jubūrī. Baghdad: Al-Irshad Press, 1971.

al-'Asqalānī, Ibn Ḥajar. *ad-Durar al-kāmina.* 5 vols. Edited by M. Sayyid Jādd al-Ḥaqq. Cairo: Dār al-kutub al-ḥadītha, 1966.

Ateş, Süleyman. *İşârî Tefsîr Okulu.* Ankara Üniversitesi İlâhiyat Fakültesi Yayınları, no. 122. Ankara: Ankara Üniversitesi Basımevi, 1974.

————. "Üç müfessir bir tefsîr." *İlâhiyât Fakültesi Dergisi* 18 (1970), 85–104.

Aubin, Jean. "Shaykh Ibrāhīm Zāhid Gīlānī." *Turcica* 21–23 (1991), 39–54.

Babs Mala, S. "Self-realization in the mystical thought of al-Kubra." *Orita* 12 (1978), 51–65.

Baǧdatlı Ismail Paşa. See Ismāʿīl Pāshā al-Baghdādī.

al-Baghdādī, Majd ad-dīn. *Tuḥfat al-barara fī-masāʾil al-ʿashara* [sic]. Translated into Persian by Muḥammad Bāqir Sāʿidī-yi Khurāsānī. Edited by Mushtāq ʿAlī. Tehran: Intishārāt-i Marwī, 1989.

Bahāristān-i Shāhī: A Chronicle of Medieval Kashmir. Edited and translated by K.N. Pandit. Calcutta: Firma KLM Ltd., 1991.

Barthold, W. *An Historical Geography of Iran.* Translated by Svat Soucek. Edited by C. E. Bosworth. Modern Classics in Near Eastern Studies. Princeton: Princeton University Press, 1984.

Bosworth, C.E. *The Islamic Dynasties.* Edinburgh: Edinburgh University Press, 1967.

Böwering, Gerhard. *The Mystical Vision of Existence in Classical Islam.* Studien zur Sprache, Geschichte und Kultur des Islamisch Orients, no. 9. Edited by Bertold Spuler. Berlin: Walter de Gruyter, 1980.

———. "The *Adab* Literature of Classical Sufism: Anṣārī's Code of Conduct." *Moral Conduct and Authority: The Place of Adab in South Asian Islam.* Edited by Barbara D. Metcalf. Berkeley: University of California Press, 1984, 62–87.

———. "ʿAlī Hamadānī." *Encyclopaedia Iranica.* Vol. 1. Edited by Ehsan Yarshater. London: Routledge and Kegan Paul, 1985, 862b–64a.

Boyle, J. A. *The Successors of Genghis Khan.* New York: 1971.

Brocklemann, Carl. *Geschichte der arabischen Litteratur.* 2 vols. 2nd Edition. Leiden: E. J. Brill, 1943–49; Supplement, 3 vols. Leiden: E. J. Brill, 1937–42.

Browne, Edward G. *A History of Persian Literature.* 4 vols. Cambridge: Cambridge University Press, 1920.

Būzjānī, Darwīsh ʿAlī. *Rawḍat ar-riyāḥīn.* Edited by Heshmat Moayyed. Persian Text Series, no. 29. Edited by E. Yarshater. Tehran: Bungāh-i tarjumān wa nashr-i kitāb, 1966.

The Cambridge History of Iran. Vol. 5: The Saljuq and Mongol Periods. Edited by J. A. Boyle. Cambridge: Cambridge University Press, 1968.

———. Vol. 6: The Timurid and Safavid Periods. Edited by P. Jackson and L. Lockhart. Cambridge: Cambridge University Press, 1986.

Chabbi, J. "Remarques sur le développement historique des mouvements ascétiques et mystiques au Khurasan III/IXe siècle." *Studia Islamica* 46 (1977), 5–72.

Chittick, William C. *The Sufi Path of Knowledge*. Albany: SUNY Press, 1989.

———. "Ibn 'Arabī and His School." *Islamic Spirituality: Manifestations*. Edited by S.H. Nasr. World of Spirituality, vol. 20. New York: Cross Roads, 1991, 49–79.

Chodkiewicz, Michel. *Le sceau des saints: prophétie et sainteté dans la doctrine d'Ibn Arabî*. Bibliothèque des sciences humaines. Paris: Gallimard, 1986.

Corbin, Henry. *En Islam iranien*. 4 vols. Paris: Gallimard, 1972.

———. *The Man of Light in Iranian Sufism*. Translated by Nancy Pearson. Boulder: Shambala Press, 1978.

———. "L'intériorisation des sens en herméneutique soufie iranienne." *Eranos Jahrbuch* 26 (1957), 57–187.

———. "Physiologie de l'homme de lumière dans le soufisme iranien." *Ombre et lumière*. Paris: Académie Septentrionale, 1961.

Cordt, H. *Die Sitzungen des 'Alā' ad-Dawla as-Simnānī*. Zurich: Juris, 1977.

Dānishpazhūh, M.T. "Khirqa-yi hazār mīkhī." *Collected Papers on Islamic Philosophy and Mysticism*. Edited by H. Landolt and M. Mohaghegh. Tehran: La branche de Téhéran de l'institut des études islamiques de l'Université McGill, 1971, 147–78.

Dārā Shikūh. *Safīnat al-awliyā'*. Cawnpore: 1906.

Davidson, Herbert A. *Alfarabi, Avicenna, and Averroes, on Intellect*. New York: Oxford University Press, 1992.

Dawlatshāh Samarqandī. *Tadhkiratu'sh Shu'ará*. Edited by E. G. Browne. Persian Historical Texts, no. 1. London: Luzac and Co., 1901.

ad-Dāwūdī, Shams ad-dīn Muḥammad b. 'Alī. *Ṭabaqāt al-mufassirīn*. 2 vols. Edited by 'Alī M. 'Umar. Cairo: Maktaba Wahba, 1972.

Dāya ar-Rāzī, Najm ad-dīn. *The Path of God's Bondsmen from Origin to Return (Mirṣād al-'ibād min al-mabdā' ila'l-ma'ād)*. Translated by Hamid Algar. Delmar: Caravan, 1982.

———. See also Algar, Hamid.

Dehghan, Iraj. "Khwādjū." *Encyclopaedia of Islam*, new edition. Vol. 4. Leiden: E.J. Brill, 1978, 909b–10a.

DeWeese, Devin. "Sayyid ʿAlī Hamadānī and Kubrawī Hagiographical Traditions." *The Legacy of Medieval Persian Sufism*. Edited by Leonard Lewisohn. London: Khaniqahi Nimatullahi Publications, 1992, 121–58.

———. *The Kashf al-Hudā of Kamāl ad-dīn Ḥusayn Khorezmī: A Fifteenth-Century Sufi Commentary on the Qaṣīdat al-burdah in Khorezmian Turkic.*" Ph.D. Diss., Indiana University, Bloomington, 1985.

adh-Dhahabī, Muḥammad Ḥusayn. *at-Tafsīr wa'l-mufassirūn*. 2 vols. 2nd edition. Cairo: Dār al-kutub al-ḥadītha, 1976.

adh-Dhahabī, Shams ad-dīn. *Maʿrifat al-qurrāʾ al-kibār*. 2 vols. Edited by Muḥammad Sayyid Jādd al-Ḥaqq. Cairo: Dār al-kutub al-ḥadītha, 1969.

———. *Siyar aʿlām an-nubalāʾ*. 35 vols. Beirut: Muʾassasat ar-risāla, 1985.

———. *Tadhkirat al-ḥuffāẓ*. 5 vols. Hyderabad: Dāʾirat al-maʿārif, 1915.

———. *Dhayl tadhkirat al-ḥuffāẓ li'dh-Dhahabī*. Damascus: al-Qudsī, 1928.

Dikhudā, ʿAlī Akbar. *Lughatnāma*. Edited by M. Muʿīn. Tehran: Dānishkada-yi adabiyyāt wa ʿulūm-i insānī, 1958.

Elias, Jamal J. "A Kubrawī Treatise on Mystical Visions: The Risāla-yi nūriyya of ʿAlāʾ ad-dawla as-Simnānī." *Muslim World* 83 (1993), 68–80.

Ernst, Carl W. *Words of Ecstasy in Sufism*. Albany: SUNY Press, 1985.

Friedmann, Yohanan. *Shaykh Aḥmad Sirhindī*. McGill Islamic Studies, no. 2. London: McGill-Queen's University Press, 1971.

Gardet, Louis. "ʿĀlam." *Encyclopaedia of Islam*, new edition. Vol. 1. Leiden: E.J. Brill, 1960, 349b–52a.

Ghanī, Qāsim. *Tāʾrīkh-i taṣawwuf dar Islām*. 2nd edition. Tehran: Kitāb-furūshī-yi Ibn Sīnā, 1951.

al-Ghazzālī, Abū Ḥāmid. *Iḥyāʾ ʿulūm ad-dīn*. 4 vols. Cairo: Maṭbaʿat al-istiqāma, n.d.

Ghiyāth ad-dīn al-Ḥasanī (Khwānd Amīr). *Dastūr al-wuzarāʾ*. Edited by Saʿīd Nafīsī. Tehran: Kitābfurūshī-yi Iqbāl, 1938,

———. *Tāʾrīkh-i ḥabīb as-siyar*. 4 vols. Tehran: Kitābkhāna-yi Khayyām, 1964.

———. *Rijāl-i kitāb-i ḥabīb as-siyar*. Edited by ʿAbd al-Ḥusayn Nawāʾī. Tehran: Sahāmī, 1955.

Gramlich, Richard. *Die schiitischen Derwischorden Persiens*. Vols. 1-3 Abhandlungen für die Kunde des Morgenlandes. Der Deutschen morgenländischen Gesellschaft. Wiesbaden: Franz Steiner, 1965–81.

Grousset, René. *The Empire of the Steppes*. Translated by Naomi Walford. New Brunswick: Rutgers University Press, 1970.

Habib, Mohammad and Khaliq Ahmad Nizami, editors. *A Comprehensive History of India*. Vol. 5: The Delhi Sultanate. New Delhi: Peoples Publishing House, 1970.

Ḥāfiẓ-i Ābrū, Shihāb ad-dīn al-Khwāfī. *Dhayl-i jāmiʿ at-tawārīkh-i rashīdī*. Edited by Khānbābā Biyānī. Tehran: Shirkat-i taḍāmunī-yi ʿilmī, 1938.

Ḥājjī Khalīfa. *Kashf aẓ-ẓunūn*. 4 vols. Istanbul: Milli Eğitim Basımevi, 1971.

Halm, Heinz. *Kosmologie und Heilslehre der frühen Ismāʿīlīya*. Abhandlungen für die Kunde des Morgenlandes, no. 44:1. Wiesbaden: Franz Steiner, 1978.

Ḥamūya, Saʿd ad-dīn. *al-Miṣbāḥ fiʾt-taṣawwuf*. Edited by Najīb Māyil-i Hirawī. Tehran: Intishārāt-i Mawlā, 1983.

———. *Kitāb baḥr al-maʿānī*. MS. 706, 1a–92a. Köprülü Kütüphanesi, Istanbul.

———. *Kitāb al-maḥbūb*. MS. 2058, Ayasofya, 1b–205a. Süleymaniye Kütüphanesi, Istanbul.

———. *Risāla fī-ẓuhūr khātim al-wilāya*. MS. 2058, Ayasofya, 206a–7b. Süleymaniye Kütüphanesi, Istanbul.

———. Untitled. MS. 3931, Serez, 33b–43b. Süleymaniye Kütüphanesi, Istanbul.

Ḥaqīqat, ʿAbd ar-Rafīʿ. *Taʾrīkh-i Simnān*. Tehran: 1962.

———. *Taʾrīkh-i Qūmis*. Tehran: 1965.

———. *Taʾrīkh-i junbish-i sarbadārān wa dīgar junbishhā-yi īrānīyān*. Tehran: Intishārāt-i āzād andīshān, 1981.

———. *Khumkhāna-yi waḥdat*. Tehran: Shirkat-i muʾallifān-u mutarjimān-i Īrān, 1983.

Harley, J.B. and D. Woodward, editors. *The History of Cartography*. Vol. 2, book 1. Cartography in the Traditional Islamic and South Asian Societies. Chicago: University of Chicago Press, 1992.

al-Ḥasanī, ʿAbd al-Ḥayy b. Fakhr ad-dīn. *Nuzhat al-khawāṭir wa-bahjat al-masāmiʿ waʾn-nawāẓir*. 8 vols. Hyderabad: Dāʾirat al-maʿārif al-ʿuthmāniyya, 1931.

Heath, Peter. *Allegory and Philosophy in Avicenna*. Philadelphia: University of Pennsylvania Press, 1992.

Hinz, Walther. *Islamische Masse und Gewichte*. Handbuch der Orientalistik, no. 1. Edited by Bertold Spuler. Leiden: E.J. Brill, 1955.

Hirawī, Najīb Mayil, "Chahār guftār-i shaykh ‘Alā’ ad-dawla-yi Simnānī." *Dānish* 3 (1985), 3–70.

———. "Kitābshināsī wa nuskhashināsī-yi ‘Alā’ ad-dawla-yi Simnānī." *Kitābshināsī*, no. 1. Edited by Akhtar Rāhī and ‘Ārif Nawshāhī. Lahore: Maktaba-yi ‘ilmiyya, 1986.

———. "Chahār naẓar pīrāmūn-i chahār athar-i mansūb bi Sayyid ‘Alī-yi Hamadānī." *Dānish* 11 (1987), 90–116.

———. See also works by Simnānī.

Hussaini, Syed Shah Khusro. *Sayyid Muḥammad al-Ḥusaynī-i Gīsūdirāz on Sufism*. Delhi: Idarah-i Adabiyat-i Delli, 1983.

Ibn Abī Uṣaybi‘a al-Khazrajī. *‘Uyūn al-anbā’ fī-ṭabaqāt al-aṭibbā’*. Edited by Nizār Riḍā. Beirut: Dār maktabat al-hayāt, 1965.

Ibn al-‘Arabī, Muḥyī ad-dīn. *al-Futūḥāt al-makkiyya*. 12 vols. Edited by ‘Uthmān Yaḥyā. Cairo: al-Hay’a al-miṣriyya al-‘āmma li’l-kitāb, 1975–89.

Ibn al-Athīr al-Jazarī, ‘Izz ad-dīn. *al-Lubāb fī-tahdhīb al-ansāb*. 3 vols. Beirut: Dār Ṣādir, 1972.

Ibn al-Fuwaṭī al-Baghdādī, Kamāl ad-dīn. *al-Ḥawādith al-jāmi‘a*. Baghdad: al-Maktaba al-‘arabiyya, 1932.

Ibn Ḥajar. See al-‘Asqalānī.

Ibn al-‘Imād, Abū Falāḥ ‘Abd al-Ḥayy. *Shadharāt adh-dhahab fī-akhbār man dhahab*. 8 vols. in 4. Cairo: Maktabat al-Qudsī, 1932.

Ibn al-Karbalā’ī-yi Tabrīzī, Ḥusayn. *Rawḍāt al-janān wa jannāt al-janān*. Edited by Ja‘far Sulṭān al-Qurrā’ī. Majmū‘a-yi matūn-i fārsī, no. 20. Edited by E. Yarshater. Tehran: Bungāh-i tarjuma wa nashr-i kitāb, 1965.

Ibn Qāḍī Shuhba, Taqī ad-dīn ad-Dimashqī. *Ṭabaqāt ash-shāfi‘iyya*. 4 vols. Edited by ‘Abd al-‘Alīm Khān. Beirut: ‘Ālam al-kutub, 1987.

Ibn Qayyim al-Jawziyya. *Madārij as-sālikīn*. 2 vols. Edited by M. Muḥyī ad-dīn ‘Abd al-Ḥamīd. Cairo: 1956.

Ibn Rāfi‘, Abu’l-Ma‘ālī Muḥammad. *Tā’rīkh ‘ulamā’ Baghdād*. Edited by ‘Abbās al-‘Azzāwī. Baghdad: Maṭba‘at al-Ahālī, 1938.

Ibn Taymiyya, Abu’l-‘Abbās Aḥmad. *Risāla ila’s-sulṭān al-Malik an-Nāṣir fī-sha’n at-tatār*. Edited by Ṣalāḥ ad-dīn al-Munajjid. Beirut: Dār al-kitāb al-jadīd, 1976.

al-Isfarā'inī, Nūr ad-dīn. *Le révélateur des mystères.* Edited and translated into French by Hermann Landolt. Lagrasse: Verdier, 1986.

————. See also Landolt, Hermann.

Ismā'īl Pāshā al-Baghdādī. *Hadiyyat al-'ārifīn.* 2 vols. Istanbul: Milli Eğitim Basımevi, 1951.

————. See also Ḥājjī Khalīfa.

Ivanow, W. "More on the Sources of Jami's Nafahat." *Asiatic Society of Bengal, Journal and Proceedings.* New Series 19 (1923), 299–303.

Izutsu, Toshihiko. "The Theophanic Ego in Sufism: An Analysis of the Sufi Psychology of Najm al-Dīn Kubrā." *Sophia Perennis* 4:1 (1978), 23–42.

Jāmī, 'Abd ar-Raḥmān. *Nafaḥāt al-uns.* Edited by Mahdī Tawḥīdīpūr. Teheran: Kitābfurūshī-yi Sa'dī, 1958.

al-Jawziyya. See Ibn al-Qayyim al-Jawziyya.

al-Jazarī. See Ibn al-Athīr al-Jazarī.

al-Jurjānī, 'Alī. *Kitāb at-ta'rīfāt.* Istanbul: Maṭba'a Aḥmad Kāmil, 1909.

Juwaynī, 'Alā' ad-dīn 'Aṭā' Malik. *Tā'rīkh-i jahāngushā.* 3 vols. Edited by Muḥammad b. 'Abd al-Wahhāb-i Qazwīnī. Leiden: E. J. Brill, 1937.

Kachawchawī, Waḥīd Ashraf. *Ḥayāt-i Sayyid Ashraf Jahāngīr-i Simnānī.* Lucknow: Sarfarāz Qawmī Press, 1975.

al-Kāshānī, 'Abd ar-Razzāq. *Kitāb iṣṭilāḥāt aṣ-ṣūfiyya.* Edited by Aloys Sprenger. Lahore: al-Irshād, rpt. 1974.

Kāshī. See Kāshānī.

Khūnjī, Faḍl Allāh b. Rūzbihān. *Mihmānnāma-yi Bukhārā.* Translated into German by Ursula Ott, *Transoxanien und Turkestan zu Beginn des sechzehnten Jahrhunderts.* Freiburg: 1974.

Khwāfī, Faṣīḥ Aḥmad b. Jalāl ad-dīn Muḥammad. *Mujmal-i faṣīḥī.* 4 vols. Edited by Maḥmūd Farrukh. Mashhad: Kitābfurūshī-yi bāstān, 1960.

Khwānd Amīr. See Ghiyāth ad-dīn al-Ḥasanī.

al-Khwānsārī al-Iṣbahānī, Muḥammad Bāqir al-Mūsawī. *Rawḍāt al-jannāt.* 8 vols. Tehran: Maktaba-yi Ismā'īlīyān, 1970.

al-Kirmānī, Aḥmad Ḥamīd ad-dīn. *Rāḥat al-'aql.* Edited by Muṣṭafā Ghālib. Beirut: Dār al-Andalus, 1967.

Kishmī, Khwāja Muḥammad Hāshim. *Zubdat al-maqāmāt.* Lahore: Bustān-i adab, 1969.

Köprülü, Mehmed Fuad. *Türk Edebiyatında İlk Mutasavvıflar.* 4th edition. Ankara: Diyanet İşleri Başkanlığı Yayınları, 1981.

Krawulsky, Dorothea. *Īrān—Das Reich der Īlḫāne: Eine Topographisch-Historische Studie*. Supplement to Tübinger Atlas des Vorderen Orients, no. 17. Wiesbaden: Dr. Ludwig Reichert, 1978.

al-Kubrā, Najm ad-dīn. *Ādāb aṣ-ṣūfiyya*. Edited by Masʿūd Qāsimī. Tehran: Kitābfurūshī-yi Zawwār, 1984.

————. *al-Uṣūl al-ʿashara*. Translated by ʿAbd al-Ghafūr-i Lārī. Edited by Najīb Māyil-i Hirawī. Tehran: Intishārāt-i Mawlā, 1984.

————. *Ijāza* granted to Saʿd ad-dīn-i Ḥamūya. MS. 2800, Şehit Ali Paşa, 29b–30b. Süleymaniye Kütüphanesi, Istanbul.

————. See also Meier, Fritz and Molé, Marijan.

Lāhūrī, Ghulām Sarwar. *Khazīnat al-aṣfiyā'*. Translated into Urdu by Pīrzāda I.A. Fārūqī. Lahore: Maktaba-yi nabawiyya, 1983.

Lambton, Anne K.S. *Continuity and Change in Medieval Persia: Aspects of Administrative, Economic and Social History, 11th-14th Century*. Columbia Lectures on Iranian Studies, no. 2. Edited by Ehsan Yarshater. Albany: Bibliotheca Persica, 1988.

Landolt, H., editor. *Correspondence spirituelle échangée entre Nuroddin Esfarayeni et son disciple ʿAlaoddawleh Semnani*. Le departement d'iranologie de l'institut franco-iranien de recherche, no. 21. Edited by H. Corbin. Tehran: L'institut franco-iranien de recherche, 1972.

————. *Kāshif al-asrār* of Nūr ad-Dīn Isfarā'inī. Tehran: Institute of Islamic Studies, 1980.

————. "Simnânî on waḥdat al-wujûd." *Wisdom of Persia. Collected Papers on Islamic Philosophy and Mysticism*. Edited by H. Landolt and M. Mohaghegh. Tehran: La branche de Téhéran de l'institut des études islamiques de l'Université McGill, 1971.

————. "Der Briefwechsel zwischen Kāshānī und Simnānī über Waḥdat al-Wuǧūd." *Der Islam* 50 (1973), 29–81.

————. See also Isfarā'inī.

LeStrange, Guy. *The Lands of the Eastern Caliphate*. Cambridge: Cambridge University Press, 1930.

Majd ad-dīn al-Baghdādī. See al-Baghdādī.

al-Maqqarī at-Tilimsānī, Aḥmad b. Muḥammad. *Nafḥ aṭ-ṭīb min-ghusn al-andalus ar-raṭīb*. 11 vols. Edited by M.M. ʿAbd al-Ḥamīd. Beirut: Dār al-kitāb al-ʿarabī, 1967.

Massignon, Louis. *Recueil de textes inédits concernant l'histoire de la mystique en pays d'Islam*. Paris: Librairie orientaliste Paul Geuthner, 1929.

————. *La passion de Husayn Ibn Mansûr Hallaj*. 4 vols. Paris: 1922; rpt. Gallimard, 1975.

————. *The Passion of al-Hallāj*. 4 vols. Translated by Herbert Mason. Bollingen Series, no. 98. Princeton: Princeton University Press, 1982.

Ma'ṣūm 'Alī Shāh, Muḥammad Ma'ṣūm Shīrāzī. *Ṭarā'iq al-ḥaqā'iq*. 3 vols. Edited by M. Ja'far Maḥjūb. Tehran: Kitābkhāna-yi Bārānī, 1921.

Mazzaoui, Michel M. *The Origins of the Safawids: Shī'ism, Ṣūfism, and the Ġulāt*. Freiburger Islam Studien, no. 3. Wiesbaden: Franz Steiner Verlag, 1972.

Meier, Fritz, editor. *Die Fawā'iḥ al-Ǧamāl wa Fawātiḥ al-Ǧalāl des Naǧm ad-Dīn al-Kubrā*. Akademie der Wissenschaften und der Literatur, no. 9. Wiesbaden: Franz Steiner Verlag, 1957.

————. *Abū Sa'īd-i Abū l-Ḫayr*. Acta Iranica, 3rd Series, no. 11. Leiden: E.J. Brill, 1976.

————. "Stambuler Handschriften dreir persischer Mystiker: 'Ain al-quḍāt al-Hamadhānī, Naǧm ad-dīn al-Kubrā, Naǧm ad-dīn ad-Dāja." *Der Islam* 24 (1937), 1–42.

————. "'Alā' al-Dawla al-Simnānī." *Encyclopaedia of Islam*, new edition. Vol. 1. Leiden: E.J. Brill, 1960, 346b–47b.

————. "The Problem of Nature in the Esoteric Monism of Islam." *Spirit and Nature: Papers from the Eranos Yearbooks*. Bollingen Series, no. 30, vol. 1. Princeton: Princeton University Press, 1954; rpt. 1972, 149–203.

Melville, Charles. "Pādshāh-i Islām: The Conversion of Sultan Maḥmūd Ghāzān Khān." *Pembroke Papers*. Edited by Charles Melville. Vol. 1: Persian and Islamic Studies in Honour of P. W. Avery. Cambridge: University of Cambridge Center of Middle Eastern Studies, 1990, 159–77.

Mīr Khwānd, Mīr Muḥammad b. Sayyid Burhān ad-dīn Khwāwandshāh. *Tā'rīkh-i rawḍat aṣ-ṣafā*. 5 vols. Tehran: Kitābfurūshī-yi Pīrūz, 1960.

Molé, Marijan. *Les mystiques musulmans*. Paris: Presses universitaires de France, 1965.

————. "La version persane du traité de dix principes de Najm al-Din Kobrā, par 'Alī b. Shihāb al-Dīn Hamadānī." *Farhang-i Irān zamīn* 6 (1958), 38–51.

————. "Un traité de 'Alā' al-Dawla Simnānī sur 'Alī b. Abī Ṭālib." *Bulletin d'études orientales* 16 (1958–60), 61–99.

————. "Les Kubrawiya entre sunnisme et shiisme aux huitième et neuvième siècles de l'Hégire." *Revue des études islamiques* 29 (1961), 61–142.

————. "Traités mineurs de Naǧm al-dīn Kubrà." *Annales islamologiques* 4 (1963), 1–78.

————. "Entre le Mazdéisme et l'Islam: la bonne et la mauvaise religion." *Mélanges Henri Massé*, 1963, 303–16.

Morewedge, Parviz, editor. *The "Metaphysics" of Avicenna (ibn Sīnā).* Persian Heritage Series, no. 13. New York: Columbia University Press, 1973.

————. *Neoplatonism and Islamic Thought.* Studies in Neoplatonism, Ancient and Modern, no. 5. Albany: SUNY Press, 1992.

Murtaḍawī, Manūchihr. *Taḥqīq dar bāra-yi dawra-yi Īlkhānān-i Īrān.* Tabriz: Kitābfurūshī-yi Tihrān, 1963.

————. *Masā'il-i aṣr-i Īlkhānān.* Silsila-yi tā'rīkh wa bāstān shināsī, no. 3. Tabriz: Intishārāt-i mu'assasa-yi tā'rīkh wa farhang-i Īrān, 1979.

Mustawfī al-Qazwīnī, Ḥamd Allāh. *Nuzhat al-qulūb.* 2 vols. Edited and translated by G. Le Strange. E.J.W. Gibb Memorial Series, 23:1–2. Leiden: E.J. Brill, 1915, 1919.

————. *Tā'rīkh-i guzīda.* Edited by 'Abd al-Ḥusayn Nawā'ī. Tehran: Intishārāt-i Amīr-i Kabīr, 1983.

Mu'tamidī, Mihīndukht. *Mawlāna Khālid Naqshbandī wa pīrawān-i ṭarīqat-i ū.* Tehran: Pāzhang, 1989.

Nafīsī, Sa'īd. "Khāndān-i Sa'd ad-dīn-i Ḥamawī." *Kunjkāwīhā-yi 'ilmī wa adabī.* Intishārāt-i dānishgāh-i Tihrān 83 (1950), 6–39.

————. "'Alā' ad-dawla-yi Simnānī." *Yaghmā* 7 (1954), 358–62.

Najm ad-dīn-i Dāya ar-Rāzī. See Dāya ar-Rāzī.

Nasafī, 'Azīz ad-dīn. *Zubdat al-ḥaqā'iq.* Edited by Ḥaqq-Wardī Nāṣirī. Tehran: Kitābkhāna-yi Ṭahūrī, 1985.

Nasr, Seyyed Hossein. *An Introduction to Islamic Cosmological Doctrines.* Cambridge, MA: Belknap Press, 1964.

Nawā'ī, Mīr 'Alī Shīr. *Majālis an-nafā'is.* Edited by A.A. Hikmet. N.p.: 1945.

Netton, Ian Richard. *Allāh Transcendent: Studies in the Structure and Semiotics of Islamic Philosophy, Theology and Cosmology.* London: Routledge, 1989.

Nicholson, R.A. *Studies in Islamic Mysticism.* Cambridge: Cambridge University Press, 1921; rpt. 1980.

Nwyia, Paul. *Exégèse coranique et langage mystique*. Pensée arabe et musulmane, no. 49. Beirut: Dar el-Machreq, 1970.

————. "Corps et espirit dans la mystique musulmane." *Studia missionalia* 26 (1977), 165–89.

Peterson, Daniel C. *"Cosmogony and the Ten Separated Intellects in the Rāḥat al-'Aql of Ḥamīd al-Dīn al-Kirmānī,"* Ph.D. diss., University of California, Los Angeles, 1990.

Petrushevsky, A.P. *Nahḍat-i sarbadārān-i Khurāsān*. Translated into Persian by Karīm Kishāwarz. 1962. Reprint. Tehran: Intishārāt-i payām, 1972.

Profitlich, Manfred. *Die Terminologie Ibn 'Arabis im ≪ Kitāb wasā'il al-sā'il≫ des Ibn Saudakīn*. Islamkundliche Untersuchungen, no. 19. Freiburg: Klaus Schwarz Verlag, 1973.

al-Qāshānī, Abu'l-Qāsim 'Abd Allāh b. 'Alī. *Tā'rīkh-i Uljāytū*. Edited by Mahin Hambly. Majmū'a-yi mutūn-i farsī, no. 40. Tehran: Bungāh-i tarjuma wa nashr-i kitāb, 1969.

Qazwīnī. See Mustawfī al-Qazwīnī.

al-Qushshāshī, Ṣafī ad-dīn Aḥmad b. Muḥammad ad-Dajjānī. *as-Simṭ al-majīd*. Hyderabad: Majlis-i dā'irat al-ma'ārif an-niẓāmiyya, 1909.

Rashīd ad-dīn Faḍl Allāh Hamadhānī. *Jāmi' at-tawārīkh*. 2 vols. Edited by Bahman Karīmī. Tehran: Kitābfurūshī-yi Iqbāl, 1959; rpt. 1988.

————. *Tā'rīkh-i mubārak-i ghāzānī*. Edited by Karl Jahn. London: 1940.

Rāzī, Amīn Aḥmad. *Haft iqlīm*. 3 vols. Edited by Jawwād Fāḍil. Tehran: Kitābfurūshī-yi 'Alī Akbar 'Ilmī, n.d.

Riḍā Qūlī Khān Hidāyat. *Majma' al-fuṣaḥā'*. 6 vols. Edited by Maẓāhir Muṣaffā. Tehran: Chāp-i Mūsawī, 1960.

————. *Tadhkira-yi riyāḍ al-'ārifīn*. Edited by Sayyid Aḥmad Muhadhdhab. Tehran: Kitābkhāna-yi mahdiyya, 1937.

Riyāḍ, Muḥammad. *Aḥwāl-u āthār-u āsh'ār-i Mīr Sayyid 'Alī-yi Hamadānī*. Islamabad: Markaz-i taḥqīqāt-i fārsī-yi Īrān wa Pākistān, 1985.

Rizvi, Saiyid Athar Abbas. *A History of Sufism in India*. 2 vols. New Delhi: Munshiram Manoharlal, 1978, 1983.

Rūzbihān Baqlī-yi Shīrāzī. *Kitāb 'abhar al-'āshiqīn*. Edited by Henry Corbin and Mohammed Moin. Tehran: Institut français d'iranologie de Téhéran, 1958; rpt. 1981.

Sadr, Sayyed Mozaffer. *Sharḥ-i aḥwāl-u afkār-u āthār-i Shaykh 'Alā' ad-dawla as-Simnānī*. Tehran: Dānish, 1955.

aṣ-Ṣafadī, Ibn Aybak. *Kitāb al-wāfī bi'l-wafayāt: Das Biographische Lexikon des Ṣalāḥaddīn Ḥalīl ibn Aibak aṣ-Ṣafadī*. Edited by Iḥsān 'Abbās. Bibliotheca Islamica, no. 7. Wiesbaden: Franz Steiner Verlag, 1969.

———. *A'yān al-'aṣr*. MS. 1809, Atif Efendi. Süleymaniye Kütüphanesi, Istanbul.

Ṣahinoğlu, M. Nazif. *Alâ al-Davla al-Simnânî: Hayatı, Eserleri, Kelâm Telâkkisi, Tasavvuf Alanındaki Görüşleri ile Beyân al-İhsân li ahl al-îkân*. Istanbul: Ṣarkiyat Araṣtırma Merkezi Kitaplan, no. 6, 1966.

———. "Alâuddevle-i Simnânî." *Türkiye Diyanet Vakfı İslam Ansiklopedisi*. Vol. 2. Edited by Kemal Güren et. al.. Istanbul: Türkiye Diyanet Vakfı, 1989, 345a–47b.

as-Sam'ānī, Abū Sa'd 'Abd al-Karīm. *Kitāb al-ansāb*. 6 vols. 'Abd ar-Raḥmān al-Yamānī. Hyderabad: Dā'irat al-ma'ārif, 1962.

as-Sam'ānī, Aḥmad. *Rawḥ al-arwāḥ fī-sharḥ asmā' al-malik al-fattāḥ*. Edited by N. M. Hirawī. Tehran: Intishārāt-i 'ilmī wa farhangī, 1989.

Samarqandī. See Dawlatshāh Samarqandī.

Saunders, John J. *A History of Medieval Islam*. London: Routledge and Kegan Paul, 1965.

———. *Muslims and Mongols*. Edited by G. W. Rice. Christchurch: University of Canterbury Press, 1977.

Schimmel, Annemarie. *Islam in the Indian Subcontinent*. Leiden: E.J. Brill, 1980.

Sezgin, Fuat. *Geschichte des arabischen Schrifttums*. 4 vols. Leiden: E. J. Brill, 1967–72.

ash-Shaybī, Kāmil Muṣṭafā. See Al-Shaibi.

Shīrāzī, 'Īsā b. Junayd. *Tadhkira-yi hazār mazār*. Edited by Nūrānī Wiṣāl. Shiraz: Kitābkhāna-yi Aḥmadī, 1985.

Shīrwānī, Ḥājjī Zayn al-'ābidīn. *Riyāḍ as-siyāḥa*. Edited by Aṣghar Ḥāmid Rabbānī. Tehran: Kitābfurūshī-yi Sa'dī, 1960.

Shpall, William. "A Note on Najm al-dīn al-Rāzī and the *Baḥr al-ḥaqā'iq*." *Folia Orientalia* 22 (1981–84), 69–80.

Shushtarī, Nūr Allāh. *Majālis al-mu'minīn*. 2 vols. Tehran: Kitābfurūshī-yi islāmiyya, 1986.

as-Sijistānī, Abū Ya'qūb Isḥāq. *Kitāb ithbāt an-nubuwāt*. Edited by 'Ārif Tāmr. Beirut: Imprimerie catholique, 1966.

Sirhindī, Aḥmad Fārūqī. *Maktūbāt-i Imām-i Rabbānī.* 3 vols. Edited by Nūr Aḥmad Naqshbandī and Shāh Abu'l-Khayr. Lahore: Rauf Academy, n.d.

Smith, John M. *The History of the Sarbadār Dynasty 1336-1381 A.D. and its Sources.* Publications in Near and Middle East Studies, Columbia University. The Hague: Mouton, 1970.

Spuler, Bertold. *Die Mongolen in Iran: Politik, Verwaltung und Kultur der Ilchanzeit 1220–1350.* Berlin: Akademie Verlag, 1955.

————. *History of the Mongols.* Translated by H. and S. Drumond. Berkeley: University of California Press, 1972.

as-Suhrawardī, Abū Ḥafṣ 'Umar. *'Awārif al-ma'ārif.* Edited by 'Abd al-Ḥalīm Maḥmūd and Maḥmūd b. ash-Sharaf. Cairo: Dār al-kutub al-ḥadītha, n.d.

as-Suyūṭī, Jalāl ad-dīn. *Dhayl ṭabaqāt al-ḥuffāẓ.* Damascus: al-Qudsī, 1928.

Tabrīzī, Muḥammad 'Alī. *Rayḥānat al-adab fī-tarājim al-ma'rūfīn bi'l-kunya aw al-laqab.* Tehran: Chāpkhāna-yi shirkat-i sihāmī-yi ṭab'-i kitāb, 1950.

at-Tahānawī, Muḥammad 'Alī b. 'Alī. *Kitāb kashshāf iṣṭilāḥāt al-funūn.* 2 vols. Edited by M. Wajīh, 'Abd al-Ḥaqq and Ghulām Qādir. Calcutta: W.N. Lees, 1862; rpt. Istanbul: 1984.

Tauer, Felix, editor. *Cinq opuscules de Ḥāfiẓ-i Abrū concernant l'histoire de l'Iran au temps de Tamerlan.* Prague: Editions de l'academie tchecoslovaque des sciences, 1959.

Teufel, Johann Karl. *Eine Lebensbeschreibung des Scheichs 'Alī-i Hamadānī.* Leiden: E.J. Brill, 1962.

Trimingham, John Spencer. *The Sufi Orders in Islam.* Oxford: Clarendon Press, 1971.

Valiuddin, Mir. "Reconciliation between Ibn 'Arabi's Wahdat-i-Wujud and the Mujaddid's Wahdat-i-Shuhud." *Islamic Culture* 25 (1951), 43–51.

Van Ess, Josef. "'Alā' al-dawla Semnānī." *Encyclopaedia Iranica.* Vol. 1. Edited by Ehsan Yarshater. London: Routledge and Kegan Paul, 1985, 774b–77a.

Wā'iẓ-i Kāshifī, Fakhr ad-dīn 'Alī b. Ḥusayn. *Rashaḥāt 'ayn al-ḥayāt.* 2 vols. Edited by 'Alī Asghar Mu'īniyān. Silsila-yi intishārāt-i bunyād-i nīkūkārī-yi nūriyānī, no. 15. Tehran: Bunyād-i nīkūkārī-yi nūriyānī, 1978.

Waley, Muhammad Isa. "Najm al-Dīn Kubrā and the Central Asian School of Sufism (The Kubrawiyyah)." *Islamic Spirituality: Manifestations.* Edited by S.H. Nasr. World of Spirituality, vol. 20. New York: Cross Roads, 1991, 80–104.

Waṣṣāf, Shihāb ad-dīn Shīrāzī. *Tā'rīkh-i Waṣṣaf.* Tehran: 1967.

Wensinck, A.J. *On the Relationship Between Ghazālī's Cosmology and His Mysticism*. Mededeelingen der Koninklijke Akademie van Wetenschappen. Afdeeling Letterkunde, vol. 75, series A, no. 6. Amsterdam: N.V. Noord-Hollandsche Uitgevers-Maatschappij, 1933.

————. *La pensée de Ghazzālī*. Paris: Librairie d'Amérique et d'Orient Adrien-Maisonneuve, 1940.

Yahia, Osman. "Theophanies and Lights in the Thought of Ibn 'Arabi." *Journal of the Muhyiddin Ibn 'Arabi Society* 10 (1991), 35–44.

Yāqūt ar-Rūmī, Shihāb ad-dīn Abū 'Abd Allāh. *Mu'jam al-buldān*. 5 vols. Beirut: Dār Ṣādir, 1979.

Yazdī, Sharaf ad-dīn 'Alī. *Ẓafarnāma*. 2 vols. Edited by Muḥammad 'Abbāsī. Tehran: Amīr-i Kabīr, 1957.

INDEX OF QUR'ĀNIC CITATIONS

2:28	. . .you were dead, and He gave you life	106
2:60	Each group knew its own drinking place	124
2:116	To Him belongs what lies in the heavens and the earth	64
2:152	Remember Me and I will remember you	125
2:255	Allāh! There is no god but Him	64
2:284	To Allāh belongs all that is in the heavens. . .	64
3:7	They are the primordial book	64
3:26	Good is in Your hand. . . Indeed You are Powerful over. . .	36
3:41	Remember your Lord much and Praise Him. . .	125
4:103	So when you have completed the prayers then. . .	125
4:171	Do not be extreme in your religion	36
5:77	Do not be extreme in your religion	36
6:59	With Him are the keys of the unseen	64
6:91	Say 'Allāh!' Then leave them to plunge in vain discourse. . .	134
7:55	Call on your Lord in humility and in private. . .	130
7:205	And remember your Lord within yourself. . .	125, 130
9:100	And the first leaders of the Muhājirūn and. . .	36
17:1	He is the Hearer, the Seer	36
17:110	Neither say your prayer aloud. . .	130
18:24	And remember your Lord when you have forgotten	125, 133
18:110	Say: I am a mortal like you	123
33:41	O You who believe! Remember Allāh. . .	125
35:32	And among them are those who are cruel. . .	116
38:26	O David! Indeed We have created you as. . .	84
40:20	He is the Hearer, the Seer	36
40:56	He is the Hearer, the Seer	36
40:65	He is the Living; there is no god but Him	65
41:53	We shall show them Our portents on the horizons. . .	68
42:11	There is no like unto Him. . . He is the Hearer, the Seer	36

42:23	Say: I ask of you no fee for it except...	36
45:23	Do you see one who takes as his god his own desire	130
53:5–7	He was taught by one mighty in power...	91
53:9	...two bows' length or near	92
53:14–15	By the Lote-tree of the utmost boundary	91
53:27	Those who believe not in the hereafter...	76
54:55	...in the seat of sincerity with a Sovereign Omnipotent	64
55:3–4	He created the human being and taught him...	93
55:22	Out of them come pearls and corral	135
55:26	Everyone that is thereon will pass away	76
56:8–10	The companions of the right hand...	110
57:1	Everything that is in the heavens and the earth...	125
57:2	His is the mastery of the heavens and the earth	62
57:20	Know that the life of this world is but play...	103
57:21	...and Allāh is of infinite bounty	102
58:19	Truly it is the party of Satan that will perish	125
59:1	Everything that is in the heavens and the earth...	125
61:1	Everything that is in the heavens and the earth...	125
61:6	And remember, Jesus, the son of Mary, said...	85
64:8	Believe in Allāh, His messenger, and the light...	110
66:8	Indeed, You are Powerful over all things	36
68:1	*Nūn*, and the pen and that which they write	89
72:18	And the places of worship are for Allāh	125
73:8	And Remember the name of your Lord...	125
75:18–19	When We have promulgated it, follow you...	93
76:1	Was there not a time in the life of man when...	133
76:25	And remember the name of your Lord...	125
87:1	Glorify the name of your Lord, most high	129

INDEX

'Abd Allāh (Shaykh), 20n. 26, 200.
'Abd Allāh b. Muḥammad b. Ibn al-Baqī, 48n. 59.
'Abd al-Wāḥid b. Zayd, 39.
Abdāl, 37n. 9, 104.
Abhar, 18, 20.
Abharī (Akhī 'Abd al-Ghaffūr al-), 47n. 52.
Abharī (Ḥājjī-yi), 18, 20.
Abharī (Ṣafī ad-dīn), 17.
Abraham, 35, 84, 86.
Abu'l-'Abbās b. Idrīs, 39.
Abū 'Alī al-Kātib, 38.
Abū Bakr aṣ-Ṣiddīq, 23.
Abū Isḥāq-i Injū, 52.
Abu'l-Muwāḥid Muḥsin ad-dīn al-Aḥmadī (Akhī). *See* Muḥsin ad-dīn.
Abu'l-Qāsim b. Ramaḍān, 39.
Abu'ṣ-ṣafā' (Simnānī's son), 25n. 47.
Abū Sa'īd (the Ilkhan), 11, 16n. 4, 29, 30, 52, 161.
Abū Sa'īd b. Abi'l-Khayr, 38, 39, 115n. 71, 145n. 111, 193.
Abū Ṭāhir, 39.
Abwāb al-birr, 30.
Act (*fi'l* pl. *af'āl*), 65; divine acts, 61, 63, 101, 105, 149, 162, 197.
Ādāb al-murīdīn, 123.
Adam, 35, 79, 84, 86, 87, 88, 101, 102, 133.
Adhkānī al-Isfarā'inī (Najm ad-dīn Muḥammad b. Sharaf ad-dīn Muḥammad al-), 47, 50, 53.
Aḥmad b. Abi'l-Ḥawārī, 135n. 73.
Aḥmad Mawlānā, 46.
Aḥmad Takūdār, 19, 44, 54, 161.

'Ajamī (Ḥabīb al-), 38, 41.
Akhfāsh (Ṣadr ad-dīn), 17.
Akhī, 46.
'Alā' ad-dīn-i Hindū, 53.
'Ālam. See Realm.
'Alī b. Abī Ṭālib, 37, 38, 39, 41, 104n. 18, 123, 126.
'Alī-yi Dūstī-yi Simnānī (Akhī Abu'l-Barakāt Taqī ad-dīn), 46–47, 50.
'Alī-yi Farāhī (Shāh), 48.
'Alī-yi Hamadānī. *See* Hamadānī (Sayyid 'Alī).
'Alī-yi Kashmīrī, 52.
'Alī-yi Lālā (Raḍī ad-dīn), 20n. 26, 38, 39, 41, 193.
'Alī-yi Miṣrī (Akhī), 47, 50.
'Alī b. Mūsā ar-Riḍā, 126.
'Alī-yi Rūmī (Akhī), 48.
'Alī-yi Sīstānī (Akhī), 48.
'Alīnāq, 17–18.
Amāna (sacred trust), 76–77, 95, 99, 106.
Amīn ad-dīn-i 'Alī, 53.
Āmul, 20.
Āmulī (Ḥājjī), 26–27, 97.
Anatolia, 47.
Angels, 64, 70, 77, 79, 91, 108, 111n. 55, 113, 153, 155, 171.
Annihilation (*fanā'*), 76, 112, 121, 122n. 19, 134, 149, 150; annihilation in God, 98, 148; annihilation through recollection, 137–38, 139–40; *halāk*, 76; levels of annihilation, 142; annihilation and resurrection, 141–44. *See* Death.
Anṣārī ('Abd Allāh al-), 115n. 71.

Antinomianism, 27n. 56, 55, 58,
   97, 110–11, 113, 129, 134, 180.
Aqkhwāja, 18, 19n. 20.
'Aql. See Intellect.
Ardabīlī (Ṣafī ad-dīn), 43, 45, 46,
   161.
Arghūn, 16, 17, 18, 25–26, 44, 54,
   161; religious policy of, 17, 18,
   26, 53; Simnānī's relationship
   with, 19n. 20, 20, 21, 161.
Aristotle, 152.
Asceticism (*zuhd*), 20, 25, 42, 66,
   124, 195; ascetic practices, 41n.
   24, 121, 142.
Āthār (effects), 61, 63, 146, 149,
   162.
 Atīqī (Mawlānā Jalāl ad-dīn), 52.
Attribute (*ṣifa* pl. *ṣifāt*), 141; divine
   attributes, 61, 63–66, 68, 76, 79,
   80n. 3, 95, 105, 106, 127, 138,
   149, 158n. 35, 162, 196; essential
   attributes, 65, 101, 107, 153.
Azarbāyjān, 17.

Bābā Ratan (Abu'r-Riḍā), 41.
Badakhshān, 50.
Badakhshī (Nūr ad-dīn Ja'far), 47.
Badakhshī (Qawām ad-dīn), 51n.
   75.
Badal. See Abdāl.
Baghdad, 17, 22, 25, 26, 27, 28, 30,
   41, 42, 48, 54, 199.
Baghdādī (Junayd al-), 38, 39, 41,
   55, 63, 129, 162; teachings of,
   98–99, 119–20, 135n. 73;
   Simnānī's attitude towards, 42,
   148.
Baghdādī (Majd ad-dīn al-), 38, 41,
   57n. 105; teachings of, 119, 130n.
   57, 193, 198; influence on
   Simnānī, 1, 44, 123, 135n. 73,
   148.
Baghdādī (Muḥammad b. 'Abd
   Allāh ar-Rāshid b. Abu'l-Qāsim
   al-), 42.

Baghnawī (Ṣadr ad-dīn Abu'l-Ma'ālī
   al-Muẓaffar al-'Adawī al-), 190.
Baḥrābād, 44, 51.
Bākharzī (Ṣayf ad-dīn), 57n. 105.
Bakhshī, 18. *See* Buddhism.
Bakhshī Parinda, 18n. 16.
Bakrī (Imām ad-dīn 'Alī al-), 53.
Baqā' (eternal abiding with God),
   98, 142.
Barā'ī (Badr ad-dīn), 53.
Barzakh (barrier), 79, 107, 139.
Barzishābādī (Shihāb ad-dīn 'Abd
   Allāh), 51.
Baṣrī (Ḥasan al-), 38, 41.
Bāybādī ('Ubayd Allāh), 52.
Being (*wujūd*), 70; contingent
   being, 98, 148, 184; necessary
   being, 98, 105, 148, 153, 184.
Bidlīsī ('Ammār b. Yāsir al-), 38,
   39, 130n. 57, 198.
Bisṭāmī (Abū Yazīd al-), 20, 42,
   97n. 55, 135n. 73.
Biyābānak, 15, 18n. 16, 28, 30n.
   70.
Body, physical human, 64, 68,
   79–81, 84, 85, 89, 90, 93, 94,
   122, 133, 136, 137, 159, 193;
   acquired body (*al-badan al-
   muktasab*), 81, 83, 89, 93, 94,
   95, 141, 185; spiritual human
   body, 81, 135, 144, 149, 185.
Buddhism, 18, 36, 110, 147;
   Buddhist monks, 18, 26, 53, 55.
Bulghārī (Ṣalāḥ ad-dīn Ḥasan al-),
   45, 53, 200.
Bustī (Abu'l-Ḥasan al-), 21n. 29.

Caliphate. *See Khilāfa.*
Chishtiyya, 49.
Chūbān (Amīr), 16n. 4, 30, 161.
Climes (*aqālīm* sing. *iqlīm*),
   85–87, 135, 149.
Colors, 127, 134–37, 139, 149;
   color symbolism, 1.

Compounds (*murakkabāt*), 76, 79, 95, 106.

Cosmology, 61, 66, 71, 150–54, 186.

Covenant (*mīthāq*), 63n. 8, 114.

Creation (*khalq*), 2, 70–71, 105, 150.

Curtain. *See* Veils.

Dahistānī ('Azīz ad-dīn Muḥammad), 47, 180.

Damascus, 53.

Daqīqa (pl. *daqā'iq*, particulars), 62, 72, 80n. 3, 94, 96.

Daqqāq (Abū 'Alī al-), 135n. 73.

Dārānī (Abū Sulaymān al-), 135n. 73.

Dargazīnī (Jamāl ad-dīn), 46.

Dargazīnī (Sharaf ad-dīn), 46n. 51.

Dastirjānī (or Dastgirdānī, Jamāl ad-dīn), 16, 54.

David, 35, 84, 86–87.

Dāwūd b. Muḥammad, 39.

Dāya (Najm ad-dīn ad-), 205, 206.

Death, 121, 142, 149, 159; voluntary death (*al-mawt al-ikhtiyārī*), 121, 142, 149; collective death of all human beings (*al-yawm al-maw'ūd al-kabīr al-'aẓīm*), 142. *See* Annihilation.

Dhahabiyya, 51, 57. *See* Kubrawiyya.

Dhāt. See Essence.

Dhawq (mystical experience or taste), 95, 112, 114, 138, 145.

Dhikr (recollection), 1, 24, 39, 112, 122, 124–34, 137, 142, 145, 198; audible and silent recollection, 45, 130–32, 139, 161–62; benefits of, 131, 189; breath control associated with, 128, 131; practice of, 23–24, 58, 115–16, 120, 148, 150, 193; rules of recollection, 124–29, 171;

recollection of Simnānī, 3, 22, 47, 55, 126–34, 178.

Dinājpūr, 49.

Dimashq Khwāja, 16n. 4, 30.

Dimensions (visible and invisible), 69–70, 72, 136, 139.

Dīnawarī (Abū Ḥafṣ 'Umar b. Karam), 42.

Dīnawarī (Aḥmad Siyāh ad-), 41.

Dīnawarī (Mamshād ad-), 41.

Discipleship (*irāda*), 37.

Divine grace (*luṭf*), 66, 95; names, 64, 95, 125–26, 129, 180; throne and footstool ('*arsh* and *kursī*), 81, 111n. 55, 126; transcendence, 61, 97; unity, 18n. 16, 61, 62, 63n. 8, 64, 97, 98, 105, 129, 146.

Ḍiyā' al-mulk Muḥammad b. Mawdūd, 15.

Diyārbakr, 17, 22n. 35.

Elements (*mufradāt*), 64, 80, 81, 85, 93; celestial elements, 66, 186.

Emanation (*fayḍ*), 61, 70–77, 81–83, 88, 92, 94, 102, 150–54, 160; divine emanation, 2, 150.

Enlightenment. *See* Ma'rifa.

Eschatology, 44n. 40, 113, 139, 171, 185, 188.

Essence (*dhāt*), 65, 93, 152; divine essence, 61, 62, 63, 64, 77, 79, 93, 94, 96, 101, 102, 127, 139, 146, 149, 162, 196.

Existence, 61, 63, 104, 139, 172; human existence, 61, 79, 102, 125, 137, 140.

Faculties. *See* Quwā.

Faghnawī-yi Mawlawī (Khwāja), 45.

Fanā'. See Annihilation.

Fārābī (al-), 150, 152.

Fārmadhī (Abū 'Alī al-), 21n. 29.

Fārs, 17, 45n. 45.

Fārūthī ('Izz ad-dīn 'Abd Allāh b. 'Umar al-), 41, 42.
Fāṭima (Simnānī's sister), 49.
Fayḍ. See Emanation.
Fi'l. See Act.
Forces. *See Quwā.*
Futuwwa, 42, 46, 50.

Galen, 152.
Gaykhātū, 38n. 13, 54.
Ghazzālī (Abū Ḥāmid al-), 152, 155–56, 159.
Ghazzālī (Aḥmad al-), 38, 191.
Ghāzān, 16, 28, 29, 38n. 13, 43, 54.
Ghayb al-ghuyūb (Hiddenmost Hidden), 85, 89, 136.
Ghurjistānī (Wajīh ad-dīn 'Abd Allāh), 48, 52, 180.
Gīlānī (Shams ad-dīn), 48.
Gīsūdarāz (Sayyid Muḥammad al-Ḥusaynī), 49, 56.
Gūrpānī (or Jūrfānī, Aḥmad), 24n. 45, 38, 39, 41, 44, 193.

Ḥabashī ('Abd Allāh al-), 48.
Ḥadīth, 42, 43, 47, 53, 65, 71, 79, 108n. 37, 121n. 13, 129, 130, 134, 145, 154, 158n. 35, 180, 183, 188, 189.
Hakkı Efendi, 191.
Ḥāl. See Mystical states.
Ḥallāj (Abū Manṣūr al-), 97n. 55, 155–56, 158.
Hamadān, 25, 47, 50.
Hamadānī (Mīr Muḥammad), 50.
Hamadānī (Mīr Sayyid 'Alī), 46, 47, 49–51, 56, 57, 115n. 71, 160, 192.
Ḥamūya (Ghiyāth ad-dīn Hibat Allāh al-Maḥmūdī), 52.
Ḥamūya (Sa'd ad-dīn), 43, 44, 57n. 105, 69, 132n. 59, 156–57.
Ḥamūya (Ṣadr ad-dīn Ibrāhīm), 43–44, 53, 54.

Ḥanawayh (Akhī Sharaf ad-dīn). *See* Sharaf ad-dīn.
Ḥaqīqa (pl. *ḥaqā'iq,* reality), 85, 89, 96, 141, 180; divine realities (*al-ḥaqā'iq al-lāhūtiyya*), 62, 80n. 3; essence of the reality of certitude (*ḥaqīqa ḥaqq al-yaqīn*), 133; the "real", 110.
Ḥasan-i Sakkāk, 21, 25.
Heart (*qalb* or *dil*), 70, 80, 85, 88, 90, 110, 113, 119, 120, 122, 131, 132n. 59, 135, 136, 138, 140, 144, 159, 160, 186; garden of the heart (*jannat al-qalb*), 85; mystical (or real) heart, 24, 85, 93, 127, 150, 159; pineal heart (*dil-i ṣanūbarī*), 24, 127.
Heresy, 27n. 56, 66, 97, 108.
Heterodoxy, 44n. 40, 51, 55, 147, 189.
Hishmī (Majd ad-dīn), 16n. 5.
Ḥulūl (indwelling), 61, 98n. 58, 155n. 17.

'Ibāda. See Worship.
Ibn 'Ajīl, 38n. 12, 46.
Ibn al-'Arabī (Muḥyī ad-dīn), 2, 9, 44, 57–58, 97–98, 147–48, 152, 156, 159–60, 193, 199.
Ibn al-I'rābiyya, 21.
Ibn Sīnā, 34n. 3, 147, 150, 152, 153, 174.
Ibn Taymiyya, 46n. 51.
Ibrāhīm b. Adham, 1, 42, 55.
Ibrāhīm Zāhid-i Gīlānī, 46.
Ilhām (inspiration), 108.
Ilkhanids, 1, 8, 55; Ilkhanid admininstration, 53; Simnānī's association with, 3, 29–30, 147; Persian families in, 1, 5, 28, 43–44, 53; scholarship under, 11; religion under, 18n. 16, 30, 43, 45, 53–54, 147, 161.
'Imād ad-dīn 'Abd al-Wahhāb, 31.

India, 18n. 16, 26, 49, 55; Sufism
   in, 2, 49, 57, 162.
Inmost being (*Sirr*), 70, 80, 85, 90,
   110, 132n. 59, 135, 136, 140, 144,
   159.
Intellect (*'aql*), 74n. 40, 80n. 3, 89,
   152–54, 159; active intellect,
   152; first intellect, 152; human
   intellect, 65, 91, 111, 131, 152,
   188; tablet of the intellect (*lawh
   al-'aql*), 81–83.
Iqbāl (Muhammad), 162.
Iqlīm. See Climes.
Iran, 1, 45, 49, 50, 54; religion in,
   51, 53, 55, 56, 57, 161.
Iraq, 1, 53.
Isfahān, 18.
Isfarā'in, 31n. 76, 47.
Isfarā'inī (Nūr ad-dīn al-), 1, 2, 25,
   26, 27, 33, 37, 38, 42, 57n. 105,
   123n. 23, 148, 181, 182, 204; his
   masters, 20n. 26, 24n. 45, 39, 41;
   relationship with Simnānī, 5–6,
   11, 22, 24, 28, 29, 37–38, 39,
   126, 172, 198; his disciples,
   22–23, 29, 38, 54; relationship
   with Ilkhanid administration,
   54–55.
Ismā'īlism, 150, 152, 153–54.

Jabarūt. See Realm.
Jabriyya, 35, 36.
Jājarmī ('Umar al-), 186.
Jalāl ad-dīn Khwārazmshāh, 15.
Jāmī ('Abd ar-Rahmān), 9, 15, 52.
Jaunpur, 49.
Jesus, 35, 44n. 40, 84, 85, 87.
Jihād, 113, 114, 161, 171.
Jinn, 70, 77, 79, 85, 113, 140, 171.
Jurjānī (Abu'l-Qāsim al-), 38.
Jurjānī ('Alī al-), 158n. 35, 159.
Juwayn, 44.
Juwaynī ('Atā Malik), 1, 43.

Kalābādhī (Najm ad-dīn), 16n. 5.
Karkahrī (or Karkarī, Tāj ad-dīn),
   46, 200.
Karkhī (Ma'rūf al-), 38, 41, 126.
Kart (Ghiyāth ad-dīn Muhammad),
   30.
Kart (Mu'izz ad-dīn Husayn), 52.
Kāshānī ('Abd ar-Razzāq al-), 43,
   156, 158n. 35, 159, 193; his
   disciples, 15, 49; contacts with
   Simnānī, 2, 9, 44, 48, 97–98,
   199.
Kashmir, 26, 50.
Khafī (mystery), 70, 85, 110, 136,
   144, 186.
Khājū-yi Kirmānī (Kamāl ad-dīn
   Abu'l-'Atā' Mahmūd), 52.
Khalīfa-yi Māzandarānī, 51, 161.
Khalq. See Creation.
Khalwa. See Seclusion.
Khānaqāh, 25, 28, 30, 31, 38, 47,
   161, 171.
Khānaqāh-i Rūda, 46.
Khānaqāh-i Sakkākiyya, 25, 28, 29,
   31.
Kharaqānī (Abu'l-Hasan al-), 111n.
   55.
Khārijiyya, 35–36.
Khidr, 138.
Khilāfa (caliphate, divine
   vicegerency), 1, 76, 84, 101, 104,
   113, 161.
Khirqa (Sufi robe), 6, 39, 41, 42,
   45, 195, 204.
Khulāṣat al-manāqib, 47.
Khurāsān, 15, 22, 44, 50.
Khuttalān, 50.
Khuttalānī (Ishāq), 50–51.
Khwāja Abu'l-Fadl Qutb ad-dīn
   Yahyā, 52.
Khwāja-yi 'Azīzān. *See* Rāmtīnī
   (Khwāja-yi 'Azīzān 'Alī
   an-Nassāj).
Khwāja-yi Hājjī, 38n. 12.
Khwārazm, 46.

Khwārazmī (Abū Ṭāhir), 52.
Kirmān, 45, 52.
Kirmānī (Ḥamīd ad-dīn al-), 153–54.
Kirmānī. *See* Khājū-yi Kirmānī.
Knowledge, 112, 138, 188; direct knowledge of the divine (*al-ʿilm al-ladunī*), 138, 146, 159.
Kubrā (Najm ad-dīn al-), 1, 38, 39, 41, 57n. 105, 149, 161, 204–5; his disciples, 43, 44n. 40; his teachings, 115n. 71, 119, 198.
Kubrawiyya, 2, 3, 6, 9, 10, 43, 44, 54, 55, 149, 156, 160, 195, 199, 204; Hamadānī branch of, 51, 52, 57; mystical theories of, 2, 119.
Kumayl b. Ziyād, 39.

Lāhūrī (ʿAlāʾ ad-dīn), 49.
Lāhūrī (Raḍī ad-dīn Ḥasan aṣ-Ṣaghānī al-), 183.
Lāhūt. See Realm.
Lālā (Raḍī ad-dīn ʿAlī). *See* ʿAlī-yi Lālā.
Laṭāʾif-i ashrafī, 46, 49, 200.
Laṭīfa. See Subtle Substance.
Light (*nūr*), 83, 96, 102, 107, 110, 124, 125, 131, 137, 139, 141, 144n. 105, 149, 185, 191; of intellect, 80n. 3, 89, 124; of faith, 107, 127; of the heart, 138, 140; of the inmost being, 140; of Muḥammad, 110, 125; of the mystery, 138, 139; of prophecy, 89; of recollection, 135; of the spirit, 138, 140; of the soul, 137, 140; of spirituality (*nūr-i rūḥāniyyat*), 80, 107; of will (*nūr al-irāda*), 19; divine light, 110, 146.

Maghribī (Abū ʿUthmān al-), 38, 135n. 73.
Mahdī, 50.
Mahdī-yi Ḥājjī, 18, 20.

Majd ad-dīn-i Shaykhān, 39.
Makkī (Abū Ṭālib al-), 21, 42.
Malakūt. See Realm.
Malwa, 49.
Mamlūks, 16, 28.
Manifestation (*tajallī*), 135; divine manifestation, 2, 61, 65, 66, 77, 79, 95, 122, 150, 154, 186, 193; manifestation of light, 122, 139–40; locus of manifestation (*maẓhar*), 61, 63, 66, 76. *See* Mirror.
Manṣūr-i Khilāf, 38.
Maqām. See Mystical stages.
Maqqarī (Rashīd ad-dīn Abū ʿAbd Allāh b. Abuʾl-Qāsim al-), 41.
Maʿrifa (enlightenment), 105, 107, 110, 111-12, 117, 127, 128, 135, 149; *ʿirfān* (realization), 102; *ʿārif* (true gnostic), 106.
Mashhad, 30.
Mawālīd (also *mutawalladāt*, progeny), 66, 74, 93, 105, 154.
Māzandarānī. *See* Khalīfa-yi Māzandarānī.
Mazdaqānī (Sharaf ad-dīn Maḥmūd), 47, 50.
Mecca, 23, 28n. 60, 30, 45n. 45.
Medina, 28.
Microcosm and macrocosm, 68–69, 84, 149, 197.
Mirror, 66, 93; mirrors in emanation, 61, 63, 64; mirrors of divine attributes, 68, 77, 101, 146, 196; subtle substance of I-ness as mirror of the divine essence, 94–96, 106, 119, 149. *See* Manifestation.
Miṣrī (ʿAfīf ad-dīn al-), 27, 97.
Mīthāq. See Covenant.
Mongols, 43, 55; invasion by, 3, 15, 53, 161. *See* Ilkhanid.
Moses, 35, 84, 86, 87, 104n. 18.
Muʿaṭṭiliyya, 35, 36.
Mubāriz ad-dīn Muḥammad-i Muẓaffarī, 52.

Mufradāt. See Elements.
Muḥammad (the Prophet), 20, 35,
    38, 39, 41, 70, 71, 85, 87–88,
    90–92, 93, 104, 110–11, 117, 123,
    124, 129, 134, 135n. 73; as
    archetypal human being, 71, 83,
    91–92, 124n. 32; light of, 71n.
    31.
Muḥammad-i Khurd, 48, 191.
Muḥammad Khwārazmshāh, 15.
Muḥammad b. Mankīl, 39.
Muḥammad Murta'ish, 39.
Muhja (innermost self), 85.
Muḥsin ad-dīn al-Aḥmadī (Akhī
    Abu'l-Muwāḥid), 47–48, 50, 173,
    183, 184, 185.
Munawwar (Nūr ad-dīn al-), 39.
Murakkabāt. See Compounds.
Mushabbihiyya, 35, 36.
Mutawalladāt. See Mawālīd.
Mystery. *See Khafī.*
Mysticism, mystical attainment
    (*wuṣūl*), 37, 121; mystical
    exercises, 122n. 19, 142; mystical
    experience, 122, 124, 134, 136,
    137, 139, 145, 185; mystical
    flight (*ṭayarān*), 37; mystical
    journey (*sayr*), 37, 71, 141;
    mystical path (*sulūk*), 37, 121,
    134, 137, 142, 146, 150, 191;
    mystical practice, 124; mystical
    quest (*ṭalab*), 37, 132, 180;
    mystical stages (*maqāmāt*), 116,
    119, 133, 137, 170; mystical
    states (*ḥāl* pl. *aḥwāl*), 116, 133,
    135, 138, 141, 170, 182.
Mystics (*ṣūfiyya*), 104, 116–17, 121;
    mystical travelers (*sayyāḥūn*),
    141.

Nafaḥāt al-uns, 9, 10.
Nafs. See Soul.
Nahrajūrī (Abū Ya'qūb an-), 39.
Nakhjiwān, 45.
Naqshband (Bahā' ad-dīn), 49.

Naqshbandiyya, 2, 45, 49, 56–58,
    161–62; Mujaddidī branch of, 2,
    56, 57, 161–62.
Nasafī ('Azīz ad-dīn), 69, 71.
Nasawī (Sharīf Muḥammad an-),
    16n. 5.
Nassāj (Abū Bakr an-), 38.
Nāsūt. See Realm.
Nawrūz (Amīr), 16, 30, 161.
Naysābūrī (Abū Ḥafṣ al-Ḥaddād
    an-), 42.
Neoplatonism, 61, 71, 147, 150.
Nishāpūrī (Tāj ad-dīn), 16n. 5.
Noah, 35, 84, 86, 87.
Nūḥ (Simnānī's son), 25n. 47.
Nūrbakhsh (Sayyid Muḥammad),
    50–51, 160.
Nūrbakhshiyya, 46n. 51, 51, 57,
    160. *See* Kubrawiyya.
Nuṣayriyya, 21.
Nūyān (Amīr Ḥasan), 52.

Oneness of being (*waḥdat al-
    wujūd*), 2; Simnānī's attitude
    towards, 27, 44–45, 57–58,
    97–99, 147–48, 162, 199.
Oneness of witnessing (*waḥdat
    ash-shuhūd*), 2, 56, 162.

Pārsā (Khwāja Muḥammad), 49, 52.
Perfect Human Being (*al-insān al-
    kāmil*), 69, 83, 101, 161; as 'seal
    of created entities' (*khātim at-
    tarākīb*), 79, 99, 106.
Prayer, 112; ritual prayer, 20, 22,
    113–16, 120, 126, 127, 148, 171;
    mystical prayer, 22, 37, 114–16.
Progeny. *See Mawālīd.*
Prophecy, 35, 86–87, 90, 97, 104–5,
    107, 110–11, 113, 173; prophets,
    84, 86–87, 90, 92, 103, 106, 109,
    149–50, 171.
Ptolemy, 150, 152.
Pūr-i Ḥasan, 24n. 45.
Purity. *See Ṭahāra.*

Qabḍ and *basṭ*, 145.
Qadariyya, 35, 36.
Qalandariyya, 21.
Qalb. See Heart.
Qarwānī (Sharaf ad-dīn Ḥasan b. 'Abd Allāh al-), 20.
Qayṣarī (Ismā'īl b. Ḥusayn al-), 39, 193.
Qazwīn, 18.
Qazwīnī (Rukn ad-dīn al-), 53.
Qazwīnī (Sirāj ad-dīn 'Umar al-), 53.
Qiyāma. See Resurrection.
Qur'ān, 3, 36, 87, 89, 92, 93, 107, 115, 116, 133, 139n. 94, 144, 154, 158n. 35, 166, 167, 180, 184, 187, 189, 203; esoteric dimension of, 107, 108; limit of (*ḥadd*), 108; point of ascent of (*muṭṭala'*), 108; as primordial book, 122.
Qushayrī (Tāj ad-dīn Muḥammad al-), 48, 179.
Qūt al-qulūb, 21, 42.
Quṭb (mystical pole), 31n. 76, 37, 105, 116, 122, 170.
Quṭb-i ā'lam Chishtī, 49.
Quwā (sing. *quwwa*, forces or faculties), 83, 86, 96, 120, 125, 150, 172; bodily forces (*al-quwā al-qālabiyya*), 107, 110, 138; celestial forces, 65, 76, 110, 111, 152; terrestrial forces, 65, 76, 110; forces that incite to evil (*al-ammāra*), 103, 121; forces that rebuke (*al-lawwāma*), 103.

Rāfiḍiyya, 35, 36.
Rāja Ganēsha, 49.
Rāmtīnī (Khwāja-yi 'Azīzān 'Alī an-Nassāj), 45, 57, 161–62, 200.
Raqīqa (pl. *raqā'iq*, fine or rare substances), 62, 72, 80n. 3, 94, 96.
Rashīd b. Abi'l-Qāsim, 53.

Rashīd ad-dīn Faḍl Allāh-i Hamadānī, 30.
Rayy, 15, 47.
Reality. *See Ḥaqīqa.*
Realm ('*ālam*), 105, 154–57; Realm of Divinity ('*ālam al-lāhūt*), 61, 62, 63, 64, 65, 72, 77, 80n. 3, 91, 94, 96, 108, 134n. 71, 135, 136, 154, 157; Realm of Kingdom ('*ālam al-mulk*), 155; Realm of Omnipotence ('*ālam al-jabarūt*), 61, 62, 63, 64, 65, 72, 77, 80n. 3, 91, 94, 96, 108, 122, 134, 135, 155, 157; Realm of Sovereignty ('*ālam al-malakūt*), 61, 62, 63, 64, 72, 77, 80n. 3, 91, 94, 96, 108, 134, 135, 155, 157; Human Realm ('*ālam an-nāsūt*), 61, 62, 63, 64, 72, 77, 80n. 3, 93, 94, 96, 108, 134, 157; finite realm or physical realm, or realm of horizons ('*ālam al-āfāq*), 68, 69–70, 72, 81, 84, 86–88, 89, 103, 104, 108–9, 120, 121, 122, 123, 136, 149–50, 152, 154, 195, 196; Invisible and visible realms ('*ālam al-ghayb wa'sh-shahāda*), 63, 66, 69, 106, 113, 122, 139, 141; spiritual realm ('*ālam al-anfus*), 37, 68, 69–70, 81, 84, 87, 88, 89, 108–9, 120, 123, 127, 136, 149–50, 154, 157, 160; sublunar or terrestrial realm, 66, 74, 81, 95, 149, 153.
Recollection. *See Dhikr.*
Religious endowments. *See Waqf.*
Resurrection, 141–44. *See* Death.
Rūdhabārī (Abū 'Alī ar-), 38.
Rūḥ. See Spirit.
Rukn ad-dīn-i Ṣā'in, 16, 42n. 29; execution of, 16, 29, 55.
Rukn ad-dīn-i Ṣā'in (Nuṣrat Allāh 'Ādil), 16n. 4.
Rukniyya, 160. *See* Kubrawiyya.
Rūzbihān Baqlī-yi Shīrāzī, 156.

Sabzawār, 52.

Sacred trust. *See Amāna.*

Saʿd ad-dawla, 16–17.

Saʿd ad-dīn Muḥammad-i Awajī, 16.

Ṣafawiyya, 45.

Sainthood. *See Walāya.*

Samāʿ (audition), 132n. 59, 171, 178.

Saqaṭī (Sarī as-), 38, 41, 135n. 73.

Sarakhsī (Abu'l-Faḍl Ḥasan), 39.

Sarāyī (Minhāj b. Muḥammad), 52, 176.

Sarbadār movement, 10, 161.

Sarrāj, 39.

Satan, 66, 85, 88, 111, 119, 121, 123, 125, 129, 134, 136, 137.

Sāwa, 47.

Sāwajī (Saʿd ad-dīn), 54.

Sāwajī (Salmān), 52.

Sāwajī (Shams ad-dīn), 38n. 12, 46.

Sayyid ʿAlī-yi Hamadānī. *See* Hamadānī (Sayyid ʿAlī).

Seclusion (*khalwa*), 119, 121, 122, 128; requirements of, 119-21, 148, 171, 182.

Senses, 131, 192; inner, 124.

Shāh Ughūl b. Qāʿid, 47.

Shāhrukh (the Timurid ruler), 51.

Shāmī (ʿAbd Allāh ash-), 31n. 76.

Shams ad-dīn Muḥammad-i Būqā, 16.

Shaqīqa (pl. *shaqāʾiq,* divisions), 62, 94, 96.

Sharaf ad-dīn-i Badīʿ, 23n. 41.

Sharaf ad-dīn Saʿd Allāh al-Ḥanawayh (Akhī), 22, 23, 24, 25, 26, 27, 29, 39, 126.

Sharīʿa, 106; accord with Sufism, 58, 129, 134, 180; necessity of abiding by *sharīʿa,* 97n. 56, 110–11, 113, 125, 148.

Sharqī (Ibrāhīm Shāh), 49.

Sharūyāz, 36.

Shaṭḥiyyāt (theophanic utterances), 97–98, 148, 180.

Shaṭṭārī (ʿAbd Allāh), 51n. 75.

Shaṭṭāriyya, 51n. 75.

Shiblī, 135n. 73.

Shīʿism, 35-36, 44n. 40, 52, 57; Simnānī's attitude towards, 10, 11, 30, 51, 54, 55, 183.

Shīrāz, 52.

Shīrwānī (Siyāwash ash-), 17–18.

Ṣifa. See Attribute.

Sijistān, 48.

Sijistānī (Abū Yaʿqūb as-), 153–54.

Sikandar-i Butshikan (Shāh), 50.

Silsila, 38–39, 41, 42.

Simnān, 1, 15, 20, 21, 22, 23, 25, 28, 44, 46, 47, 49, 53.

Simnānī (ʿAlāʾ ad-dawla as-); attitude towards Shīʿism, 10, 11, 30, 51n. 75, 54, 55, 147, 183; his disciples, 7, 15, 43, 44–53; his family, 15–16; his masters, 37–42, 43, 195, 197; mystical conversion of, 5, 19, 20, 21, 22, 148, 182; mystical experiences of, 21, 22, 24, 55, 147; meditational exercises of, 29; relationship with the Ilkhanid court, 29–30, 55, 147.

Simnānī (Ashraf Jahāngīr), 15, 46, 48, 49, 50, 56, 57, 200.

Simnānī (Ḍiyāʾ ad-dīn Biyābānakī), 16.

Simnānī (Jalāl ad-dīn) 16, 54; offices held by, 16, 26; execution of, 16, 17.

Simnānī (Sayyid Ibrāhīm), 15, 17.

Simnānī (Sayyid ʿImād ad-dīn), 15.

Simnānī (Sharaf ad-dīn) 16, 38n. 12, 54; offices held by, 16, 26; execution of, 16, 28, 54.

Sirhindī (Aḥmad), 2, 56, 57, 162.

Sirr. See Inmost being.

Sīsī (Majd ad-dīn Ismāʿīl), 52.

Sīstānī (or Sijistānī, Iqbāl Shāh Jalāl ad-dīn b. Sābiq), 7, 9, 46, 48, 55, 177.

Sobriety (*sahw*), 99, 148.
Somnāth, 18n. 16.
Soul (*nafs*), 37, 68, 80, 88, 90, 110, 131, 136, 144n. 105, 159, 160, 186; celestial soul, 153; cosmic soul, 102; human soul, 65, 70, 85, 87, 96, 103, 123, 128, 153; rational soul, 94; lower or appetitive soul, 119, 120, 121–22, 138, 141, 149.
Spirit (*rūh*), 70, 80, 85, 90, 107, 110, 120, 132n. 59, 136, 144, 159, 160, 183; Holy Spirit, 85, 138; supportive spirit (*ar-rūh al-muttaki'a*), 37.
Substance (*jawhar*), 64.
Subtle substance (*latīfa* pl. *latā'if*), 1, 61, 72, 76n. 44, 81–91, 102, 109–10, 135, 137, 149–50, 157–60, 172, 185; subtle substance of I-ness (*al-latīfa al-anā'iyya*), 4, 61, 66–68, 93–97, 98, 101, 119, 135, 141, 149, 179, 185; subtle human substance (*al-latīfa al-insāniyya*), 160, 174; higher and lower substances (*al-latā'if al-'ulwiyya wa's-sufliyya*), 72, 88, 95, 107; subtle substance of the animal spirit (*latīfa-yi rūh-i hayawānī*), 120; of the body (*al-latīfa al-qālabiyya*), 81, 84, 85, 87–88, 89, 138, 146; of the heart (*al-latīfa al-qalbiyya*), 83, 84, 85, 87, 88, 92, 94, 138, 146; of the inmost being (*al-latīfa as-sirriyya*), 83, 84, 85, 87, 88, 91, 138, 146; of the mystery (*al-latīfa al-khafiyya*), 83, 85, 87, 88, 91, 98, 138–39, 146; of the "real" (*al-latīfa al-haqqiyya*), 83, 85, 87–93, 95, 96, 98, 110, 111, 136, 138, 144, 146; of the soul (*al-latīfa an-nafsiyya*), 81, 84, 85, 87, 88, 138, 146; of the spirit (*al-latīfa ar-rūhiyya*), 83 , 84, 85, 87, 88, 91, 138, 146.

Sufism. *See* Mysticism.
Sūfīyābād-i Khudādād, 28, 30n. 70, 31, 47, 48.
Suhrawardī (Abu'n-Najīb as-), 38, 39, 41, 123.
Suhrawardī (Shihāb ad-dīn Abu Hafs 'Umar as-), 41, 42, 44, 155, 192.
Suhrawardiyya, 41, 42.
Sulamī (Abū 'Abd ar-Rahmān as-), 130.
Sultāniyya, 26, 29, 30.
Sūsī (Abū Ya'qūb as-), 39.
Suwaydā' (deepest core of the self), 85.
Syria, 28, 29, 47, 55, 161.

Tabriz, 20, 21, 26, 45.
Tabrīzī (Shams ad-dīn at-), 45.
Tafrīd (isolation), 114, 120, 146; inner isolation (*tafrīd al-bātin*), 104, 119.
Tahāra (purification or purity), 33, 35, 120, 122n. 19, 181.
Tā'ī (Dāwūd at-), 38, 41.
Tā'ibābādī (Zayn ad-dīn Abū Bakr 'Alī), 52.
Tajallī. See Manifestation.
Tajrīd (divestment), 104, 112.
Theophany. *See* Manifestation.
Tilimsānī ('Afīf ad-dīn Sulaymān b. 'Alī at-), 27n. 56.
Tīmūr (Tamarlane), 3, 50.
Transoxiana, 17, 18n. 16, 47, 49, 50, 56–57, 162.
Tuhfat al-barara fi'l-masā'il al-'ashara, 123, 130n. 57, 148.
Tūs, 48.
Tūsī (Bābā Muhammad), 52.
Tūsī (Rashīd ad-dīn), 20n. 26.
Tustarī (Sahl at-), 135n. 73, 158.

Ūjān, 21.
Uljāytū Khudābanda, 20, 29–30, 52.

Uways-i Īlkānī (the sultan), 52.
Uzbek Khanate, 57.

Veils, 85, 88, 92, 107, 111, 135–38, 159.
Visions, 124, 125, 127, 134–41, 144, 148, 149.

Waḥdat ash-shuhūd. See Oneness of witnessing.
Waḥdat al-wujūd. See Oneness of being.
Wajīh ad-dīn. *See* Ghurjistānī.
Walāya (sainthood), 97, 104, 173; *walī* (accomplished mystic or saint), 83, 104–5, 106, 123.

Waqf (religious endowment), 25, 46, 54, 165.
World. *See* Realm.
Worship (*'ibāda*), 33, 35, 113, 115, 124, 133, 139, 171.
Wujūd. See Being.

Yemen, 46.

Zāhid-i Gīlānī. *See* Ibrāhīm Zāhid-i Gīlānī.
Zanjānī (Akhī Faraj az-), 41.
Zaynabī (Najm ad-dīn Bashīr b. Abū Bakr az-), 205n. 197.
Zuhd. See Asceticism.